Bourdieu in Africa

Studies of Religion in Africa

SUPPLEMENTS TO THE JOURNAL OF RELIGION IN AFRICA

Edited by

Benjamin Soares (*African Studies Center, Leiden, The Netherlands*)
Asonzeh Ukah (*University of Cape Town, South Africa*)
Shobana Shankar (*Stony Brook University, New York, USA*)

VOLUME 44

The titles published in this series are listed at *brill.com/sra*

Bourdieu in Africa

Exploring the Dynamics of Religious Fields

Edited by

Magnus Echtler
Asonzeh Ukah

BRILL

LEIDEN | BOSTON

Cover illustration: *Taking a picture of the 'Scottish' dancers (isikoshi) in the Nazareth Baptist Church*, eBuhleni, South Africa, July 2008. Photograph by Magnus Echtler. Reproduced with kind permission.

Library of Congress Cataloging-in-Publication Data

Bourdieu in Africa : exploring the dynamics of religious fields / edited by Magnus Echtler (Universitat Bayreuth, Germany), Asonzeh Ukah (University of Cape Town, South Africa).
  pages cm. — (Studies of religion in Africa, ISSN 0169-9814 ; volume 44)
  Includes bibliographical references and index.
  ISBN 978-90-04-30306-5 (hardback : alk. paper) — ISBN 978-90-04-30756-8 (e-book : alk. paper)
  1. Christianity—Africa. 2. Islam—Africa. 3. Religion and sociology—Africa. 4. Bourdieu, Pierre, 1930–2002. I. Echtler, Magnus, editor.

BR1360.B68 2015
200.96—dc23

2015035044

This publication has been typeset in the multilingual "Brill" typeface. With over 5,100 characters covering Latin, IPA, Greek, and Cyrillic, this typeface is especially suitable for use in the humanities.
For more information, please see www.brill.com/brill-typeface.

ISSN 0169-9814
ISBN 978-90-04-30306-5 (hardback)
ISBN 978-90-04-30756-8 (e-book)

Copyright 2016 by Koninklijke Brill NV, Leiden, The Netherlands.
Koninklijke Brill NV incorporates the imprints Brill, Brill Hes & De Graaf, Brill Nijhoff, Brill Rodopi and Hotei Publishing.
All rights reserved. No part of this publication may be reproduced, translated, stored in a retrieval system, or transmitted in any form or by any means, electronic, mechanical, photocopying, recording or otherwise, without prior written permission from the publisher.
Authorization to photocopy items for internal or personal use is granted by Koninklijke Brill NV provided that the appropriate fees are paid directly to The Copyright Clearance Center, 222 Rosewood Drive, Suite 910, Danvers, MA 01923, USA. Fees are subject to change.

This book is printed on acid-free paper.

Contents

Acknowledgements IX
List of Contributors X

1 Introduction: Exploring the Dynamics of Religious Fields in Africa 1
    Magnus Echtler and Asonzeh Ukah
Social Fields 2
Religious Fields 7
Religions in Africa 10
Religious Fields in Africa 14
Conclusion 22
References 26

2 Pierre Bourdieu and the Role of the Spirit in Some Zulu/Swathi AICs 35
    Jonathan A. Draper
Introduction 35
A Framework Suggested by Bourdieu's Concept of Field 37
Habitus and Cultural Capital in the Context of African Initiated Churches 41
Contestation in the Religious Field and Bourdieu's Concept of *Doxa* 45
Le Roux and the Zulu Congregation at Wakkerstroom as a Contested Field 51
Color Coding in Enyonini 54
Choice of Strategic Weapons in Enyonini 58
Prohibition of Pork 61
Bare Feet in Worship 61
Prohibition on Smoking 62
A Brief Note on the Red Robed Zionists: Cekwane, Vilikazi and the AmaJericho Church 63
Conclusion 65
References 67

3 Re-Imagining the Religious Field: The Rhetoric of Nigerian Pentecostal Pastors in South Africa 70
    Asonzeh Ukah
Introduction 70
Of Field and Subfields 74
The Field of Religion in (South) Africa 76

Nigerians in South Africa   78
Missionaries to Our Brothers & Sisters: Nigerian Churches in South Africa   80
Contesting Legitimacy: Self-Narration of Nigerian Pastors in South Africa   84
Conclusion   91
References   93

4   **The Faraqqasaa Pilgrimage Center from Bourdieu's Perspectives of Field, Habitus and Capital**   96
    Gemechu Jemal Geda
Introduction   96
Aayyoo Momina: Origin, Early Life, and Career   97
The Advent of *Aayyoo* Momina to Arsi: Two Different Perspectives   98
Religious Beliefs and Rituals at the Pilgrimage Center   100
Traditional Medicines   104
Spirit Possession Cult: Zar   105
Origin of Zar   106
Ways of Possession by Spirits   109
Natural Conditions   109
Inheritance   109
The Spirit's Own Choice   110
Symptoms of Possession   111
Methods of Healing the Possessed   111
Conclusion   113
References   114

5   **Fielding for the Faithful: A Tale of Two Religious Centers in a Small Muslim Town in Kenya**   117
    Halkano Abdi Wario
Introduction   117
The Context   118
The Contest in the Field   125
The Strategies of the Contests and Collaborations   131
Conclusion   135
References   135

6 The Bishop and the Politician: Intra- and Inter-Field Dynamics in
   19th Century Natal, South Africa   139
   Ulrich Berner
   Introduction: Agents in Different Fields: J. W. Colenso and
   Th. Shepstone   139
   The Bishop and the Politician in Cooperation (1854–1873)   140
   The Bishop and the Politician in Conflict (1873–1883)   147
   Conclusion: Bourdieu on the Social Functions of Religion, and the
   'Alternative Tradition' in the History of Religions   157
   References   162

7 Healers or Heretics: Diviners and Pagans Contest the Law in a Post-1994
   Religious Field in South Africa   166
   Dale Wallace
   Preamble   166
   Introduction   166
   The Genesis of a 'Religious Field'   168
   African Mediation with the Spirit Realm   173
   Witchcraft in the African Context   176
   Izangoma and the Witchcraft Suppression Act (3) of 1957   178
   South Africa Pre- and Post-1994   180
   Contemporary Paganism   182
   New Legislation Changes the Field   186
   Conclusion   190
   References   193

8 The False Messiah—Evangelicalism, Youth and Politics in Eritrea   195
   Magnus Treiber
   National Myth and Project   199
   Crackdown on Evangelical Churches   200
   Revolutionary Prophecy and the Mergence of the Political and the
   Religious   202
   Views from Below   203
   Alternative Evangelicalism   206
   Outbound Migration   210
   References   212

9 **Seclusion versus Education: Bourdieu's Perspective on Women Continuing Education Centers in Northern Nigeria** 217
   Chikas Danfulani
   Introduction 217
   Women's Education in Northern Nigeria: Problems and Prospects 220
   Impact of Sharia 224
   Description of Women Centers—Zamfara and Kano States 225
   Arguments for the Existence of Women Centers 227
   Seclusion or Education? 228
   Implications of Bourdieu's Perspective 231
   Conclusion 233
   References 234

10 **Shembe is the Way: The Nazareth Baptist Church in the Religious Field and in Academic Discourse** 236
    Magnus Echtler
    Introduction 237
    The Nazareth Baptist Church (NBC) in the Religious Field 238
    The NBC in the Academic Field 249
    Emic Views of the NBC 254
    Conclusion 261
    References 263

Index 267

Acknowledgements

As editors, we thank the Bayreuth International Graduate School of African Studies (BIGSAS) for financing the 2010 workshop "Continuity and Change in the Religious Field: Perspectives from Africa" at Bayreuth University which formed the starting point of the present volume, as well as for enabling some of our authors (Danfulani, Geda, Wario) to pursue their research, and the German Research Foundation (DFG) for funding our own research project in South Africa (Berner, Echtler, Ukah).

We also thank all our colleagues, especially the peer reviewers and the Brill series editors, whose critical comments enabled us to sharpen our argument, i.e. our cultural capital finally objectified in form of this book.

List of Contributors

Ulrich Berner
professor em. of the History of Religions (Religionswissenschaft), University of Bayreuth; affiliated senior fellow of BIGSAS (Bayreuth International Graduate School of African Studies). His main interests are European religious history, African Christianity, and method and theory in the study of religion. His recent publications include: "Religious Traditions: Kinship-based and/or Universal?" in *Critical Reflections on Indigenous Religions*, ed. James L. Cox, 49-62 (Burlington: Ashgate, 2013).

Chikas Danfulani
is lecturer at the Department of Religion and Philosophy, University of Jos, Nigeria. She holds a PhD in Religious Studies from the Bayreuth International Graduate School of African Studies (BIGSAS), University of Bayreuth, Germany. Her areas of specialization are religion, gender and education; Christian-Muslim relations; children in society; and religion in everyday life. Her publications include "'Education is Education': Contemporary Muslim Views on Muslim Women's Education in Northern Nigeria" in *Sharia in Africa Today: Reactions and Responses*, ed. John Chesworth and Franz Kogelmann, 103–124 (Leiden: Brill, 2014).

Jonathan A. Draper
is senior professor in New Testament and fellow of the University of KwaZulu-Natal, Pietermaritzburg Campus, South Africa. He has published on South African missionary history, African Initiated Churches, oral tradition and African reception of the Bible, and edited among other volumes, *Orality, Literacy and Colonialism in Africa* (Leiden: Brill, 2004) and *The Eye of the Storm: Bishop John William Colenso and the Crisis of Biblical Interpretation* (London: T&T Clark, 2003).

Magnus Echtler
works as research fellow in a project on sacred space in Durban, South Africa. Previously, he taught African Religions at the University of Bayreuth for nine years. He has published on popular Islam in Zanzibar and African Christianity in Nigeria and South Africa, and co-edited *Unpacking the New. Critical Perspectives on Cultural Syncretization in Africa and Beyond* (Berlin: LIT, 2008) and *Alternative Voices. A Plurality Approach for Religious Studies* (Göttingen: Vandenhoek & Ruprecht, 2013).

LIST OF CONTRIBUTORS

Gemechu Jemal Geda
recently completed his PhD at Bayreuth International Graduate School of African Studies (BIGSAS), University of Bayreuth, Germany. A native of Ethiopia, he has conducted field studies on indigenous religions of the Arsi Oromo. His academic interests include indigenous religions, pilgrimages, syncretism and religious transformation. His recent publications include "Momina," in *Encyclopaedia Aethiopica*, Vol. 5, ed. Alessandro Bausi, 438–440 (Wiesbaden: Harrassowitz, 2014) and "Irreecha: An Indigenous Thanksgiving Ceremony of the Oromo to the High God Waaqa," in *Critical Reflections on Indigenous Religions*, ed. James L. Cox, 143–158 (Surrey: Ashgate, 2013).

Magnus Treiber
holds a PhD in Anthropology from Munich University (2005). He has successively taught at Munich, Bayreuth and Addis Ababa Universities and is affiliated to the Felsberg Institute (FI). His main fields of interest are urban anthropology, migration, anthropological theory and methodology as well as political conflict in the Horn of Africa. Recent publications are: "Becoming By Moving. Khartoum and Addis Ababa as Migratory Stages between Eritrea and 'Something,'" in *Spaces in Movement. New Perspectives on Migration in African Settings*, ed. Mustafa Abdalla et al., 189–205 (Köln: Köppe, 2014) and "Grasping Kiflu's Fear—Informality and Existentialism in Migration from North-East Africa" in *Modern Africa. Politics, History and Society* 1/2 (2013): 111–139.

Asonzeh Ukah
is a sociologist/historian of religion. He joined the University of Cape Town, South Africa, in 2013. He taught at the University of Bayreuth, Germany, from 2005 to 2013. He earned an honors degree in Comparative Religion, and an M.A. in Sociology of Religion as well as an M.Sc. in Sociology at the University of Ibadan in Nigeria. He further earned a doctorate (2004) and habilitation (2013) in History of Religions from the University of Bayreuth, Germany. He has done fieldwork in Nigeria, Cameroon, Uganda, South Africa, Germany, and England. In addition to numerous peer-reviewed essays published in international journal (in English, German and Spanish), he is the author of *A New Paradigm of Pentecostal Power: A Study of the Redeemed Christian Church of God in Nigeria* (Trenton: Africa World Press, 2008).

Dale Wallace
obtained her PhD on Religion and Social Transformation from the University of KwaZulu-Natal in 2006. Her research focus has been on traditional African religion(s) and religious identity constructions in post-colonial South Africa,

and she has recently completed a post-doctoral project on witchcraft discourses in South Africa today. In 2009 she published "The Modern Pagan Witch: Negotiating a Contested Religious Identity in Post-Apartheid South Africa," in *Religion and Spirituality in South Africa: New Perspectives*, ed. Duncan Brown, 124–144 (Scottsville: UKZN Press).

Halkano Abdi Wario
is a lecturer in Islamic Studies at the Department of Philosophy, History and Religion, Egerton University, Kenya, and also an affiliate Volkswagen Foundation Humanities Research Fellow at St. Paul's University in Limuru, Kenya, with postdoctoral project on Muslim prints cultures and epistemologies of religious knowledge in Kenya. He completed his doctoral studies at Bayreuth International Graduate School of African Studies (BIGSAS), University of Bayreuth, Germany, focusing on localization of a translational Islamic movement called Tablīghī Jamāʿat in Kenya. His research interests include mediation and mediatization of religious knowledge, religious transnationalism, religion and spatiality, Islamic reformism in Eastern Africa and emerging trends in Islamic law in Africa.

CHAPTER 1

Introduction: Exploring the Dynamics of Religious Fields in Africa

Magnus Echtler and Asonzeh Ukah

Religion can be considered as both central and marginal with regard to the work of Pierre Bourdieu: marginal because in his overall oeuvre only few publications are explicitly concerned with religion, and central because he developed some of the central concepts of his theory of practice—field, habitus and symbolic power—against the backdrop of the sociology of religion of Marx, Durkheim and especially Weber.[1] One critical question raised with regard to his treatment of religion is whether his conceptualization of the religious field is applicable outside modern Western states with institutionalized churches and demarcated religious spheres. In this volume, we relate Bourdieu's theory to the various religious fields of sub-Saharan Africa in which we work. For him, religious fields are just one variant of social fields. In our introduction, we therefore discuss his general conceptions of social fields first, before turning to Bourdieu's specifications regarding the religious field and to the question of its applicability to the study and practice of religions in Africa. Based on the contributions in this volume, we argue that Bourdieu's theory, with its focus on specific actors and practices, does not lend itself to construct unitary, homogeneous entities like African Traditional Religions, African Christianities or African Islam. Rather, it deconstructs these and other essentializing categories by conceptualizing specific religious spheres as fields of social forces and social struggles whose dynamics are based on the relations of exchange between religious experts and laity, and on the competition amongst the specialists (Bourdieu 1991: 17). In conclusion, we highlight some problems with Bourdieu's approach, namely the significance of inter-field dynamics, the impact of deliberate interventions and discourses on the structure of social fields, and the dynamic potential of ruptures between objectified and subjectified social structures.

---

1   See Dianteill (2003). For Bourdieu on religion see Bourdieu (1971a/1987a, 1971b/1991, 1987b, 1987c, 1998: 112–126); Bourdieu & de Saint Martin (1982); see also Corso (2012), Egger (2011), Egger, Pfeuffer & Schultheis (2000), Engler (2003), Hutt (2007), Rey (2004, 2007), Schultheis (2008), Urban (2003, 2005), Verter (2003, 2004).

Social Fields

According to Bourdieu, all theodicies are sociodicies (Bourdieu 1991: 16), and, moving from the beliefs to the practices, he claims that the "specifically religious rite is simply a particular case of the social rituals whose magic does not reside in the discourses and convictions which accompany them (in this case, religious representations and beliefs) but in the system of social relations which constitute ritual itself, which make it possible and socially operative (among other things, in the representations of the beliefs it implies)".[2] Following from this insistence on the social dimension of religion, we find it most fruitful to base our discussion of African religious fields on Bourdieu's conceptualization of social fields generally, before engaging critically with his specifications regarding the religious field.

The social, for Bourdieu, is relational, as captured in spatial metaphors, primarily one of relatively autonomous social fields in which different social games are played. A field is understood "both as a field of forces, whose necessity is imposed on agents who are engaged in it, and as a field of struggles within which agents confront each other, with differentiated means and ends according to their position in the structure of the field of forces, thus contributing to conserving or transforming its structure" (Bourdieu 1998: 32).

On the one hand, there are the social structures that define the game social actors play; and on the other hand, these social structures are produced through the strategic practices of the actors, their struggles over positions in the field, as well as over the borders of the field and the rules of the game. On the side of social structure, Bourdieu distinguishes between the objectified structure, the relations between the positions of the actors in the field and the specific regularities that define the possible interactions between them, and the subjectified structure, the habitus of the actors, "systems of durable, transposable dispositions, structured structures predisposed to function as structuring structures, that is, as principles which generate and organize practices and representations" (Bourdieu 1990: 53). Habitus is arguably Bourdieu's most famous concept, and it takes center stage in his theory of practice, because its dispositions inscribed in the bodies and cognitions of the actors define their practice and drive their strategies. With regard to Bourdieu's spatial conceptualization of both objectified and subjectified structure in the form of social fields, it is important to note that this concept forms "an abstract

---

2 Bourdieu (1992b: 116/268n6). Corso (2012: 232) criticizes Bourdieu's emphasis on social interaction as "overly reductivist", because it misses the symbolic interactionism specific to religion as analyzed by Weber.

representation, deliberately constructed, like a map, to give a birds-eye view, a point of view on the whole set of points from which ordinary agents (including the sociologist and his reader, in their ordinary behavior) see the social world" (Bourdieu 1984: 169).[3] Decisive for Bourdieu's theory of action is the temporal immediacy of practice. Terms like 'practical sense' or 'practical mastery' refer to the concept of actions generated by the habitus of the actors, their internalized dispositions, rather than by deliberate and detached calculations, as well as to the 'magical' fit between subjectified and objectified structure, between habitus and field. This incorporated 'feel for the game' is "what gives the game a subjective sense—a meaning and a *raison d'être*, but also a direction, an orientation, an impending outcome, for those who take part. Therefore, it acknowledges what is at stake (this is *illusio* in the sense of investment in the game and the outcome, interest in the game, commitment to the presuppositions—*doxa*—of the game)", but also an objective sense, a meaning shared among the players. This is so "because the sense of the probable outcome that is given by practical mastery of the specific regularities that constitute the economy of a field is the basis of 'sensible' practices, linked intelligibly to the conditions of their enactment, and also among themselves, and therefore immediately filled with sense and rationality for every individual who has the feel for the game" (Bourdieu 1990: 66).

Thus, the actors buy into the *illusio* of the social game they play, and they are bound by the underlying *doxa*, the objectified and subjectified structures that cannot be easily challenged, but they also confront each other in their struggles over positions within the field. Moreover, it is this aspect of practice that introduces dynamic into the field that moves practice beyond the pure reproduction of social structure. Through this competition, by playing

---

3   Lizardo (2010: 666) argues that Bourdieu is "committed to the methodological structuralist principle of keeping a clear conceptual and practical barrier between *structural models* (and their principles of functioning and presumed properties) constructed by the analyst and the *practical models* deployed by the social agent in routine activities and ultimately responsible for the production of social practices (which can then be represented *in toto* by some structural model)", but he also notes that Bourdieu contributes "to the conceptual cacophony associated with the term 'structure' […] by using it both to refer to really-existing social and cognitive orders and not just to models constructed by the analyst" (ibid.: 678). In a lecture given in 1986 Bourdieu defined his own position as structuralist constructionism, meaning "that there exist, within the social world itself and not only within symbolic systems […], objective structures independent of the consciousness and will of agents" and "that there is a twofold social genesis" of both habitus and social fields (Bourdieu 1989: 14), but also insisted that the theoretical model is separated from practical mastery "by the infinitesimal but infinite distance that defines awareness" (Bourdieu 1990: 270).

for keeps or pressing for gain, the actors reproduce or alter the structure of the field in and through actual practice. Every action players take redefines their position in relation to the other players, and both their position and their ability to act is characterized by the economic, cultural, social and symbolic capital they possess. All forms of capital are accumulated labor, either in material, objectified form, or in incorporated, subjectified form. Economic capital entails control over productive forces. Cultural capitalia are skills and knowledge, personally acquired at the cost of time and effort. Social capital consists in the actualization of resources inherent in a network of relations with other actors. Symbolic capital is not an autonomous form, but consists of other capitalia that are acknowledged by other actors as authority, prestige, status or honor (see Bourdieu 1984; 1990: 112–122). Of special interest for us here is the notion of symbolic capital, i.e., the standing of an actor as acknowledged by the other actors in the field, because this recognition which forms the basis of most modes of domination depends on mis-recognition, i.e. on the recognition of the legitimacy of the actor's position and power.

> Symbolic capital [...] is not a particular kind of capital but what every kind of capital becomes when it is misrecognized as capital, that is, as force, a power or capacity for (actual or potential) exploitation, and therefore recognized as legitimate (Bourdieu 2000: 242, see also Bourdieu 1977: 171–197).

As such symbolic capital forms the basis for the social function of the religious field, namely to inculcate a "system of consecrated practices and representations whose structure (structured) reproduces, in a transfigured and therefore misrecognizable form, the structure of economic and social relations in force in a determinate social formation" (Bourdieu 1991: 14). However, with regard to the dynamics of practice, what is at stake in the social game are not only the positions of the players, but also the 'rules of the game,' the forms of capital relevant to the field, just as the borders of the field itself. It is thus the strategic aspect of practice that drives social change, albeit limited change based on the actors' conditional freedom "as remote from creation of unpredictable novelty as it is from simple mechanical reproduction" (Bourdieu 1990: 55).

If metaphors help understanding certain aspects of a concept or thing at the cost of hiding others, the question is what is hidden by the metaphor of playing competitive social games in spatially circumscribed fields (Lakoff & Johnson 1980: 5, 10). One frequent charge against the Bourdieu's model of the economy or logic of practice is the over-emphasis on self-interested, profit-oriented actors, players who employ strategies to compete over positions in the field.[4] Nevertheless, Lebaron (2003: 563) refutes the charge of economic reductionism by drawing attention to Bourdieu's "double move—the formal economicization of his analysis of the symbolic order and the symbolic explanation of the foundation of economic reality". Thus, the concept of field takes into account the variable cultural context of specific practices. A field is "a relatively autonomous universe of specific relationships" or more specifically the "structure of objective relationships" between the actors involved (Bourdieu 1985: 17). Each field of practice is characterized by its specific regularities that define the possible interactions between the actors, the actors' interests or investments in the field, and the kinds of capital that are at stake within the field. The main purpose of the concept is "to avoid all kinds of reductionism" and "to wrest the producers' actions and the works they produce from the absurdity of arbitrariness and of motivelessness" (Bourdieu 1985: 20). Bourdieu analyzed a variety of different fields, not least those associated with disinterested, selfless actors, e.g. the religious, the scientific, or the artistic field (Bourdieu 1987a, 1988, 1991, 1996). Accordingly, actors may have to be disinterested in order to serve their interests, as only a bad captain leaves the sinking ship before the women and children, and only a mystic who rejects worldly gain and status and lives in the desert may become a famous holy man:

> Agents that clash over the ends under consideration can be possessed by those ends. They may be ready to die for those ends, independently of all considerations of specific, lucrative profits, career profits, or other forms of profit. Their relation to the end involved is not at all the conscious calculation of usefulness that utilitarianism lends them, a philosophy that is readily applied to the actions of others. They have the feel for the game; for example, in games where it is necessary to be "disinterested" in order to succeed, they can undertake, in a spontaneously disinterested manner,

---

4   See e.g. Ortner (1984: 151), Urban (2005: 163), Warde (2004: 15). On the other hand, Bourdieu is criticized for his overly deterministic view of social action. See e.g. Comaroff (1985: 4), Jenkins (1992: 175), Moebius (2006: 64), Ortner (2005: 33f). Bourdieu claims that his concept of strategic practices generated by habitus moves beyond the subjectivist vs. objectivist dichotomy, and the fact that he is criticized from both directions points to his intermediate position (see e.g. Bourdieu 1977: 3, 24–27; 1985: 12f.; 1990: 25, 52; 2000: 63f.) This insistence on a logic of practice with the critique of scholastic theories resonates with Marxist considerations of praxis (see e.g. Schmidt 1973: 1115). Whether Bourdieu manages to synthesize the epistemological dualities or merely oscillates between them remains contested (see e.g. Berard 2005, Evens 1999, Gerrans 2005, Vandenberghe 1999).

actions in accordance with their interests. There are quite paradoxical situations that a philosophy of consciousness precludes us from understanding (Bourdieu 1998: 83).

Another side effect of the metaphor of the field is the spatial imagery it invokes, which implies a clearly delineated playing field. According to Bourdieu, the concept of field of practice is a flexible tool adjustable to the scope of analysis, and the borders of any given field are established empirically only. In our view, the relative autonomy of the field is based on the existence of a group of actors who play a social game, players who interact, who understand the moves of the other players, the 'official' rules of the game, as well as the possibilities to break the rules and win the game. It is consequently the coherence of the game in practice that makes the field a useful analytical model. This, however, that does not mean that the actors are playing this one game only, nor that the game is isolated from other parts of society. Here, Bourdieu's concept of the field shares in the problem of all social analysis below the macro-level, as, for example, with the extended case study approach of the Manchester school, where "anthropologists may want to study a particular group, or set of relationships, or domain of activities, which is only part of a larger or more complex social field. How far is it possible to isolate these areas of the field for significant study?" (Gluckman 1964: 15; see also Evans & Handelman 2006).

It follows, therefore, that the borders of fields are bound to be fuzzy because the borders, as well as the entry requirements form part of the 'rules of the game' that are contested by the players. Consequently, the contextualization of practice requires that the more general concepts like economy of practice or habitus are modified according to the specific field they refer to. In order to interpret a social action it is necessary to reconstruct the habitus of the actor, his/her position within a field of practice, the borders of the field of practice, as well as the genesis of the field, i.e., the historical process by which it gained autonomy, as exemplified by Bourdieu's analysis of Flaubert and the literary field (Bourdieu 1996, Müller 2002: 167–8). Even so, there remain the questions of the convertibility of the field-specific capitalia between different fields and of the meta-rules that govern the interaction between the different fields. This aspect of inter-field relations Bourdieu addresses by linking field-specific symbolic capital to an overarching field of power, wherein symbolic violence is the "coercion which is set up only through the consent that the dominated cannot fail to give to the dominator (and therefore to the domination) when their understanding of the situation and relation can only use instruments of knowledge that they have in common with the dominator" (Bourdieu 2000: 170). The emergence of a unified social space and field of power "goes hand in hand with the progressive constitution of the state monopoly of legitimate physical and *symbolic* violence" (Bourdieu 1998: 33, emphasis in original). For our analysis of religious fields in Africa, both the question of the borders of the field and of the interests of the actors need to be addressed with regard to the specifics of the religious field, before critically assessing its applicability to African contexts.

Religious Fields

What, then, are the specifics of the religious field? The religious field is defined by "[…] the fact that what is at stake is the *monopoly of the legitimate exercise of the power to modify, in a deep and lasting fashion, the practice and world-view of lay people*, by imposing on and inculcating in them a particular *religious habitus*" (Bourdieu 1987a: 126, emphasis in original). The prerequisite for the genesis of the religious field is therefore a division of labor with the development of a body of specialists and the corresponding disempowerment of the laity.

> Inasmuch as it is the result of the monopolization of the administration of the goods of salvation by a body of religious *specialists* […] the constitution of the religious field goes hand in hand with the objective dispossession of those who are excluded from it and who thereby find themselves constituted as the *laity* […] dispossessed of *religious capital* (as accumulated symbolic labor) and recognizing the legitimacy of that dispossession from the mere fact that they misrecognize it as such (Bourdieu 1991: 9, emphasis in original).

As religious experts, Bourdieu identifies sorcerers, priests and prophets, whereby the relations between sorcerers and priests are based on the distinction between the illegitimate and legitimate manipulation of the sacred, or between magic and religion, a distinction created by the suppression of one religious tradition by another, which then forms the basis for the (mis)recognition of the legitimacy of the successful specialist, the priest (Bourdieu 1991: 12–13). In the relation between the priest and the prophet, on the other hand, the legitimacy of the priest, based on his position within an institution, the church, is challenged by the charismatic prophet (ibid., 22–25). Charismatic leadership, for Bourdieu, raises "the problem of the *initial accumulation of the capital of symbolic power*," a problem that can only be solved by relating the prophet to his followers, by explaining "why a particular individual finds himself *socially* predisposed to live out and express […] ethical or political dispositions that are already present in a latent state amongst […]

his addressees" (Bourdieu 1987a: 130f. emphasis in original, see also Bourdieu 1991: 34–37). The dynamic of the religious field is produced through the competition amongst the specialists, and on the exchange relations between specialists and the various sections of the laity (Bourdieu 1991: 17). Religion thus produced is "predisposed to assume an *ideological function, a practical and political function of absolutization of the relative and legitimation of the arbitrary*" through the exertion of symbolic violence with the power to define what is worthy of acknowledgement, through religious practices and representations that reproduce social structure "in a transfigured and therefore misrecognizable form" (ibid. 14, emphasis in original). "Theodicies are always *sociodicies*" because they provide justifications for social inequalities (ibid., 16, emphasis in original).

With the foregrounding of the social function of religion, Bourdieu's conception of a religious field with interested actors competing for positions invites the charge of being reductionist, a charge he counters with the assertion that theories of religion that emphasize psychological functions or identify personal salvation as the core of religion are far from universal but reflect and justify the social position of an urban bourgeoisie (Bourdieu 1991, 16f). Nevertheless, the cast of characters in the religious field, Weber's priests, prophets and sorcerers, owes a lot to the Western conceptualization of world religions, or in Bourdieu's case, specifically French Catholicism. Though Bourdieu's early work on Algeria included some reflections on Protestantism and capitalism as well as Islam and society (Bourdieu 1958: 43–47, 96–107), these considerations did not move him beyond the Weberian framework and had little impact on his conceptualization of the religious field (see Egger and Schultheis 2011: 253). His only empirical work on religion was concerned with the French episcopacy (Bourdieu and de Saint Martin 1982), but he called into question his own delineation of the religious field when he discussed the role of new actors—new 'priests' like psychoanalysts, social workers, etc.—in an expanded field of symbolic manipulation, concerned with the 'healing of souls', in which the former, more clearly delineated French religious field increasingly dissolves, i.e. he addressed the question of the historic change of the borders of the religious field (Bourdieu 1987c: 118).

Because of this Western, or perhaps better Abrahamic taint, as well as the emphasis on social inequality, Rey (2007: 83–4) argues that Bourdieu's concept is well suited for analyzing religion in colonial contexts. When applied to non-Western, and especially pre-colonial contexts, it is important to heed Bourdieu's critique of anthropology's "reverse ethnocentrism of imputing to all societies, even the most 'primitive,' forms of cultural capital that can be constituted only by a determined level of the development in the division of labor" and his suggestion to "relate the structure of the system of religious practices and beliefs to the division of religious labor," as these form the prerequisites for the development of a relatively autonomous religious field (Bourdieu 1991: 10). In any case it is useful to start the analysis of religious fields in Africa and elsewhere by providing "systematic information about the complete universe of religious agents, about their recruitment and training, their position and function in the social structure" (ibid: 11), as this forms the basis for evaluating the degree of autonomy of the religious realm, for determining its social function, and for specifying the regularities of the social game the actors are involved in.

What makes Bourdieu's early articles on religion central for his theory of practice generally, despite the historical limitations of his model of the religious field, is the fact that he developed for the first time an extended vision of a social field of practice driven by the habitus of the players. The dynamics of the field are based on the exchange relations between experts and laity, and on the relations of competition between the experts. Here the conflict between priest and prophet serves as a model for conflicts driving the dynamics of all social games, namely the conflicts between established players, whose position is legitimized by both objectified and subjectified structures of the field, and the new players, whose only chance to capture a dominant position in the field is dependent on their ability to undermine the legitimacy of their opponents. This conflict pertains thus to the basic question of how social structure is produced and altered. The analytical strength of Bourdieu's approach draws from his concept of limited innovation, where the structuring force of the actor's dispositions (habitus) is limited by the fact that they are structured by the field, and where the position of innovators, even if they delegitimize established players and alter the rules of the game and the borders of the field, is still based on their ability to mobilize social networks and generate acknowledgement (social and symbolic capital). In discussing Weber's prophet, Bourdieu insists on the social character of charismatic power: this is his solution to the "problem of the *initial accumulation of the capital of symbolic power*" (Bourdieu 1987a: 130 emphasis in original), which forms the core of his endeavor to show the logic of practice, to show how interested players employ strategic moves in their struggles over positions in a field of practice, even if the social game in question requires the disinterestedness of the participating players. Bourdieu certainly liked to analyze these types of social games because his critical intent would be most visible or shocking for bourgeois audiences. While religion remained marginal within his work, his early articles on the religious field developed the blueprint for later engagements, as, for example, when he analyzes the artist Flaubert within the field of cultural production, a social game based on the "charismatic ideology of 'creation' [...] which directs the gaze towards the apparent producer—painter, composer, writer—and prevents us from asking who has created this 'creator' and the magic power of transubstantiation with which the 'creator' is endowed" (Bourdieu 1996: 167).

Religions in Africa

After discussing the historical limitations of Bourdieu's concept of the religious field as well as the logic of social fields and its problems generally, it becomes now possible to consider the analytical usefulness of Bourdieu in the African context. When talking about religions in Africa, problematic borders abound. There is the big question of the definition of religion in a non-western context (e.g. p'Bitek 1971; Asad 1997; Smith 1998; Lambek 2008; Riesebrodt 2010; Chidester 2014), and the battle over derogatory terms like fetishism or idolatry by post-colonial African scholars of religion in the attempt to reclaim the label 'religion' for the African Traditional Religions (e.g. Mbiti 1969, Idowu 1973, Ikenga-Metuh 1987). On the other hand, there is the topic of the 'holistic African worldview', linked with the question if there existed anything like 'relatively autonomous' religious fields in pre-colonial times in Africa (Ruch & Anyanwu 1981; Peel 2000), or whether it makes sense to consider religion and politics as separate fields in Africa today (Ellis & ter Haar 1998, 2004, 2007).

These questions notwithstanding, the advent of Muslim and Christian actors, and the establishment of colonial states certainly changed the configurations of religious fields in African societies. When considering the appropriateness of the concept 'religion' for Africa, it is important to keep in mind that in West and East Africa contact with Abrahamic religions in the form of Islam—with the accompanying reconfigurations of the religious fields, its experts, capitalia, and the very conceptions of 'religion'—predated the encounter with Western missionaries by up to a thousand years. Worthy of note, also, is that these Islamic religious fields in Africa were not static but changed as frequent waves of reformers challenged the legitimacy of established experts and their expertise, and shifted the borders of the religious sphere by excluding or including African elements, fluctuations reflected in scholarship by the universalizing and particularizing conceptualizations Islam in Africa and African Islam.[5]

---

5 For Islam in Africa see e.g. Horton (2001), Insoll (2003: 1–35), Levtzion & Powels (2000), Masquelier (2009), McIntosh (2009), Robinson (2004), Schulz (2003), Seesemann (2006), Soares (2000), Westerlund & Rosander (1997). There is, of course, also the case of Ethiopian Christianity, see e.g. Moore (1936), Parry (2010).

As the later newcomers in various African societies, Christian missionaries established themselves by pushing experts of indigenous traditions outside the borders of redefined religious fields, by labeling them as charlatans or devil-worshippers, i.e., non-religionists or anti-religionists. European settlers and missionaries first claimed Africans had no religion;[6] when later they grudgingly recognized and admitted that indigenous populations had religion, it was termed the wrong type of religion such as 'idol worship', 'animism', 'idolatry'. Illuminating examples of this type of redefinition of religious fields can be found in the work of David Chidester (1996, 2012, 2014) and J. D. Y. Peel (1990, 1995, 2000). By redefining religious fields, the missionaries also attempted to control access to a significant segment of emergent Christian fields; they were in control of the cultural capital relevant for these fields, acquired in the mission schools, and they controlled the symbolic capital, as they, and only they, ordained Christian religious leaders. Evidently, Islamic religious professionals as well as different categories of specialists in the indigenous religions contested the character and prerequisites for engaging with the new, vibrant and increasingly pluralized religious fields. In many African societies success of the Christian mission came with the destruction of pre-colonial social formations, when the role of the missionaries was not restricted to religious fields but formed part of the power relations of the colonial states, where new 'rules of the meta-game' structured their involvement in the educational, administrative and political fields.

Further reconfigurations of African religious fields took place when new players challenged the position of the missionaries: the founders of the African Initiated/Instituted/Independent/Indigenous Churches (AICs). These newcomers did not claim existing positions in the religious fields; they changed the structure of the fields by their practice. They changed the borders by founding new churches and re-introducing certain cultural aspects into Christianity, e.g. indigenous musical styles and instruments forbidden in liturgical worship by western missionaries; by emphasizing neglected cosmological elements like the importance of ancestors; by redefining what capitalia were relevant to the fields, e.g. cultural capital in the form of spiritual healing or the communicative or revelatory powers of dreams and visions, or social capital in the form of membership in specific descent groups. As the leaders of AICs became established, they were in turn challenged by newer players in the

---

6 In an era when having the 'correct' kind of religion was an index of a people's humanity, the claim that Africans had no religion came with huge implications such as that Africans were less than human or permanently children and could be killed or dispossessed of their property with impunity (Chidester 1996: 56; 2014: 193).

guise of Pentecostal or Charismatic leaders, who strove to discredit the AICs by once again reconfiguring the borders of the religious fields. In addition, as the structures of religious fields changed, so did their relations with other fields, as the new players could make use of their status acquired within religious fields to further economic or political ends. These changes in turn prompted reactions from actors in other fields, and most notably from the state, who in its colonial and post-colonial form strove to implement its visions for the significance of religious players in the political fields. The reconfigurations of the African Christian fields have been reflected in various trends in scholarship, in the shift in focus from AICs to Pentecostal/Charismatic churches (Meyer 2004), the 'Pentecostalization' of early African churches (Anderson 2000) or the 'Africanization' of Pentecostalism (Kalu 2008), or the attempt to apply the more neutral term of New Religious Movements (Hackett ed. 1987, Larkin & Meyer 2006), among many others (see Kollman 2010a,b). Likewise, the interrelatedness of religion with politics and economics has been considered with regard to a wide variety of actors and traditions (see e.g. Comaroff & Comaroff 1999, Ellis & ter Haar 2007, Marshall 2009, Ukah 2008).

Various African traditions have played important roles in the variously configured religious fields, and they have also been reflected upon in scholarship, although in a somewhat marginal position, possibly due to the ongoing Christian predominance in the sector of academia concerned with religion in Africa.[7] Throughout, the academic treatment has been suspect of 'othering' African traditions, ranging from the denial of religion proper to Africans in colonial times (Chidester 1996, 2014; Pels 1998) to the recent controversy over exotizing tendencies in the writings on the occult in Africa (Meyer 2009, Ranger 2007, ter Haar & Ellis 2009). Conversely, one of the most significant reformulations of religion in Africa was what Rosalind Shaw (1990) aptly describes as "the invention of African Traditional Religion", following V. W. Mudimbe's critique of the construction of Africa in western academic discourses. Shaw appropriately indicates that "the term 'religion' itself is absent from the languages of many of the peoples whose practices and understandings we describe as

---

7 In the leading *Journal of Religion in Africa*, in the 10 years from 2004 to 2013 (Vol. 34–43), Christianity featured in 97 articles, Islam in 35, African Traditional Religion in 31 (including 9 on Afro-American Religions). We suggest that this reflects not only the more or less objective state of African religions out there, but also the structure of the academic sub-field concerned with the study of African religions, its funding institutions and research interests of its players, i.e. "the social world that has made both the anthropologist [or scholar of religion] and the conscious or unconscious anthropology that she (or he) engages in her anthropological practice" (Bourdieu 2003: 283).

their 'religion' " (Shaw 1990: 339). Because in pre-colonial Africa, what came to be known later as 'religion' was not a specific field of activities or belief but a totality of life encompassing *fields* of conduct, thought and analysis (Ruch & Anyanwu 1981: 77–99), the residual of such comprehensive understanding is still evident in how Africans engage spiritual categories in dealing with life's exigencies (Ellis & ter Haar 2004). Shaw effectively argues that what came to be known as 'African Traditional Religion' was "largely a product of the paradigmatic status accorded in religious studies to Judeo-Christian tradition and of the associated view of 'religion as text' " (Shaw 1990: 339). Thus, religion in Africa was constructed according to templates provided by the Judeo-Christian religious studies: "The images of African religious forms constructed in early studies were thus informed by missionary interests in cultural translation, and were based upon a Judeo-Christian template" (ibid., 343). Evident in the process of the invention of 'religion' in Africa was its external impetus; it was not only Judeo-Christian inspired, it was also a western, colonial project partly designed to selectively privilege certain religious forms while denigrating or ignoring others. It was ideological in that it reconstituted and contested the field of power and capitalia in favor of western cultural, colonial discourses. A Euro-American interpretation of Christianity and religion remapped the field of 'religion' in Africa by producing concepts and analyses which have so far influenced how religion is view, lived, and interpreted in Africa till the present times. The invention of African Traditional Religion can thus be analyzed as "reverse ethnocentrism" (Bourdieu 1991: 10), as pointed out above. But while Shaw's critique is primarily concerned with academic discourse, Bourdieu insists that it is necessary to move beyond the scholastic view if one is to understand the logic of practice of real-life actors bound and active within specific social fields (Bourdieu 2000: 50), which leads to the final issue in the present discussion of religions in Africa.

The privileging of ideas over practice constitutes a high point in western/Christian/scholastic influence: religion is primarily interpreted as belief, as doctrines, as ideas and only secondarily as practice, lived expression, everyday encounters of ordinary people instead of a privileged class of professionals and scribes. This western bias is evident in the work of African pioneers in the studies of 'African Traditional Religion' such as Bolaji Idowu (1962), John Mbiti (1970), or Emefie Ikenga-Metuh (1981), and was criticized as such by Okot p'Bitek (1971).[8] These scholars all devoted considerable energy to the project of

---

8   For the conceptualization of African Religions in African and Western scholarship see also Adogame, Chitando and Bateye (eds. 2012), Ludwig and Adogame (eds. 2004), Platvoet, Cox and Olupona (eds. 1996), Westerlund (1985).

distilling what 'Africans' think about 'God'; in other words, the idea and nature of God in African indigenous cultures and religions which qualify Africans for being removed from the class of a 'Godless people' and their religions from the class of 'Godless religions'. Prioritizing ideas, doctrines, beliefs rather than practice is an ideological carry-over from the Euro-American and colonial past. Bolstering this point is David Morgan's (2005: 6) apt observation that "[b]elief is...a *Christian* way of thinking of religion" (emphasis in original). We therefore suggest to consider belief not as an internal state or creedal affirmation, but "situationally and behaviourally" (Ruel 1997: 37), as "practice of cyclically regenerating a condition of internalized 'believing'" (Kirsch 2004: 700), as structured and structuring dispositions corresponding to the configurations of particular social fields. This departure redraws the border of what 'religion' is through shifting emphasis and focus on the specifics of various religious fields and practices in Africa.

Religious Fields in Africa

After all these considerations, we finally turn to our explorations of the dynamics of African religious fields. We propose that it does make sense to talk of religious fields, making use of something like the working definition proposed by Ellis and ter Haar (2007: 387), according to which "religion in sub-Saharan Africa is best considered as a belief in the existence of an invisible world, distinct but not separate from the visible one, that is home to spiritual beings with effective powers over the material world." We consider this definition useful even if the emphasis on belief and the material—spiritual dichotomy are of Western provenance, because in all African societies, pre-contact cultural traditions, whether 'religion' or not, had to come to terms with Abrahamic religions for a rather long time. In practice, all these traditions have been located in religious fields, and their experts have become partisan players in the struggles over the borders of these fields. But unlike ter Haar and Ellis, who emphasize the belief in spiritual beings, we hold with Bourdieu that while beliefs as part of the subjectified structure contribute to the dispositions that structure action, they are also structured structures that are produced in practice, and therefore cannot be considered as something given that explains action, but as part of a dialectical process, changed and retained in and through practice. Our notion of religious fields includes all actors with a vested interest in the social game of religion, and that includes those who are explicitly rejected from the game by the hegemonic players because the very rejection establishes their interest in the form of negative symbolic capital, and it even includes the avowed unbelievers who call into question the social game itself. Further, it includes all scholars of religion, who define and redefine the borders of the religious field and thus exert considerable symbolic violence, a power misrecognized as legitimate thanks to their apparent disinterestedness as players in the scientific field and its doxa of scientific objectivity. Within this reflexive frame it is also necessary to take heed of the postcolonial critique and of what Bourdieu calls the danger of "reverse ethnocentrism" (Bourdieu 1991: 10). Consequently, the genesis of religious fields, their histories, the reconfigurations of their borders, and all the actors involved have to be specified for each socio-cultural context. Are there specialists who establish a relatively autonomous field of social practice? To what extent does the social game they are playing confirm to concepts of 'religion'? This specificity produces a diversity that does not only call into question the usefulness of the concept of religious field, but also that of 'Africa'. Pragmatically, the collection of essays in this volume reflects the structure of the scientific field: all authors are part of the African Studies subfield.[9] More specifically, the volume originates in a workshop and research collaboration between the Universities of KwaZulu Natal (South Africa) and Bayreuth (Germany), which led to its focus on Southern Africa. Nevertheless, the diversity of religious fields described here suffices to deconstruct the assumed socio-cultural homogeneity of sub-Saharan or Black Africa, and while this might be useful to dispel concepts of an essential African religiosity, it certainly makes the limitation to African contexts an arbitrary one.

The chapters of this book are diverse not only with regard to their specificity to various socio-cultural contexts, encompassing West, East, and South African examples, but also with regard to their thematic focus. Bourdieu provides a unified, coherent theoretical frame, but this frame is wide enough to allow for the discussion of a wide range of topics, from the analysis of structures, like the significance of the colors of the priests' garments, the cultural context of ritual practices establishing 'spirit possession,' or linguistic practices producing or subverting authority, to the analysis of the dynamics of practice, like the shift from Saudi Arabian to Indian references in order to challenge established Muslims, the varied interaction of African diviners and Pagans with state law, or the de-legitimizing strategies of Pentecostal pastors. Central part of the common frame is the emphasis on the social nature of religious action, and on the interested, competitive actors, even if the religious game is played behind the screen of disinterestedness. Every theory focuses on certain aspects of reality and ignores others, and Bourdieu's approach is strongest if one is interested

---

9 The male bias, as well as the predominance of essays concerned with Christianity, reflects fairly accurately the structure of the academic sub-sub-field on African Religions.

in religion as a field of social relations, understood as a field of forces imposed on actors as well as a field of struggles between actors (Bourdieu 1998: 32). This aspect of Bourdieu's theory has been criticized as reductionist, but we hold that it is its major strength as argued above.

Our volume starts out with a section considering dynamics within religious fields. In the following second chapter, Jonathan Draper discusses the emergence of African Initiated Churches in Southern Africa, one of the most important reconfigurations of the Christian religious fields in Africa, or indeed their 'Africanization.' He argues that the concept of 'spirit' draws upon both Christian/Pentecostal and Zulu/Swathi habitus. These concepts represent the structural forces imposed on the actors, and, at the same time, the cultural capital inscribed in the dispositions of potential followers that the prospective religious leaders can draw upon and play around with in their struggles over positions in the field. Draper then shows how the bi-polar structure lends itself to distinctive and divisive practices that mark the foundation of independent and indeed African churches, practices that turn cultural capital into symbolic capital, into the acknowledged positions of new church leaders, practices that alter the structure of the religious field, both with regard to the rules of the game and the position of the players. Thus the decision not to eat pork, to wear a white or blue robe instead of a black one, to carry a staff and to walk barefoot become practices that alter the structure of the field, and they can do so, they are successful, they are recognized as significant because they draw upon the habitus of the laity. At the same time they are contested practices that draw into the open the implicit bi- or multi-polarity of the structural forces, they challenge the doxa of the religious field, and are thus labeled as syncretic and either condemned as the return to heathenism or hailed as the genesis of African Christianity.

In the third chapter, Asonzeh Ukah takes us into the religious field of contemporary South Africa, or rather into the peculiarities of one of its sub-fields, Pentecostal-Charismatic Christianity. In focusing on the churches of Nigerian migrants, he analyses the church leaders' strategy of de-legitimizing established players, thereby legitimizing their own intrusion into the field. In their narratives, the Nigerian pastors present themselves as missionaries, as following a calling made necessary by the serious mutilation of the South African religious sphere because of the history of apartheid. As both Mission and Pentecostal Christianities are implicated in this history and thus found wanting in spiritual strength, it is only Nigerian Pentecostalism that can liberate the superstitious South Africans from the stranglehold of heathenism. In moving beyond Bourdieu and the religious field, Ukah focuses on the rhetorical strategies of migrants in delegitimating the authority and capital of the religious leaders of their host society in the competition for economic and symbolic resources in South Africa.

Moving to East Africa, Gemechu Jemal Geda is concerned with the Faraqasa pilgrimage center in Ethiopia, especially the healing practices and spirit possessions that take place there. What is striking about this center is its ambivalent position within the religious field. This ambivalence is reproduced through conflicting versions of the life history of the center's founder. As a religious leader wielding spiritual power, she is linked with indigenous religious traditions, but she is also related to Islam and Christianity, as well as to various ethnic groups. While these multiple identity ascriptions allow various sections of the laity to connect with the center and participate in its rituals, they are also used to produce symbolic capital, to privilege one's own position among the experts associated with the center. Turning to the religious practices, Geda analyzes how spirit possession is inscribed in the actors' habitus as a form of embodied cultural capital, how forms of capital are transformed through practice, e.g. economic capital into symbolic capital through sacrifice, and he explores the central significance of healing practices and points out how the symbolic capital of the center and its experts is produced through miracles, or more precisely through the discursive practices of telling stories or singing hymns about miracles.

In the fifth chapter, Halkano Abdi Wario investigates the religious field in Merti, a Muslim town in northern Kenya. He is mostly concerned with the religious field as a field of struggles, as he describes the strategies of a group of newcomers, members of the Tablīghī Jamāʿat, who compete over positions with the established leadership of the Muslim community. This is a conflict primarily over what kind of cultural capital forms the basis for religious authority. Wario argues that since the 1980s, Muslim leaders in northern Kenya strove to deepen religious persuasion in the laity through Islamic learning. Consequently, the position of the religious leaders, their legitimacy, is based on this kind of cultural capital, knowledge of the Quran and other Arabic texts, cultural capital acquired at *madrasa* schools and Islamic universities, especially in Saudi Arabia, Egypt and the Sudan. Their endeavor modified the habitus of the laity, and included the call to become more actively involved in religious matters. However, for a section of the laity, this increased personal involvement, and especially the access to leading positions, was barred by their lack in Islamic learning. This discontented part of the laity formed the basis for the success of the Tablīghī Jamāʿat, who offered another way to legitimize religious leadership. What is required of members is to dedicate time to God, to travel away from home in order to preach and spread the tenets of the movement. What they gain through this personal investment is cultural capital in the form of oratory skills and knowledge in the Quran, the *Hadith*, and the movement's religious teachings, as well as social capital in the form of the networks of the movement that support the travelling members. As everyone can preach according to their teachings, Tablīghī Jamā'at can be considered as a lay movement that produces self-made sheiks, who challenge the positions of the established leaders of the *umma*. What is striking about the case discussed by Wario is that the classic strategies of the religious establishment for dealing with deviant newcomers, incorporation or excommunication, do not work here. Tablīghī Jamā'at cannot be incorporated, because it relies on its own teachings, and its own international connections, centered on India rather than Arabia / North Africa. And its members cannot be excluded from the religious field, because both parties share in the doxa of the field, both support the practice of *da'wa*—to spread the truth of Islam—though they disagree on who is entitled to do so.

In the sixth chapter, the first of the second part of our volume on inter-field dynamics, Ulrich Berner is exploring the formative period of the religious field proper in colonial South Africa. He discusses the interaction of the political and the religions fields by concentrating on the relationship between two outstanding actors, John William Colenso, bishop of Natal, and Theophile Shepstone, Secretary for Native Affairs. Berner presents the religious field, or rather the field of Anglican Christianity in South Africa, as a field of struggles in which divergent theological positions led to the excommunication of Colenso; but even here the dynamic was not religious only, because Colenso kept his diocese despite the excommunication because of political intervention. His good standings, and indeed friendship with Shepstone, however, deteriorated rapidly when Colenso publicly opposed the colonial state in the prosecution of a Zulu chief for treason, and in the invasion and eventual annexation of Zululand. Berner shows that the actors from the political field acknowledged the autonomy of the religious field—and that this relative autonomy indeed forms the basis of the social function of religion—but also, as representatives of the state, insisted that the actors from the religious field keep within the boundaries of their constituency, and, in the case of a conflict between religious and political interests, submit to the supremacy of the state. Berner argues that it were these very conflicts that negotiated the borders of the fields, or set the rules for the games played in the borderlands between the religious and the political. He also criticizes Bourdieu's emphasis of the opposition between church and prophet, whereby the established church provides the legitimacy for the social order, and the prophets challenge it: in this case, it was the bishop who turned heretic.

INTRODUCTION

In the seventh chapter, we stay in South Africa, but we jump to present times. Dale Wallace analyses the conflicts over the definition of what constitutes 'witchcraft' between African diviners (*izangoma*), Pagans of European traditions, and South African commissions of law. While Wallace uses primarily Bourdieu's 'field of struggle' metaphor to explore the competitions over the power to define what is worthy of acknowledgement, her chapter, together with Berner's, make an interesting argument for the 'field of forces' aspect of Bourdieu's theory, because they provide a striking example for the continuity of structural forces in the religious field, as well as its relations to the wider field of power. In Berner's chapter, the conflicts between actors from the religious and the political field were often linked to instances of witchcraft (*umthakathi*), an anti-social force within Zulu views of the world which called for violent counter measures, which in turn forced or permitted the colonial state to intervene. Likewise, the post-apartheid state had to deal with the issue of witchcraft against the backdrop of anti-witchcraft violence in the mid-1990s, although within a pluralistic and post-colonial frame, in which Pagans with a completely different, Wiccan, conception of witchcraft want to be heard as well. Wallace argues that the struggles over the definition of terms like 'witchcraft' concern the ability to exert symbolic violence, and need therefore be connected to the emergence of the South African religious field within a wider field of power that includes the conceptualization of African Traditional Religions in the colonial context, incorporating layers of historical connotations dating back to the witch-hunts in early modern Europe, as well as the emergent study of religion as academic discipline with an evolutionary framework, all of which needs to be deconstructed from a post-colonial position. She points to two more or less 'religious' experts from pre-colonial African traditions, the herbalists (*izinyanga*) and diviners (*izangoma*), and their anti-social opponents, the witches (*abathakathi*), and argues that colonial / apartheid legislation criminalized both diviners and witches, but not herbalists, because it enforced a conceptual differentiation between science, magic and religion, closely related to the one proposed by Frazer. With the state exerting symbolic violence on the religious field, actors reacted, in part by inventing a new type of expert, the Christian diviner, who could deal with witches while at the same time belonging to religion proper as protected by state law. For the post-apartheid context, Wallace discusses the competition over symbolic capital at the 1999 World Parliament of Religions in Cape Town, where established players demanded that African diviners and Pagans should be excluded, which led to cooperation between the two 'newcomers.' Nevertheless, this alliance was short-lived, as representatives of both groups clashed when trying to influence state legislation on 'witchcraft' with diametrically opposed concepts.

Magnus Treiber analyses the interrelations between religious, political and domestic fields in Eritrea. He notes the strategic aspect of linguistic practices when he describes how young people ridicule their elders in English, which the elders do not understand, because they could not show such disrespect openly. This generational conflict is one of the driving forces behind the recent antagonism between the religious and political fields, according to Treiber. He argues that the Maoist Eritrean People's Liberation Front (EPLF) developed a charismatic political prophecy corresponding to the structural requirements of the guerrilla war leading to independence, a political ideology that effectively merged the religious and political field after independence in 1991 and the establishment of an autocratic single-party state. Within that frame, political actors could not accept an autonomous religious field, and while Islam and other Christian denominations were tolerated, Pentecostal Churches were singled out for state prosecution in 2002, despite their leaders' protestations of their apolitical nature. Treiber shows the political significance of the churches by exploring their significance to young urbanites. From their perspective, the Pentecostal churches offer a view of the world that breaks with the political ideology of the older generation, that indeed identifies the state president as the "false Messiah", and they provide new communities separated from the paternal kinship ties, social capital that also entails international connections that might be mobilized to migrate to Europe, the US or Canada.

In the ninth chapter, Chikas Danfulani analyzes the interrelations between the religious field and the field of education in northern Nigeria since the re-introduction of Sharia in 1999 by focusing on the practices taking place at Women Continuing Education Centers (WCECs). Danfulani points to the difficulties in distinguishing social fields in the Muslim context, where a single, religiously derived law is thought to govern all areas of social life, but also points to the impact of Western education in Nigeria, a secular state according to its constitution, with a concept of education that promises to empower women. In the WCECs, married women, who dropped out of formal education because of their marriage, receive Western education while conforming to religious and cultural practices, especially to the practice of seclusion (*kulla*). Following Bourdieu's emphasis on the role of education in imposing symbolic violence and reproducing social structure, Danfulani examines the actual educational practices at these centers and concludes that they serve to reproduce male dominance rather than empower women.

In the final chapter, Magnus Echtler returns to the opening chapter by discussing the position of an AIC in the South African religious field, but maintains the frame of the book's second half—inter-field dynamics—by discussing the feedback loops between the academic and religious fields. He argues how certain practices, Sabbath worship and religious dances, positioned the Nazareth Baptist Church (NBC) in the religious field in relation to both missionaries and Zulu diviners, thereby altering the regularities of the social game and the boundaries of the field itself. He argues with Bourdieu that the mobilizing force of the charisma of Isaiah Shembe, the founder of the NBC, was based on the dispositions of parts of the laity, on its link with the authority of Zulu diviners and lineage heads. However, Isaiah Shembe founded a new church; he did not simply reproduce traditional forms of symbolic capital, but transformed them by disconnecting them from their link with social capital in the form of descent group membership. The further development of the NBC was shaped by the structure of the religious field, by its regular transformations: as a newcomer, Shembe used his charisma to establish his position in opposition to the established players from Mission Christianity. However, in order ensure the reproduction of his symbolic power his charisma had to become routinized, and in the NBC this process led to the establishment of hereditary charisma in the form of a dynasty of church leaders, and to the increasing importance of traditional and bureaucratic leadership within the church. The character of the charisma of the church's leadership was also decisive for the church's treatment within academic discourse. On the one hand, Echtler argues that the confrontations over the messianic character of Isaiah Shembe and the classification of the church had more to do with the structure of the academic than the religious field. On the other hand, he focuses on the interrelations between the two fields, and shows how the apparently disinterested and objective scientific classifications exert symbolic violence on the religious field, and how the inclusive and exclusive academic classifications of the NBC as Christian or Non-Christian represent the classic reactions of established churches to prophetic newcomers: canonization or excommunication. The issues of classification form part of explicit discourses that intersect the academic and religious fields, and church members challenge the legitimacy of academic classifications. Lastly, Echtler turns to the emic discourses on the church leader's charisma, which center on the notion of a singular and eternal spiritual Shembe present in the succession of church leaders. This notion is somewhat ambivalent with regard to the issues of classification, an ambivalence whose strategic value lies in the fact that it can relate to the dispositions of various sections of the laity. With this form of hereditary charisma, the NBC is prone to succession conflicts over who incarnates the singular spiritual Shembe. These issues are decided, and symbolic capital thus produced, through public acclaim at the major festivals of the church.

Conclusion

Taken together, the chapters of this volume do not add up to provide the structure of an African religious field in the singular—and indeed we hold that any such endeavor would be looking for essentials where there are none. Rather, each chapter explores some aspects of the structure and the dynamics of a particular religious field. At best, several chapters taken together reach the density to reconstruct part of the history of a specific religious field, in our case the South African one. From the practices and discourses that established a relatively autonomous religious field in colonial times (Berner), its reconfigurations through the impact of African Independent Churches (Draper, Echtler), to the migrant churches, the African healers and Pagans whose struggles alter its structure and borders (Ukah, Wallace), our combined analysis highlights some of the structural continuities and dynamic processes that shaped—and are still shaping—the South African religious field—with the obvious privilege granted to Christianity at the expense of ATRs, Islam, and Hinduism, a feature of our analysis that must be questioned in the context of the structures of the scientific field concerned with religions in Africa.

If one moves beyond the analysis of the individual religious fields (or subfields), there are some conclusions we can draw from our work with regard to Bourdieu's theory of practice generally, and his notion of social field in particular. The first of these is the emphasis on the importance of inter-field dynamics. Looking at the contributions to our volume, it is striking that half of our authors make sense out of the actors' practices by explicitly addressing the inter-relations between two or more fields. If one follows Lizardo's (2010: 679) argument that Bourdieu's structural models work on the heuristic rather than the ontological level, it is the epistemological value of the concept of social field that is called into question here. Of what use is a model that proposes distinguishable social games played in relatively autonomous fields when one constantly has to take into account the interdependence of the fields in order to explain the actors' behavior? This problem calls for closer investigation of the inter-field dynamics (see Thomson 2008: 80). What are the rules of the game played in-between fields, how are the borders of the fields negotiated? Bourdieu offers the concept of a field of power as a general frame, and points to the central role of the modern state within it.[10] The importance of

---

10   See Bourdieu (1989, 1998: 35–63). What needs to be developed further is the link between the vertical and horizontal axis in Bourdieu's theory (see Müller 2002: 165–168). However, Rehbein (2003: 89) argues that there is a contradiction between the Euclidian concept of vertical social space and the relational conception of social fields.

state actors in determining the boundaries of a religious sphere is supported by many of our contributors (e.g. Berner, Danfulani, Treiber, Wallace), but there are also other areas that have to be considered, e.g. the economy, especially in contexts where the state chooses to deregulate its involvement in the religious market (Ukah). What gives credence to the continued use of the concept of social fields, or at least religious fields in the context of modern states, is their status on the ontological level in the form of rather similar concepts used by the actors themselves when they claim, challenge or defend autonomy for a religious sphere (e.g. Berner, Echtler, Treiber, Wallace). This leads us to the fundamental problem of the relation between conscious and unconscious aspects of the actors' habitus.

Habitus, for Bourdieu, conceptualizes the actors' disposition to act, the "systems of schemes of perception, appreciation and action [that] enable them to perform acts of practical knowledge [...] and, without any explicit definition of ends or rational calculation of means, to generate appropriate and endlessly renewed strategies" (Bourdieu 2000: 138). The concept is aimed against the twin scholastic fallacies of mechanism and finalism (ibid). In his attack on finalism, utilitarianism, rational choice theory, or "the old philosophy of the subject or of consciousness, that of classical economy and of its *homo economicus*" (Bourdieu 1985: 12), Bourdieu characterizes the practical sense of habitus as "ways of being that result from a durable modification of the body through its upbringing [which] remain unnoticed until they appear in action" (Bourdieu 2000: 138). Our findings here suggest that Bourdieu overemphasized the unconscious, embodied aspects of the structuring structures that generate action, or, to put it the other way around, that he neglected the impact of deliberate interventions on the production of fields of practice. Which brings us back to the question of inter-field dynamics discussed above, and to the question to what extent the concepts employed by the actors resemble the structural models of Bourdieu. In colonial South Africa, the decision of a missionary to bodily defend alleged witches against physical harm might well be interpreted as the immediate reaction of a practical sense, though the missionary's conviction that witches do not exist might better be specified as a cognitive rather than simple bodily disposition.[11] But the action of the missionary

---

11 From a cognitive perspective, Strauss and Quinn (1997: 46–47) criticize Bourdieu's concept of habitus for overemphasizing the dichotomy between conscious discourse and embodied practice, for disregarding emotions and motivations, and for marginalizing the intentions of the actors. For a reading of Bourdieu as cognitive sociology see Lizardo (2004, 2011), for the use of Bourdieu to criticize a cognitive theory of religion see Echtler (2010).

eventually led to the intervention of the Secretary of Native Affairs, who in the written communications of state bureaucracy explicitly rejects any religious considerations interfering with state administration, demanding that the actors from the religious sphere keep within the boundaries of their constituency, and, in case of conflict, submit to the state (Berner). In Eritrea, religious leaders demand autonomy for the religious field, and are supported in their struggle by international organizations promoting freedom of religion, but these claims are ignored by political leaders who regard the religious actors as trespassing into the political realm and prosecute them accordingly (Treiber). In Post-Apartheid South Africa, African diviners and Pagans address the symbolic violence inherent in the concept of 'witchcraft' in the public sphere, and indeed take their contestations of the structure of the religious field to court (Wallace). In these cases it might be argued that we overemphasize the role of intellectuals, and, for the intellectuals themselves, the importance of conscious, deliberate action. But we hold that strategic interventions performed in a conscious mode of operation have effects on social fields and their practices and should not be ignored only because they do not conform to Bourdieu's notion of habitus.[12]

Another reason why we emphasize conscious and reflective aspects of habitus driven practice might be due to another characteristic of religious fields in Africa. Throughout, we encounter hysteresis, mismatches between habitus and field, typical of "situations of crisis or sudden change, especially those seen at the time of abrupt encounters between civilizations linked to the colonial situation or too-rapid movements in social space" (Bourdieu 2000: 161, see also Hardy 2008). It is in such situations of rupture between subjectified and objectified structure that practices, otherwise taken for granted, become problematic and the subject of reflection and discourse, especially in religious fields where there are actors with time on their hands and dispositions to move into scholastic modes of viewing the world. Typical examples for these dynamics are the African Independent Churches and their leaders, whose success as newcomers in Christian fields was based on their reverence to pre-existing habitus in the African laity when they (re-)introduced certain practices and concepts, like color-coding, sacred places, dancing, or sacrifices to ancestors,

---

12   According to Bourdieu (1990: 53), "[i]t is, of course, never ruled out that the responses of the *habitus* may be accompanied by a strategic calculation tending to perform in a conscious mode the operation that the *habitus* performs quite differently," but he also insists that the theoretical model "is separated from what the agents master in the practical state [...] by the infinitesimal but infinite distance that defines awareness or (it amounts to the same thing) explicit statement" (ibid., 270).

into the religious field (Draper, Echtler). In a way, these innovations overcame the earlier mismatches between Christian fields and African dispositions, but they immediately created a new rift between the reconfigured religious field and the missionaries' habitus. Moreover, the missionaries reacted by explicitly attacking these practices and beliefs: If Africans were to save their souls, and thereby, in terms of the structural model, belong to the religious field proper, they had to abandon them. These dynamics are not restricted to the colonial situation either. In contemporary Kenya, members of Tablīghī Jamā'at introduce new practices, and new types of cultural capital as the basis for religious leadership, innovations that create a mismatch with the habitus of the established leadership who attack the newcomers as uneducated and unqualified (Wario). We do not argue that the discourses about practices in the religious fields indicate that the actors' struggle over positions is the result of deliberate strategies; indeed, most of them serve to misrecognize the actors' interest. Nor do we hold that the discourses determine the practices, far from it, but they are nevertheless not without impact on the structure of the field.

A consequence of this, together with the importance of inter-field relations, is the possibility of feedback loops between religious fields and academic practices, the asymmetrical power relations between the subaltern and the scientist that play a major role in postcolonial studies of Africa and elsewhere (Spivak 1988). We argue that the position of the leader of the Nazareth Baptist Church, his symbolic capital, is primarily based on the acknowledgement of his followers, on their bodily practice of falling on their knees and shouting "You are holy" whenever they encounter him. But we also hold that the academic discourse on the Christian character of the church and the messianic character of its leader have an influence on the field, especially since the church leaders perceive academic classifications as "the stick and the carrot", i.e. as the exertion of symbolic violence (Echtler). Bourdieu addressed this need for reflexivity with the concept of participant objectivation where he argued that what needs to be objectivized is "the social world that has made both the anthropologist and the conscious or unconscious anthropology that she (or he) engages in her anthropological practice" (Bourdieu 2003: 283). To that, we would add the importance of reflecting on the inter-relations between the academic and religious fields. Thus, we end with two questions. How does our use of Bourdieu in analyzing African religions relate to our position in the academic field? How does our analysis of religions as strategic practice effect social actors in Africa? We cannot even begin to answer these questions here, but we suspect that the answers will be related to what we hold to be the central tenet of Bourdieu's theory for analyzing the dynamics of religious fields, namely, that these dynamics are driven by the *"exchange* relations established between specialists and laypersons on the basis of different interests, and the relation of *competition*, which oppose various specialists to each other inside the religious field" (Bourdieu 1991: 17, emphasis in original). The same holds true for the scientific field. With this book we take a stand in competitive relations with our colleagues, we showcase our particular cultural capital, acquired in research in African religions and in reading Bourdieu, in the hope of converting it into scientific fame and well-paid positions, that is, into symbolic and economic capital. In the exchange relations with the scientific laity, we offer a critical rather than apologetic view on religion in the hope that this agrees with the interests of a sizable portion of the laity who will use our findings to further their own ends and continue to invest society's surplus in funding scholars of religion in turn.

References

Adogame, Afe, Ezra Chitando and Bolaji Bateye, eds. 2012. *African Traditions in the Study of Religion in Africa: Emerging Trends, Indigenous Spirituality and the Interface with other World Religions; Essays in Honour of Jacob Kehinde Olupona*. Farnham: Ashgate.

Anderson, Allan. 2000. *Zion and Pentecost. The Spirituality and Experience of Pentecostal and Zionist/Apostolic Churches in South Africa*. Pretoria: Unisa Press.

Asad, Talal. 1997. *Genealogies of Religion. Discipline and Reasons of Power in Christianity and Islam*. Baltimore: John Hopkins University Press.

Berard, T. J. 2005. Rethinking Practices and Structures. *Philosophy of the Social Sciences* 35 (2): 196–230.

p'Bitek, Okot. 1971. *African Religions in Western Scholarship*. Kampala: East African Literature Bureau.

Bourdieu, Pierre. 1958. *Sociologie de l'Algérie*. Paris: Presses Universitaires de France.

———. 1971a. Une interpretation de la théorie de la religion selon Max Weber. *Archives européennes de sociologie* 12: 3–21.

———. 1971b. Genèse et structure du champ religieux. *Revue Française de Sociologie* 12 (3): 295–334.

———. 1977. *Outline of a Theory of Practice*. Cambridge: Cambridge University Press.

———. 1982. Les rites d'institution. *Actes de la recherche en sciences sociales* 43: 58–63.

———. 1984. *Distinction. A Social Critique of the Judgment of Taste*. Cambridge: Harvard University Press.

———. 1985. The Genesis of the Concepts of Habitus and Field. *Sociocriticism* 2: 11–24.

———. 1986. The Forms of Capital. In *Handbook of Theory and Research for the Sociology of Education*, edited by John Richardson, 241–258. New York: Greenwood Press.

———. 1987a. Legitimation and Structured Interests in Weber's Sociology of Religion. In *Max Weber, Rationality, and Modernity*, edited by Scott Lash and Sam Whimster, 119–136. London: Allen and Unwin.

———. 1987b. Sociologues de la croyance et croyances de sociologues. In *Choses dites*, 106–111. Paris: Éditions de Minuit.

———. 1987c. La dissolution du religieux. In *Choses dites*, 117–123. Paris: Éditions de Minuit.

———. 1988. *Homo Academicus*. Stanford: Stanford University Press.

———. 1989. Social Space and Symbolic Power. *Sociological Theory* 7 (1): 14–25.

———. 1990. *The Logic of Practice*. Stanford: Stanford University Press.

———. 1991. Genesis and Structure of the Religious Field. *Comparative Social Research* 13: 1–44.

———. 1992a. Price Formation and the Anticipation of Profits. In *Language and Symbolic Power*, 66–89. Cambridge: Polity Press.

———. 1992b. Authorized Language: The Social Conditions for the Effectiveness of Ritual Discourse. In *Language and Symbolic Power*, 107–116. Cambridge: Polity Press.

———. 1996. *The Rules of Art. Genesis and Structure of the Literary Field*. Stanford: Stanford University Press.

———. 1998. *Practical Reason. On the Theory of Action*. Stanford: Stanford University Press.

———. 2000. *Pascalian Meditations*. Stanford: Stanford University Press.

———. 2003. Participant Objectivation. *Journal of the Royal Anthropological Institute* (N.S.) 9: 281–294.

Bourdieu, Pierre, and Monique de Saint Martin. 1982. La sainte famille: L'épiscopat français dans le camp du pouvoir. *Actes de la recherche en sciences sociales* 44/45: 2–53.

Bourdieu, Pierre, and Loïc Wacquant. 1992. *An Invitation to Reflexive Sociology*. Cambridge: Polity Press.

Chidester, David. 1996. *Savage Systems. Colonialism and Comparative Religion in Southern Africa*. Charlottesville: University Press of Virginia.

———. 2012. *Wild Religion. Tracking the Sacred in South Africa*. Berkeley: University of California Press.

———. 2014. *Empire of Religion: Imperialism and Comparative Religion*. Chicago: The University of Chicago Press.

Comaroff, Jean. 1985. *Body of Power, Spirit of Resistance: The Culture and History of a South African People*. Chicago: University of Chicago Press.

Comaroff, Jean, and John L. Comaroff. 1999. Occult Economies and the Violence of Abstraction: Notes from the South African Postcolony. *American Ethnologist* 26 (2): 279–303.

Corso, John. 2012. In Defence of Symbolic Interactionism: A Theoretical Response to Bourdieu. *Max Weber Studies* 12 (2): 225–239.

Dianteill, Erwan. 2003. Pierre Bourdieu and the Sociology of Religion: A Central and Peripheral Concern. *Theory and Society* 32: 529–549.

Echtler, Magnus. 2010. A Real Mass Worship They Will Never Forget. Rituals and Cognition in the Nazareth Baptist Church, South Africa. In *Body, Performance, Agency, and Experience.* Vol. 11 of *Ritual Dynamics and the Science of Ritual,* edited by Angelos Chaniotis, Silke Leopold, Thomas Quartier, Joanna Wojtkowiak, Jan Weinhold and Geoffrey Samuel, 371–397. Wiesbaden: Harrassowitz.

Egger, Stephan. 2011. Pierre Bourdieus Religionssoziologie. Eine werkbiographische Skizze. In *Religion. Schriften zur Kultursoziologie 5,* by Pierre Bourdieu, 257–278. Frankfurt a M: Suhrkamp.

Egger, Stephan, Andreas Pfeuffer and Franz Schultheis. 2000. Vom Habitus zum Feld. Religion, Soziologie und die Spuren Max Webers bei Pierre Bourdieu. In *Das religiöse Feld. Texte zur Ökonomie des Heilsgeschehens,* by Pierre Bourdieu, 131–176. Konstanz: UVK.

Egger, Stephan and Franz Schultheis. 2011. Editorische Anmerkungen. In *Religion. Schriften zur Kultursoziologie 5,* by Pierre Bourdieu, 252–256. Frankfurt a M: Suhrkamp.

Ellis, Stephen, and Gerrie ter Haar. 1998. Religion and Politics in Sub-Saharan Africa. *Journal of Modern African Studies* 36 (2): 175–201.

———. 2004. *Worlds of Power: Religious Thought and Political Practice in Africa,* New York: Oxford University Press.

———. 2007. Religion and Politics: Taking African Epistemologies Seriously. *Journal of Modern African Studies* 45 (3): 385–401.

Engler, Steven. 2003. Modern Times: Religion, Consecration and the State in Bourdieu. *Cultural Studies* 17 (3/4): 445–467.

Evens, T. M. S. 1999. Bourdieu and the Logic of Practice: Is All Giving Indian-Giving or is "Generalized Materialism" Not Enough? *Sociological Theory* 17 (1): 3–31.

Evans, T. M. S. and Don Handelman. 2006. Introduction: The Ethnographic Praxis of the Theory of Practice. In *The Manchester School. Practice and Ethnographic Practice in Anthropology* edited by T. M. S. Evans & Don Handelman, 1–11. New York: Berghahn.

Gerrans, Philip. 2005. Tacit Knowledge, Rule Following and Pierre Bourdieu's Philosophy of Social Science. *Anthropological Theory* 5 (1): 53–71.

Gluckman, Max (ed.) 1964. *Closed Systems and Open Minds. The Limits of Naivety in Social Anthropology.* Edinburgh: Oliver & Boyd.

Haar, Gerrie ter and Stephen Ellis. 2009. The Occult does not Exist. A Response to Terence Ranger. *Africa* 79 (3): 399–412.

Hackett, Rosalind IJ, ed. 1987. *New Religious Movements in Nigeria.* Lewiston: Edwin Mellen Press.

Hardy, Cheryl. 2008. Hysteresis. In *Pierre Bourdieu. Key Concepts*, edited by Michael Grenfell, 131–148. Stocksfield: Acumen.

Horton, Mark. 2001. The Islamic Conversion of the Swahili Coast 750–1500; Some Archaeological and Historical Evidence. In *Islam in East Africa: New Sources*, edited by B. S. Amoretti, 449–469. Rome: Herda.

Hutt, Curtis. 2007. Pierre Bourdieu on the Verstehende Soziologie of Max Weber. *Method and Theory in the Study of Religion* 19: 232–254.

Idowu, E. Bolaji. 1962. *Olodumare: God in Yoruba Belief*. London: Longman Publishers

———. 1973. *African Traditional Religion: A Definition*. London: SCM Press Ltd.

Ikenga-Metuh, Emefie. 1987. *Comparative Studies of African Traditional Religions*. Onitsha: IMICO Publishers.

———. 1981. *God and Man in African Traditional Religion: A Case Study of the Igbo of Nigeria*. London: Geoffrey Chapman.

Insoll, Timothy. 2003. *The Archaeology of Islam in Sub-Saharan Africa*. Cambridge: Cambridge University Press.

Jenkins, Richard. 1992. *Pierre Bourdieu*. London: Routledge.

Kalu, Ogbu. 2008. *African Pentecostalism. An Introduction*. Oxford: Oxford University Press.

Kirsch, Thomas G. 2004. Restaging the Will to Believe: Religious Pluralism, Anti-Syncretism, and the Problem of Belief. *American Anthropologist* 106 (4): 699–709.

Kollman, Paul. 2010a. Classifying African Christianities: Past, Present, and Future: Part One. *Journal of Religion in Africa* 40: 3–32.

———. 2010b. Classifying African Christianities, Part Two: The Anthropology of Christianity and Generations of African Christians. *Journal of Religion in Africa* 40: 118–148.

Lakoff, George and Mark Johnson. 1980. *Metaphors We Live By*. Chicago: University of Chicago Press.

Lambek, Michael. 2008. Provinzializing God? Provocations from an Anthropology of Religion. In *Religion. Beyond a Concept*, edited by Hent de Vries, 120–138. New York: Fordham University Press.

Larkin, Brian, and Birgit Meyer. 2006. Pentecostalism, Islam and Culture: New Religious Movements in West Africa. In *Themes in West African History*, edited by Emmanuel Kwaku Akyeampong, 286–312. Oxford: James Currey.

Lebaron, Frédéric. 2003. Pierre Bourdieu: Economic Models Against Economism. *Theory and Society* 32: 551–565.

Levtzion, Nehemia and Randall L. Powels. 2000. Patterns of Islamization and Varieties of Religious Experience Among Muslims of Africa. In *The History of Islam in Africa*, edited by Nehemia Levtzion and Randall L. Powels, 1–20. Athens: Ohio University Press.

Lizardo, Omar. 2004. The Cognitive Origin of Bourdieu's Habitus. *Journal for the Theory of Social Behaviour* 34 (4): 375–401.

———. 2010. Beyond the Antinomies of Structure: Levi-Strauss, Giddens, Bourdieu, and Sewell. *Theory and Society* 39 (6): 651–688.

———. 2011. Pierre Bourdieu as a Post-Cultural Theorist. *Cultural Sociology* 5 (1): 1–22.

Ludwig, Frieder and Afe Adogame, eds. 2004. *European Traditions in the Study of Religion in Africa*. Wiesbaden: Harrassowitz.

Marshall, Ruth. 2009. *Political Spiritualities: The Pentecostal Revolution in Nigeria*. Chicago: University of Chicago Press.

Masquelier, Adeline. 2009. *Women and Islamic Revival in a West African Town*. Bloomington: Indiana University Press.

Mbiti, John S. 1969. *African Religions and Philosophy*. London: Heinemann.

———. 1970. *Concepts of God in Africa*. London: SPCK Publishers.

McIntosh, Janet. 2009. *The Edge of Islam: Power, Personhood, and Ethnoreligious Boundaries on the Kenya Coast*. Durham: Duke University Press.

Meyer, Birgit. 2004. Christianity in Africa: From African Independent to Pentecostal-Charismatic Churches. *Annual Review of Anthropology* 33: 447–474.

———. 2009. A Response to ter Haar and Ellis. *Africa* 79 (3): 413–415.

Moebius, Stephan. 2006. Pierre Bourdieu: Zur Kritik der symbolischen Gewalt. In *Kultur. Theorien der Gegenwart*, edited by Stephan Moebius and Dirk Quadflieg, 51–66. Wiesbaden: Verlag für Sozialwissenschaften.

Moore, Dale H. 1936. Christianity in Ethiopia. *Church History* 5 (3): 271–284.

Morgan, David. 2005. *Sacred Gaze: Religious Visual Culture in Theory and Practice*. Berkeley: University of California Press.

Müller, Hans-Peter. 2002. Die Einbettung des Handelns. Pierre Bourdieus Praxeologie. *Berliner Journal für Soziologie* 12 (2): 157–171.

Ortner, Sherry B. 1984. Theory in Anthropology Since the Sixties. *Comparative Studies in Society and History* 26: 126–166.

———. 2005. Subjectivity and Cultural Critique. *Anthropological Theory* 5(1): 31–52.

Parry, Ken, ed. 2010. *Blackwell Companion to Eastern Christianity*. West Sussex: Blackwell Publishing Ltd.

Peel, J. D. Y. 1990. The Pastor and the Babalawo: The Interaction of Religions in Nineteenth-Century Yorubaland. *Africa* 60 (3): 338–369.

———. 1995. For Who Hath Despised the Day of Small Things? Missionary Narratives and Historical Anthropology. *Comparative Studies in Society and History* 37 (3): 581–607.

———. 2000. *Religious Encounter and the Making of the Yoruba*. Bloomington, Indiana: Indiana University Press.

Pels, Peter. 1998. The Magic of Africa: Reflections on a Western Commonplace. *African Studies Review* 41 (3): 193–209.

Platvoet, Jan, James Cox and Jacob Olupona, eds. 1996. *The Study of Religions in Africa. Past, Present and Prospects*. Cambridge: Roots & Branches.

Ranger, Terence. 2007. Scotland Yard in the Bush: Medicine Murders, Child Witches and the Construction of the Occult: A Literature Review. *Africa* 77 (2): 272–283.

Rehbein, Boike. 2003. 'Sozialer Raum' und Felder. In *Pierrre Bourdieus Theorie des Sozialen. Probleme und Perspektiven*, edited by Boike Rehbein, Gernot Saalmann and Hermann Schwengel, 77–95. Konstanz: UVK.

Rey, Terry. 2004. Marketing the Goods of Salvation: Bourdieu on Religion. *Religion* 34: 331–343.

———. 2007. *Bourdieu on Religion: Imposing Faith and Legitimacy*. London: Equinox Publishers.

Riesebrodt, Martin. 2010. *The Promise of Salvation: A Theory of Religion*, translated by Steven Rendall, Chicago: The University of Chicago Press.

Robinson, David. 2004. *Muslim Societies in African History*. Cambridge: Cambridge University Press.

Ruch, E. A. and K. C. Anyanwu. 1981. *African Philosophy: An Introduction to the Main Philosophical Trends in Contemporary Africa*, Rome: Catholic Book Agency.

Ruel, Malcolm. 1997. *Belief, Ritual and the Securing of Life: Reflective Essays on a Bantu Religion*. Leiden: Brill.

Shaw, Rosalind. 1990. The Invention of 'African Traditional Religion'. *Religion* 20: 339–353.

Schmidt, Alfred. 1973. Praxis. In *Handbuch philosophischer Grundbegriffe*, edited by Hermann Krings, Hans Michael Baumgartner and Christoph Wild, 1107–1138. München: Kösel.

Schultheis, Franz. 2008. Salvation Goods and Domination: Pierre Bourdieu's Sociology of the Religious Field. In *Salvation Goods and Religious Markets. Theory and Applications*, edited by Jörg Stolz, 31–50. New York: Peter Lang.

Schulz, Dorothea E. 2003. 'Charisma and Brotherhood' Revisited: Mass-Mediated Forms of Spirituality in Urban Mali. *Journal of Religion in Africa* 33 (2): 146–171.

Seesemann, Rüdiger. 2006. African Islam or Islam in Africa? Evidence from Kenya. In *The Global Worlds of the Swahili. Interfaces of Islam, Identity and Space in 19th and 20th-Century East Africa*, edited by Roman Loimeier and Rüdiger Seesemann, 229–250. Münster: Lit.

Smith, Jonathan Z. 1998. Religion, Religions, Religious. In *Critical Terms for Religious Studies*, edited by Mark C. Taylor, 269–284. Chicago: University of Chicago Press.

Soares, Benjamin. 2000. Notes on the Anthropological Study of Islam and Muslim Societies in Africa. *Culture and Religion* 1(2): 277–285.

Spivak, Gayatri. 1988. Can the Subaltern Speak? In *Marxism and the Interpretation of Culture*, edited by Cary Nelson and Larry Grossberg, 271–313. Urbana: University of Illinois Press.

Strauss, Claudia and Naomi Quinn. 1997. *A Cognitive Theory of Cultural Meaning*. Cambridge: Cambridge University Press.

Swartz, David. 1996. Bridging the Study of Culture and Religion. Pierre Bourdieu's Political Economy of Symbolic Power. *Sociology of Religion* 57: 71–85.

Thomson, Patricia. 2008. Field. In *Pierre Bourdieu. Key Concepts*, edited by Michael Grenfell, 67–81. Stocksfield: Acumen.

Ukah, Asonzeh FK. 2008. *A New Paradigm of Pentecostal Power: A Study of the Redeemed Christian Church of God in Nigeria*. Trenton: Africa World Press.

Urban, Hugh B. 2003. Sacred Capital: Pierre Bourdieu and the Study of Religion. *Method and Theory in the Study of Religion* 15: 354–389.

———. 2005. Spiritual Capital, Academic Capital and the Politics of Scholarship: A Response to Bradford Verter. *Method and Theory in the Study of Religion* 17: 166–175.

Vandenberghe, Frédéric. 1999. "The real is relational": An Epistemological Analysis of Pierre Bourdieu's Generative Structuralism. *Sociological Theory* 17 (1): 32–67.

Verter, Bradford. 2003. Spiritual Capital: Theorizing Religion with Bourdieu against Bourdieu. *Sociological Theory* 21: 150–174.

———. 2004. Bourdieu and the Bauls Reconsidered. *Method and Theory in the Study of Religion* 16: 182–192.

Westerlund, David. 1985. *African Religion in African Scholarship. A Preliminary Study of the Religious and Political Background*. Stockholm: Almqvist & Wiksell.

Westerlund, David and Eva Evers Rosander, eds. 1997. *African Islam and Islam in Africa*. London: Hurst & Company.

Inner-Field Dynamics

CHAPTER 2

Pierre Bourdieu and the Role of the Spirit in Some Zulu/Swathi AICs

Jonathan A. Draper

Introduction

Since the groundbreaking work of Bengt Sundkler in *Bantu Prophets in South Africa* (1948), the position of the Holy Spirit in African Initiated Churches has long been a point of discussion. It formed the focus of a study I undertook in response to an invitation to a Conference on the Holy Spirit and Worship at Yale University in 2008, which left me feeling that I still had not fully grasped the dynamics of the field (Draper 2009). My study was provoked also by the thesis of Anders Fogelqvist (1986) on the AmaJericho Church in Swaziland, which takes up the pioneer work of Bengt Sundkler in *Zulu Zion* (1968). Fogelqvist rightly sees the relationship between the Holy Spirit and power, but wrongly, in my opinion, *reduces* the Holy Spirit to power. After noting that Elias Vilikati, the founder of the church, experienced conversion as the reception of the Spirit and that this was associated by him with power, he comments briefly: "In the context of the Jericho Church, as well as among other Swazi Zionists, the two terms appear to be interchangeable. When an attempt is made to define them, it is usually done by referring one to the other" (Fogelqvist 1986: 124). The word Spirit or *uMoya* is, he argues, of missionary origin, so that they are "two terms of different origin to describe the same concept" (ibid.: 125; cf. Kiernan 1990, though his study is more nuanced). After this, he speaks only of power and never of Spirit. There are two points to be made against this reductionist position. The first is that, while the earliest Zulu dictionary published by Bishop John William Colenso (1861) on which the later dictionaries cited by Fogelqvist depend does suggest that the use of Spirit to refer to numinous agency is of missionary origin, it ignores the role of African agents who were the source of the choice of this word to render the English word Spirit (or the Afrikaans word Gees, since this was the first European language in the field). Secondly, it is challenged by a statement of one of our own informants, asked to say what his church believed about the Spirit, that "The Spirit is everything".[1]

---

[1] The data for this chapter is derived from fieldwork on African Initiated Churches funded by a National Research Foundation grant on Indigenous Knowledge Systems. Besides myself,

That would be to say, according to Fogelqvist's definition, "Power is everything". Well, obviously, power or contested hegemony is a fundamental part of all human behavior, but that does not explain the specific role of Spirit in the universe of meaning constituted by Zulu Zion—it becomes a tautology. Holy Spirit (*uMoya oyiNcwele*) is only half of the power equation, if one puts it like that. The other half is constituted by evil spirit (*umoya omubi*) with its corollaries of *uSatan*, witchcraft (*umthakati*) and demons (*amadimoni*) in general. In addition, Fogelqvist does not take account of the specifically *embodied* nature of spirit, good and evil, in Zionist understanding, its essential materiality in that it inheres in bodies, objects, places and other *materia*.

While Fogelqvist essentially dismisses the relevance of the Christian concept of the Holy Spirit in his equation of the term with pre-Christian concepts of power, Allan Anderson (2000) conflates the concept of Holy Spirit in African Initiated Churches with the Holy Spirit in modern Western Pentecostalism. His concern is to undo the stigmatization of Zionist churches by traditional mainline Christian churches and to view it as part of a worldwide phenomenon of Pentecostal experience (which is fast becoming a new and accepted "mainline" Christian phenomenon of the West). However, there is a certain "imperialism" of the West latent in this attempt also, which downplays the differences and the specifically African cultural nuances in Zionist understandings of the Spirit and its rebellion against Western imperialism and domination. There is no denying the early links between American Pentecostalism and the emergence of Zionism in Africa, highlighted already by Sundkler (1948: 47–50; 1976: 1–67), and this chapter certainly has no desire to continue the marginalization of Zionism as an expression of Christian experience, nor to minimize the ground-breaking "boundary jumping" of the early Pentecostal missions, but the specific character of Zionist appropriation of the concept of Holy

---

the fieldwork was undertaken by Dr. Kenneth Mtata and Ms. Queen Masondo. Fieldwork consisted of qualitative interviews of leaders and members of selected churches focusing on their understanding of Holy Spirit, guided by a series of structured questions, as well as observation of communal worship and ritual. Signed informed consent was obtained for each interview in accordance with the ethics policy of the University of KwaZulu-Natal, as well as permission from the 'gatekeepers' of the churches to attend gatherings. The research focused on two churches claiming their origin from the breakaway of Daniel Nkonyane from Pieter le Roux's Apostolic Faith Mission: the Christian Catholic Apostolic Holy Spirit Church in Zion (CCAHSCZ), the Zion Combination Church founded in 1906; as well as the Jericho Church of Elias Vilikazi in Swaziland founded in 1948. This fieldwork builds on earlier fieldwork and archival research also funded by the National Research Foundation on the *iBandla Labancwele* (Church of the Saints) founded by George Khambule in 1918 and now defunct.

Spirit and its relation to pre-colonial African culture should not be too quickly passed over either.

'Spirit' is central to an understanding of the success of the Zionist Churches in the religious field. 'Spirit' represents cultural capital that draws simultaneously on the Christian/Pentecostal *habitus* and the Zulu/Swathi *habitus*. It is a key instance of the negotiation of power for Africans caught between the two worlds of the colonizers and the colonized, which Jean Comaroff has portrayed with respect to the Baralong, "as determined, yet determining, in their own history; as human beings who, in their everyday production of goods and meanings, acquiesce yet protest, reproduce yet seek to transform their predicament" (Comaroff 1986: 10–11). Since 's/Spirit'[2] is regarded as a 'legitimate' source of power by both parties in the emergent religious field in colonial southern Africa, the missionaries and their converts, and is (in theory) regarded as beyond the control of either party by definition, and since its relation to culture and to colonial power relations is misrecognized by both parties, it changes the balance of power in the contestation of the religious field. This can be demonstrated in the precise historical context of the emergence of Daniel Nkonyane's Zionist church from the Dutch Reform Mission (and its Pentecostal breakaway) at Wakkerstroom in 1906. The success of the Zionist movement can be seen to be linked to the connection with the experience of the numinous and its symbolic representation in two (religious) traditions that determine the (objective) structure of the field. Consequently, this chapter rejects the positions of Fogelqvist, who argues for a simple continuity of the African strand in the concept of power-spirit, and Anderson, who argues for the success of Zionism as part of the world-wide phenomenon of the spread of American Pentecostalism, without taking proper account of the specificity of the Nguni cultural *habitus*.

A Framework Suggested by Bourdieu's Concept of Field

It seems to me that the work of Pierre Bourdieu offers a helpful way to assess this data, because his own work begins, as he repeatedly reminds his readers, with an attempt at "escaping both the objectivism of action understood as a

---

2 The use of the capitalized 'Spirit' rather than spirit/s obviously suggests the Christian doctrine of 'Holy Spirit' and presents a problem in a discussion of the intersection of the missionaries and their African converts. In the context of this contribution, given its location within missionary discourse, the uncapitalized 'spirit' will be used except for specific references to Christian usage—accepting the ambiguity this leaves in research into AICs.

mechanical reaction 'without an agent' and the subjectivism which portrays action as the deliberate pursuit of a conscious intention, the free project of a conscience positing its own ends and maximizing its utility through rational computation" (Bourdieu and Wacquant 1992: 120). Fogelqvist confuses the *field of religious contestation* with the *universe of discourse* within that field and its contestation by reducing everything to do with Spirit to relations of power. Anderson does not recognize the extent to which the emergence of African Initiated Churches is an exercise of limited agency in the disposition of *cultural capital* in the contestation of the religious field, since he assumes a unity of understanding and practice of Spirit among those claiming to exercise its power. African Initiated Churches become allies in a broad based but fissiparous front against 'mainline' churches. Possession of 'spirit' is a potent form of African cultural capital, maybe a 'trump card,' in the religious field once it is introduced as a legitimate currency, but even a cursory reading of the data shows that the breakaways of black Pentecostals not only from missionary led churches but also emerging 'mainline' white Pentecostal churches were more fundamental than a 'storm in an apartheid teacup'. The arrival of Pentecostal Zionism from the United States in the late nineteenth and early twentieth centuries proved explosive because it changed the boundaries[3] of the religious field and hence changed the balance of power in the contested religious field between the missionaries and their converts irrevocably:

> As a space of potential and active forces, the field is also a *field of struggles* aimed at preserving or transforming the configuration of these forces. Furthermore, the field as a structure of objective relations between positions of force undergirds and guides the strategies whereby the occupants of these positions seek, individually or collectively, to safeguard or improve their position and to impose the principle of hierarchization most favorable to their own products. The strategies of agents depend on their position in the field, that is, in the distribution of the specific capital, and on the perception that they have of the field depending on the point of view they take *on* the field as a view taken from a point *in* the field (Bourdieu and Wacquant 1992: 101).

Since it is a relational space in which agents exercise the force of the capital available to them to transform it to their advantage, field is also a dynamic

---

3   Bourdieu sees the field as a site of "endless change" in which, "Every field constitutes a potentially open space of play whose boundaries are *dynamic borders* which are the stake of the struggles within the field itself" (Bourdieu and Wacquant 1992: 104).

locus of "endless change" (Ibid.: 103). Spirit is central in the *symbolic capital* deployed successfully by the Zulu/Swathi Zionists in contested power relations with the missionaries and other imperial agents in the colonial situation. Leadership and 'ministry' within the community is based on its recognition of an individual's possession and exercise of 'spirit' which does not depend on the validation of colonial agents, since it is perceived as derived from the God on whom the colonial agents themselves base their claim to derive their authority. At the same time, the Zionist communities misrecognize the 'interestedness' of personal claims to possess 'Spirit' in the contestation of power and leadership within the community. The endless splintering of the Zionist churches is nearly always around the issue of succession after the death of the leader. 'Spirit' comes to be understood as an inherently personal quality, and leadership therefore becomes hereditary, while the financial interest and incentive at play in maintaining leadership within a self-perpetuating elite is misrecognized.[4] Hence, in Bourdieu's terms, Fogelqvist confuses the *habitus*— the structuring structures and competencies of the game—with the field, with the game in itself. He does not allow for the nature and significance of the social construction and embeddedness of power within specific cultures, so that its exercise is both enabled and misrecognized in social relations. His assumption seems to be that 'spirit' is simply a synonym for the traditional Zulu concept of power without any discernible influence from Christianity. I consider this to underestimate the fluid and dynamic nature of culture and of social agency, especially in times of rapid social change. It also excludes the possibility and diversity of experience of the numinous in and across cultures.

On the other hand, Anderson's argument that the impact of global Pentecostalism effected a complete change of *habitus* in which the influence of continuing African religious practice is marginal, seems equally implausible on detailed examination. Instead, I argue that the prolonged contestation of the religious field in southern Africa during more than 350 years of colonial occupation[5] presents a more nuanced and complex scenario than either Fogelqvist or Anderson allow. Far from being a "syncretistic sect.... the bridge over which Africans are brought back to heathenism" (Sundkler 1948: 297,

---

4 This is aggravated by the non-stipendiary nature of Zionist ministry, without the benefit of housing or transport even when full-time. The boundaries between personal and church property are often blurred.

5 Although the Portuguese had established trading posts and forts along the Mozambique coast much earlier, the organized settlement of the Cape by the Dutch, which began with the arrival of Jan van Riebeeck in 1652, initiated a much more prolonged and intense colonial occupation of southern Africa.

subsequently retracted), Zionism signifies the emergence of a new African social capital which enabled black African people in southern Africa to counteract the 'symbolic violence' (Bourdieu and Passeron 1977) inflicted on them by the colonial experience in general and the missionary experience and missionary education in particular, and to regain their autonomy without surrendering the new cultural capital they had acquired with their conversion to Christianity which also enabled them to compete more effectively in the contestation of the colonial field.

My discussion is informed largely by the work of Bourdieu in *Outline of a Theory of Practice* (1977), in which Bourdieu contrasts *doxa*, as the unrecognized and therefore undiscussed universe of meaning obtaining for participants in a given field, with *opinion* as the universe of discourse, in which meaning becomes contested because it becomes the known. The contest takes the form of argument over the definition of what is accepted (orthodoxy) and what is rejected (heterodoxy)—which, despite appearances, is never fixed or defined as if it were a system of rules or laws. This struggle over orthodoxy and heterodoxy is, in reality, a struggle over the boundaries of the field, over what constitutes legitimate 'play' in the 'game' (*ludus*), since for play to take place there has to be some measure of 'collusion' (agreement to play) about the boundaries for a field to be active and activated or 'the effects of the field cease' (Bourdieu and Wacquant 1992: 100). Nevertheless, Bourdieu insists that, despite the attempts of those who dominate the field to define its boundaries by force, "it is a limit that is never actually reached, even under the most repressive 'totalitarian' regimes" (ibid.: 102). The missionaries attempted to define the 'orthodoxy' or boundaries of the religious field, but they were never able to do so in any definitive sense.

Bourdieu sometimes seems to use the concept of 'capital' rather fluidly, but insists on the existence of multiple sub-types of capital, more specifically economic, cultural and social capital (the sum total of resources of the individual or group), to which he adds symbolic capital as the form any capital takes when its specific logic is (mis)recognized (Bourdieu and Wacquant 1992: 119). The most important of these for our purposes is cultural capital, that is, "[c]apital, which in its objectified or embodied forms, takes time to accumulate and which, as a potential capacity to produce profits and to reproduce itself in identical or expanded form, contains a tendency to persist in its being, is a force inscribed in the objectivity of things so that everything is not equally possible" (Bourdieu 1986: 241). It is embodied because it is learnt and accumulated in relation to a body in the world, so that the "social order inscribes itself in bodies through this permanent confrontation" until the body becomes a kind of "memory pad" (Bourdieu 1990: 141). For this reason, cultural capital and the *habitus* constitute each other in a field of social 'play' which both enables and limits the spontaneous human agency of a given 'socialized body' in the collective 'socialized body'. Cultural capital and *habitus* constitute the *doxa* which is unknown to its community because it is taken for granted, as the nature of things. When contact with other cultures and contestation of field bring the constructed nature of cultural capital into contestation and thus to conscious recognition, this necessitates a conscious re-ordering of social capital.

Habitus and Cultural Capital in the Context of African Initiated Churches

Cultural capital (symbolic capital inasmuch as it is (mis)recognized and discussed by participants in the game) is not directly exchangeable for, but is nevertheless the precondition for, the accumulation of economic and material capital: for instance, it is the condition for economic and material accumulation and social hierarchy in the Maghreb (Bourdieu 1977). Kinship, marriage and fertility are related to and in a certain way translatable into 'rifles' and hence applicable to larger power contests and protection, and hence to material capital. But they are not reducible to it. They constitute the *habitus* or structuring structures of life within the Maghreb, the rules of the game and the competencies or 'feel for the game' learned by socialization and participation in the field of play. The *habitus* is indeed the product of the material conditions in which it arises and tends to reproduce those same material conditions which produced it, but it cannot be reduced to a deterministic set of laws. Participants in a given field are socialized into a given set of structuring structures from earliest childhood, so that it becomes the condition of their participation in life and obtains the force of *doxa*, the undiscussed universe of meaning that has the force of the obvious and inevitable, even though it is contingent and "the product of history, produces individuals and collective practices, and hence history, in accordance with the schemes engendered by history...a post which survives in the present and tends to perpetuate itself into the future by making itself present in practices structured according to its principles" (Bourdieu 1977: 82). In the Maghreb, the *habitus* constitutes the means for survival in the specific and harsh terrain of the semi-desert conditions in which the people live, constituted over millennia and yet continually contested and evolving in practice in the face of 'objective events'. In other conditions the *habitus* will reflect and reproduce the different circumstances of its production, including but not reducible to its material and economic circumstances, in a constantly evolving and dynamic way.

The situation in the Maghreb is comparable to the religio-cultural *habitus* of the African peoples in sub-Saharan pre-colonial Africa, which reveal similar features related to life in small villages and towns, competition over scarce resources, the unpredictability of rain and the various dangers of their habitat (such as lightning). In an oral culture such as that of the Zulu and Swathi people, the *habitus* is implicit in story, proverb, ritual, dance and song, movement and a host of practices oriented towards successful competition in the field under the conditions which produced it. However, southern Africa also was subject to imperial and colonial invasion by force of arms by European societies which had a sophisticated and reflexive system of legitimation underpinning and misrecognizing the exercise of brute force in their conquest of the indigenous peoples. This intrusion was spear-headed by the missionaries, who were concerned precisely with the subversion of the *habitus* of the indigenous people, with the devaluation of their cultural capital as part of a sustained attempt to redefine the field and insert their own Western Christian cultural capital as the currency of power and contestation. The earliest missionary endeavor was a precursor to the physical and military domination and the appropriation of the economic and material capital of the African people, even if the missionaries themselves may have entirely or partly misrecognized the role they were playing.[6] Naturally, this enforced interaction redrew the boundaries of the *field* of contested power relations for both parties—even if the impact was far greater for the conquered than for the conquerors. Pre-colonial sub-Saharan Africa was not characterized by a religious field separate from the rest of social and economic life, since religion was embedded in other/all activities. However, in line with Bourdieu's suggestion of *multiple fields* emerging under

---

6 Even 'enlightened' missionaries open to the humanity and culture of the African people they sought to Christianize, such as Bishop John William Colenso, were 'blind' to the nature of imperial domination in their own work. See Jeff Guy (1983, esp. 350–360) and various essays in Jonathan A. Draper (2003a). Jean and John Comaroff (1991) in their discussion of this question emphasize the extent to which both the missionaries and the indigenous peoples were unaware and experimental in their interaction, and they may have overstated the case. Bourdieu does not seem so far from this in his insistence that so-called rules and taxonomies do not govern behavior but are a feature of the reality of practice, or of the sense of the game in a given *habitus*, and "owe their value to the fact that they are 'practical,' that they make it possible to bring in just enough logic for the needs of practice, neither too much—fuzziness is often indispensable, particularly in negotiations—not too little, because life would become impossible" (in an interview with Lamaison 1986: 118). However, Bourdieu also insists that colonial repression in Algeria was "knowingly and methodically produced in order to ensure the control of the dominant power and to further the interests of its own nationals" (1962: 120).

the conditions of modernity, one can meaningfully speak of an emerging *field of religious contestation* under colonial conditions and the beginning of the incorporation of the indigenous peoples of Africa into the global structures of 'modernity'. However, it is unlikely that the early Christian converts made a distinction between 'strictly religious' and economic, territorial, or other social goals in the manner of modern complex 'differentiated' societies with their "totality of the practices which, although objectively economic are not and cannot be socially recognized as economic, and which can be performed only at the cost of a whole labor of dissimulation, or, more precisely, *euphemization*" (Bourdieu 1986).

In order for there to be any meaningful engagement between missionaries and indigenous peoples in this emerging religious field, there was necessarily a process of (mutual) definition of their religious *habitus*. The *habitus* had to be negotiated between missionaries, outsiders viewed with suspicion, and indigenous *agents* who could mediate access for them to the African *field*. In this delicate situation, the African agents could exercise a power invisible for the most part to historical investigation, since the words suggested for equivalency, the explanations provided for the religio-cultural symbols and activities, the accounts of the indigenous belief systems were impervious to Western gaze, except through their eyes and their mediation. The result was intense contestation not merely between indigenous agents but also between the missionaries themselves, as for example the debate over the name for God in Zulu between *uNkulunkulu, umVelingcangi, uThixo, uDio, uThongo* and so on, admirably set out in David Chidester's, *Savage Systems* (1996). Some of the missionaries were more sensitive and open to the Zulu *habitus* than others, more able and willing to engage in language acquisition, conversation, observation and more open to the intrinsic merits of the local culture (such as Bishop John William Colenso). In other words, a few of the missionaries were open to the possibility of becoming players in the existing field of the indigenous people in terms of their own *habitus*, but they were the minority. For most missionaries, their strategy was designed to strip their converts of their own and draw them into the missionary's religious field and school them in an acquired religio-cultural *habitus*. For most missionaries, there was a systematic misrecognition of what they were doing, just as for many 'native agents' and Christian converts (*Amakholwa*) who "became a de facto comprador class trafficking in the modernity of the colonial political system while simultaneously speaking on behalf of and representing native opinion" (Mokoena 2011: 23). However, their hybrid identity, situated between and mediating two worlds, also placed them in a unique position as 'players of the game' familiar with two sets of rules and possessing a *feel for the game* or fluency in code switching between them.

In any case, what resulted from the missionary activity was the superimposition and interplay of two competing constructions of the *habitus* in one common religious field. The early colonial situation was fluid and the social standing and identities of colonists and the indigenous people was constantly negotiated. For instance, missionaries might initially have come from despised and economically disadvantaged groups back home but have a new and elevated social status in the mission field (Comaroff and Comaroff 1991). However, that status depended on recruiting and retaining converts, on the myth of the triumph of the gospel over the entire world and the 'civilizing' of the savage 'other'. The indigenous people initially controlled the land and the means of production and might also have a high social status in their own communities, but had a low social status within the mission compared with the status of the missionary. However, their own sense of worth and their standing with their non-Christian peers demanded recognition from the missionaries. The terms and definitions of the game were also subject to the dynamics of the imperial and colonial domination as the material resources which formed the basis for the embedded religious field in African society were gradually but systematically wrested from their control (e.g. cattle and grazing rights). Social and economic positions began to change as the white colonial government gained full control of the natural resources and labor market, which tended to reverse the positions of the early mission field. The missionary now controlled the mission land (often the only land available to converts), 'discipline', hierarchy and the decision making apparatus of the church, and those who had joined them were essentially disempowered. The *Amakholwa*, like the missionaries, sought to position themselves within the changing political landscape, initially seeking unsuccessfully to gain full acceptance and equality, and when this failed sought ways of redrawing the boundaries of the field, to construct alternative identities and status within alternative hybrid structures. African Zionism represents one such avenue designed to re-assign value markers in the colonial field. While at the outset the African 'players' may have held the balance of social and economic capital in the pre-colonial period, with possession of land and cattle as well as high status in their own community, their embedded and oral culture put them at a disadvantage in a contestation over the new Christian cultural and symbolic capital vested in a book whose interpretation was controlled by literate missionaries. But knowledge of the Bible, whether appropriated orally or by the ability to read it, offered a strategic counterpoint to white domination in contestation of the religious field. The battle over the symbolic capital of the Bible intensified when combined with unmediated access to the legitimating power of Holy Spirit offered by the new Pentecostal Zionism originating in the United States, where initially African Americans played leading roles in the Azuza Street Revival. The Bible and the Christian faith could be appropriated now as *African* cultural capital and used in contestation with the missionaries for control of the religious field.

The missionaries were not, on the whole, in a strong position to counter this new strategy. Their conflict with Enlightenment rationalism led them to a literalism in interpretation of the Bible, so that they had no real answer when their converts now began asking why the biblical injunctions to worship on Saturday, to avoid pork, to avoid alcohol, to stop cutting "the forelocks of one's hair," were not carried out; why polygamy should not be permitted when it clearly was so in the Bible; why shoes were worn in the presence of God despite the command to Moses; why demons were not being cast out, the sick healed and the dead raised simply in the name of Jesus; why baptism was not done in the river as it had been in the Jordan for John and Jesus. The Bible seemed to legitimate their experience of the numinous more than the teaching of the missionaries. When black leaders were directly endowed with the power of healing and exorcism and prophecy, the missionaries could no longer justify withholding from such men and women an equal role in leadership of the church and fell back on their control of education, ordination, mission land and their influence with the colonial government to try and regain control of the field. The emerging leaders of the African Initiated Churches, on the other hand, were in a strong position to deploy the symbolic capital of the Christianity, which they had adopted and internalized, in the contestation of the religious field, since the world of the spirit was only too real to African people and African culture had well-established cultural knowledge on how to manipulate it. In this new situation where Holy Spirit was available directly to all, their adopted Christian understanding of Spirit merged with understandings of spirit at the unrecognized level of *doxa* to produce innovations which nevertheless were experienced as 'natural'. In this way, their participation in the contestation of the religious field gave them a strategic advantage over the missionaries. Their cultural capital concerning spirit, drawn from their indigenous knowledge system, when fused with the Christian teaching of the gift of the Spirit to every Christian which was amply attested in the Bible, enabled them to redraw the boundaries of the field and to reconfigure the *habitus* in a way that 'fitted' perfectly and had a 'taken for granted' feel for their followers. Consequently, African Zionism spread rapidly and with a bewildering variety of forms and practices in the twentieth century.

•

Contestation in the Religious Field and Bourdieu's Concept of *Doxa*

As missionaries and Africans squared up in the contest over the religious field, two options suggested themselves: to accept and attempt to adopt the *habitus* of the Western missionaries (*alternation of social universe* in the terms of Berger and Luckmann 1966), which involved not merely a religious switch but also a switch of socio-cultural universe. In a crude form it might be described as an attempt to become English in culture and citizenship within the colonial establishment in Natal as fully acculturated 'exempted natives,' black citizens of the empire (Welsh 1971; Marks and Rathbone 1982: 1–44; Marks 1970). The *Amakholwa*, detribalized and Westernized Christians, sought not only religio-cultural recognition but also to compete in terms of economic capital and production by buying land all over Natal. This had begun with James Allison's Methodist settlement at Edendale in Pietermaritzburg in 1848, and proved a highly successful strategy. The realization that neither colonial society nor the missionaries had any intention of allowing such a cultural and economic intrusion to become a genuine escape from—or inclusion as equals within—white hegemony led first to the formation of breakaways from mainline churches to form independent/ 'Ethiopian' churches (see Sundkler's taxonomy 1948: 38–64). However, since they were still essentially craving equality with the settlers/missionaries according to the same rules, this was in the long run not an effective strategy, and their gradual decline has shown this to be the case.

Another option presented itself with the appearance of American Pentecostal Revivalism in South Africa at the end of the nineteenth century, through Dowie's Christian Zion in Chicago, which was taken up and promoted especially by Pieter le Roux at Wakkerstroom in the independent voortrekker Transvaal Republic—a small town at the intersection of the Dutch and English colonial enterprises (Hofmeyr and Smith 2009). The new possibility of understanding the Holy Spirit as a direct experience of the numinous and as an immanent possession of an individual, related to ecstatic prophetic speech, healing and exorcism, opened up the possibility of a different strategy for contesting the religious field which was far more effective. The possibility of direct revelation of the meaning of the Bible mediated through the Spirit subverted the fundamental presuppositions of mission schools that conversion necessitated Western education to enable converts to read the Bible and understand it. Anderson argues that the American Zionist missionaries did not worry about learning the indigenous languages because they believed that the Holy Spirit would give them the gift of tongues to preach to the people in their own language. This, however, was certainly not the case with the two most important of the Zion missions which concern us here, since the Mahons among the BaSotho at Harrismith and the Le Rouxs among the Zulu in Wakkerstroom certainly became fluent linguists. They did not put much emphasis on speaking in tongues either—something Le Roux never mastered, according to Sundkler (1976: 47)—but rather on prophecy and healing. For this reason they did not stress literacy and therefore schools and education to learn to read the Bible like the other missionaries. They stressed immediate and unmediated access to the Spirit of God and the gifts and power of the Spirit.

Pierre Bourdieu distinguishes between *doxa* as the universe of the 'undiscussed' and therefore the accepted understanding of the way the world is, and 'opinion' as the universe of 'discourse' or discussion and argument of what is contested.[7] Such contestation arises most naturally through the crisis brought on when a particular way of life ceases to be 'self-evident' as a result of 'culture contact' or through "the political and economic crises correlative with class division", both of which result in "competing discourses—whose political truth may be overtly declared or may remain hidden even from the eyes of those engaged in it, under the guise of religious or philosophical oppositions" (1977: 168). The relevance of Bourdieu's model for the African mission field is obvious. The taken-for-granted way of life or *habitus* for African people, in which religion was embedded unreflectively in ritual and custom, and in which the spirit world was pervasive, was confronted with a highly reflective rationalist world view which problematized the African *habitus* and sought to replace it. For those converted to Reformed Christianity in the early missionary period in South Africa, the broad outline of Calvinist theology constituted the *doxa* of the missionaries and was rarely questioned—and therefore brought into the realm of opinion—except where 'idiocentric' figures like Bishop Colenso made an impact. However, the tenets of American Zionist Pentecostalism as mediated by Le Roux and Mahon matched the unstated and undiscussed tenets of Zulu culture far better than those of the Western mission culture. The exclusivist and agonistic nature of Dowie's Zionist Pentecostalism as a medium for accessing Spirit and therefore power for healing and for combating the devil redrew the boundaries of the field and provided African mission Christians with a strategic option in which they were better qualified to compete than the missionaries.

For the mainline missionaries Holy Spirit was an article of doctrine but hardly of practice, while Satan, the devil, and demonic possession were a largely redundant, even repugnant, inherited tradition (witches and witchcraft having emigrated to the realm of folk tale and superstition in England and the Netherlands). Nevertheless, Holy Spirit, Satan and hell were embedded in the Christian tradition, part of the *doxa* of Western Christianity. When it

---

7 Comaroff and Comaroff (1991) make the same distinction, but use the term *hegemony* for the unseen and unspoken universe of meaning, which controls our normal thought and action unless it is challenged, and *ideology* for the debates and discussions which emerge once hegemony is challenged and brought into the realm of consciousness.

was made the subject of contestation, and therefore of *opinion*, by Bishop Colenso in his *Commentary on Romans* (1861), Colenso was subjected to a heresy trial for among other things denying [the devil], hell and damnation. Colenso affirmed the Zulu experience of God and the Zulu ethical tradition as largely positive, he defended their social, cultural, economic and political rights as best he could, but ultimately the Christianity of his Western European Enlightenment convictions—which make him a figure of admiration for me personally—was ill-suited as a *habitus* in the field of religious contestation in southern Africa.[8] It is interesting to note that the products of his own rather brief missionary work—before it was largely terminated by his heresy trial and the withdrawal of funding—became leaders among the 'native intellectuals' increasingly able to compete in the political field (see here the excellent work of Vukile Khumalo 2003 and Hlonipha Mokoena 2008, 2011) rather than leaders in the production of a counter Christianity able to contest the religious field. Where these *Amakholwa* intellectuals did break away from the mission churches, they tended either to abandon the Christian faith or to replicate the churches they came from rather than to find a new synthesis.[9] For the missionaries, literacy, education and fluency in the Western socio-cultural idiom, supplemented by convictions of racial superiority, provided the (mis-recognized) strategies of domination and control. The irruption of American Pentecostalism, with its teaching of the availability of the Holy Spirit and power to all, provided the impetus for a shift in the balance of power in the religious field under colonial conditions, even if the Pentecostal missionaries were as loathe to relinquish power as their mainline colleagues. So it is hardly surprising that in approximately 1906, Daniel Nkonyane rejected the authority of Pieter le Roux at Wakkerstroom on the basis of a dream.

For those African Christians who remained within the mainline churches it was only the (partial) collapse of imperial domination which enabled them to contest the field effectively. The current crisis in the Anglican Church over the issue of the ordination of gays and lesbians could be analyzed as a continuing aspect of these currents in the field of religious contestation.

For African mission Christians, the active and powerful presence of good spirit/Holy Spirit—and the possibility of possession by, and manipulation of, good spirit by human agents—was a fundamental and unquestioned aspect of their world view/*doxa*. So too, and equally, was the active and powerful presence of evil spirit—and the possibility of possession by, and manipulation of, evil spirit by human agents. This fundamentally agonistic binary opposition

---

8   Although Colenso's ideas and commitments have stood the test of time and he still excites interest and admiration today from both scholars and churchmen (see Draper 2003b).

9   Sundkler (1948: 39–47) calls such churches "Ethiopian" rather than "Zionist".

was—and still is in my opinion—fundamental to the *habitus* of African cultures, on which other binary oppositions were structured. Spirit has its source in the idea of a remote, high, creator god. Not to say there may not have been more gods in the system—I do not really want to enter the fray over monotheism or polytheism in African religion—the existence of *Nomkubelwana* or Queen of Heaven in Zulu culture makes it likely that monotheism was not straightforwardly understood, if at all. Good/Holy Spirit/spirit(s) is the source and protector of life, the fertility of living beings and land alike, as well as health, success and well-being for human beings. This well-being is, however, constantly under threat from evil spirit(s) and those who manipulate it for harm. Death, disease, failure and disaster are primarily seen as originating in witchcraft, the manipulation of evil spirit by those hostile to one. Protection has constantly to be actively sought from good spirit(s), especially as mediated by the ancestors, against the possibility of such evil attacks from outside. Human agents are understood to be especially the gateway for the intrusion of evil spirit destructively in people's lives.

Once possession by and manipulation of spirit as a legitimate expression of Christian experience and practice entered into the religious field of the missionary-indigenous dialogue in southern Africa, it changed its 'boundaries' and also changed the 'rules of the game' and the 'feel for the game'. Dreams, visions and communication with the world of spirit, good and bad, together with the access to numinous power (as Fogelqvist rightly notes) is a central aspect of Zulu-Swathi culture. The role of the medium or *isangoma* is well defined and to some extent coterminous with that of the prophet as defined by Dowie's Zionism. Unlike Le Roux, however, in terms of their cultural capital, Daniel Nkonyane and those who followed him knew the spiritual properties of trees, animals, herbs, stones and waters within the religious field. They also knew how to open themselves to possession by good spirit and how to combat or ward off evil spirit—what diet to follow, which mountains to climb, etc. If the religious field was dominated by combat between Holy Spirit and *uSatan*, then they had the cultural capital and the 'feel for the game' in which they had no need for instruction, guidance or assistance, let alone control, from the missionaries. What remained was to convert this cultural capital into symbolic capital which was accepted as legitimate within their community and could form the basis for a counter community. The main question was to determine which aspects of their indigenous cultural capital could be legitimately used and for what purpose,[10] and likewise, which aspects of the cultural capital of

---

10 As I will demonstrate later, I do not think these decisions were always made on the basis of conscious reflection or even awareness of their underlying cultural basis, but rather on the basis of their "feel for the game".

the Western missionaries should be retained or developed in the formation of new symbolic capital as the basis for the new community and which abandoned. In other words, which behaviors constituted what Bourdieu terms 'orthodoxy' and which constituted 'heterodoxy,' which symbols were to be associated with *uMoya oyiNcwele* and which with *umoya omubi*, and whether the ancestors were to be seen as *amadimoni* (demonic) or as co-operative powers with the Holy Spirit.

Possession by spirits—and exercising spirit-power—can be good or bad. There is an ambivalence arising from the exercise of spirit, especially as this is linked with the ancestors or the *amakhosi* (ruling spirits who are not family ancestors). People are wary of *izangoma* because even if they use their spirit power for good, they may use it for harm. But good spirit cannot work harm, just as the ancestors do not work harm on the living, even if they may be severe to bring people to book and warn them of their current behavior. The purpose of the intervention of the ancestors is to restore community. At least this is the common understanding. Nevertheless there is a certain ambivalence around power which may also spell danger.

It appears that most African Christians accept the existence of good and evil spirit—they identify the good spirit with Holy Spirit and/or a plurality of good spirits with angels,[11] but many would still not deny that even non-Christians might be able to exercise control of good spirit for the healing and weal of people. This would be the distinctive mark of good spirit. So some mainline Christians will ask for prayer in church, go to a doctor and also consult a traditional healer without feeling any major contradiction.

Bourdieu points out that cultural capital produced by socialization into a social universe of meaning may have a certain fuzziness: since its terms may have different properties, relationships and analogies in difference universes of practice. Practical ends "are such as to impose on them a *necessity* which is not that of logic" (1977: 113; Bourdieu in Lamaison 1986: 111):

> The universes of meaning corresponding to different universes of practice are both self-enclosed—and therefore protected against logical control through systematization—and objectively adjusted to all the others in so far as they are loosely systematic products of a system of practically integrated generative principles that function in the most diverse fields of practice.... This is why they can only generate systematic products,

---

11   See already Sundkler 1948: 249–253. The distinction between Holy Spirit, angels and ancestors is often, but not always, blurred (Draper 2009).

but with an approximate, fuzzy coherence that cannot withstand the test of logical criticism (1990: 87).

Victor Turner (1967: 19–47)—admittedly speaking from a structural functionalist world that Bourdieu rejects—also speaks of the necessary imprecision of ritual symbols, because they express what cannot be expressed, at least in words, and he points to a link between the material associations of symbols and their symbolic reference, so that they always have both a sensory pole and an ideological pole. This necessary 'fuzziness' is an important factor when considering the Zionist response to colonial missionary domination.

Le Roux and the Zulu Congregation at Wakkerstroom as a Contested Field

Pieter Le Roux and his wife lived and worked very closely with their Zulu congregation, to the point where he shared with them every step of the agonized path he followed as he worked out the consequences of his conviction (partly mediated to him by his mentor and friend in the Dutch Reformed Church, Andrew Murray) concerning divine healing, his contacts with the American Zionists and his final break with the Dutch Reformed Church.[12] However, as he joined the American Pentecostals from the Azuza Street revival in Los Angeles and became part of the Apostolic Faith Mission (and indeed its President in 1913–1943) a rift opened up with his Zulu followers at Wakkerstroom. The majority of his congregation had joined him and his wife in their rebaptism by total immersion in the Snake River by Daniel Bryant of the Christian Catholic Church in Zion in 1904 (141 of them according to Bryant in Sundkler 1976: 38). He had insisted on the primacy of the Spirit and healing and prophecy and his teaching had been welcomed, but there came a day when he arrived to find half of his Zulu congregation at Wakkerstroom wearing white robes. His response to the independent exercise of Spirit, healing and prophecy by his African congregants was written in the margins of his Zulu New Testament beside Hebrews 9:10, as Sundkler (1976: 51, the explanatory remarks in square

---

12   Le Roux and his family were subjected to considerable harassment for this move, as were their Zulu congregants. For an account of these events focused on Le Roux, see the study written by his grandson, Harold Le Roux (2007), drawing in part on family and archival sources. I am grateful to him for making available some of his sources. See also G. C. Oosthuizen (1987) drawing heavily on the reports of Dowie's Chicago Zion news letter, *Leaves of Healing*.

brackets are his) describes it: "The worship of the *first tabernacle* [which was replaced by Christ] 'stood only in meats and drinks and divine immersions, and carnal ordinances' ". Sundkler also records that written in Zulu beside this text were the words, "*Carnal ordinances*: white robes, pork, tobacco, to carry the 'cross' (or holy staff); taking off shoes" (1976: 51). The adoption of these symbolic representations was prohibited by Le Roux to his congregation and became the cause of the secession of the first group of Zulu Zionists to form the Christian Catholic Holy Spirit Church of Zion. The date of this is contested, but members of the churches interviewed insist on the date of 1906. It is highly significant that the group added the words 'Holy Spirit' to the title derived from Dowie's Christian Catholic Apostolic Church of Zion (CCACZ)—it came to be called in Zulu *Enyonini* ("the place of the bird", with the double reference of the Holy Spirit as dove and the symbolism of flying away to a place of refuge). It was an act of contestation of symbolic capital in the religious field, but why were these five symbols (white robe, prohibition of pork and tobacco, staff and bare feet) so significant to both parties? Ironic, in any case, that the prohibition of tobacco should form part of the list, since Le Roux himself had already forbidden it in 1902, along with alcohol and Western medicine (Sundkler 1976: 25). Clearly they signaled something different on each side, which was (mis)recognized but instinctively apprehended. The five symbols represent the bringing into the field of play of Zulu cultural capital, not for the most part consciously or rationally, but not irrationally either. The creative agency displayed by Nkonyane and his community was no "unpredictable novelty" but "the conditioned and conditional freedom" facilitated by the Zulu *habitus* whose "limits [were] set by the historically and socially situated conditions of its production" (Bourdieu 1990: 55).[13] Le Roux demonstrated similar creative agency with respect to the Reformed tradition in his participation in the formation of the Apostolic Faith Mission, but there was a mutual inability to comprehend or accept each others' bona fides on both sides. The introduction

---

13   Jean Comaroff (1985: 19) makes the same point with respect to the Barolong: "The particular constitution of the Tshidi social order, c. 1800–1830, was formative in important respects of the subsequent conjuncture with external forces and agencies". The transformations which occurred under imperial domination were not simply imposed but subject to repeated assertions of agency by the dominated, so that "incorporation into colonial society was not a onesided process of domination: it was a conjuncture in which existing cultural structures were deployed by Tshidi so as to develop novel modes of practice; practice that expressed resistance to the self-image bred by proletarianization and subordination" (ibid.: 22).

of Zion and Pentecost had changed the boundaries of the religious field in a way which resonated with the *habitus* of the African Christians and enabled them to make strategic moves in the contestation for advantage in the setting of colonial domination. It also inevitably alienated them from their missionary 'overseers'.

From the point of view of Le Roux, as recorded in an interview with Sundkler (1976: 50–51) much later in 1940, the white robes represented making "the outward show". The use of crosses and colors also represented Roman Catholic influence. In other words, these things activated the unrecognized *doxa* of the Reformation pastor, part of the cultural capital of the Reformers in their contestation of the religious field of Europe. They represented things outward as opposed to the rationalism of the internal, which underpinned the Cartesian world view. For the devout this meant, at the end of the day, rational piety even for the Pentecostal pastor: "God is not a God of confusion but of peace" (1 Cor 14:33). Robes and staffs (even when recommended to black Christians by the Holy Spirit in visions and prophecies) evoked the danger signals of the quite different religious field in Europe. In particular, the white robes, as opposed to the sober black academic gown of the Reformed pastor, might have been an alarming reminder of the white albs and surplices of Roman Catholic (and Anglican) Christianity, to which the Reformed Christians were implacably opposed. A photograph of the first Zion baptism in the Snake River show the Zion City overseer Daniel Bryant baptizing the scores of white clad black Christians wearing his black gown in the water—an ironic commentary on this later quarrel. Leaving aside Le Roux's puzzling comment on tobacco (for or against would signal something different?), the prohibition of pork, which he does not address in the interview, activates quite different danger signals arising from the conflict between Christians and Jews in the religious field in Europe, nearly two millennia of Christian supersessionism and anti-Semitism. The insistence of Zionists and Adventists later on that worship should be on the true Sabbath (i.e., Saturday) would have activated the same signals. His response to worship in bare feet (unless he was objecting to its association with Moses) has probably no basis in the religious field, but everything to do with the 'civilizing' mission and supremacy of European culture. It is interesting that no point of doctrine was at stake in this contestation of the religious field. The outsider to Zion, Dlamini (1976) writing much later, is struck by how close the teaching and worship of the CCACZ is to that of standard evangelical Protestantism. In any case, Le Roux was in no doubt that these new rules of the black Zionists represented a contestation of the religious field. His response was to make a characteristic move of the white missionaries, to expel the black

Christians from the mission at Wakkerstroom and re-assert the dominance of colonial authority over the colonial subjects, revealing what was at stake beyond the religious field, namely political power, appropriation of the land, control of black bodies by white bodies. It is also significant that the response of the Zulu Zion congregation was to rename their church the Christian Catholic Apostolic *Holy Spirit* Church of Zion and purchase land to re-locate their community just across the border of the Transvaal Colony (as it had become after the Boer War) to Charlestown in the Natal Colony, where 'exempted natives' had already been purchasing land and pursuing political and economic equality for half a century. Here their headquarters remained in Charlestown until the next wave of neo-colonialism, apartheid, dispossessed them and drove them into a black 'township' near Newcastle, where they became known as *Enyonini*.

Color Coding in Enyonini

What exactly was the source of these prohibitions and rules for the black Zionist breakaways from Le Roux's Apostolic Faith Mission? The Reformed missionaries used the black gown of Geneva, which continued to be used by the first white leaders of Zion, but the black leaders of Zion chose the white robe ostensibly because of the imminent end of the world. Sundkler (1976: 48) attributes this to a vision or dream experienced by Michael Ngomezulu and confirmed by a reading of the book of Revelation. However, from the perspective of Bourdieu, the choice of colors would be part of the *habitus* of the player in the religious field, a sense of what is right, of what works, of a feel for the game which would have deeper roots than the experience of an individual. Indeed, the *habitus* would circumscribe and interpret the experience of the individual. In the Christian Catholic Apostolic Holy Spirit Church of Zion (CCAHSCZ) it was soon combined with blue/green (*uhlaza*, there being no primary distinction in Zulu culture between these colors) to create the uniform characteristic of many if not most Zulu Zionist groups. The opposition of white to black in the contested religious field would be natural and not without consequences, since these form a part of a 'structuring system of structures which structure,' not as taxonomies or rules, but as dispositions of choices strategically made within culturally determined possibilities. As Bourdieu finds that gendered opposites do have a structuring significance in the Maghreb, but a shifting one, depending on the location and circumstances, so white and black play a structuring and gendered role in Zulu culture, especially in combinations of colors.

Within a short time, the Zulu Zion community of *Enyonini* added a second color to the white robe of members, a green/blue sash, worn differently by men and women, in response to a vision of Andries Nkonyane in 1924 (Dlamini 1976: 45). This also clearly resonated with the Zulu *habitus* and 'felt natural' in Bourdieu's sense of a feel for the game. The color combination of white and blue/green has become standard for the many African Zionist groups who owe their origin and inspiration to the Nkonyane church. However, neither the white robe nor the blue/green sash or stole owe anything to the distant conflicts of the Reformation which so alarmed Le Roux.

In an oral culture such as that of the amaZulu before colonization, the only records are those of the outsiders—which are not always reliable. A. T. Bryant in his *The Zulu People as They Were before the White Man Came* (1949) does, however, provide a compendium of information on colored beads from early reports. Bishop Colenso reports in 1855 that the three preferred colors in use for beads are red (*umGazi*—blood), white (*Tambo*—bone) and blue (*amaQanda*—eggs). King Mpande reserved the large red beads for himself (*iMfibinga*). Ludlow in 1880 notes also that black and white beads are preferred in some kraals, while pink (which are equivalent to red—there being no Zulu equivalent to pink), green and blue are in others. Bryant gives his own experience as being that black (*isiTimane*) and white (*iTambo*), blood red (*umGazi*) and blue (*uZulu-cwatile*), together with transparent crimson (*umLilwana*) were mostly used, while pink, yellow, green and clear transparent beads were "in small demand". He notes that these beads were used in combination by Zulu girls to send letters (*izincwadi*), which have subsequently been the study of Stan Schoeman (1983) which is still often cited and is readily available on the web in simplified form.[14] While he identifies seven colors in symbolic use, he also notes that black, white and blue form the standard colors used in combinations. What is particularly helpful is his observation that there is both structure and innovation in the use of beads, though since he is studying the love letters of women his interpretation is overly determined by their reference to marriage, when clearly they would also have some kind of symbolic value outside of the realm of courtship also. His representation (Schoeman 1983: 150) of their relationship follows:

---

14 (http://www.marques.co.za/clients/zulu/bead.htm)

TABLE 2.1 *Colour coding in Zulu beadwork (Schoeman)*

Color Coding Positive	Color	Color Coding Negative
marriage, regeneration	black	death, sorrow, despair
fidelity, a request	blue	ill-feeling, hostility
wealth, a garden, domestic, industry, fertility	yellow	thirst, withering away, badness
contentment, domestic bliss	green	illness, discord
high birth/rank, an oath, a promise	pink	poverty, laziness
violent love, strong emotion	red	anger, heartache, impatience
spiritual love, purity	white	[*passivity*—my addition]

These representations are helpful in showing that, although there is some kind of symbolic meaning attached to each color, it is in combination that they articulate the system.

What Schoeman does not consider is the use of white and black in combination with the other colors in Zulu rituals associated with the ancestors and with ritual experts, the *isangoma* (medium for contact with the ancestors) and the *inyanga* (ritual expert in herbs and traditional medicines). White and black, red and green/blue, play especially important roles in these circumstances. Positive dreams associated with the ancestors are associated with white and with the feminine, and are common in descriptions of calls to become *isangoma* and also a prophet in an AIC (Oosthuisen 1992: 22–23). Oosthuisen's fieldwork highlights the role that maternal grandmothers play in such a call. One of the earliest oral accounts of a call given by Nomguqo Pauline Dlamini (c.1858–1942), once a member of the *isigodlo* (harem) of King Cetshwayo, characterizes her call to mission as coming from a woman in white and as opposed by a male in black (Draper 2002), which has quite different connotations than those given by the missionary, Heinrich Filter, who recorded them. Both white and black or red play a role in the process of becoming *isangoma*, as they do in rituals of initiation. The naked initiand is daubed with white all over when he joins the initiation school in Xhosa[15] and Pedi culture and remains so until he completes the ritual, which is symbolized

---

15   King Chaka abolished initiation rituals and circumcision for Zulu males and substituted military service as the entry point to manhood, but it would originally have been the same.

by being daubed with red all over before he rejoins his community. Young Zulu girls symbolically decorate their faces with white patterns even today, though these may be alternated with red spots in some circumstances. The association of red with the Zulu and Swazi kings is well-known and continues (symbolized by the head adornment with the wing feather of a Loeri bird), which is why Mpande reserved a particular red bead to himself and his immediate retinue as noted by Bryant. White is closely associated with blue/green, as Schoeman has noted. Blue/green is associated with the female deity/ancestor, Nomqublwane. So that there does seem to be some kind of binary structuring of color codes related to the gendered body.

While color codes should not be construed as laws, as Bourdieu reminds us, it may be helpful to try and provide some kind of a structure of colors, which suggests the strategic role that colors might play in the *habitus* and hence in the contestation of the religious field which we have been exploring in the origin of the AICs. This could be arranged in a modification of the diagram offered by Bourdieu in his *Theory of Practice*:

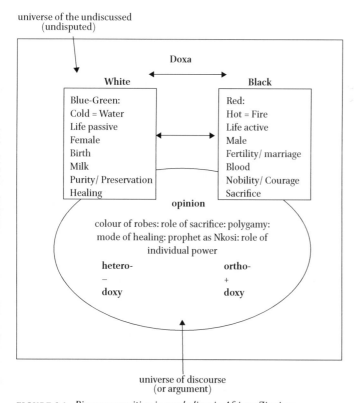

FIGURE 2.1 *Binary opposition in symbolism in African Zionism*

When the members of Le Roux's Zulu Zion in Wakkerstroom chose to wear white they made a choice which 'seemed natural' to them, which articulated their 'feel for the game' at multiple levels. Of course, it opposed the white robe of their baptism to the black robe of their overseers, and did so with the sanction of the Apocalypse in the Bible as appropriated by them and as revealed by the Spirit. However, it also opposed the male black/red symbolism of Zulu color coding with the female white/blue. This celebrated and appropriated the properties of healing, life and fertility in a time of death and confusion brought by colonial domination and war in their own daily experience. But it implied also passivity and sustenance rather than activity and passion: milk over blood, healing over sacrifice. This does not imply any value judgment, but rather an exploration of the possibility of a historical strategy for survival of the dominated. That the choice made by this small group of African Christians or *Amakholwa* in Wakkerstroom had an instant and irrevocable success indicates the way in which it articulated the innate undiscussed power of the *habitus*, which Bourdieu characterizes in his discussion of *doxa*.

Choice of Strategic Weapons in Enyonini

When Le Roux objected to the use of staffs by his black congregants, he was responding in all likelihood to the same set of signals from his Reformed *habitus* in opposition to the *Roomse gevaar*—the fear of Roman Catholicism which had deep roots particularly in the Afrikaans community with its background of bloody, historical struggle in the Netherlands and France (the Huguenots). Crosses from ceremonial processions, jeweled crooks of powerful prince bishops and their alliances with the imperial powers of the 'Holy Roman Empire' remained deeply embedded in the *habitus* of Reformed Christianity—perhaps revitalized by the alliance of Anglican Christianity and its ceremonial rituals with the imperial British conquest and overlordship of the defeated Boer Republics still powerfully emblazoned on the memory of Afrikaners like Le Roux in Wakkerstroom. But he (mis)recognized the applicability of this relationship between Christianity and empire to his own situation as an 'overseer' of African Christianity. So he instinctively felt rather than understood the connection between the appearance of staffs in his black congregation and the emergence of resistance to himself as an agent of empire.

For the black Christians of Wakkerstroom, the use of staffs of power was legitimated by the use of such staffs by Moses, when he was given the staff by God to confront Pharaoh after his vision of God in the burning bush. Just as he had to take off his shoes, so the community of *Enyonini* would take off their shoes in worship as a sign that they were in the presence of the divine revelation of the Spirit. Lifting up the staff of Moses, they would confront the death dealing experience of colonial oppression and mediate healing life. This explanation of the use of the staff is given whenever its use is questioned, as our interviews showed consistently. It is also explicitly mentioned by George Khambule to justify his own use of the great metal staff he carried, surmounted by a serpent. He claimed to incarnate Moses and to exercise his power. Interestingly, though, *Enyonini* granted the power of the staff of Moses to all its members, and claimed a biblical warranty for the practice. It was a powerful rebuttal of the arguments of the white 'overseers'.

However, the staffs resonated at a different and deeper level in the Zulu *habitus*, since they were called by the name of the traditional sign of numinous power and protection in Zulu culture, which were particularly utilized by the *isangoma*, namely the *izikhali* or "weapons". This was a sign of taking up the struggle against the oppressive power of *uSatan* but also the oppressive power vested in the colonial system which mediated death and even against the missionaries who had converted them to Christianity but continued to be 'overseers' of Pharaoh. The self-evident nature of the strategic use of staffs in Zulu/Swazi AICs in the contestation of the religious field in the Zulu *habitus* is shown by the choice of the particular trees from which the staffs are made in *Enyonini*. While originally only one staff was allowed, ultimately two were permitted (to form the *izikhali*). The original staffs were made of the wood of *uSondeza*, the Wild Caper Bush (*capparis sepiaria* and/or also the *capparis tomentosa* which are a Western generic distinction and they were not necessarily differentiated at the time since their range overlaps) and they are often simply called by this name. Keith Coates Palgrave's *Trees of Southern Africa* (1983) says of this tree that,

> This is one of the best-known trees among African peoples for its supposed magico-medicinal properties and has the reputation of curing a variety of complaints ranging from coughs and colds to barrenness and impotence. Moreover, if a stick is coated with a paste made from the powdered root and other ingredients and pointed towards storm clouds, it is believed to act as a safeguard against floods. The Venda make a ritual remedy for pneumonia by combining parts of this tree with dried hyena and antelope blood and mixing the concoction together with ox fat (1983: 185).

Elsa Pooley confirms this evaluation of the ritual use of the Wild Caper Bush: "Medicinal and magical properties; traditionally used as protection from lightning and to ward off evil" (1993: 104). This connection between protection from lightning and ritual performance in the use of the wood as a staff has deep roots in Zulu-Swazi culture and the choice of such a staff coincided with the biblical legitimation of the Moses story, except for the availability of such a staff to every member of the church. The power of the staff in warding off the aggression of evil intention from outside, symbolized and embodied by lightning, is reflected in the way members of *Enyonini* understand their use of the staffs as *izikhali*. The practice of touching the affected part of the body in illness with the staff is an important part of healing. So highly was the staff of the *Enyonini* regarded that, after laying hands on the Swazi King Sobuza in 1923, Daniel Nkonyane presented him with the *uSondeza* staff, named it *Litfusi*, and advised him to use it in public on all state occasions, which he did from then onwards (Dlamini 1976: 9).

It was not long before members were allowed to use a second staff, made from the wood of the *umNquma* or Wild Olive (*olea europaea* local subspecies *africana*). Again the choice of this tree is drawn from the Zulu-Swazi *habitus*, since again it has traditional properties associated particularly with healing, as Coates Palgrave confirms: "Africans drink an infusion of fresh bark to relieve colic; they use an infusion of the leaves as an eye lotion for both humans and animals, while a decoction of the leaves provides a gargle for sore throats" (1983: 759). Pooley comments that "Bark and leaves use medicinally for headaches, respiratory and renal ailments" (1993: 412). Again, members of *Enyonini* are well aware of the tree's identity and call the staff by this name to distinguish it from *uSondeza*. It has the additional advantage that whenever the olive tree is mentioned in the Bible, always positively, the word *umnquma* is used and it resonates with Zulu cultural capital. When a person joins the church they have to obtain the staff from a ritual expert who selects these sticks from the wild after fasting and abstaining from sexual relations, according to the leaders of the church. The staffs are on offer at the appropriate price (R10, R20 or R30, depending on size and quality) at the great Easter celebration of the Church in Madadeni. Which of the two are taken is a matter of vision and calling, or whether both are used. The story goes that if a member chooses the wrong staff it will break in the hands of the initiand at the initiation. Two sticks were carried by *izangoma* and also by the praise poet, who is also considered to be "not held responsible for what he says, since he is in a semi-ecstatic state with loud voice, gestures and movement" (see Jeff Opland 1983: 67; for an example of the use of two sticks, see the photograph of a performance in the South African Parliament on the cover of Opland's book, *Xhosa Poets and Poetry* 1998). In any case, the use of staffs designated *izikhali* thus brings into play the ecstatic state of the *isangoma* (see, for instance the painting *Isangoma* by Gerard Bhengu,

1910–1990). Hence the choice to permit and even encourage the use of two sticks, either in the form of a crude cross or two separate sticks, resonates in the Zulu *habitus* with the powerful symbol of the *izikhali* and draws on the medicinal properties of the wood used.

Prohibition of Pork

The disapproval of the prohibition of pork by Le Roux has its roots in the supersessionist and anti-Semitic tendencies and teachings of European Christianity, which was given a fresh incentive by Luther's appropriation of Paul in his *sola fide-sola gratia* teaching. Jews were made the great foil of this teaching, the 'others' in terms of which the Protestant Christians defined themselves in the dichotomy between law and grace, which served them as an analogy in their battle against their perception of the 'works-based' justification of Roman Catholicism. Hence Le Roux would have sniffed out a latent tendency to 'works of the law' in a prohibition of pork, as he would no doubt have done in the case of the sabbatarian tendencies of many AICs and adventist churches. However, pigs are regarded as particularly unclean animals already in Zulu culture and this would also have resonated with the Zulu *habitus* in their strategic contestation of the field with their European 'overseers'. It would have had a particular resonance with Le Roux, in addition, in that he was indicted by the Dutch Reformed Committee investigating his case in 1901 concerning his position on the teaching of John Alexander Dowie's Chicago Zion. One of the charges was that he advocated "the teaching that the eating of flesh was against Holy Scripture and therefore sinful" (Sundkler 1976: 23). It was probably the eating of pork that was at issue and it is likely that this was suggested to his congregation by the visit of Rev. Daniel Bryant, Dowie's South African emissary and other leaders of the Chicago Zion. Le Roux's ambivalent position on this would have given black members of Zion a strategic advantage in their confrontation with their 'overseer'.

Bare Feet in Worship

While bare feet in worship are not specifically commented on by Le Roux, they are taken up by *Enyonini* as part of the Moses typology, as we have seen. Under the influence of the new Azuza Street Pentecostalism from Los Angeles, Le Roux claimed of himself that he woke up in the middle of the night and, "The next moment, the Lord spoke to him in a clear voice: 'Said I not to thee that if thou wouldest believe, thou shouldest see the glory of God?' " (Sundkler 1976: 53). In his contestation with his restive congregants at Wakkerstroom who were not willing to follow him into the newly formed Apostolic Faith Mission (AFM), it is probable that Le Roux shared his experience of the revelation of the glory of God and of the emphasis on this kind of revelation in the AFM. The insistence that shoes should be removed in the presence of the glory of God on the part of the converts—many of whom would have been unshod in any case out of poverty—would have been a potent riposte to these kind of claims to bring the Zulu Zion at Wakkerstroom under the control of the white dominated and increasingly segregationist AFM. It would also resonate at deeper levels with Zulu culture where shoes were a Western import and not a part of home life but of public demonstrations of adherence to the colonial system—shoes being worn especially in church was a sign of adoption of the Western *habitus* and of belonging to the Westernized mission elite (*Amakholwa*).[16] In the Natal Colony, this was expressed by the fight for legal recognition as 'exempted natives' who were free from traditional Zulu law and who were recognized as citizens of the colony (Welsh 1971: 51–66; 235–49).

Prohibition on Smoking

As I have indicated, it is not clear to me whether and on what basis Le Roux was opposed to a prohibition on smoking, since he himself expressly forbade it to his congregants. However, the importance of its prohibition to black members of the Wakkerstrom Zion was deeply rooted in cultural questions relating to the use of smoke in ancestor rituals and the use of *dagga* (cannabis) in warrior traditions of the Zulu *impi*. The members of Shembe's *amaNazaretha* use *imphepho* (smoke from burning herbs) in the annual pilgrimage to Nhlangakazi mountain, which enhances trance state and 'altered states of consciousness,' particularly with the use of drums (see Sundkler 1948: 199). Perhaps the strategic decision of *Enyonini* to follow the 'female' trajectory of the gendered oppositions suggested a 'cool' or 'white' response which lowered the level of ecstatic behavior and emphasized order. Our fieldwork observations of the church note the highly ritualized worship with little emphasis on spontaneous and emotional behavior. Drums and ecstatic dance were no longer practiced. Use of *isiwasha* (the administration of an emetic mixture of water, ashes and sometimes other herbs) was discouraged, though not prohibited. Education

---

16 Even today I have noticed rural Congregants of mainline churches carrying their shoes to church while they walk there barefoot.

was highly valued and several members of the church were highly qualified professionals.

A Brief Note on the Red Robed Zionists: Cekwane, Vilikazi and the AmaJericho Church

As a corollary to the case study in *field, habitus* and their contestation, it may be helpful to conclude by pointing out that the strategic choices made by Nkonyane's *Enyonini* were not the only possibilities. They were clearly not, to that extent, made by laws governing behavior. The choice of a red robe was also a possibility. There is no space in this chapter to chart the historical and historicizing strategic choices of the 'red robe' Zionists, but a brief sketch points the way in which the use of the same analytical tools from Bourdieu might apply (a wealth of data on the red-robed *AmaJericho* is supplied by Fogelqvist 1986). Already in 1910, Timothy Cekwane, also coming out of a Reformed church near Himeville in the Drakensberg (the Presbyterian Church of Africa) led his followers in a wild ecstatic appropriation of the Spirit which culminated in beating one another with bushes on the mountain, drawing blood, which manifested itself on Cekwane in a kind of stigmata of a wound on his hand. He chose to use red robes for his *Ibandla loku Khanya* (Sundkler 1976: 108–118). He claimed to have been conceived by a drop of blood inserted by God into his mother's womb and blood is the central symbol. Other African Zionist groupings were horrified at the choice of red, according to Sundkler, designating it the 'wrong' color—the equivalent of 'foul play' in their 'feel for the game.' However, it is a meaningful move in the 'structuring structure.' The choice of red from the Zulu *habitus* was a strategic move which had consequences in their behavior, which are unsurprising if our strategic representation in Diagramme 3 has any validity. According to Sundkler, there were always more men than women in the church pilgrimage of red robed Zionists and in the worship (60 percent), and it is men who are the most active in Spirit possession. This is a contrast to *Enyonini*, where Sundkler records Elizabeth Nkonyane (Daniel's wife) as saying in response to the predominance of women who experienced ecstatic states, "[l]et now the Holy Spirit enter the men rather than the women" (1976: 47). The worship of red robed Zionists consisted of violent movements under the possession of Spirit (jumping, screaming, shaking all over, falling prostrate and rigid on the floor, swaying 'as if drunk'). This is 'hot possession' by *uMoya* (Spirit) as opposed to the 'cold possession' of the *Enyonini*. Sacrifice of cattle and symbolic kindling of fire became also central ritual actions in the annual gathering at the Temple.

Fieldwork data on the *amaJericho* church of Elias Vilikazi in Swaziland, who specifically chose the red robe in opposition to the white robe of the *Enyonini* presents an interesting study in contrast to *Enyonini*, as a church in which ecstatic, emotional and even violent behavior is encouraged and practiced (for accounts see Sundkler 1976: 217–8; Fogelqvist 1986).

Elias Vilikazi (c.1925–2006) converted in 1947 while working in Johannesburg, South Africa. He was first protected and then favored by the Swazi King. In 1951 he adopted the red dress/robe for himself and his followers (a photograph of Elias Vilakazi on the church's Calendar for 2008 shows him almost entirely in red with narrow white fringes). The color red matched and perhaps encouraged his church's alliance to the traditionalist and absolute Swazi monarchy. Nevertheless, the uniform of the church also adds strips of blue and white to the fringes of the red. Our analysis of the *habitus* would suggest that the inclusion of these is significant in combination. Using the suggested connotations of colors in Schoeman's article, red by itself would positively connote 'violent love, strong emotion,' but blue and white in combination denote 'fidelity in marriage.' The addition of blue and white fringes to red might indicate an emphasis on faithfulness as well as violent emotion, and represent a strategic move to moderate potentially erratic behavior. His church is now probably the biggest in Swaziland and is very close to the royal family, but split into two factions after his death, between two of his sons over the issue of succession to Vilikazi. Their law cases against each other and the violence of their conflict and its impact on Swaziland has occasioned concern and attempts to mediate by the Swazi monarchy.[17] Here groups of men 'drink the Spirit' together in extremely noisy, aggressive circles, and prophecy may be practiced in an agonistic mock conflict style between two prophets. When they are not in uniform, the *amaJericho* members choose their own uniform based on the Spirit possessing them (Archbishop Bhekibandla Vilikazi in an interview outlined thirty two different forms of *uMoya* which possessed members, each with their own possible colors). The *izikhali* of the *amaJericho* often resemble offensive weapons, especially knobkerries, and whose group marching and dancing most obviously resembles the movement of warriors.[18] Further, the men

---

17 King Mswathi called our fieldworker, Queen Masondo, for an interview in the hope that she might be able to engineer a reconciliation between the two parties.

18 Three excellent and fascinating videos of the worship of *amaJericho* are available commercially, produced for *amaJericho* by "Sbu". One of them covers a meeting in the Edendale Lay Ecumenical Centre on 23 June 1990, addressed by Elias Vilikazi himself before he died (entitled *The Lion of Jericho Bishop E. Vilakazi*); a second covers the participation of *amaJericho* in the Good Friday gathering of AICs in Swaziland before King Mswathi in 2007,

conspicuously wear the *isicoco*, the head ring of the Zulu warrior, although made of colored rope. The members of the church explicitly practice animal sacrifice and offerings for their ancestors, in which individuals continue to practice the 'home altar' to the ancestors or *iladi* which is known as the *msamo* in Zulu homesteads. Again, the consequences of activating the 'masculine' or black/red side of the gendered symbolic system of Zulu-Swazi culture had consequences for the contestants in the religious field, in suggesting their strategy and 'feel for the game.'

Conclusion

In this chapter we have argued that Spirit is a fundamental aspect of the Zulu-Swazi *habitus* and studies of the African Initiated Churches should neither reduce *uMoya* to a disguised manipulation of relations of power nor to the spontaneous experiences and choices of individuals participating in a worldwide religious phenomenon of Holy Spirit in some kind of universal form or denomination of Christianity. Bourdieu's model has highlighted that *umoya* at the level of *doxa* has to do with meaning, values integrated in a system validated by an embedded communal experience of the numinous (cf. Comaroff 1985: 176). In this respect it cannot be reduced to power. On the other hand, in the context of the strategic contest of field, it is intimately related to power. The historical experience of Christianity in its different historical forms is an important aspect of the religious *field* and its *habitus*, partly determining the strategic choices made by the 'players in the game' and their 'feel for the game.' Moreover, *umoya* as an aspect of the Zulu-Swazi *habitus* is itself a 'structuring structure which reproduces structure.' It can only be understood within the *field* of religious contestation by understanding its location within a complete set of gendered structural choices which have deep socio-cultural historical and historicizing roots in the indigenous African cultural matrix. On the other hand, as we have seen, the creativity which so marked the exercise of agency on the part of the Zionist churches was also circumscribed by their adoption of their Christian faith into (unconscious) dialogue with their Zulu *habitus*. They did *not* simply 'walk over a bridge back to heathenism,' but underwent a fusion which incorporated and re-interpreted the Christian faith and its book as an aspect of their strategic contestation of the religious field and indeed the colonial field in general. A new consciousness emerged from the fusion

and a third covers the festivals of Christmas and *Ulwandle* (*Christmas and Ulwandle 2008*). The descriptions sketched here are amply demonstrated in these videos.

of the experience of Holy Spirit and spirit within the African *habitus* which enabled members of AICs to recover a measure of agency in colonial and neo-colonial South Africa. 'Spirit' was now no longer *umoya* of African Traditional Religion nor simply *uMoya* of Western Christianity, but something creatively informed by both of them.

While the findings of this study of the religious field using Bourdieu's theory of practice are suggestive for addressing the question raised by the late Rob Garner (2004) concerning the difference between Zionists and Apostolics in terms of economic progress, it is premature to draw any conclusions. Strategic choices relating to the cultural capital available to the players would have economic consequences, but it would require an in depth statistical study and analysis of particular AICs and their choices to begin to answer the question. What is clear is that the first leaders of the African Zion and its various subsequent manifestations were not unaware of the economic aspects of their struggle. For instance, their attempts to contest the religious *field* of the *habitus* were always accompanied by attempts to gain control of geographical space by purchasing land for their Zion, a material representation of their freedom from the white 'overseers' with whom they contested. However, these rural Zions were usually linked also in intricate ways with patterns of migratory labor to the cities and the generation of economic capital.[19] Zion has become big business for some leaders (e.g. *amaNazaretha* of the Shembe family, the Zion Christian Church of the Lekganyane family). The success of members of the different AICs will be the result of their strategic choices as individual players in the economic *field* in terms of their *habitus*. Choices concerning *uMoya* made by their churches will influence their strategic moves, to the extent that they remain faithful to the group—and this cannot be taken as a given. Different members in interviews expressed different relations to the group mores, and there is a certain tacit flexibility which allowed them to do so. For instance, different members of *Enyonini* have expressed different positions with respect to animal sacrifice in relation to the ancestors (*umsebenzi*). However, the relation between an emphasis on possession by 'hot' Spirit or by 'cold' Spirit, with all their potential combinations, and economic success or failure in the new globalized economy would provide a fascinating and valuable study.

The question of the economic profile of Zionist churches is raised in the context of development in the ethnographic study of Robert Garner (2004: 61–103) into all churches in a defined area of Mbali, Pietermaritzburg, which suggested an emerging difference between Zionists (such as *amaJericho*) and Apostolics

---

19   See Jean Comaroff (1985: 165–199) for a detailed analysis of these factors in the Tshidi context.

(such as *Enyonini*). He notes that while Zionist churches seem to inhibit the economic performance and social mobility of their members, the Apostolic churches seem promote their members' success in engaging with aspects of modernity such as education and active participation in the economy. In what way does their respective deployment of the Spirit as symbolic cultural capital differ if at all? Is this indicative of a major shift brought about by the emergence of a new democratic and postcolonial situation, even if it has to be conceded that many of the forces existing under colonialism and apartheid continue to affect the lives of ordinary black South Africans today? The application of Pierre Bourdieu's theory of field and cultural capital to this question should prove to be productive.

References

Anderson, Allan. 2000. *Zion and Pentecost: The Spirituality and Experience of Pentecostal and Zionist/Apostolic Churches in South Africa*. Pretoria: University of South Africa Press [AICM 6].

Berger, Peter and Thomas Luckmann. 1967. *The Social Construction of Reality: A Treatise in the Sociology of Knowledge*. New York: Anchor Books.

Berglund, Axel-Ivar. 1976. *Zulu Thought-Patterns and Symbolism*. Bloomington: Indiana University Press.

Bourdieu, Pierre. 1962 [1958]. *The Algerians*. Translated by Alan C. M. Ross. Boston: Beacon.

———. 1977. *Outline of a Theory of Practice*. Cambridge: Cambridge University Press.

———. 1986. The Forms of Capital. In *Handbook of Theory and Research for the Sociology of Education*, edited by John Richardson, 241–258. New York: Greenwood.

———. 1990. *The Logic of Practice*. Stanford University Press.

Bourdieu, Pierre and Jean Claude Passeron. 1977. *Reproduction in Education, Society, and Culture*. London: Sage Press.

Bourdieu, Pierre and Loïc J. D. Wacquant. 1992. *An Invitation to Reflexive Sociology*. Chicago/Cambridge: University of Chicago Press/Polity.

Bryant, A. T. 1949. *The Zulu People as They Were before the White Man Came*. Pietermaritzburg: Shuter and Shooter.

Chidester, David. 1996. *Savage Systems: Colonialism and Comparative Religion in Southern Africa*. Charlottesville/London: University Press of Virginia.

Comaroff, Jean. 1985. *Body of Power, Spirit of Resistance*. Chicago: University of Chicago Press.

Comaroff, Jean and John Comaroff. 1991. *Of Revelation and Revolution. 1. Christianity, Colonialism, and Consciousness in South Africa*. Chicago: University of Chicago Press.

Dlamini, Timothy L. L. 1976. "The Christian Catholic Apostolic Holy Spirit Church in Zion: Its Development, Life and Worship." Two Volumes. Unpublished MA Dissertation, University of Botswana and Swaziland.

Draper, Jonathan A. 2002. The Bible as Onion, Icon and Oracle: Reception of the Printed Sacred Text in Oral and Residual-Oral South Africa. *Journal of Theology for Southern Africa* 112: 9–56.

———, ed. 2003a. *The Eye of the Storm: Bishop John William Colenso and the Crisis of Biblical Interpretation*. London: T&T Clark [JSOTSup 386].

———. 2003b. Bishop John William Colenso and History as Unfolding Narrative. *Journal of Theology for Southern Africa* 117: 97–105.

———. 2009. The Holy Spirit in the Worship of Some Zulu Zionist Churches. In *The Spirit in Worship—Worship in the Spirit*, edited by Teresa Berger and Bryan D. Spinks, 261–284. Collegeville, Minnesota: Liturgical.

Fogelqvist, Anders. 1986. *The Red-Dressed Zionists: Symbols of Power in a Swazi Independent Church*. Uppsala: Uppsala Research Reports in Cultural Anthropology.

Guy, Jeff. 1983. *The Heretic: A Study of the Life of John William Colenso 1814–1883*. Pietermaritzburg/Johannesburg: University of Natal Press/Ravan.

Hofmeyr, H. and K. Smith with C. Smit. 2009. *Wakkerstroom: Jewel of/Juweel van Mpumalanga*. Pretoria: Mediakor.

Khumalo, Vukile. 2003. The Class of 1856 and the Politics of Cultural Production(s) in the Emergence of Ekukhanyeni, 1855–1910. In *The Eye of the Storm*, edited by Jonathan Draper, 207–241. London: T&T Clark.

Kiernan, James E. 1990. *The Production and Management of Therapeutic Power in Zionist Churches within a Zulu City*. Lewiston, New York: Edwin Mellen.

Lamaison, Pierre. 1986. From Rules to Strategies: An Interview with Pierre Bourdieu. *Cultural Anthropology* 1(1): 110–120.

Le Roux, Harold. 2007. White Afrikaner Zionist Pieter Louis Le Roux (1865–1943). *Studia Historiae Ecclesiasticae* 33(2): 45–65.

Le Roux, Pierre Louis. 1996. *Geskiedenis van die Voor-en Nageslagte van Pieter Louis Le Roux (a2b2c1od2e2fig2h1) vanaf 1669 tot 1996*. Bloemfontein: Private Publication.

Marks, Shula. 1970. *Reluctant Rebellion: the 1906–8 Disturbances in Natal*. Oxford: Clarendon.

Marks, Shula, and Richard Rathbone. 1982. *Industrialisation and Social Change: African Class Formation, Culture, and Consciousness, 1860–1930*. London: Longman.

Mokoena, Hlonipha. 2008. The Queen's Bishop: A Convert's Memoir of John W. Colenso. *Journal of Religion in Africa* 38: 312–42.

———. 2011. *Magema Fuze: The Making of a Kholwa Intellectual*. Pietermaritzburg: University of KwaZulu-Natal Press.

Oosthuizen, G. C. 1987. *The Birth of Christian Zionism in South Africa*. KwaDlangezwa: NERMIC [Series T14].

Schoeman, Dan. 1983. Eloquent beads: the semantics of a Zulu art form. *Africa Insight* 13(2): 147–51.
Sundkler, Bengt. 1948. *Bantu Prophets in South Africa*. Oxford: Oxford University Press.
———. 1972. *Zulu Zion*. Oxford: Oxford University Press.
Turner, V. W. [1964] 1967. *The Forest of Symbols: Aspects of Ndembu Ritual*. Ithaca, NY: Cornell University Press.

CHAPTER 3

Re-Imagining the Religious Field: The Rhetoric of Nigerian Pentecostal Pastors in South Africa

Asonzeh Ukah

I came to South Africa in a difficult and mysterious way; God sent me as a missionary to bring a better life to our suffering brothers and sisters in South Africa. Since I came here in 2005, God has confirmed [...] that he sent me with a message of power, authority, healing, salvation and miracles. [...] A woman with HIV/AIDS was healed in my church; another [who was] barren for 7 years, just had a baby. These are confirmations that God sent me as a missionary to this land that has suffered so much.
   BISHOP CHRIS (A Nigerian church founder-owner in Yeoville, Johannesburg, 2009)[1]

I used to attend a Nigerian church at Berea. I attended for about a year and really enjoyed the lively music and choruses. I stopped because of too many demands for money. [...] It surprises us [South Africans] that after two months a pastor that just arrived here will buy a big car and will be living an extra-ordinarily flashy lifestyle. [...] They should make our lives better; instead, they are taking away the little we have.
   JOHN (A South African ex-member of a Nigerian church, Hillbrow, Johannesburg, 2011)

Introduction

One of the increasingly visible exports of Nigeria in the 21st century is religion, specifically a brand of evangelicalism sometimes called Pentecostal/charismatic Christianity. With well over a million Nigerian nationals (both documented and undocumented) living in South Africa in 2014, the Nigerian diaspora in post-apartheid South Africa represents a significant proportion of the overall immigrant population in the country. A remarkable feature of the Nigerian community in South Africa—as is the case elsewhere in Europe and North America—is the ease and resolve with which its members establish

---

1 Names of interview partners have been changed to maintain anonymity.

their own worship communities, strongly asserting their religious sensibilities and dynamics as well as at the same time altering the socio-religious ecology of the host society. In mid-2014, there were well over 600 Pentecostal-charismatic formations and ministries—as some are called—founded and headed by Nigerians in South Africa, 70 percent of which were concentrated in Johannesburg. Using Bourdieu's concept of the *field*—with its obvious limitations as highlighted in chapter 1 of this volume—and data from an ongoing research project involving interviews with more than fifty Nigerian church founder-leaders, this chapter examines the rhetoric of legitimacy and arguments which these church founders deploy in justifying their presence in South Africa as deliberate, even if pragmatic, attempts to reimagining and redefining the local religious field and ecology.

The presence of Nigerian migrants in South Africa, which is now almost socially inescapable, meets with a variety of reactions and responses from host South Africans as well as other African migrants. The religious ecology of post-apartheid South Africa is dramatically changing in response to the presence and activities of migrant communities. One sphere in which Nigerian nationals in South Africa are increasingly asserting their presence—and which local reactions are equally becoming strong and vehement—is within the emergent local religious marketplace. Religious institutions, founded and headed by Nigerian migrants, have achieved social visibility, generating mixed reactions from different sectors of the host society. For the Nigerian diaspora community in South Africa—as well as elsewhere—religion is a core element in identity formation and self-representation. Wherever they emigrate to, Nigerians are in the business of establishing churches and para-church organizations. Anecdotal evidence indicates that it is more likely for a Nigerian than a Ghanaian or a Cameroonian or even a South African to establish a church outside their country of origin. All over Western Europe and North America, Nigerian-founded/owned churches have achieved social visibility and academic attention (Ugba 2009; Ludwig & Asamoah-Gyadu 2011). For African migrants in general and for Nigerian migrants in particular, religion is an important institution of identity politics, social negotiation and economic resource. The practical and pragmatic role of religion in African migrant life resonates strongly with the view of the British sociologist Bryan Turner (2011a: 103) who writes that, "diasporic communities are typically held together by their religious beliefs and practices in such a way that in modern societies the distinction between ethnicity and religion begins to become irrelevant". As religion has become a strong and important structure of identity politics for Nigerian migrants in South Africa, so also it has become a site of contestation with South Africans. While some South Africans express awe and excitement about the religious and economic energy of many Nigerians living in their midst, others react with characteristic resistance and skepticism. Apart from the general atmosphere of xenophobia and afrophobia that pervades South African cities and townships,[2] for Nigerian church owners and leaders, different segments of the local society perceive them with a generalized feeling of hostility. This hostility is often attributed to the perception of many members of the Nigerian community as engaged in criminal activities many of which are financial in nature. Church owners and leaders are not exempt from the stereotypical perception of using their organizations to extract financial resources from the local population. Explicitly, many South Africans accuse Nigerian pastors of turning religion into a veritable commercial enterprise with the primary aim of recruiting economic resources from the locals and repatriating these to their home country. Further, the pastors are accused of masking illegal, corrupt activities as religion. Historically, the South African state perceives new religious movements with a great deal of suspicion and unease (Oosthuizen 2000; Pretorius 2007); migrant religious organizations are particularly so viewed in the light of many media stories regarding abuses of authority and members. However, the sheer number of Pentecostal organizations founded and owned by Nigerians attracts rigorous scrutiny and unease as some are alleged to be involved in a variety of unethical conducts (Laniel 2001).

Nigerian pastors who often face hostile charges and allegations deploy a range of strategies and rhetoric in bolstering their claims and religious messages in order to reaffirm their beliefs and withstand negative publicity.

---

2   Xenophobia, in its most general meaning refers to the fear of foreigners. In South Africa, however, the targeting, attacking and killing of citizens of other African countries—in April and May 2008 and again in April 2015—is more complicated than can be summarised by the fear of foreigners. Because the killings and looting of businesses owned by citizens of other black African countries is not completely captured by xenophobia, afrophobia has been used in the discourse about South African national chauvinism where state policies target citizens from black African countries for exclusion from the new South Africa. The fear of foreigners does not involve or warrant the physical attacks, wanton killings and destruction of businesses and property of citizens of other African countries. Not even afrophobia or "negrophobic xenophobia" captures the full ramifications of these events. If genocide is the targeted killing of a people based on ethnicity, religion, social status or political opinion, etc., then that comes frighteningly close to capturing the meaning of the frequent and often unchecked attacks and killings of black non-nationals and the looting of businesses, homes and property. The deliberate misrepresentation and misrecognition of this phenomenon is a conscious effort by the South African state, government departments and financial institutions, key political figures, and civil society at denying the underlying causes of such attacks and perpetuating a rhetoric of 'othering' and national exceptionalism. For the South African state and many of its citizens, the black immigrant is the ultimate Other, the terror at the soul of the nation. (See Els 2013; Manik and Singh 2013; Maluleke 2010.)

Frequently, they resort to exploiting local histories as ideologies of legitimation. The most important legitimation strategy used by these pastors is to dismiss South African Christianity as vacuous and powerless because of its intimate relationship with traditional cultural practices, particularly ancestral veneration and the ambivalent role of missionary Christianity in the brutal process of colonization of consciousness (Comaroff & Comaroff 1991) and the subsequent justification of apartheid policies. Furthermore, they claim black South African hostilities against an "empowering message" to emanate from "contamination" of local Christianity through the incorporation of aspects of ancestor worship and other intermingling of African traditional religious practices and beliefs. For the migrant pastors, the hostilities they encounter are orchestrated by "principalities and powers" (Eph. 6:12) emanating from 'dark forces' of traditional, 'pagan' practices. This chapter proposes to demonstrate how the rhetorical strategy employed and deployed by Nigerian pastors in South Africa serves as an instrument of class consciousness and classification of the religious communities as well as social division intended to contest and restructure the post-apartheid religious field. The rhetoric is not simply an observation of objective differences in the quality of spiritual capital; it is also a clear claim to religious and social superiority by the Nigerians. As Pierre Bourdieu (1984: 7) argues in *Distinction*, rhetorical discourses serve "to fulfil a social function of legitimating social difference". In the face of increased economic hardship and xenophobic violence, migrant life in South Africa is characterized by social uncertainty, economic marginality and ontological precariousness. Migrants often are victims of increasingly harsh immigration regimes and hostile reactions from sections of the local population. Rhetorics of difference and superiority as espoused by Nigerian church-owners serve as a resource and form of empowerment. The rhetorical strategies used by Nigerian pastors are shaped and informed by, but also directed at reimagining, contesting and reshaping the local religious field. By valorizing certain spiritual distinctions and characteristics, the migrant clergy struggle to carve out a subfield of competence, control and power for themselves. Nigerian pastors channel their rhetorical discourse towards pushing the dominant structures of (religious) power to a position of powerlessness and invert their marginality into a structure of privilege and influence. In this way, they claim a visibility that complexifies the religious field and conflates religious capital with economic capital.

An important implication of such arguments and counterarguments is the reimagining of the local field of religion. According to Bourdieu (1988: 782), "Social action is guided by a practical sense, by what we may call a 'feel for the game' ". Bourdieu (1998: 113) argues that for a religious actor such as a sacristan to "play the religious game", he "would reject the comparison of his work of religious service to that of a cleaning man or woman". The deployment of delegitimating and legitimating discourses and authenticating self-narrations by Nigerian pastors in their engagement with religious individuals and institutions in South Africa can be conceptualized as a demonstration of a practical sense or reason necessitated by their 'feel for the game' of effectively competing for a niche in the religious field characterized by endless competition and contestation. Nigerian church-owners constitute a professional class of religious entrepreneurs whose primary function is the production and distribution of religion, and in so doing, make a living. For these religious leaders in South Africa, part of their feel for the religious game and active engagement with the religious field is "the avoidance of rendering their truth explicit" by using euphemisms and adopting "structural double game" (Bourdieu 1998: 113). To disentangle the elements of this field of religious culture, the concept of field from Pierre Bourdieu's theory of social practice will be utilized in providing insights into this aggressively contested arena of migrant Pentecostal practice in post-apartheid South Africa.

Of Field and Subfields

Byran Turner (2011b: 228) contends that although Bourdieu produced a very small number of essays on religion, his conceptual framework—encapsulated in such concepts as habitus, hexis, capital and field—provides "a powerful perspective" on religion in contemporary society.[3] Bourdieu's interest in religion is generally confined to organizational or institutional religion and specifically on Western Christianity or French (Roman) Catholicism. In this sense, he is solely interested in the monopolization of sacred power or hierocratic authority by a single institution in Western Europe. Even though Pentecostalism had developed and achieved social and academic visibility in Western society during his lifetime, Bourdieu completely ignored it, perhaps because of his general belief that a sociology of religion is impossible, and religion—just like Karl Marx had maintained—is on a declining trajectory in contemporary society. Pierre Bourdieu's theory is often dense and hard to condense in a summary such as intended in this brief presentation, which builds on the introductory chapter of this volume. His theory of fields, first worked out in the mid-1960s in relations to the worlds of art and literature, was slowly refined and extensively

---

3 According to Terry Rey (2007) Bourdieu produced about ten essays on religion although Turner (2011b: 231) says Bourdieu published thirteen essays on religion.

elaborated upon and formalized over a long period to encompass the analysis of the field of cultural production. Bourdieu's concept of field builds on Weber's (1991 [1922]: 20–59) conceptualization of the conflicts over symbolic capital, which pervade and structure the interactions between prophets, priests, magicians/sorcerers. The concept of field is directed towards understanding how social groups struggle over symbolic capital. This concept may provide some helpful insights into the struggles migrants engage with when they (re)position religion as a central organizing institution and practice in socially and economically unstable contexts such as post-apartheid South African society is. To understand migrant religious tastes and practices, it is important to factor in the role of religious institutions, micro-organizations and collective and personal religious interests in (re)structuring the religious field.

For Bourdieu, social space is not a neutral, undifferentiated environment. The concept of "field" is frequently deployed as an analytical category, "a thinking tool", to frame a distinct microcosm embodying or characterized with its own peculiarities such as rules, regularities (or regulations), and authority structure. Different aspects of social life, such as politics, art, science, economy, literature, the law as well as religion constitute different fields with distinct rules, demands, characteristics and structures. Bourdieu (1998: 113) describes "institutions" as "fields". The field is composed of "occupants", agents, institutions and the network of interactions between them; it is "a network, or a configuration, of objective relations between positions" (Bourdieu and Wacquant 1992: 97). It is, Bourdieu (1985: 17) writes, "a relatively autonomous universe of specific relationships". The positions occupied by agents in the field are defined by the type and amount of power—or capital—they bring into it the possession of which grants access to certain profits, privileges or benefits available in the field. These are resources of the field over which there is an endless competition and contestation among agents and players. Because agents possess an unequal and limited amount of power, capital or resources, struggle to maximize self-interest in order to ensure self-reproduction is an inherent feature of the field. The field is, therefore, structured and determined by self-interest, which drives competition over limited resources and gains. The different forms of capital—economic, social, symbolic and cultural—exist and function only within a specific field. A field has its own logic, which transcends individual agents or institutions within it. In order to be an effective player within the field and a master of the game, an agent will "recognise and comply with the demands immanent in the field" (Bourdieu 1990: 58). As a force field, therefore, with the capacity to impose its rules on all who enter within its milieu, the field exhibits a conditioning and determining effect on all agents and institutions that interact within its boundary. The degree of autonomy of a field varies according to how it can impose the demands of its specific logic on those participating in it.

Each field of social formation conceived as a structure of objective relationships has subfields which have their "own logic, rules and regularities [which]...entail a genuine qualitative leap" (Bourdieu and Wacquant, 1992: 104). The analysis of each field or subfield involves three separate but related processes, namely: i) the study of the position of an agent in relation to other agents as a field of power; ii) the mapping out of the objective structure of relationships among competing agents within the field for legitimate form of specific authority; and iii) the analysis of agents' *habitus*—the different systems of internalized dispositions acquired through relating to their social and economic conditions. The position of an agent in the field informs, defines and determines the strategies or "position-taking" which s/he assumes.

The Field of Religion in (South) Africa

Although the people of South Africa were intensely religious before the first arrival of Europeans in 1652,[4] a distinct and delineated field of practice and knowledge known as "religion" did not exist. As Bolaji Idowu adequately and extensively describes in his now classic *Africa Traditional Religion: A Definition* (1972), a central pillar of the legitimizing rhetoric of the first Europeans that encountered Africans was the assertion—with an unusual categorical certainty—that Africans had no religion. David Chidester traces the emergence of comparative study of religion to "European discoveries of the absence of religion [in Africa]" (Chidester 1996: 11). Although this assertion claimed to be a statement of knowledge, it was in reality a performance of power and violence on Africans. European missionaries, white settlers, colonial agents, and travelers proceeded thereafter to invent the category of "religion" and foisted it on the "natives" as an integral component of their "civilising mission" and containment strategies (Chidester 2014: xi). To understand what the locals did not have was in itself a powerful knowledge; to invent and give it to them was not an exercise of benevolence but a performance of control and domination. Religion was, and has since remained, an instrument of creating distinctions, classes and classifications as well as empowerment. If it is an instrument of empowerment, it is also equally a structure of disempowerment. During the colonial onslaught on Africa, indigenous African cosmovisions

---

4   The first Christian missionary in South Africa was George Schmidt who arrived in Cape of Good Hope in 1737 to establish a Moravian church.

resisted obliteration and asserted its intensely religious underpinnings at every juncture. Through conversations and conflicts, dialogue and violence, co-optation and resistances, Europeans inevitably engaged indigenous religious adherents and professionals such as the *babalawo* (the diviner) and the *onisegun* (the healer) who provided the religious infrastructure and intellectual framework upon which a new contested field or category of religion were to emerge (Peel 2000). The presence of "religious outsiders" who were interested in the contest over power, prestige and other forms of resources through the deployment of legitimate and non-legitimate means helped in the invention of the field of religion.

As David Chidester persuasively argues in his seminal work, *Savage Systems* (1996: xiii–xiv), the practice and study of "religion" as well as the discoveries of the categories of "religion" and "religions" were "entangled in the power relations of frontier conflict, military conquest and resistance, and imperial expansion". In the interaction and encounter with indigenous South African peoples, a range of personages such as missionaries, adventurers, traders, travelers and colonial interventionists all participated actively and in varying degrees in the production of the category of religion and the delineation of the field of religion. The principles, interpretations, explanations and definitions of religion were articulated and "entangled in social, economic, and political conflicts of colonial situations" (Chidester 1996: xiv). More importantly, Chidester (1996: 3) argues, "The discovery of local religious systems in southern Africa can be precisely correlated with the establishment of local control over Africans". The delineation of the field of religion, therefore, was a dominating purpose, an outcome that has remained tenuous and contested ever since. Indigenous religious practices were dismissed as primitive/infantile mentality, fetishism, animism or magic while the religion of the Europeans was "religion proper" which approximates closely to "civilized science".

The structure of the religious field that emerged through the encounters between imperialist agents and indigenous peoples was made up of discourses, ideas, practices, agents or actors and institutions and the complex or diverse— sometimes conflicting—networks of relations among these structures. The sub-fields of the religious field could be conceptualized as discrete or disparate sections such as "colonial/imperial religion" or what is alternatively called "Mission Christianity", African Indigenous/Independent/Initiated/Instituted Churches (AICs), African Indigenous religious or healing systems; similarly, African Pentecostalisms represent a subfield of African Christianity. An important feature of the religious (sub-)field such as this is that it is, in the words of Chidester (1996: 21), "an open, contested zone of intercultural contact". Because it is open, it allows new entrants or religious agents/professionals who must deploy specific strategies—in the form of actions and practices, ideas or discourses—to contest for a position of power or influence within the field in general or within a sub-field. The instruments or actions adopted by agents and actors in this field are not necessarily a product of rational choice, but more importantly, they are guided by a practical or pragmatic sense, a "feel for the game" (Bourdieu 1988: 782). As shall be adumbrated shortly, self-interest is a strong driving and structuring force within the field.

In this conceptualization, where do migrant religious formations such as Nigerian founded-and-headed churches fit in? Generally, migrant churches belong to the sub-field of Pentecostal-Charismatic Christianity. Through their rhetoric of legitimation and delegitimation, Nigerian pastors contest the structure of the field by highlighting the distinctive character and value of religious capital they bring to the field of play. They likewise underscore the validity of their claims to superiority by delegitimating existing religious capital of the host clergy, and by so doing reconfigure the entire South African religious field with its constituent sub-fields. By self-presenting as missionaries with a divine authorization, these pastors make claims that shift their social perception as economic actors and reinterpret the functions of religions and why things are as they are in the post-apartheid South African society.

Nigerians in South Africa

The official (that is, political) end of apartheid in 1994 marked the beginning of a reconfiguration of social, economic and political structures in South Africa. This epic transformation also has ongoing cultural and religious ramifications. With the influx of migrants from the troubled Congo DR as well as the traditional neighbors in the Southern Africa Development Community (SADC) region, South Africa was in practice becoming a new environment. Nevertheless, the presence of immigrants from western Africa, specifically, Ghana, Cameroon and Nigeria, soon became a fresh yeast or catalyst speeding up the religious and cultural transformation of the country. With the presence of large numbers of transnational migrants, a truly multicultural society emerged, partly fuelling episodes of xenophobic violence targeted specifically against nationals of other black African countries who were suspected to be responsible for the upsurge in crimes and the exacerbation of poverty. Poor black migrants are frequently accused of taking jobs from the local black population, illegal practices such as drug smuggling, human trafficking and prostitution, among others (Tevera 2013).

The mid-1990s was a particularly fraught period in the history of contemporary Nigeria. It was the period of unprecedented political and economic turmoil precipitated by the annulment of the 12 June 1993 elections by the Ibrahim Babangida military junta, an event that ultimately propelled Sanni Abacha—unkindly known in some quarters as the "Butcher of Abuja" because of the numerous assassinations of opposition politicians attributed to his hit squad—to power. Abacha's reign of terror was a push factor in compelling some Nigerians to emigrate. The "New Face of South Africa" represented by the newly elected ANC government of Nelson Mandela was enough attraction for many professionals and businesspersons to come to South Africa for business and professional career. The shortage of qualified black South Africans to take up employment in the health sector, manufacturing, justice department as well as in different disciplines in the academia was the main reason for the first ANC government to liberalize immigration rules. The relaxation of visa requirements at this time was also a goodwill and appreciation gesture by the ANC government to other African countries who participated in the struggles against the apartheid regime.[5] Nigeria has the largest pool of intelligentsia in Africa. Many Nigerian lawyers, professional court translators, engineers, computer scientists and media entrepreneurs—or small business owners—came to South Africa in this period to contribute to the development of the host society and make a decent livelihood by so doing. These professionals were the first responders to the call of the ANC government for skills in rebuilding the nation away from the skewed structures of apartheid. In addition to the professional class that emigrated from Nigeria, a large number of students came to avail themselves of the opportunities to study at the generally renowned tertiary educational institutions in the country.

There are no reliable figures about the population of Nigerians in South Africa. Between January 1994 and April 1997, a total of 2,862 Nigerians was recorded as applying for political asylum in South Africa (Shindondola 2007: 6). Considering that Nigeria was facing concrete political challenges due to the repressive, highhandedness and a violent political culture of the mid-1990s, it is understandable that some Nigerians fled to South Africa in search of political refuge. This situation correlates very well with much of the literature on migration that describes points of departures as contexts of political turbulence, economic upheaval or cultural subjugation (Kelly and Lusis 2006). The last official figure for foreigners living in South Africa comes from the 2011 census that put it at 2.2 million residents, up from 1.1million a decade earlier. According to the 2011 census figures, nationals from 53 African

---

5   Within three months of his release from prison in February 1990, Nelson Mandela visited Nigeria as a show of gratitude for the country's contribution to the fight to end apartheid. He also received the sum of US$10 million from the government of general Ibrahim Babangida as campaign contribution to the ANC (for more details, see Adebajo 2007: 213–235).

countries reside in South Africa; the largest cohort comes from Zimbabwe (605,416), followed by Mozambique (377,021), and then Lesotho (142,694).[6] In 2008, Johannesburg—the largest city in South Africa—was estimated to have a population of 3.9 million people between 500,000 to 550,000 of which were foreign nationals.[7] Nigerian nationals constitute the third largest group of immigrants in Johannesburg after Zimbabweans and Mozambicans. The official figure from the 2011 census of Nigerians resident in South was 23,757, much lower than popularly thought. This figure does not include those Nigerians who have now naturalized as South African citizens or who were using the passports of other countries such as Liberia or Ghana.[8] However, some scholars estimate that there are about "1.5 million Nigerians who now live in South Africa"—documented and non-documented.[9] The influx of Nigerians (and nationals of other African countries) into South Africa, particularly middle-aged males, provided an impetus that increasingly altered the social ecology of urban South Africa. The large number of Nigerian migrants in South Africa is the motor that drives the expansion of Nigerian founded churches in the country.

Missionaries to Our Brothers & Sisters: Nigerian Churches in South Africa[10]

Expansion of Nigerian Pentecostal/Charismatic churches and ministry outside of Nigeria usually follows migration pathways of the economically active

---

6 http://www.sowetanlive.co.za/news/2012/11/02/nationals-from-53-african-nations-stay-in-sa (accessed 26.07.2014).

7 Centre for Development and Enterprise (CDE), *Immigrants in Johannesburg: Estimating Numbers and Assessing Impacts* (Johannesburg: August 2008), p. 6.

8 In the wake of the afrophobic violence of April 2015, the South African Home Affairs Department released some limited statistics about foreigners living and working in South Africa in the past five years. According to the figures, "between 2010–2015, there were 889,943 foreigners legally in South Africa, including 104,332 refugees, 273,563 asylum seekers and 434,650 with valid work permits" (see: Marianne Merten, "Security Crackdown aims to Boost Nation's Image", *Cape Argus* (Cape Town), (Wednesday 29 April 2015), p. 1).

9 Chimamanda Ngozi Adichie "Why do South Africans Hate Nigerians?" *The Guardian* (London), Monday, 5 October 2009. Unfortunately, the author of this piece, a renowned Nigerian novelist, failed to indicate her source for this figure which may be closer to the reality on ground in South Africa.

10 Between 2006 and 2011 a total of 94 in-depth interviews were conducted in four different South African cities: Johannesburg, Pretoria, Durban and Boksburg. Forty-eight of the

population (Ukah 2009). Religious professionals were not among the first batch of Nigerian migrants who came to South Africa between 1993 and 1994. The first Nigerian church in South Africa was a congregation of Zoe Ministries Worldwide (ZMW) established in 1996 at Nmabatho, on the South African border with Botswana. ZMW was first established in Nigeria in November 1990 by a businessman-turned preacher from Delta State in Nigeria, Patrick Anwuzia. Anwuzia was one of the early popularizers of the prosperity gospel in Nigeria who claimed to have received three specific missions from God for humanity, namely: to save souls, "to redeem humankind from the shackles of poverty" through prosperity preaching, and lastly, "to liberate [human]kind from demonic oppressions, afflictions, and possessions of demons".[11] He is, however, better known for his flamboyant and extravagant lifestyle; his promise to produce wealth for those who made huge financial contributions to his ministry attracted many followers and admirers. According to some of those who frequented his preaching events in Johannesburg in the late 1990s and early 2000s, Anwuzia would instruct his audience to donate handsomely to his ministry and then take home some pebbles, which they must place under their pillow at night while they sleep. It was believed the pebbles would miraculously turn to gold nuggets by the next morning. The popularity of ZMW in South Africa resulted in the proliferation of parishes such that in 2004, the church had established eight separate congregations—or parishes, as they are called by the pastors

    interviewees were Nigerians; all but ten were pastors or church owners. Of the pastors, all but one were male. These founders were properly educated; all but four have a university degree mainly in law, economics and marketing, social and the human sciences; two have doctorates in the sciences (geology and metallurgy), some had higher degrees too or were in the process of acquiring them at one of the universities in Johannesburg. Only one had a degree in theology! One was a professional accountant before becoming a pastor and now doubles as a bishop and regional coordinator of a conglomerate church with more than twenty branches in southern Africa. The pastors were in mid-life with a median age of 35. Twenty-seven (or 75%) of the thirty-eight pastors were church founder-owners and head their own churches; the remaining 11 were in charge of branches or congregations of conglomerate churches such as the RCCG or Winners Chapel or Overcomers Christian Mission. Majority of them were self-trained as pastors or were trained on the job. Membership in the churches in Johannesburg is majority Nigerian; 10% or less is South African spouses or girlfriends of Nigerians. The rest are drawn from the Zimbabwean, Zambian, Cameroonian or Ghanaian immigrant communities. Reflecting the demographics of the Nigerian immigrant communities in South Africa, these churches are made up of more than 60% young, male Nigerians with an average age of 34 particularly in Johannesburg but less so in Durban, for example.

11   http://www.zoeministriesworldwide.org/about_zoe_ministries.html (accessed 16.03.10).

in charge—many of these in Johannesburg.[12] By 2008, there were 14 separate branches of ZMW in the country. However, by 2009, only two of these parishes existed, the rest had folded up or were appropriated through schisms by the pastors in charge. In the late 1990s and early 2000s, ZMW was the Pentecostal flagship of the swelling Nigerian immigrant community in the country. To demonstrate the authenticity of his brand of message and divine approval, Patrick Anwuzia recorded many television programs in South Africa which he broadcast on Nigeria television networks in the late 1990s, stimulating interest and competition—some would argue, envy and jealousy—from other rival Pentecostal entrepreneurs in Nigeria. Soon, however, tales of success and profit saw a large number of religious entrepreneurs scrambling to open churches and religious firms in South Africa.

By late 2009, there were well over 300 Nigerian churches in South Africa, more than half of these established in Johannesburg alone. By mid-2014, this figure has grown to over 600 discrete churches or congregations. The Believers LoveWorld (BLW), better known by the moniker of Christ Embassy, is arguably the most popular and populous of the lot—with close to 400 separate satellite parishes. In Cape Town alone, Christ Embassy has 25 satellite parishes and 72 others in Johannesburg and Pretoria combined.[13] The Redeemed Christian Church of God (RCCG) has established 40 parishes of its own in the country. Winners Chapel has nine large congregations in nine cities[14] while Lazarus Muoka's The Lord's Chosen Charismatic Revival Church, originally founded in Lagos in December 2002, has four branches. Similarly, Overcomers Christian Mission has three congregations in three cities: Johannesburg, Cape Town and Durban. The controversial but media savvy Synagogue Church of All Nations owned by Prophet T. B. Joshua has a single congregation in South Africa that is located at Bellville in Cape Town (established in 2005). These are some of the big players in the Pentecostal field; there are, in addition, hundreds of upstart or storefront churches jostling for a foothold in the emergent post-apartheid religious marketplace. In both local media and popular discourse,

---

12   Personal interview with Pastor Trinity Mosetlhi, ZOE parish Yeoville, Johannesburg, 19.09.08.
13   Thanks to Bernard M. for providing the statistics on Christ Embassy (personal communication, 26.06.2014).
14   The congregations are sited in the following cities: Johannesburg, Cape Town, Pretoria, Port Elizabeth, East London, Polokwane, Nelspruit, and Bloemfontein. There is a resident bishop who is in charge of these and other winners Chapel congregations in Southern Africa. He is based in Johannesburg (Personal interview with Bishop Thomas Aremu, Louise Botha Avenue, 09.03.09).

many of these churches are characterized by allegations of maleficence usually of financial and sexual nature. Some of the churches are alleged to be fronts for drug dealing or smuggling and money laundering. For example, Christ Embassy and Overcomers Christian Ministries are inundated with allegations of financial manipulation and exploitation, trickery involving the production of miracles—or stage-managed miracles—and sexual misconduct among its clergy (on fiscal practices of some of the Nigerian churches in South Africa, see Ukah 2013; cf. Belk and Wallendorf 1990).[15]

Nigerian churches in South Africa proliferate more by fission or schism rather than by church planting. The contest for the control of resources and authority is an important reason for the breakup of churches. The explosion of Nigerian churches in South Africa may be explained by a convergence of factors but for the present purposes, the theory of path dependence offers some useful insights. Originally developed in economics, path dependence is utilized to explain institutional continuity as well as stability, the bandwagon and the imitation of successful firms, businesses and technologies (Boas 2007; Magnusson and Ottosson 2009). Nigerian church owners in South Africa have taken the same path and method of establishing and running Pentecostal formations in Nigeria. In Nigeria, Pentecostal pastors recruit their largest followers from their ethnic base. This pattern of recruitment is applied in South Africa. Even though the pastors claim to be missionaries sent by God to South Africans, their churches are first founded within the migrant community within which they recruit their first members. To understand the organizational behavior of Nigerian churches in South Africa, it is important to factor in their histories and background in Nigeria as well as the political economy of Nigerian Pentecostalism. The interface between political regulations and economic behavior frequently influences religious vitality such as church affiliation, participation and the character of a religious economy (Gill 2002: 115–132). In Nigeria, the explosion of Pentecostalism has been driven by stiff competition on the part of religious suppliers and producers who operate in a *laissez-faire* religious economy. Although the government (both at the federal and state levels) expends astoundingly huge sums of tax money on religious events—for example, in subsidizing pilgrimages to Mecca for Muslims and to Jerusalem and Rome for Christians—there is no intervention or supervision of the activities, management and mobilization of funds of religious

---

15   There is been a range negative media publicity involving Christ Embassy both in Nigeria and in South Africa. For details, see, for example, Ukah (2007a, b); Sam Eyoboka "South Africans vow to sack Nigerian Pentecostal Church", *Vanguard* (Lagos), 11 April 2009 (http://www.vanguardngr.com/content/view/33302/139/) (accessed 4.11.2009).

organizations. Furthermore, religious entrepreneurs account for their actions neither to members of their congregations nor to any government agency or body. To be a church founder-owner effectively means being a Chief Executive Officer of a non-profit organization with tax-exempt status who accounts to no one for the resources of the organization which are normally directed towards personal use. The exception to the open and free religious economy, of course, is in the twelve Sharia states of northern Nigeria where since 1999, Islam has been privileged as the "state religion".[16] As the capacity of the government to perform its statutory responsibilities to its citizens dwindles under the weight of economic difficulties, corruption and impunity, so the scope and privileges of religious authority and activities expand.

Following Jonathan Fox (2008: 27), religious authority is defined here as "a structure that attempts to reinforce order and reach its end by controlling the access of individuals to some desired goods, where legitimation of that control includes some supernatural component, however weak". The symbolic and material advantages attached to such authority—which include unchecked access to funds, social respect and deference—have made it very attractive and alluring, thus predisposing many individuals to seek entry into the new religious class of "pastors" and church-founder-owners (Okwoi 1995; Hackett 1995). Part of the attraction of establishing religious organizations in Nigeria (and elsewhere by Nigerian migrants), therefore, is that religion is directly and indirectly subsidized with public money and public accountability is almost completely absent. Many South Africans and a significant segment of Nigerians themselves believe that many of the church-owners are economic migrants and are specifically interested in a religiosity of the belly. The pastors, however, insist that they are missionaries working in a fraught, hostile environment, spreading a much-needed message of salvation, health and prosperity.

Contesting Legitimacy: Self-Narration of Nigerian Pastors in South Africa

For Nigerian Pentecostal pastors in South Africa, self-narration is not only an instrument of self-presentation but, more importantly, it is a tool of self-conceptualization and competition. The narration of the self is an important process and strategy of reconfiguring the South African society modeled after

---

16   On the issue of the implementation of an expanded version of Sharia in northern Nigeria as well as the constitutional treatment of religion in Nigeria, see Ilesanmi (2001); Kalu (2003); Bolaji (2010).

their ambition and aspiration, or the sort of frustrations they experience in the society. For Pentecostal pastors, many of whom could be realistically called church-owners, the public presentation of the self is a performance of resistance in an unstable and uncertain social world of South African cities conceived as a stage of ontological angst (Goffman 1959). Experience and aspiration are at the centre of the narratives of why, how and what Nigerian pastors are doing in South Africa; in other words, the practice of Nigerian Pentecostal pastors in South Africa is guided by their background experience in Nigeria and their aspiration to reconfigure the South African society into a new, firebrand nation laden with Christian power. At least, this intention or aspiration is what many of them are eager to communicate to the larger society: They are in South Africa to propagate an empowering religious message and practice, which will in future transform the society, its citizens and its potentials. Through such narratives, these pastors develop rhetorical strategies for representing their experiences of local life and history; impose a certain order on these experiences but also on disconnected events. These perspectives are forms of "technologies of the self on the self" which socialize pastors' attitudes and identities and produce dynamics of multiple selves as well as imagined worlds.

In an important essay that discusses the competitive strategies of religious organizations, Kent D. Miller (2002: 440) identifies three important conditions that underlie the competitive advantage of religious organizations, namely: the production of credible commitment and social perceptions of legitimacy; the production of inimitable goods; and market segmentation and product positioning. While all three factors feature prominently in the practices of Nigerian pastors in South Africa, the first—the search for social legitimacy—is the most important and figures most noticeably in the self-narration of pastors. Almost all the pastors interviewed during recent fieldworks in South Africa insisted God instructed them to come to South Africa for evangelical work. Their self-chosen term was "missionary": they are in South Africa as Pentecostal missionaries with a message of salvation and power. Many painted the image of Jonah in the Bible who rejected a divine mission in Nineveh and was consequently afflicted by tribulations (cf. Matt 12: 39–41; Jonah 1–2). The "divine call to mission", they claimed, were given in visions, dreams, or "word of knowledge" from a renowned "man of God" (rarely woman of God). Only four pastors agreed that they came for other reasons such as education (1), medical treatment (2), and work (1). Two pastors attended a conference in South Africa and returned to Nigeria afterwards. Later they received a "call" to return to South Africa as "missionaries" and founded their own churches as platforms for their missionary activities. As missionaries, they were instructed to help "educate" and "disciple" black South Africans about the power in the Word of God; they bring physical healing to the sick, and empower the poor to the path of prosperity. Miracles of different types are certifications and proofs of their missionary mandate. The production of miracles authenticates the gospel message and improves the life of local converts. One of the missionary-pastors, for example, calls his church, "better life ministry", insisting that although life is generally good in South Africa, it is God's purpose to make it better through the activities of Nigerian missionaries. By casting themselves in the mould of missionaries, which is a valorized category connoting self-sacrifice for the good of others, the Nigerian pastors engage in an active process of identity formation and transformation guided by what Bourdieu appropriately calls "a feel for the game".

It is significant that virtually all the pastors spoken to make different claims to special powers, or commissions from God to come to South Africa. The missionary message they brought is intended to rescue local citizens and prepare them for the actualization of divine purpose, which is greater missionary work with global impact. Knowledge of the Bible, the capacity to pray for extended periods of time, endless cycles of prayer sessions and night vigils and more importantly, the power to work miracles (of healings, deliverances and prosperity) are some of the external validating marks of the claim to distinction and superiority over local clergy. An informant summarizes this distinction in the following way.

> I can tell you, there is a huge difference between Nigerian pastors and local pastors. South African pastors do not even know how to pray. We have challenged them on television on how to pray but within 10 minutes of praying, they are exhausted. But our [Nigerian] pastors pray for more than one hour non-stop. We pray with power and energy, and people see the results. Even though they know this is true, South African leaders do not want to accept it; it is bad for their business. Nigerians know how to pray; we pray for results, and we get results from praying.

Such claims may be construed to constitute "religious capital" which Bourdieu (1991: 9) aptly describes as the "accumulated symbolic labor" and "specific competence necessary for the production and reproduction of a deliberately organized corpus of secret (and therefore rare) knowledge [which is necessary for] the constitution of a religious field". These claims, often supported by a plethora of internally generated narratives such as testimonies and in-house media production such as magazines, bulletins, DVDs and CDs, constitute the qualification and competences of the claimants to compete effectively in the local religious field. The flipside of such claims, as Bourdieu rightly recognized, is the deliberate exclusion or dispossession of certain classes of people of religious capital who are now deemed not to have such knowledge or are incapable of producing miracles or messages of empowerment. As Max Weber (1991 [1922]: 47) points out, prophets have historically been demanded by their followers to authenticate their charismatic authority, "a proof of their possession of particular gifts of the spirit, of special magical or esthetic abilities". Failure to provide charismatic authentication usually results in a diminished authority and influence as well as followership. Nigerian pastors insist their ability to produce miracles and recruit large followership are the proof of their divine mandate; inversely, the lack of such proof from local clergy is interpreted as their lack of power, training, preparedness and ability to play an effective role in the new Pentecostal field. The claim by migrant pastors of power and distinctiveness dispossesses and delegitimizes local pastors of their place of influence within the field. Not being able to produce supporting authentication or proof of possession of special magical and aesthetic abilities is a symptom of lacking the feel for the game within the emergent Pentecostal subfield.

To understand purpose is to know design. It is God's purpose to designate South Africa a mission field for Nigerian Pentecostal missionaries even when Pentecostalism emerged in South Africa before it did in Nigeria (see Oosthuizen 1975; Anderson 2007: 149–185; Marshall 2009). It is intriguing that northern Nigeria, with more than 80 million non-Christians (far more than the entire South African population of 52 million) is not designated as a "mission field" by Pentecostal pastors. In God's design, South Africa is a mission field because of the purpose of God for both Nigeria and South Africa. Some informants claim that God's destiny for Nigeria (with fervent and ardent believers/preachers and numerical strength) is to trigger a Christian revival in South Africa while South African resources such as communication technology, engineers and a strong economy would be mobilized for spreading the gospel to the rest of the continent and the world at large. Such eschatological speculation that accommodates the instrumental role host pastors play in actualizing a divine purpose guarantees a superior function for migrant missionaries.

There are three related discourses presented by Nigerian migrant preachers to account for the attenuated or truncated character of Pentecostal practice and religiosity in South Africa. The first of these is that black South Africans are believed to be superstitious and culturally conservative; they are thought of as being closely related to the traditional religious and cultural practices.[17] South Africans, the argument elaborates, have not successfully made any clean break, complete or incomplete, with their cultural past, a fact that hinders them from

---

17 In a similar way, the entire complex of the AICs is dismissed as traditional religion with a veneer of Christianity and so is hardly worth the label of Christian organizations.

appropriating the firepower inherent in the gospel. Born-Again Nigerians are in South Africa to liberate their brothers and sisters from the stranglehold of traditional cultural and religious practices and ushering them into the new dispensation of Pentecostal power and transformation.

A second argument reinforces the charge that South African Christianity is vitiated through cultural contamination, this time, it is with respect to mission Christianity. Mission Christianity is charged with compromising its mandate because it was the structure and foundation of the apartheid system. Because there were strenuous arguments and sustained construction of blacks as people without religion, and hence without law or customs and therefore without rights or entitlements, Europeans aggressively expropriated the land and used Christianity to justify such an extractive system. Mission Christianity, which is an offshoot of European missionary activities, had compromised the power and vigor of the word of God, the Nigerian pastors insist. Here, the migrants point to local history, or their unique interpretation of it, to delegitimize the local clergy and at the same time account for why their new role as missionaries is necessary and needed for the actualization of divine soteriological purpose. The popular history of South Africa is attractive to migrants who appeal to it to account for why things are as they are: a means of gaining an understanding of their experience in an alien land with alien laws and systems.

The third argument specifically targets local Pentecostal organizations. Black South African Pentecostal pastors are characterized by Nigerian pastors as lax, undisciplined and laid back, afraid to exercise firm leadership and authority. Above all, black South African pastors are spiritually weak because they lack firm authority of the scriptures; this accounts for why they cannot pray with power, "signs and wonder". This argument, which hacks back on the claim of lack of spiritual capital, is not merely stereotyping local Pentecostal elite but subtly dismembering the infrastructure of charismatic authentication. By accounting for why what is on ground is a form of "powerless Pentecostalism", the Nigerian pastors are explicitly establishing difference and arguing for its superiority over their competition.

Considering these arguments as a whole shows how migrant religious leaders almost completely dispossess the principal actors within the Christian religious field of their charismatic authority. Nigerian pastors in South Africa, as part of the larger immigrant community, try to make sense of their lifeworlds through contesting the meaning and field of religion. The rhetoric of a divine message laden with charismatic power fulfils the social function of legitimating cultural, social and religious difference. It is a powerful rhetorical strategy that generates class and classification different from how the locals or even state actors (such as the officials of the Home Affairs Department and the Police) classify them. Migrants from other sub-Saharan Africa are not simply called 'aliens', or 'foreign nationals', but *makwerekwere*.[18] Nigerian pastors come to South Africa with pre-existing, culturally formed dispositions, attitudes, perceptions, tastes, which they acquired while in Nigeria. The specific, assertive and intuitive responses that characterize them are a part of their habitus. By producing specific rhetoric or discourse of classification, which is a counter-labeling strategy, they reconfigure and reassert their public image as missionaries in order to engage with the religious field of the host society. This social field of action necessitates playing "a structural double game" of denying the economic basis of their practice while at the same being driven by the logic of the religious economy. Pastors' framework of expectations, priorities, evaluations and reactions are reworked according to the new context and rule of the game, which structures the new field of play. This new field of religion demands new forms of religious capital and skills: intense, vigorous, long hours of prayers, ceaseless cycles of vigils, production of miracles. Capital is power and the types and degrees of social, cultural or economic competences pastors possess that enable them to contest for more power within the religious field is critical to their survival and success. As "a potential capacity to produce profits", the cultural/religious capital of Pentecostal knowledge enables pastors to remold themselves relative to members of the host society who are not as socially vulnerable as immigrants.

The claim to be missionaries is central to the self-understanding and self-presentation of Nigerian pastors in South Africa. It is important in their struggle to generate their peculiar form of class and classification, structures of distinction and difference, of power and empowerment and superiority. This self-perception gives the impression that, contrary to local ideology of *makwerekwere*, they are not in the country because of self-interest or economic accumulation. Missionaries are social actors generally guided by self-sacrificing, altruistic purpose. Missionaries are generally perceived as humanitarians at the service of a higher, nobler, sacred objective; they are individuals who have left so much

---

18   *Makwerekwere* is a local slang for "foreigners" in South Africa; however, the word is not used to describe any or all foreigners. It is used derogatorily to designate (undocumented) foreigners from other black African countries, who are supposedly inferior to citizens. *Makwerekwere* is an ideology—albeit a racialized one—of classification, difference, delegitimization, of violence and dispossession directed by mostly black South Africans against other black Africans from outside the borders of South Africa. The *Makwerekwere* label instills utmost fear in the hearts of black migrants, documented or not. It is the rhetoric of national chauvinism, superiority, non-belonging and exclusionary logic in contemporary South Africa. (On the rhetoric and practices of Makwerekwere, see Matsinhe 2011; Nyamnjo 2012; Isike and Isike 2012).

for the benefit of their host communities. Deconstructing the old order enables the missionary to reconstruct a new order, to *reorder social knowledge*, where he would privilege his own brand of sacred discourse or ideas. Strategically, "the constitution of claims" which the new Nigerian entrants make regarding both their abilities to remake the religious field and the deficiencies of the local enterprises of salvation and their clergy are "specifically developed in view of the production, reproduction, or diffusion of religious goods" (Bourdieu 1991: 7). These goods are important because they authenticate charismatic authority; to undermine the claims of one's competition is to effectively reposition oneself to fracture and reconstitute the structures of the religious field.

According to Bourdieu (1998: 114), "The religious discourse which accompanies practice is an integral part of the economy of practice as an economy of symbolic goods". The discourse, which revolves around the economic character of religious enterprise such as establishing and running a church or being a missionary, rather than an economic migrant, is complex and multi-layered. For Bourdieu, (1998: 112) religious practice is an "enterprise with an economic dimension founded on the denial of the economy". The missionary language appropriated by Nigerian pastors is a creative strategy that prepares them to play "the religious game" that mystifies the objectification of their activities as an economic enterprise. The use of such rhetoric is to make their hosts and detractors "forget that it is an economic enterprise that can only function as it does because it is not really a business, because it *denies* that it is a business" (Bourdieu 1998: 113, emphasis in original). To insist on being a missionary as opposed to a *makwerekwere* is "the work of euphemization of the economic relationship" which cloaks the relationship between pastor-church-owners and their followers or clientele. This is the point which many black South Africans explicitly and implicitly emphasize in their discussions about Nigerian churches in their midst. The missionary discourse is the perspective the church-owners emphasize because it conceals and denies the economic character of their practice and also highlights and valorizes its self-abnegating qualities. However, consistent with Bourdieu's (1998: 115) theory of social practice, the missionary enterprise "is an enterprise with an economic dimension which cannot admit to so being and which functions in a sort of permanent negation of its economic dimension". Herein lies the subtlety of migrant Pentecostal action and its relative success in South Africa as Ilana Van Wyk's (2014) recent ethnography of The Universal Church of the Kingdom of God makes clear.

Conclusion

The field, in the conceptualization of Bourdieu, is a competitive arena of social relations where agents/institutions/organizations/entities deploy immense physical, mental, symbolic, and strategic resources in the production, acquisition and control of capital. By delegitimizing religions of their host society, Nigerian pastors in South Africa contest structural power relations by asserting the value of the skills and capital they possess. Whatever they construct their South African counterparts of lacking, they make a bold claim to have in abundance. These claims are rooted on the value the pastors assign to the social, economic, cultural capital they possess, which enable them to compete with other agents in the field of religion or the sub-field of the production of Pentecostal goods and services. By framing themselves as missionaries, they valorize their position and claim to be respected and protected because they are bringers of valued goods of salvation, and not mere *makwerekwere*. By deconstructing the South African religious field, they underscore the meaning and value of the religious stock of knowledge and power they possess. The relative success of the missionary discourse is that its proponents believe in its veracity and consistently confront their detractors with narratives of its reality: *makwerekwere* are now lifesaving missionaries. The truth of the practice of the pastors is anchored on their rejection of the economic definition of their practice by the host society as well as the rejection of the ideology of *makwerekwere* as defined and propagated by members of the local society as well as the operators of its power apparatus such the immigration and police forces. Rejection or resistance is not enough; the missionary definition is a counter-force that repositions migrant pastors to offer their services unashamedly and with a claim to respect and entitlement.

Nigerian pastors innovate within the religious field of their host society. They produce new religious ideas, practices, organizations and symbols; in short, new religious and spiritual capital. By innovating, they become better equipped to contest the resources and boundaries of the religious field. However, the existing structures of the religious field constrain and determine these innovations. Within this structured field, pastor-missionaries effectively play the game of being religious leaders by utilizing acquired skills and capitals. In other words, migrant religious leaders lack the capacity or wherewithal to radically change the "structuring structures" (Bourdieu 1992: 164) within the religious field of competition generally and subfield of Pentecostal and charismatic activities specifically. Hence, these pastors re-imagine the religious field rather than practically changing it. Such the rhetorical device of re-imagination often empowers those who are marginalized and threatened by political and cultural or social and economic forces.

Some scholars such as Turner (2011b: 241) may claim "Bourdieu did not make a major contribution to the sociology of religion. Nevertheless, his key conceptual tools, such as embodiment, habitus, practice and field, offer a fruitful way of thinking about religion." As the foregoing discussion indicates, deploying one of Bourdieu's concepts—field—in understanding the endless competition and contestation which pervade post-apartheid religious fields in South Africa, where migrants are increasingly using religious practice as an instrument of self-assertion and livelihood has some merits. This chapter argues that a good starting point to exploring the relationship between the actions and lived experiences of Nigerian pastors in South Africa is to examine and articulate how these actions and rhetoric challenge and reframe the religious field; in this respect, Bourdieu's lexicon of fields, sub-fields, habitus as well as the different forms of capital are insightful. Rhetorical discourses revolving around the missionary status of Nigerian preachers in South Africa serve the social function of legitimating their self-representation. Inversely, the same devices fulfill the additional function of reclassifying and delegitimizing their competition within the religious field. Such (re)classification and production of distinctions effectively re-imagine the religious field even though they may not permanently restructure the field because of the inherent determinism within the field. Although the immigrant pastors respond to a new kind of religious context in which they find an appropriate feel of the game, many of the strategies deployed are guided more by habit than reason. Such habit includes siting their operational base in cities and recruiting membership first from their compatriots and structuring their organization like family firms according to the dictates of the Nigerian political economy of religion rather than paying critical attention to the structures of a new context and culture of operation. The pastors learn this habit of practice, which indeed is an epistemology, through training and experience back home, which are then transposed almost wholesale and uncritically to their new context. Reason would suggest a different course of action, for example, to understand local culture and organizational practices, integrating these into the cultivation of alliances and networks with local actors. Rather, they choose to delegitimize the religious capital possessed by their host, and thereby alienating them. This partly explains how and why after nearly two decades of operating in South Africa, Nigerian churches are still urban-based and marginal to South African society and lacking cultural depth and revolve around a central founder-owner who must produce charismatic authentication or lose relevance and competitive edge within an intensely competitive and dynamic religious field.

References

Adebajo, Adekeye. 2007. South Africa and Nigeria in Africa: An Axis of Virtue? In *South Africa in Africa: The Post-Apartheid Era*, edited by Adekeye Adebajo, Adebayo Adedeji and Chris Landsberg, 213–235. Durban: University of KwaZulu-Natal Press.

Anderson, Allen. 2007. *Spreading Fires: The Missionary Nature of Early Pentecostalism*. Maryknoll, New York: Orbis Books.

Belk, Russell W., and Melanie Wallendorf. 1990. The Sacred Meaning of Money. *Journal of Economic Psychology* 11: 35–67.

Boas, Taylor C. 2007. Conceptualizing Continuity and Change: The Composite-Standard Model of Path Dependence. *Journal of Theoretical Politics* 19(1): 33–54.

Bolaji, M. H. A. 2010. Shari'ah in Northern Nigeria in the Light of Asymmetry Federalism. *Publius: Journal of Federalism* 40(1): 114–135.

Bourdieu, Pierre. 1984. *Distinctions: A Social Critique of the Judgement of Taste*, trans. Richard Nice. Cambridge: Harvard University Press.

———. 1985. The Genesis of the Concept of *Habitus* and of *Field*. *Sociocriticism* 2: 11–24.

———. 1990. *The Logic of the Practice*, trans. Richard Nice. Cambridge: Polity Press.

———. 1991. Genesis and Structure of the Religious Field, *Comparative Social Research* 13: 1–44.

———. 1998. *Practical Reason: On the Theory of Action*. Stanford: Stanford University Press.

Bourdieu, Pierre, and Loïc Wacquant. 1992. *An Invitation to Reflexive Sociology*, Cambridge: Polity Press.

Chidester, David. 1996. *Savage Systems: Colonialism and Comparative Religion in Southern Africa*. Charlottesville: University Press of Virginia.

———. 2014. *Empire of Religion: Imperialism and Comparative Religion*. Chicago: The University of Chicago Press.

Comaroff, Jean, and John Comaroff. 1991. *Of Revelation and Revolution: Christianity, Colonialism and Consciousness in South Africa*. Volume 1. Chicago: University of Chicago Press.

Els, Carla. 2013. "Constructing Xenophobic Discourses: The Case of the Daily Sun", *Language Matters: Studies in Languages of Africa*, vol. 44, no. 2: 47–67.

Fox, Jonathan. 2008. *A World Survey of Religion and the State*. Cambridge: Cambridge University Press.

Gill, Anthony. 2002. A Political Economy of Religion. In S*acred Markets, Sacred Canopies: Essays on Religious Markets and Religious Pluralism*, edited by Ted G. Jelen, 115–132. New York: Row &Littlefield Publishers, Inc.

Goffman, Irving. 1959. *The Presentation of Self in Everyday Life*. London: Penguin Books.

Hackett, Rosalind I. J. 1995. The Gospel of Prosperity in West Africa. In *Religion and the Transformations of Capitalism: Comparative Approaches*, edited by Richard H. Roberts, 199–214. London: Routledge.

Idowu, Bolaji. 1972. *African Traditional Religion: A Definition*, London: SCM.

Ilesanmi, Simeon O. 2001. Constitutional Treatment of Religion and the Politics of Human Rights in Nigeria. *African Affairs* 100: 529–554.

Isike, Christopher and Efe Isike. 2012. A Socio-Cultural Analysis of African Immigration in South Africa. *Alternation: Interdisciplinary Journal for the Study of the Arts and Humanities in South Africa*, vol. 19, no. 1: 94–116.

Kalu, Ogbu U. 2003. Safiyya and Adamah: Publishing Adultery with Sharia Stones in Twenty-First-Century Nigeria. *African Affairs* 102: 389–408.

Kelly, Philip, and Tom Lusis. 2006. Migration and the Transnational Habitus: Evidence from Canada and the Philippines. *Environment and Planning A* 38: 831–847.

Laniel, Laurent. 2001. Drugs in Southern Africa: Business as Usual. *International Social Science Journal* 53: 407–414.

Ludwig, Frieder, and J. Kwabena Asamoah-Gyadu, eds. 2011. *African Christian Presence in The West: New Immigrant Congregations and Transnational Networks in North America and Europe*. Trenton: Africa World Press.

Magnusson, Lars, and Jan Ottosson, eds. 2009. *The Evolution of Path Dependence*. Cheltenham Glos: Edward Elgar Publishing Ltd.

Maluleke, Tinyiko Sam. 2010. Of Africanised Bees and Africanised Churches: Ten Theses on African Christianity. *Missionalia*, vol. 38, no. 3: 369–379.

Manik, Sadhana and Anand Singh. 2013. Editorial: Love your Neighbours—Exploring and Exposing Xenophobia in Social Spaces in South Africa. *Alternation: Interdisciplinary Journal for the Study of the Arts and Humanities in South Africa*, vol. 7: 1–8.

Marshall, Ruth. 2009. *Political Spiritualities: The Pentecostal Revolution in Nigeria*. Chicago: The University of Chicago Press.

Matsinhe, David Mario. 2011. Africa's Fear of Itself: The Ideology of *Makwerekwere* in South Africa. *Third World Quarterly* 32(2): 295–313.

Miller, Kent D. 2002. Competitive Strategies of Religious Organizations. *Strategic Management Journal* 23: 435–456.

Nyamnjo, Francis B. 2012. Intimate Strangers: Connecting Fiction and Ethnography. *Alternation: Interdisciplinary Journal for the Study of the Arts and Humanities in South Africa*, vol. 19, no. 1: 66–92.

Oosthuizen, G. C. 1975. *Pentecostal Penetration into the Indian Community in Metropolitan Durban, South Africa*. Pretoria: Human Sciences Research Council.

———. 2000. The African Independent Churches in South Africa: A History of Persecution. *Emory International Law Review* 14: 1098–2000.

Peel, J. D. Y. 2000. *Religious Encounter and the Making of the Yoruba*. Bloomington: Indiana University Press.

Pretorius, Stephan P. 2007. Seemingly Harmless New Christian Religious Movements in South Africa Pose Serious Threats of Spiritual Abuse. *HTS Theological Studies* 63(1): 261–281.

Rey, Terry. 2007. *Bourdieu on Religion: Imposing Faith and Legitimacy*. London: Equinox Publishing Ltd.

Shindondola, Hilma. 2007. Chasing an Illusion and Being Trapped in the Social and Economic Obligations: The Case of Cameroonians in Johannesburg. Paper presented at the Anthropology and Development Studies Seminar, University of Johannesburg, 09 March.

Tevera, Daniel. 2013. African Migrants, Xenophobia and Urban Violence in Post-apartheid South Africa. *Alternation* (Special Edition), vol. 7: 9–26.

Turner, Bryan S. 2011a. *Religion and Modern Society: Citizenship, Secularisation and the State*. Cambridge: Cambridge University Press.

———. 2011b. Pierre Bourdieu and the Sociology of Religion. In *The Legacy of Pierre Bourdieu: Critical Essays*, edited by Simon Susen and Bryan S. Turner, 223–245. London: Anthem Press.

Ugba, Abel. 2009. *Shades of Belonging: African Pentecostals in Twenty-First Century Ireland*. Trenton: Africa World Press.

Ukah, Asonzeh. 2007a. Piety and Profit: Accounting for Money in West African Pentecostalism (Part 1). *Nederduitse Gereformeerde Teologiese Tydskrif* 48(3–4): 621–632.

———. 2007b. Piety and Profit: Accounting for Money in West African Pentecostalism (Part 2). *Nederduitse Gereformeerde Teologiese Tydskrif* 48(3–4): 633–648.

———. 2009. Reverse Mission or Asylum Christianity? African Christian Churches in Britain. In *Africans and the Politics of Popular Cultures*, edited by Toyin Falola and Augustine Agwuele, 104–132. Rochester: University of Rochester Press.

———. 2013. Prophets for Profit: Pentecostal Authority and Fiscal Accountability among Nigerian Churches in South Africa. In *Alternative Voices: A Plurality Approach for Religious Studies Essays in Honor of Ulrich Berner*, edited by Afe Adogame, Magnus Echtler and Oliver Freiberger, 131–159. Göttingen: Vandenhoeck & Ruprecht Publishers.

Van Wyk, Ilana. 2014. *The Universal Church of the Kingdom of God: A Church of Strangers*. Cambridge: Cambridge University Press.

Weber, Max. 1991 [1922]. *The Sociology of Religion*, translated by Ephraim Fischoff. Massachusetts: Beacon Books.

CHAPTER 4

The Faraqqasaa Pilgrimage Center from Bourdieu's Perspectives of Field, Habitus and Capital

Gemechu Jemal Geda

Introduction

This chapter tries to utilize Bourdieu's concepts of the field, habitus, and capital as tools for explaining and analyzing the Faraqqasaa pilgrimage center in the religious field of Ethiopia, the life and career of Momina (the founder of the center), the *karaama* (the spiritual power) of Momina and the other leaders, and the various rituals and healing methods as practiced at the Faraqqasaa pilgrimage center. The aforementioned concepts outlined by Bourdieu are relevant and crucial for the analysis of the data on the Faraqqasaa pilgrimage center for various reasons. The concept of habitus which Bourdieu (1985: 13) defines as an experience and possession of a tradition by an agent is important to analyze the rituals performed at the center. It is the habitus of the pilgrims which drives their practices at the center, their participation in the various rituals and their singing of songs praising the miracles performed in the name of the center and its various leaders. As embodied dispositions habitus is especially salient in analyzing the practice of spirit possession. The concept of the field is also significant in relation to the data gathered on the Faraqqasaa pilgrimage center. It can treat the center as an independent entity within the religious field in Ethiopia competing with the two dominant religions in the country, Islam and Christianity as well as other shrines established by Momina and other notable religious personalities. The concept can also be applied to treat the center as an independent field with various agents such as the religious leaders and pilgrims of various religious, social, political, and geographical backgrounds. This chapter, however, mostly treats the center in the sense of the later. The concept of capital, which according to Bourdieu und Wacquant (1992: 101) does not exist and function except in relation to a field is also indispensable to analyze the coming to dominance of the pilgrimage center in Ethiopia as well as the power of its subsequent ritual leaders, which are claimed to have supernatural powers, which they use as their capital to exercise authority.

Some of the rituals to be analyzed include *wadaajaa, arhibu,* and *zar*. An attempt will also be made to show how the spiritual leaders use different forms of capital (social, cultural, and symbolic) at their disposal to their and the pilgrimage center's advantage. The chapter will also try to show how pilgrims use various controversies concerning the early life and religious background of Momina to justify their involvement in her cult as well as to increase their status within the religious field. The Faraqqasaa Pilgrimage center is situated at a place called Faraqqasaa in Arsi zone of the region of Oromia, 225 kilometers south east of Addis Ababa, the capital of Ethiopia. It was established by Momina, affectionately called *Aayyoo*[1] Momina, in the first quarter of the twentieth century. Her early life and religious background is very controversial.

Aayyoo Momina: Origin, Early Life, and Career

The reconstruction of the early life and career of *Aayyoo* Momina was quite challenging to undertake. The main reason for this is that she was a very mobile person. According to informants,[2] she traveled from one part of the country to the other because her spirit did not allow her to stay at a single place for a long period of time. Added to this is that there is a lack of consensus among many of the informants on her religious and family background. This seems to originate from the informants religious background itself. For instance, the majority of Muslim informants stated that Momina was born Muslim, while Christian informants stated otherwise. As a result of the lack of informants who lived contemporaneously with her, fragmented oral information, and the scarcity of written sources made the reconstruction of the early life and career of *Aayyoo* Momina quite challenging. This challenge is, however, not limited to the study of the topic under discussion. For example, Gore (2002: 207) clearly indicates that the majority of local indigenous kinds of religious beliefs and rituals depend on oral traditions, which makes it challenging to study their historical roots and later development.

There are different traditions—or controversies—concerning Momina's origin, religious and family background. The first controversy revolves around her original homeland and family background. Some writers (Braukämper 1984: 769 and Habib 2002: 6) claim that Arsi is her original homeland. Some

---

1 *Aayyoo* is an Oromo honorary term with an equivalent meaning of 'mother.'
2 The informants include individuals who assist the spiritual leader and who have been at the center for a very long period of time, as well as some of her relatives.

informants, especially her relatives, however, claim that her original homeland was at a place called Sanqa in what is today the Amhara region. The second controversial point is the date of her birth which is still contested. Habib states that Momina was born in the last quarter of the 19th century (2002: 7). But this does not seem plausible since it is believed that the last quarter of the 19th century was the time when Momina came to Arsi. It seems to me, however, that she was born earlier than the last quarter of the 19th century. The third, and yet the fundamental controversy, is about her religious background. The religious background of Momina is a point of argument among Christians and Muslims of the area.

These controversies in the religious field regarding the origin and the early faith of Momina are important for the pilgrimage center as well as the pilgrims themselves. The center became appealing for people of various regions, ethnic groups, and religions. The pilgrims, be it Muslims or Christians, also use the controversy surrounding the early faith of Momina as a strategy to probably achieve two goals. First, it is a way of justifying or legitimizing pilgrims' participation on the various rituals and involvement in the pilgrimage center. Secondly, by associating their origin as well as ethnic and early faith backgrounds with that of Momina, pilgrims are trying to increase their own status and distinguish themselves from the others.

The Advent of *Aayyoo* Momina to Arsi: Two Different Perspectives

As pointed out in the previous section, there are two divergent views about the original homeland of *Aayyoo* Momina; Arsi on one hand, and Wollo on the other. Most informants and all her relatives, however, agree on her Wollo origin and her ensuing migration to Hararge and finally to Arsi. If we also agree on her Wollo origin, we will face one major unavoidable question: Why did she leave Wollo and go to Hararge and then to Arsi, where she settled for the rest of her life? There are three possible explanations for this. First, her constant movement was attributed to her *Karaamaa*.[3] It is said that a *bala-karaamaa*,[4] like *Aayyoo* Momina, cannot stay at one place permanently because of a tremendous pressure from the spiritual power they posses. Second, her migration is attributed to the political situation of the country at that time. During the reign of Emperor Yohannes IV (r.1872–1889), the Muslims of Wollo were ordered to abandon their religious belief and adhere to Christianity or

---

3   It means "spiritual power".
4   It refers to someone with a *Karaamaa* or spiritual power.

confront alienation of their property and land rights. This can be seen in the light of what Bourdieu and Wacquant (1992: 102) term as a struggle within a certain field, in this case the religious field, where the Christian empire as the dominant power in the field was in a position to impose its principles on the people of Wollo and punish those who resist this domination. The reaction of the people of Wollo to this order was diverse. Some, especially the ruling elites, renounced Islam and embraced Orthodox Christianity. Others declared that they were converted just to escape persecution and became Christians praying to the Christian God in the day time and Muslims praying to Allah in the evening. Others, however, opted for exile (Bahru 2001: 43–49). Thirdly, her move from Wollo to Hararge and subsequently to Arsi is explained in light of her marriage to a certain *Girazmach*[5] Wolde-Ghiorgis, governor of Hararge at the time. These controversies have placed Momina and her pilgrimage center in a suitable position in the religious field. The belief that she possessed a strong *Karaamaa* made her appealing to diverse group of people regardless of their religious affiliations. Similarly, her adherence to Islam attracted large number of moderate Muslim followers while her marriage to a Christian exposed her cult to Christians who later joined it.

Momina is said to have travelled to and stayed at different places in Arsi and Bale regions. Informants state that *Aayyoo* Momina left Hararge and came to Arsi in the last quarter of the 19th century. She came to Arsi, accompanied by her *kaddamis* (servants at the pilgrimage center) and *Aggaafaariis*[6] (those who supervise work at the pilgrimage center) around 1884/1885 and settled at a place called Gado-Galama. From here she is said to have proceeded to places such as Badu, Ittisa, Zaliba, Sole-Qawe, Guna-Gannate and finally to Faraqqasaa, which became the apex of indigenous pilgrimages in Ethiopia and where she stayed for the remaining part of her life. Even if the Faraqqasaa pilgrimage center is the last to be established by Momina, it is by far the most famous of all. The main reason for this is the presence of her burial site and memorial at Faraqqasaa, which could be described as the objectified form of cultural capital. According to Bourdieu (1986: 246–247), the objectified form

---

[5] It was a political and military title with a meaning of 'commander of the left' (Bahru 2001: 276).

[6] It refers to those who supervise work at all the pilgrimage centers established by Momina. Its singular form is *aggafari*. They have played a crucial role as intermediaries between pilgrims and local officials on one hand and Momina on the other hand. This tradition persisted even after the death of Momina and her successors. They are also responsible for receiving guests who came with different types of votive gifts. They also facilitate accommodation for the pilgrims.

of cultural capital refers to the cultural capital "objectified in material objects such as [...] monuments, and which is transmissible in its materiality".

Religious Beliefs and Rituals at the Pilgrimage Center

Before discussing the religious beliefs, various rituals and healing methods, it is necessary to look briefly into the major pilgrimage dates. One of the most important dates when large numbers of pilgrims gather at Faraqqasaa, is October 29 of each year.[7] It is the annual celebration of the anniversary of the death of *Aayyoo* Momina. In addition, one of the informants claimed that October 29 is celebrated at Faraqqasaa because it was the day when Momina arrived at Faraqqasaa. The other periods which attract a large crowd of pilgrims are associated with Islam such as *Mawlid*[8] and *Id al-fitr*.[9] In addition, large number of pilgrims congregate at Faraqqasaa on December 28 and May 27 (the days of St. Gabriel),[10] and the month of *Pagumen*.[11] In addition to these days pilgrims also visit the center at any time. There are no official records of the number of pilgrims who visit the center each year. Informants said that on the 29th of October of each year, at least 30,000 pilgrims visit the center. In terms of sex ratio, women took the upper hand over men. This seems to be the result of the very nature of labor division in Ethiopia where looking after children and household choirs is in most cases the responsibilities of women. When children are sick, mostly it is up to women to take them to health centers or traditional healing centers such as Faraqqasaa. Hence, large number of women visit Faraqqasaa pilgrimage center.

Pilgrims gather from all corners of the country and all walks of life to take part in various rituals such as singing of hymns praising the power of the spiritual leaders and narrating the miracles they have performed, reciting the Qur'an by the *Darasaa*,[12] praying, *Arhibu* (coffee ceremony), fasting, exorcising and/or harmonizing spirits with the possessed, votive offerings, burning

---

7   All dates are given in the Gregorian calendar if not stated otherwise.
8   Bosworth (1991: 895) defined *Mawlid* as "a term for the time, place, or celebration of the birth of a person, especially that of the prophet Mohammed or of a saint".
9   It is the festival of the breaking of Muslim fast (Lewis et al., 1986: 1008).
10 The death of Momina on 29 October, the other day for the veneration of St. Gabriel by Christians in Ethiopia resulted in the selection of St. Gabriel's days as days of congregation at Faraqqasaa.
11 The Ethiopian calendar has thirteen month and *Pagumen* is the thirteenth month. It is made up of only five days and it has six days every four year.
12 It is an Arabic word meaning "to study". It also refers to young Muslim religious scholars.

of incense and joss sticks under big trees (*adbars*), chewing of *khat* (*Catha edulis*). All of these share most of the defining characteristics of a ritual. First, a ritual is repeated and it takes place at some time of each year. Second, it is sacred and related to the sanctified with the greatest significance. Third, it is formalized and composed of fixed and unchanging actions such as kneeling and bowing. Fourth, it is traditional, claiming an ancient history or authority by myth. Fifth, it is intentional and it is done with a specific meaning or intention (Grimes 1982: 541).

The spiritual leaders, especially Momina, are believed to have supernatural powers and they are viewed with the utmost respect by their followers. As a result of this respect and reverence which followers have for their religious leaders, the pilgrims do not even look straight into the eyes of the leaders. The fundamental and most popular belief is that Momina and her descendants who succeeded her as spiritual leaders possess the power to solve various problems of their followers: heal the leper and the crippled, the infertile, and provide prosperity for the poor. Some even claim that faith may help to raise the dead. Pilgrims therefore flock to all the shrines established by Momina to get one of the above benefits for themselves and/or for their relatives. It is not always necessary to visit the pilgrimage centers in person ask for help. Believers may ask for help wherever they are by invoking such names as *ye Tayye Karaamaa* "Tayye's *karaamaa*", *Ennate Momina* "My mother Momina", *Ye-Arusiwa Emebet* "The Lady of Arsi", *and Ye-Shibbash Karaamaa* "Shibbash's *Karaamaa*. The other popular belief among the devotees is to consider Momina's and the other spiritual leader's words as *baraka*, "blessing".

There seems to be a mutual relationship between spiritual leaders and their followers. The allegiance which the followers show by attending various rituals and votive offerings helps them win the favor of the leaders whose power protects their followers from various catastrophes and endow them with children, health, and wealth. It is believed that anyone who dare to attack these spiritual leaders or any of the shrines will be cursed, and a bad luck will befall upon them and sometimes even on their descendants. Stories narrating the power of the leaders and the center are presented and popularized in hymns sung at the center. Informants could not tell the original composers of the hymns. What is known is that they were there since the time of Momina. Some informants said that there are new hymns added from time to time. Yet, they are not able to identify the original composers. Hymns that revolve around the leaders' spiritual power and performance of miracles contributed a great deal to the success and coming to regional dominance of the Faraqqasaa pilgrimage center and its popularity in Ethiopia. Hymns are usually recited from memory when pilgrims gather to take part in various ritual ceremonies at Faraqqasaa.

It seems the hymns are choreographed but they are not. The hymns recited and the other rituals and practices are good example of a habitus, which is elaborated by Bourdieu as follows:

> Objectively regulated and regular without being in any way the product of obedience to rules, they [habitus] can be collectively orchestrated without being the product of the organizing action of a conductor. The habitus, a product of history, produces individual and collective practices—more history—in accordance with the schemes generated by history. It ensures the active presence of past experiences, which, deposited in each organism in the form of schemes of perception, thought and action, tend to guarantee the 'correctness' of practices and their consistency over time, more reliably than all formal rules and explicit norms (Bourdieu 1990: 53–54).

Pilgrims habitus at Faraqqasaa conforms to the above statement by Bourdieu. Pilgrims conformity of practices and actions while performing various rituals, singing hymns in praise of the shrine as well as the power of its past and present leaders, narrating the stories of various religious personnel at the shrine and miracles these individuals said to have performed are good examples of habitus at Faraqqasaa.

The hymns sung by pilgrims at Faraqqasaa also help to produce symbolic capital for the leaders because they are mostly narrations of the miraculous deeds and healing prowess of the spiritual leaders. This production of symbolic capital through hymns in return justifies and acknowledges the position of the leaders' vis-à-vis ordinary pilgrims.

The other events which gather pilgrims together during the major pilgrimages or at any time are the *wadaajaa* and *arhibu* ceremonies. At Faraqqasaa, *wadaajaa* is a religious assembly at one of the religious houses called *Hadraa Masgid*. The *wadaajaa* ceremony is led by the *Hadraa-Mari*[13] who beats the drum on the occasion. Even if informants did not ascertain the origin of the term, it seems, however, evident that the practice existed among the Oromo even before the advent of Momina. Trimingham stated that the *wadaajaa*, which is the principal religious phenomenon of the Oromo, is a type of family or communal prayer gathering which go along with a feast, coffee and sometimes sacrifices of sheep (1952: 262). However, at Faraqqasaa it refers to praying, chewing *chat*, drinking coffee, singing of hymns, and reciting the

---

13   *Hadraa-Mari* is an Amharic term which means the leader of the *Hadraa* or the religious assembly.

miraculous deeds of Momina and Tayye, which are referred to as *qissa*. One popular belief about the *wadaajaa* ceremony is that seriously ill people will get remedies for their sickness and other earthly problems by reciting the names of Momina and Tayye. On this event, evil spirits such as *budaa*[14] and *Djinni*[15] are exorcised and *zar*[16] is harmonized with the possessed with the help of the spiritual leader and his assistants. In addition to sick and possessed people, anyone who is interested can take part on the *Wadaajaa* ceremony.

Arhibu is a call made by the *kaddamis* (servants at the pilgrimage center) to welcome or summon the pilgrims to drink coffee which is a three times a day event: in the morning, mid day, and evening. Coffee is prepared by males only and there will be absolute silence during the whole ceremony.

Another common practice during the major pilgrimages is the handing over of votive offerings. At Faraqqasaa gifts are offered by pilgrims to show devotion and to give weight for their prayers. It is up to pilgrims to decide what they want to bring but they have to bring exactly what they have promised during their prayers. The value, amount, and type of pilgrims' gifts do not affect the outcome of their prayers. Some pilgrims, however, bring expensive gifts such as gold, car, and/or large sum of money, hoping it results in quick reply to their prayers. At Faraqqasaa, pilgrims mostly present offerings in the form of money, oxen, joss sticks, incense, perfume, carpets, gold, silver, umbrellas, butter, honey, milk, coffee beans, and other items, for the favor they claimed to have received from their prayers using Momina's or Tayye's *Karaamaa*. Pilgrims also offer gifts when they make a wish at the center. When pilgrims' prayers are fulfilled they bring the votive gift they pledged and hand it over publicly announcing the miracles, which are referred to as *aja'bat*. Sometimes pilgrims who promised to offer gifts on the fulfillment of their wishes may not be able to show up during the pilgrimage events due to various personal, family, and social problems such as sickness, funerals and so on. Under these circumstances, they can send the gift with a relative, a friend, or any pilgrim going to the center. The delegated pilgrims would then publicly announce the miracle and offer the gift. If pilgrims failed to hand over the promised gifts for their fulfilled wishes, it is widely believed that some misfortune will befall the individual or one of his/her relatives.

---

14   It means evil eye. In this case, misfortune is blamed on envy, especially, "the fear of envy in the eyes of the beholder" (Helman: 1994: 108).
15   For *Djinni* and their subclasses in Arabic mythology see Lewis, Pellet and Schacht (1965).
16   In Ethiopia, *zar* is an Amharic term used both in the singular and plural to refer to a possessing spirit/possessing spirits.

This handing over of gifts by pilgrims is an excellent example of Bourdieu's concept of the convertibility of cultural and social forms of capital into economic capital (1986: 243) as well as into symbolic capital because of pilgrims' public declaration of miracles, which in turn strengthens the status of the spiritual leaders. The credibility which the spiritual leaders at Faraqqasaa acquire because of their social capital (being the descendants of the founder of the pilgrimage center) and cultural capital, such as the ability to talk with spirits, enables them to collect large amounts of votive gifts (material and money) from the pilgrims who invoke the name of the leaders in their prayers. Here, it can be argued that it is the structure of the field that exerts pressure on pilgrims to conform and deliver economic capital, which is of course disguised in the form of votive offerings.

Some of the oxen obtained from the pilgrims are slaughtered for the occasion. Some of the blood is mixed with perfume and sprinkled around the pilgrimage center while the rest is kept in a little hut near Momina's shrine for the spirits. There is also a kind of feast for the *Darmu*[17] and part of the meat is given. In return, the *Darmu* does not harm the pack animals of the pilgrims as well as the pilgrims who sleep in the open space in the evening.

The other event during the pilgrimages is the burning of incense and joss sticks by pilgrims under giant trees called *adbars*. They also smear the trunk of these trees with butter. It is widely believed that Momina once sat under these trees, which grew to be giant trees through time, healed the sick and performed various forms of miracles. It is also believed that many ancient spirits have resided on the *adbars*. These *adbars* are so revered that worshippers have to take off their shoes before coming close to them. They have to bow down and kiss the ground under the trees and they also kiss the trunk of the *adbars*.

Traditional Medicines

As discussed in the previous section, the spiritual power of the leaders is crucial for healing. In addition there are various forms of healing methods, such as traditional medicine and the possession cult, *zar*. There are three kinds of traditional medicines used to heal patients at Faraqqasaa. These are *tabal, emat,* and *hawza*. The first of these is *tabal* "holy water". *Tabal* is found in many pilgrimage centers and it is believed that it can cure various forms of sicknesses including headaches and intestinal problems (Pankhurst 1994: 948). Informants also claim that it can be used to cure possession by evil spirits such

---

17   *Darmu* is the term used by the local people to refer to an ordinary hyena.

as *budaa* (evil eye). At Faraqqasaa it takes more than an hour's journey to fetch the water to be used as *tabal* from the springs which are located in a deep valley. Pilgrims then either drink it or wash themselves with it as a medicine. Pilgrims are not allowed to take the holy water to their homes. Informants said that it was very recently that it was forbidden to take the holy water away from the pilgrimage center. Previously, pilgrims used to take the holy water for themselves, as well as sick relatives and friends. Some informants said that the reason for the restrictions is that some people started selling the holy water.

The second item used as a traditional medicine is *emat*, which is obtained after burning incense and mixing the ash with water, usually holy water from the spring at the center. It is only the water fetched from the spring which can be used as holy water. The spring water became holy water because of the blessings of Momina for it to have a curative effect. Pilgrims use *emat* as a medicine either by ingesting it or applying it externally on their faces, and/or body. They can also bring it to their sick relatives who could not manage to come to the center. The third item used as a traditional medicine is *hawza*, which is prepared from boiled water mixed with *chat* and drunk by sick as well as healthy pilgrims at the center as a medicine. Pilgrims buy the *chat* and incense from the traders who come to the pilgrimage center to sell their items. *Emat* and *hauza* can be prepared either by the *Aggaafaariis* (assistants at the center) or by the pilgrims themselves. It is not known why the above items are chosen as medicines but it is said that they have been used since the time of Momina.

Spirit Possession Cult: Zar

According to Klass (2003: 67) belief in the presence of spirits is the precondition for belief in spirit possession. Belief in sprit possession also exists throughout the world (Al-Adawi et al., 2001: 47, Bourguignon 1995: 71). The idea of spirits possessing a human body temporarily prevails among 90% of the world's population (Al-Adawi et al., 2001: 47). In sub-Saharan Africa, belief in possession exists among 66 percent of the population (Bourguignon 1995: 71). The tradition of belief in spirits and their capability to possess human beings has its roots in ancient times, and its influence and significance continued to spread well into the twentieth century (Lewis 1984: 419). Natvig (1987: 677), however, challenged this view of the origin of *zar* in the ancient times and stated that the oldest scroll mentioning the term *zar* goes back well into the sixteenth century.

The word *zar* refers to the possession by the spirit as well as the rituals to either exorcize the possessing spirit or to harmonize it with the possessed. It is related to the whole experience of an individual possessed by spirits (Al-Adawi et al., 2001: 48, Natvig 1987: 670, Boddy 1989: 131, El Guindy and Schmais 1994: 107). The *zar* cult refers to a religious group where the criterion for membership is possession by a *zar* spirit, and where regular ceremonially provoked spirit possession is the basis to maintain meaningful and long lasting relationship with the possessing spirits (Natvig 1987: 670). *Zar* is a type of dance performed with the purpose of healing and it is widely practiced in Egypt, the Sudan, and its country of origin, Ethiopia among Christians, Muslims, and Jews. Regardless of the countries where they are practiced, rhythm and rituals remained important characteristics of a *zar* dance (El Guindy and Schmais 1994: 107).

The origin of the term *zar* itself is debatable. Many scholars assume that the word *zar* derived from the Persian and not the Arabic language by looking at the word etymologically. Another suggestion is that it derives from Amharic, the official language of Ethiopia as a consequence of the long standing existence of the cult in Gondar and the surrounding areas. But it is generally believed to be a corruption of *zahr*, an Arabic word meaning "he visited" (Boddy 1989: 132; Al-Adawi et al., 2001: 48; El Guindy and Schmais 1994: 107).

Origin of Zar

The origin of the belief in *zar* is debatable.[18] It is widely believed that *zar* originated in Ethiopia and at the beginning it was related with the cult of a deity which was reduced to the position of a demon after the population embraced Christianity (Sengers 2003: 89). Based on an Abyssinian myth other writers also agreed that *zar* originated in Ethiopia[19] and then spread to other areas such

---

18 There are different views with regard to this. The first group of scholars state that it originated in Ethiopia and spread to the Middle East and other parts of North Africa through the Nile valley. (Al-Adawi et al., 2001: 48). It was suggested that this belief in possession by *zar* originated from the name of an ancient deity in Abyssinian myth (Al-Adawi et al., 48–49). The second group of scholars argues that the belief originated in Iran (Al-Adawi et al., 2001: 49). The third group still argues that this belief in possession by a *zar* spirit originated in the Sudan (Al-Adawi et al., 2001: 49). Others still believe that it originated in Zanzibar (Al-Adawi et al., 2001: 49).

19 According to the Abyssinian myth, the story of a *zar* spirit goes back to the narration of the Garden of Eden, where it was assumed that Eve had lived with 30 of her children. According to this narration, one day God came to visit the Garden of Eden and asked Eve to show him her children. Eve was afraid that God might take her children and decided to hide fifteen of the most beautiful and successful of her children. God however found out what she did and decided to turn the children that she hidden into unseen spirits

as Egypt, the Sudan, Iran, the Middle East, and even Nigeria (El Guindy and Schmais 1994: 107). According to my informants, the story about the origin of spirits conforms to the literature. Accordingly, they stated that the story of the origin of spirits was the Garden of Aden, where Eve lived with her 30 children. One day God disguised himself as a human being and came to visit Eve and her children. Eve was, however, unwilling to show him her beautiful children and she showed him the ugly ones only. Then he asked her whether or not she had hidden some but she told him that she did not. God knew that she was hiding half of the children he gave her. He then cursed the hidden children to be invisible and hostile to the children she showed him. *Zar* is therefore believed to be the descendant of those children turned to spirits by God.

At Faraqqasaa, *zar* refers to spirits as well as the ceremony to harmonize spirits and the possessed. Having seen this, I will turn to my own observation of the *zar* ceremony at Faraqqasaa on 27 May 2006. I was sitting in the *Sagannat*.[20] Present were Hajji Sirak, the great great grandson of Momina and now the cult leader, his family, and many attendants of the pilgrimage center. Around 7:30 in the evening, the sound of a drum begun to echo on all corners of the pilgrimage center. In the house I was sitting, people begun to pour perfumes from bottles into a large bucket. The sound of the drum is believed to enable possession by the spirits, while the perfume would be used as a feast for the guardian spirits and a way of identifying evil spirits.

The noise outside gradually grew louder and louder. Pilgrims possessed by all types of spirits were running to the compound from different directions. They were shouting and screaming as a result of the possession they were experiencing following the sound of the drum. This was the time to deal with people possessed by the spirits. I was invited to go out and watch the event. I stood close to Hajji Sirak to be able to hear what he said. He did not directly talk with the possessed and give orders. He gave the instructions or orders to his closest aide and it was this man who shouted orders to the spirits possessing the individuals.

The *Aggaafaariis* (supervisors) shouted out orders as given by Hajji Sirak. The pilgrims were in trance possession and dancing the *zar* dance, and orders

---

which became active during the night time only. The *zar* spirits are believed to be the descendants of these children turned to spirits by God. Even if they were given immortality and other powers, they are taught to be jealous of the other children (Al-Adawi et al., 2001: 53, El Guindy and Schmais 1994: 109).

20   *Sagannat* is the name of one of the religious houses. The spiritual leader and his associates spend most of the time in this house. In addition, the coffee ceremony, healing, as well as the handing over and collection of votive gifts takes place in it.

were given for the *budaa* and *djinn* spirit to be separated. Threats of being burned were given for failing to do so. Meanwhile, some of the aides at the center brought the perfume to the possessed. They sprinkled the perfume on all the people with a fly whisk. The people were sitting there calmly on instructions to behold and sit silently. I saw some people asking the people who sprinkled the perfume to sprinkle them some more. According to my informants it was the *zar* which asked for more, as it was not satisfied at the beginning. Some people started to scream when the perfume touched them. These were people possessed with *budaa* and *jinn*, which are believed to be evil spirits. The belief is that these evil spirits do not like a good smell, but they are not immune to it. I was informed that the perfume burns these evil spirits and defeats them, hence the screaming. It is believed that it was the spirit which was screaming using the body of the possessed as a medium.

The people possessed with evil spirits were then identified and taken away by the *Aggaafaariis*. The rest, who were considered to be possessed by guardian spirits stayed, and were told to "play without bumping into one another". This meant to continue the *zar* dance, revolving the head and shaking the torso. Although there were many people at the event, there were no incidents of bumping into each other during the *zar* dance, even if the possessed were revolving their heads and shaking their torsos violently. Then orders were given for silence. Every order was directed to the spirits again. The spirits were told that they would receive offerings, usually sacrifices of animals of different colors once a year. The spirits were also told not to trouble their *feres* "horses" until next year, to leave them and stand by their side. Blessings were made for peaceful meetings next year, and for peace for the country and the families of all those who were present there. On each blessing the pilgrims simultaneously said "amen". Finally order was given to the possessed. They were told to offer their spirit what they used to offer it before. Then the spirits were told to mount their "horse" and play at their respective places. With this instruction, the possessed left the compound and dispersed into their camps. This whole ceremony did not take more than half an hour.

After the ceremony came to an end, the people possessed with evil spirits which were already identified during the sprinkling of perfume were taken to the *Hadraa bet*[21] for healing. The spiritual leader ordered the spirits to leave their 'human horses'. At the beginning the spirits were not willing to leave the

---

21   *Hadraa bet* is one of the religious houses at Faraqqasaa where pilgrims sing hymns praising the life and miracles performed by Momina and other spiritual leaders of the center, chew *chat*, and drink *hauza* (a kind of tea prepared from boiled chat leaves). It is also the main house of healing activities, mainly exorcizing evil spirits.

persons they possessed. The leader then made bribes promising that the individuals will offer different material things such as wearing clothes of certain colors, sacrificing animals of various colors. In some cases, the spirits accepted the offer and leave the persons. There were, however, cases where the spirits refused to accept the bribe and leave the possessed. In such instances, the leader threatened the spirits including burning them with fire (warm iron). It is said that the spirits leave the persons they possessed finally through either one of the above ways.

Ways of Possession by Spirits

There are diverse views of how one can be attacked or possessed by a spirit. Human beings are believed to be exposed to being possessed by a spirit/spirits of one sort or the other (Messing 1958: 1121, El Guindy and Schmais 1994: 110). There is, however, individual variation in terms of the extent of exposure or predisposition to attack by *zar*.

Natural Conditions

There are some natural conditions that attract *zar*. Some of these are geographical areas, particularly bushes. It is here where the spirits supposedly live, riding wild animals, milking them, and also defending them from hunters (Messing 1958: 1121). Informants also state that individuals going to bushes, rivers, valleys, garbage disposal sites, and graveyards alone at midday or midnight can be attacked by the spirits who consider this an intrusion.

Inheritance

The other view is that *zar* can be inherited (Al-Adawi et al., 2001: 49). Research shows that some people encourage this inheritance intentionally, especially, if the spirit has been changed to some kind of protective spirit (*Wuqaabii*) and this can be achieved through promises of future devotion (Messing 1958: 1121, El Guindy and Schmais 1994: 110). This possession by spirits hereditarily usually passes through the female members of the family such as mothers, aunts and grandmothers (El Guindy and Schmais 1994: 111). This story of inheriting spirits is also a case at point at Faraqqasaa. However, at Faraqqasaa, a spirit can possess any member of the family regardless of their gender. For instance, after the death of Momina, it was her great-grandson who inherited the powerful spirit that had possessed her when she was alive. After his death this spirit possessed her great-great-grandson, who is the spiritual leader at the moment.

The Spirit's Own Choice

The third view is that spirits usually possess people of their own choice (Al-Adawi et al., 2001: 49). Some spirits may possess people for certain good qualities such as their beauty or the beauty of their voice (Al-Adawi et al., 2001: 49, Messing 1958: 1121). Sometimes, however, people with weak personalities are targeted by spirits (Al-Adawi et al., 2001: 49). An individual can also be possessed by spirits accidentally. According to informants, zar also attack people who mock the worshippers as well as the whole institution. Apart from possession, mockery may also result in very serious sickness.

It is widely believed that *zar* may cause very serious problems and even death if the individual resists possession. The possessed have to pass through a series of ritual ceremonies to exorcise spirits (Al-Adawi et al., 2001: 49). Here, Al-Adawi's explanation is applicable at Faraqqasaa only if the possessing spirits are evil spirits that must be exorcised. If the possessing spirits are guardian spirits, an attempt is made to harmonize the spirits and the possessed in which case the spirits protect the people they possess and the possessed offer material things mostly sacrifices of chickens and sheep of different colors. Resistance to possession is very risky at Faraqqasaa. The people resisting possession usually had to be tied up not to hurt themselves by throwing themselves hard on the ground. For the spirits to be exorcised or appeased, the possessed have to take part in various ritual ceremonies under the auspices of the spiritual leader.

Al-Adawi suggests that women are especially susceptible to spirit possession as a result of their low status in the community. In most cases, the afflicting spirits are, however, males (2001: 54). Lewis also states that the bases of most possessions in Ethiopia are associated with various forms of psychosocial deprivation such as feeling of inferiority, and low status in the society. He further assumes that possession by spirits may help women and people of low social status or people who would like to improve their social or economic status (1984: 419). Men are generally hesitant to acknowledge the existence of spirits. This led to the assumption that the *zar* experience is exploited by men to exercise their authority over women minimizing the risk of facing a serious opposition from them. In the short-term, the women will also benefit from the *zar* phenomenon. (Al-Adawi et al., 2001: 54). This explanation about women possession, however, is not fully applicable as it is practiced at Faraqqasaa. Faraqqasaa is different when it comes to possession by *zar*. Here, it is believed that *zar* possess people regardless of their age, sex, religion, and ethnic, social and economic backgrounds.

Symptoms of Possession

Possession by a spirit is marked by a number of serious mental and physical problems such as loss of sense of time, inability to work, sleepiness during day time, dizziness, serious and continuous headaches, lack of appetite, and restlessness (Al-Adawi et al., 2001: 50). Lambek (1996: 239) has also identified trauma, temporary dissociation, physical pain, convulsive behavior, occasional auto-aggression as additional symptoms of possession where as Messing (1958: 1120), and Al-Adawi et al. (2001: 48) mentioned extreme lack of interest in most of the day to day activities, sterility, proneness to accidents, and raging as additional indicators of possession by spirits. Occasionally, the afflicted may start to shout, become insistent and use some obscene words, hitting the head against a wall, singing, and also laughing and crying at the same time (Al-Adawi et al., 2001: 50). The possessed individual's misbehavior is usually associated with the *zar* spirit communicating via the individual. When the possessed talks with himself it is assumed that it is the spirit talking through the individual (Klass 2003: 37, Al-Adawi et al. 2001: 50). The possessed may sometimes talk with different tones. This is attributed to the belief that many spirits may possess a single individual simultaneously (Al-Adawi et al., 2001: 50).

Methods of Healing the Possessed

People usually start to suspect that an individual is possessed by *zar* after all treatments had failed. Ultimately, either a friend or relative of the afflicted would suggest that possession by *zar* might be the cause of the illness and recommend visiting a professional healer. The possessed will be taken to the healer's place and he/she will be interviewed and a series of ritual ceremonies will be arranged to try to exorcise the spirit. The focus of the healer is usually to encourage or force the unknown spirit to possess the afflicted to be able to know the type of possessing spirit. The healer then uses his own spirit to exorcise the unknown spirit of the possessed (Al-Adawi et al., 2001: 50). The healer makes use of his own *zar* language to speak with the possessing spirit and ultimately expel it.

At Faraqqasaa, both the possessed and the professional healer are referred to as *bale-zar*.[22] The professional healer at Faraqqasaa is the spiritual leader of the center itself. The healer was also once a patient who learned how to control his *zar* spirit and use his spirit to exorcise or harmonize other spirits that possess other individuals. The healer is believed to have stronger and more powerful spirits and he uses these to exorcise the lesser sprits that attack other people. Momina was believed to have the strongest spirit which she used to heal patients possessed with lesser spirits. After her death, her spirit was said to have passed over to her descendants who succeeded her as spiritual leaders. The leaders also have a strong staring and verbal ability. When they interviewed the possessed, they looked directly into the eyes of the possessed and gave instruction to the spirits with a language full of strong wordings including threats of being burnt.

The spiritual leaders themselves are trained to communicate with spirits and identify various types of spirits by looking at the trance dance of the possessed. This training takes a long time and is supervised by knowledgeable people, mostly by preceding spiritual leaders. This ability of the leaders to communicate with and identify various spirits can be seen as the embodied form of cultural capital. Bourdieu aptly states that the embodied form of cultural capital is

> ... linked to the body and presupposes embodiment. The accumulation of cultural capital in the embodied state, i.e., in the form of what is called, culture, cultivation, bildung, presupposes a process of embodiment, incorporation, which, insofar as it implies a labour of inculcation and assimilation, costs time, time which must be invested personally by the investor (1986: 244).

The embodied form of cultural capital possessed by various spiritual leaders at Faraqqasaa such as an intense staring ability and command of a special language to communicate with spirits conforms to Bourdieu's proposition that it is associated with a body, which means with a spiritual leader who intern learned the skill from others. This skill cannot be directly inherited rather acquired through intensive training. Current leaders at Faraqqasaa teach the aforementioned skills to their potential predecessors.

The first activity in the attempt to heal the possessed is to interview the sick at the healer's own house and find out the type of spirit causing the sickness.

---

22   In Amharic, the official language of Ethiopia *bale-zar* has an equivalent meaning of 'someone with a zar'.

The type of the *zar* possessing a certain individual is identified by the nature of the dance performed by the possessed under the direction of the possessing spirit (Messing 1958: 1120). The *zar* dance is a diagnostic method. The speed and the difficulty in which a person enters into possession trance in reaction to a certain song verify whether or not that specific individual is possessed, and the kind of the *zar* spirit that caused the illness. It is believed that there are around 162 kinds of *zar* in Ethiopia (Gemechu 2003: 50). The possessed encourages the spirit by dancing to possess her/him and show itself. It is said that the identification of the type of the spirit that attacked the individual is the first and the most important step to healing (El Guindy and Schmais 1994: 113).

When a spirit expresses itself and begins to talk through the individual, the reason for the attack will be known, and the healer makes promises or threats to exorcise it (Al-Adawi et al., 2001: 49–51). However, this is not always the case at Faraqqasaa. The spiritual leader exorcises only evil spirits. The leader does not recommend exorcism once it is known that the possessing spirit is a guardian one. It is also believed that it is not possible to exorcise a guardian spirit permanently. In this case worshippers have to take part in group healing rituals. What the healers do at Faraqqasaa is to appease the spirit and to order the spirit not to harm its human "horse" until the next pilgrimage, usually a year after each pilgrimage. During that period of a year, the possessed had to fulfill what he/she promised to the spirit. Otherwise, the spirit would become angry and make the possessed sick again. Under this circumstance, the possessed has to go to the pilgrimage center for healing again.

Conclusion

It has been mentioned in the introductory part that the Faraqqasaa pilgrimage center is an independent field which can be seen in two different perspectives. First, it can be seen as a field within the religious field of Ethiopia competing with other actors, mainly Islam and Christianity. The relationship between the center and moderate actors from Islam and Christianity is relatively harmonious. However, the center is mostly demonized and regarded as backward by orthodox actors within Islam and Christianity. Second the center can also be seen as an independent field with many actors such as the spiritual leader, overseers of various rituals, and pilgrims of diverse religious, ethnic, socio-political, and geographical backgrounds. The relationship between these actors at the center is harmonious and tolerant. Although pilgrims come from various backgrounds they are in unison in their adherence to the cult. They all accept and respect the authority of the religious leader and they share the place of pilgrimage. The practice of sharing a sacred spaces and places of pilgrimages, however, is not limited only to Faraqqasaa. Limor (2007: 219) states that one of the most fascinating phenomena in the study of sacred space and pilgrimage to holy places is how believers of different faiths may share sanctity. However, her suggestion that sharing traditions has become a point of contention, argument, and rivalry is not applicable at Faraqqasaa where pilgrims from diverse backgrounds venerate the cult peacefully.

To sum up, it is possible to apply Bourdieu's concepts of field, habitus, and capital (social, cultural, symbolic and economic) as tools to explain and analyze the controversies surrounding the life and early belief of *Aayyoo* Momina, the founder of the Faraqqasaa pilgrimage center, the miracles attributed to her and her successors as leaders, as well as the various rituals and healing methods as practiced at Faraqqasaa. An attempt has been made to show how pilgrims use the controversy surrounding the original homeland and religious background of Momina to their advantage in an attempt to improve their status (position) in the religious field and justify their participation in the cult. It has also been indicated how subsequent spiritual leaders use their social capital (being descendants of Momina), the cultural capital (the ability to talk *zar* language and identify the type of possessing spirits from the nature of trance dance), as well as symbolic capital (production of hymns glorifying the spiritual leaders and their supernatural powers) to their advantage and how they convert the above mentioned forms of capital in to economic capital in the form of votive gifts handed over by pilgrims whose wishes are fulfilled. Bourdieu's concept of habitus is also used to explain various aspects of rituals and the entire religious experience at the Faraqqasaa pilgrimage center. In short, Bourdieu's concepts of the field, habitus, and capital can be indispensable tools of explanation and analysis of the various aspects of the Faraqqasaa pilgrimage center.

References

Al-Adawi, Samir H., Rodger G. Martin, Ahmed Al-Salmi and Harith Ghassani. 2001. Zar: Group Distress and Healing. *Mental Health, Religion and Culture* 4(1): 47–61.

Bahru Zewde. 2001. *A History of Modern Ethiopia 1855–1991*. Addis Ababa: Addis Ababa University Press.

Boddy, Janice. 1989. *Wombs and Alien Spirits: Women, Men, and the Zar Cult in Northern Sudan*. Wisconsin: The University of Wisconsin Press.

Bosworth, C. E., E. van Donzel, B. Lewis, and Ch. Pellat, eds. 1991. *The Encyclopaedia of Islam*. New Edition, Vol. 6. Leiden: Brill.

Bourdieu, Pierre. 1985. The Genesis of the Concept of *Habitus* and of *Field*. *Sociocriticism* 2: 11–24.

———. 1986. The Forms of Capital. In *Handbook of Theory and Research for the Sociology of Education*, edited by John Richardson, 241–258. New York: Greenwood Press.

———. 1990. *The Logic of Practice*. Stanford: Stanford University Press.

Bourdieu, Pierre, and L. J. D. Wacquant. 1992. *An Invitation to Reflexive Sociology*. Cambridge: Polity Press.

Bourguignon, Erika. 1995. Possession and Social Change in Eastern Africa: Introduction. *Anthropological Quarterly*. 68(2): 71–74.

Braukämper, Ulrich. 1984. The Islamization of the Arssi-Oromo. In *Proceedings of the Eighth International Conference of Ethiopian Studies*, edited by Taddese Beyene, 767–778. Addis Ababa: Addis Ababa University Press.

El Guindy, Howaida, and Claire Schmais. 1994. The Zar: An Ancient Dance of Healing. *American Journal of Dance Therapy* 16(2): 107–120.

Gemechu, Jemal. 2003. "A History of the Gado-Galama Pilgrimage Center from its foundation to 2002." BA Senior Essay, Addis Ababa University.

Gore, Charles. 2002. Religions in Africa. In *Religions in the Modern World*, edited by Linda Woodhead, Paul Fletcher, Hiroko Kawanami and David Smith, 235–265. London and New York: Routledge.

Grimes, Ronald L. 1982. Defining Nascent Ritual. *Journal of the American Academy of Religion* 50(4): 539–555.

Habib Qasim. 2002. *Seenaa Muuda Faraqqasaa, Jalqaba-2001* [A Historical Survey of Faraqqasaa Pilgrimage Center, from its foundation—2001]. Asella: Arsi Cultural and Information Office.

Helman. C. G. 1994. *Culture, Health and Illness*. London: Butterworth-Heinemann.

Klass, Morton. 2003. *Mind Over Mind: The Anthropology and Psychology of Sprit Possession*. Oxford: Rowman and Littlefield Publishers, Inc.

Lambek, Michael. 1996. Afterword: Spirits and Their Histories. In *Spirits in Culture, History, and Mind*, edited by Jeannette Marie Mageo and Alan Howard, 237–249. New York and London: Routledge.

Lewis, Herbert H. 1984. Spirit Possession in Ethiopia: An Essay in Interpretation. In *Proceedings of the Seventh International Conference of Ethiopian Studies*, edited by Sven Rubenson, 419–427. Lund: Berlings.

Lewis, B., Ch. Pellet and J. Schacht. 1965. Djinn. In *The Encyclopaedia of Islam, New Edition*, Vol. 2, edited by C. E. Bosworth, H. Pearson, E. J. van Donzel and H. A. R. Gibb, 546–550. Leiden: Brill.

Lewis, B., V. L. Menage, Ch. Pellat and J. Schacht, eds. 1986. *The Encyclopaedia of Islam*. New Edition, Vol. 3. Leiden: Brill.

Limor, Ora. 2007. Sharing Sacred Spaces: Holy Places in Jerusalem Between Christianity, Judaism, and Islam. In *In Laudem Hierosolymitani: Studies in Crusades and Medieval Culture in Honour of Benjamin Z. Kedar*, edited by Iris Shagrir, Ronnie Ellenblum and Jonathan Riley-Smith, 219–231. Surrey: Ashgate.

Meagher, P. K., T. C. O'Brien and S. C. Maria Aherne, eds. 1979. *Encyclopedic Dictionary of Religion*. Vol. O–Z. Washington D.C.: Corpus Publications.

Messing, Simon D. 1958. Group Therapy and Social Status in the Zar Cult of Ethiopia. *American Anthropologist* 60(6): 1120–1126.

Mohammed Hassen. 1998. "A History of the Guna-Gannate Pilgrimage Center, from its foundation to 1997." BA Senior Essay, Addis Ababa University.

Natvig, Richard. 1987. Oromos, Slaves, and the Spirits: A Contribution to the History of the Zar Cult. *The International Journal of African Historical Studies* 20(4): 669–689.

Pankhurst, Alula. 1994. Reflections on Pilgrimages in Ethiopia. In *Papers of the 12th International Conference of Ethiopian Studies*, Vol. 2: Social Science, edited by Harold G. Marcus, 933–953. New Jersey: Red Sea Press, Inc.

Sengers, Gerda. 2003. *Women and Demons: Cult Healing in Islamic Egypt*. Leiden: Brill.

Trimingham, J. S. 1952. *Islam in Ethiopia*. London: Oxford University Press.

CHAPTER 5

Fielding for the Faithful: A Tale of Two Religious Centers in a Small Muslim Town in Kenya

Halkano Abdi Wario

Introduction

Aw Kombola is a self-made sheikh.[1] He is considered part of the clerical class at Merti Quran Center (MQC). Though he did not attain the required *madrasa* (Islamic schools) education in Merti or elsewhere, he is very religiously observant and commands immense respect as a mosque elder. From time to time Aw Kombola breaks into powerful spontaneous sermons after *farḍ* (obligatory) prayers at the Merti Jamia Mosque.[2] Often his pep talks end with announcements about an upcoming Tablīghī Jamāʿat activity in the region. Be it national *ijtimāʿ* (country-wide Tablīghī gatherings), regional *jor* (regional gathering) or just a call for a local neighborhood tours called *jowla*; he represents the very embodiment of the lay-run transnational movement in a small town. Aw Kombola mobilizes, preaches, coordinates, informs on everything Tablīghī. The sole aim of his group of itinerant preachers and by extension the 'sedentarized' *ʿulamāʾ* of MQC is *daʿwa* (proselytism) which is *amr biʾl-māʿrūf wa al-nahī ʿan al munkar*, that is, enjoining good and forbidding evil among the Muslim faithful.[3] How to go about this ambitious task forms the basis of contention between the lay preachers of the movement and the leaders of the established

---

[1] For confidentiality, pseudonyms have been used in reference to individuals unless indicated otherwise.
[2] There are two basic kinds of prayers in Islam, *farḍ* and *sunna* prayers. The former are the obligatory and congregational five daily prayers required of every one and the latter are supplementary and individual prayers considered as highly rewarding as they were done by Prophet Muhammad. Merti Jamia Mosque is the central Friday prayer mosque and the seat of town's *ʿulamāʾ*. It is managed by the dominant *Salafi* influenced sheikhs of Merti Quran Centre.
[3] *Daʿwa* has multiple meanings ranging from prayer to calling people to the path of Islam. Edgunas Racius (2004) outlines two types of *daʿwa*, intra-ummaic and extra-ummaic *daʿwa*. The former is about inviting and reminding Muslims to be steadfast in their faith, and in our case a specialty of Tablīghī Jamāʿat, and the latter calling Muslim and non-Muslims to the truth of Islam, which the *Qalole* see as their mandate.

religious institutions in town. Similar scenarios are replicated in other areas. This chapter examines the nature of relations between members of the lay movement and the established *'ulamā'* as they target to influence religious practices of the laity.

Based on ethnographic field research among Muslims of Northern Kenya, the chapter explores the strategies and nature of competition and collaboration in Islamic field between members of Tablīghī Jamā'at and established scholars in Merti town. It examines how Tablīghī Jamā'at, a new entrant into the field alternates between co-opting the local religious scholars and utilizing their mosques to unilaterally mobilizing lay Muslims to partake in their *da'wa* missions. The chapter finally explores the nature of polemics and counter polemics employed by each group in order to delegitimize their opponents religious practices and depict their own as based on the traditions of pristine Islam. Pierre Bourdieu's concepts of field and theory of practice would be used in the analysis. However it should be born in mind that despite divergence of the preaching strategies, the two groups have been able to mute their explicit differences for the sake of common good.

Between April 2009 and January 2012, the author conducted several field trips to Kenya totaling to 12 months and conducted 30 in-depth interviews with Tablīghīs, religious scholars and ordinary Muslims in Moyale, Isiolo, Merti, Garba Tulla, Kinna and Nairobi. As a participant observer, he took part in religious congregations of Tablīghī Jamā'at at their headquarters in Nairobi, travelled with them for missionary tours and listened to a number of sermons and religious motivational talks offered in various mosques by the Tablīghīs and local religious scholars.

The Context

The field in Bourdieuan sense is a social arena within which struggle takes place over specific resources or stakes and access to them. The field, hence, is a structured system of social positions occupied either by individuals or groups, nature of which determines the situation for their occupants. The field is also structured internally by power relations and the positions occupied by the agents determine their access to resources at stake be it economic capital, social capital (various kinds of valued relations with significant others), cultural capital (legitimate knowledge of one kind or another) and symbolic capital (prestige and social honor). As a field of struggle the agents' strategies are concerned with the preservation or improvement of their own positions with respect to the defining capital of the field. In other words, agents occupy certain positions in the field which are determined by how much capital they possess (Jenkins 2002: 44–45).

What could be called religious field? The Religious field is characterized by "the fact that what is at stake is the *monopoly of the legitimate exercise of the power to modify, in a deep and lasting fashion, the practice and world-view of lay people*, by imposing on and inculcating in them a particular *religious habitus*" (Bourdieu 1987: 126). The struggle within the field is, hence, over production, administration and consumption of religious capital and the adherence of the laity to whom it is marketed. The *'ulamā'* as a class of religious specialists, are wary of any class of 'non-professionals' purporting to give religious guidance to the masses. They tend to view such attempts with suspicion doubting rivals as lacking in competence and legitimacy. The quotation below perhaps captures this notion clearly:

> Over and above everything that sets them against one another, specialists agree at least in laying claims for a monopoly of legitimate competence which define them as such and in reminding people of the frontier which separates professionals from the profane. The professional tends to 'hate the common layman' who negates his professional status by doing without his services: he is quick to denounce all forms of 'spontaneism' (political, religious, philosophical, artistic) that will dispossess him of his monopoly of the legitimate production of goods and services. Those in possession of competence are ready to mobilize against everything that might favour popular self-help (magic, 'popular medicine', self-medication, etc.) (Bourdieu 1990a: 150–151).

Within this theoretical frame the Tablīghī Jamā'at can be considered a sort of lay-driven revivalist movement, and this contribution shall discuss how the *'ulamā'* in Merti try to render the movement as nothing more than a dubious Do-It-Yourself pan-Islamic spirituality in need of their constant supervision. It is self-organized, trans-national, and relatively independent of religious supervision of the *'ulamā'* and seeks its legitimacy for its programs in the core texts of Islam an interpretive task monopolized for a longer time by the *'ulamā'*. One must take note that the religious specialists are themselves differentiated and are not a homogenous group. As we shall see, the Tablīghī Jamā'at not only contest to use sacred spaces managed by these *'ulamā'* but also recruit membership on continuous basis from among the lay with relative success.

To get an in-depth understanding of the issue at hand, one needs to examine the competitive and collaborative structure of the religious field, the habitus of the practitioners, their interests and strategies, the forms of capital at stake and the exercise of domination and symbolic violence. Merti has been chosen as an appropriate site for the analysis of the field for three main reasons: first it has a rich history of Islamic learning and adherence in the Upper Eastern part of Kenya, second, there is an institutionalized and active presence of both Tablīghīs and *Qalole* (sheikhs) of mainstream *salafī* inclined tradition, and thirdly, the population is largely Waso Borana, a section of Borana historically cut off from cultural attachments to their ancestral lands and customs in Ethiopia.[4]

Among the Borana, the period from the mid-1980s to the year 2000 represented the growth of *salafī* inclined religious persuasion. Before 1986, there was only one mosque in Merti town. Currently the town has a population of around 6000 people. It is situated by the seasonal Waso Nyiro River. The town serves as the link between the pastoral economy of the Waso Borana and the outside world. Though largely Muslim, the adherence to the tenets of the faith among the populace was lukewarm up to the 1980s. Many factors accounted for that, namely the low levels of Islamic learning, the strong attachment to Borana customs and the lack of connection to outside reformist influences. The period since then has seen the establishment of Merti Quran Centre, reference point for all matters Islamic in the region. It was founded by a local cleric returning from Sudan with help from Islamic humanitarian organizations such as Al Muntada Trust, and African Muslim Agency. The establishment and consolidation of the center had significant effects on a number of fronts. The center runs a host of schools, secular and Islamic, primary and secondary, a health center, a water project, and feeding program for children of the poor, a relief distribution center, an adult learning center, an orphanage and the Merti Jamia Mosque and supports most of the outlying mosques within the region. Merti *madrasa*, one of the most sought after institution of Islamic education in Isiolo and Marsabit Counties, runs from nursery to high school level and a number of its graduates have directly joined Islamic universities and colleges in Kenya, Saudi Arabia, Egypt and the Sudan.

The *Qalole* from the center sit on various town boards ranging from water management, security, education, health to development agencies in the area. In sum, the center established itself as an influential factor in all facets of local life. It oversaw the growth and establishment of the local *Qalole* class with its strong commitment to the ethos of religious revivalism of their community. In

---

4 *Qalole* (singular: *Qalich*) is the term used by Borana Muslim to refer to religious leaders. Waso Borana are the Borana who live around Waso Nyiro River in North Kenya and who originally migrated from Southern Ethiopia. The Waso area includes the Merti, Garba Tulla, Kinna and Sericho divisions (Aguilar 1998).

simple words, a foundation of a stable and durable disposition—a habitus—was laid.

Over the years, there has been heightened religious adherence due to increased Islamic education and gradual abandonment of Borana customs and traditions. The number of mosque and *madrasa* attendance rose drastically among the common people. There also increase in number of largely secular educated but religiously observant individuals who though do not belong to the class of religious specialists wished to contribute to religious change and expand their religious capital. Such persons became receptive to alternative reform ideas and wanted to impact the efforts of *da'wa* in their own niche and way. These individuals were to become stalwart of transnational Islamic movement Tablīghī Jamā'at. It is to this group do the likes of Aw Kombola belong. In Merti, gradual rise of the *Qalole* as hegemonic dominant category was smooth until the appearance and recruitment of local Tablīghī activists.

From a one-mosque town in the 1980s, Merti witnessed a boom in sacred spaces under the supervision of the Merti Quran Centre (MQC). Currently there are seven mosques in the town, namely Jamia, Khalifa, Taqwa, Ola Ganna, Ola Sakuye, Gammachu, and Secondary school mosque. Smaller settlements like Korbesa, Basa, Bulesa or Biliqo have mosques that were established with support from MQC. The only formal Islamic place of worship to be established in the area without explicit support of MQC is Masjid Quba, a Tablīghī Markaz (Centre). Similar to the agenda of Merti Quran Centre, the Markaz disseminate Islamic teachings, network with local and translocal religious activists and aims to bring about qualitative change in adherence to Islamic tenets among the Borana of Waso. The Markaz was built in 2009 by a Tablīghī benefactor who hails from outside the town. It is a kind of victory over the monopoly of discourse on Islamization dominated by the clerics from MQC. Commenting on the new Markaz, one informant aptly observes:

> Oh... that is their new Markaz as they call it. They have built a big mosque for themselves. Remember this is the first and only mosque that has not been built or initiated by the Quran Centre. Now they can do their things way from the glare of the *Qalole*. They can now preach freely without having to ask for permission and with no fear of being told 'do it this way or that way'. I heard that it is going to be headquarters for their activities in the whole of Waso region.[5]

---

5 Sheikh Abdub, personal communication, August, 2009, Merti.

For some time, the local members of Tablīghī Jamā'at have been engaged in subtle contest over use and management of sacred spaces. They believe that the *Qalole* are but managers of these spaces and that such space cannot be privatized. The local members of the movement always actively utilize their Markaz as well as the other mosques for their form of *da'wa*. As members of any mosque community, they recruit new members, do impromptu sermons about adherence to the tenets of faith to willing mosque attendants, conduct weekly *da'wa* patrols that end in short talks at the mosque, receive and accommodate foreign as well as regional Tablīghī teams from outside the town at their mosques, and conduct weekly *shūrā* (consultative meetings). Through these practices they not only changed the nature of religious practices that can be conducted in a mosque but what practices ordinary believers can take home as reform agenda for household religious change.

Let us briefly examine the Tablīghī Jamā'at in a historical setting. It is a lay-run, voluntary, apolitical and pietistic transnational Islamic movement (Masud, 2000; Dickson, 2009; Janson, 2005). It is a preaching party that seeks to bring nominal Muslims to the path of practical faith as based on the life model of the Prophet, as they define it. As such, the movement is a process and a product that is related with the inculcation of new habitus. It requires that the ordinary believers join together, form a group, travel for stipulated numbers of days so as to transform their practice and become better Muslims. During such a travel from home the adept is required to preach to mosque attendants on fundamentals of faith. A travelling team is also expected to mobilize local Muslims to constitute groups for similar tours and motivate them to be steadfast in their religious observance. On regular basis, a Tablīghī individual is expected to commit 40 days to 4 months yearly to missionary travels and also attendance of Tablīghī activities at his local mosques. These intense religious and social networking and travels gradually transform adherent's habitus and strengthen his bonds with fellow Tablīghīs.

Though it originated in India in 1926, the movement today is considered as one of the most active Islamic movement in the world with presence in Sub-Saharan and North Africa, South and South East Asia and Europe and North America (Dickson 2009; Horstmann 2007; Janson 2005; Metcalf 2003; Moosa 1997; Reetz 2008; Sikand 2002, 2006). After the death of the founder Maulana Muhammad Ilyas in 1945, second leader of the movement Mawlana Muhammad Yusuf oversaw the transnationalization of the movement outside Indian sub-continent. It first targeted to establish presence in Saudi Arabia and United Kingdom in late 1940s and early 1950s and later relying on networks of migrant South Asian Muslims dotted all over the world penetrated areas such South and East Africa in late 1950s. When Maulana Muhammad Ilyas initiated it to transform the practice of largely religious lax Mewati community, he did not imagine that the grass root movement would rise to such heights replicating itself in many locations and maintaining distinctive local as well as South East Asian features. Its revolutionary approach to proselytism in which the laity take the front seat, has been seen as a subversion of the religious authority of the *'ulamā'* class. It shunned materialism and other forms of classification. Though influenced strongly by purist Deobandi tradition and with distinctive South Asian Hanafi jurisprudence, the global spread of the movement has been facilitated by its adaptive mechanism to existing Islamic traditions in an area. In this respect, its ability to shun doctrinal and sectarian controversies has seen it make in road into many Muslim societies.[6] It transformed the duty of preaching which had always been the preserve of the *'ulamā'* into the ultimate duty of every Muslim, male and female, who by teaching others may get a deeper knowledge of the fundamentals of Islam.[7] Central to the ideology of the Jamā'at is the role of travel as the most effective tool of personal reform (Masud 2000). The main teachings of the movement are summarized under six principles popularly known as *siffa sittah*: One, article of faith (*shahāda*); two, five daily ritual prayers (*ṣalāt*); three, knowledge (*'ilm*) and remembrance of God (*dhikr*); four, respect and honor for every Muslim (*ikrām-i Muslim*); five, emendation of intention and sincerity (*ikhlās-i niyyah*) and six, spare time (*tafrīq-i waqṭ*). (Jan Ali, 2010) The last principle is the hallmark of the movement. It is also known as *khurūj fī sabīl lillāh* (going out for the sake of God) and involves volunteers sparing time and resources to travel away from home for different durations such as 3 days, 10 days, 40 days, 4 months and even a year.

---

6 One sheikh criticizing the Tablīghīs for all-inclusive approach that does not discriminate between what he considers as deviant groups and orthodoxy admonishes them for recruiting members irrespective of their sectarian persuasions. He says 'The Tablīghīs have a belief that anyone who has said *lā ilāha illālllāh* (proclaiming of faith in Islam—There is no god but Allah) is our brother, that we should forget our differences, our different schools of thought, and our doctrinal uniqueness. That we should just stay firm and united under the flag of *lā ilāha illālllāh*. In the movement, they have accommodated all kinds of deviant groups. *Shia* are inside, *Qādiriyya* are inside, *Shahamiyya* are inside, *Nakshbandiyya, Tijānī*, Sufi are in, *Qurāfī* are in and in other everyone and everything is in it.' Sheikh Said Bafana, 'Criticism against the Tablighi Jamaat', Video CD, Wa'Haqq Films Production, August 2006.

7 The Tablīghī informants I interacted with posited that the obligation of inviting others to the faith is not *farḍ kifāya* (duties that can be done by few on behalf of the *umma*) but *farḍ 'ayn*, an obligation compulsory on each and every individual (Interviews with Mohamed Qalla September 2009, Moyale; Aw Gombore April 2009, Isiolo; Mohamed Arero September 2009, Moyale; Hassan Doda, April 2009, Isiolo and June and July 2010 Nairobi and Merti; Aw Bidu April 2009, Isiolo and Sheikh Abdi May 2010, Moyale).

The movement came into Kenya in 1956, largely through contacts between Kenya's Asian Muslim communities from Indian Subcontinent and pioneer Tablīghī preachers.[8] Historically, mercantile Indian Ocean trade brought traders of various origins to the coast of East Africa. Among them are Indians of various religious persuasions. British Colonial administration also brought large number of Indians as indentured railway laborers to construct Kenya-Uganda Railway from Mombasa to the shores of Lake Victoria at the turn of the twentieth century. A number of the laborers went back home while others made Kenya their home. Subsequent migration increased the population of this diasporic and heterogeneous community. The Kenyan Asians are relatively wealthy traders and industrialists. Various Muslim communities are represented within them including Ismailis, Ithna Asharis, Ahmadis and Sunni Memmons, Punjabi Muslims, Cutchis, Baluchis and Kokanis. (See Salvadori 1989, 2000) It is among the Sunni groups that the Tablīghī Jamā'at found ardent supporters.

The movement is active in most parts of Kenya, especially in Northern Kenya, at the Coast, in Nairobi and the major towns in Central and Western Kenya. Among the Borana community of Isiolo and Moyale, the Jamā'at has an active history of about 17 years.[9] Its national annual *Ijtimā'* in Nairobi attracts up to 15,000 adherents not only from Kenya but also from neighboring countries such as Tanzania, Uganda, Rwanda, Burundi, Somalia, Ethiopia, Djibouti and eastern Democratic Republic of Congo. In the 1970s and 80s, preachers of Tablīghī Jamā'at from the Indian peninsula frequented the region. By the 1990s, a number of indigenous Kenyans had been recruited into the lay missionary movement and became its representatives and proselytizers in the area. In every area it establishes itself; the movement creates a network of committed activists who proselytize in their mosque area jurisdiction. These individuals also conduct *da'wa* tours in their region; attend national and regional gatherings, recruit new activists, travel across national and international boundaries and network with local, regional, national and international Tablīghī committees and *dā'ī-s*.[10]

---

8   Sheikh Naushad, a sermon at Bait ul Maal, Nairobi, 18.04.2009.

9   Some informants approximate the arrival of the first Asian Tablīghī groups in early 1970s. One of the most ardent supporters of the movement in Kenya, the Muslim Asians from the town of Meru had initial contacts with local Borana communities. They for instance established the first formal *madrasa* in town of Kinna and also toured the areas with foreign *jamā'ats*. Some informants recall travelling in mid-1980s with such teams from Meru to as far as Uganda. (Hassan Dida, personal interview Isiolo, 14.04.2009. Abdi Boru, Kinna, 26.09.2009.)

10 *Dā'ī* (plural-*du'āh*) is an Arabic word that means a caller or inviter. The term is related with *da'wa*, the duty of inviting others back to the path of faith. The Tablīghī activists are

The Contest in the Field

As seen above, the Islamic field in Merti is occupied by at least two major groups of individuals. On one side are the *Qalole*, who are the guardians of the locally dominant *salafī* tradition, the pioneers in the field of revivalism and the founders and managers of several Muslim sacred spaces. On the other side of the field are the lay preachers of Tablīghī Jamāʿat. Both groups of individuals are representative of two centers, Merti Quran Centre and newly constructed Tablīghī Markaz. Both groups of individuals are interested in the monopoly over the legitimate production of religious capital, and in the institutionalization of their dominance in the field, that is, in what Bourdieu calls 'the legitimization of the arbitrary' (Bourdieu 1990b: 123).

The game or process of delegitimizing the other is a core strategy of agents in the field. From the very beginning the Tablīghīs have drawn themselves and act not as a sect or a separate stream of thoughts but as a partner to the local *Qalole* in reviving religion among the nominal lay.[11] At doctrinal levels some of the major differences between the two groups are overlooked as local Tablīghīs do not necessarily subscribe to school of jurisprudence as followed by the Tablīghīs in South Asia. The movement has distinct South Asian influence emanating from the Deobandi purist traditions while the current crop of *Qalole* are products of similar *salafī* traditions emanating from Middle East. The former is aligned at least theoretically in South Asian to the Hanafī school of Islamic jurisprudence while majority of Muslims in East Africa subscribe to Shāfiʿī school. As mentioned previously the Tablīghī Jamāʿat accommodates itself to existing doctrinal and sectarian traditions predominant in an area. It includes within its rhetoric a tacit recognition of their success being dependent upon cooperation with *Qalole* in preaching to the laity. They require the permission of the *Qalole* to use mosques for *daʿwa* as the use of pulpit is a fiercely regulated practice with sanction and approval being in the hand of an imam, the prayer leader. Except in their Markaz, the Tablīghī *dāʿī-s* have to cultivate friendly relations and give recognition to the authority of the mosque custodians in order to carry out *daʿwa* that involves giving speeches, holding weekly consultative meetings, hosting visiting fellow dais and recruitment drives. These collaborative strategies reduce the tendencies for outright contests and competition laying foundation for culture of mutual cooperation and coexistence.

---

on lifelong *daʿwa* path and hence call themselves *dais*. The term shall used in this study to refer to the Tablīghī workers.

11   Abdi Abgudo, personal conversations, September, 2009.

However despite the confluence of their objectives manifested as a concern over the religious practice of the laity, the methods they arrive at differ. This brings us to the competitive nature of the field which may require certain forms of censorship or declaration of unorthodoxy of the other. The nature of the debates between the local Tablīghī *dāʿī-s* and the *Qalole* over *daʿwa* concerns six thematic issues, namely: religious knowledge (*ʿilm*); debates over primacy of new and innovative religious practices associated with the movement; concerns over legitimacy of select Tablīghī religious text usage; discourses over political engagements and social activism, concerns over primacy of travels as the best means of proselytism and conflict over origin and transnational affiliation to movements and Islamic trends beyond the region.

The first concerns, religious knowledge (*ʿilm*). The movement targets to mobilize every Muslim irrespective of his levels of *ʿilm* to leave his home to preach. They argue that one does not require to be a religious scholar to preach; one can just inform an audience of the fundamentals of faith in local dialect. Thereby, they lower the threshold of participation and open the use of the pulpit to every willing individual. To the *Qalole*, preaching requires an individual to have vast amount of cultural capital, for instance a deep knowledge of the Quran, the prophetic traditions, and jurisprudence, among others. The discomfort of the *Qalole* originates from the blurred boundaries as to who can preach and the resulting subversion of their privileged role as custodians of the faith and sole body of religious authority. Some members of the *Qalole* are of the opinion that among the local as well as national Tablīghī requisite religious knowledge is lacking. One Sheikh of MQC sums up the state of *ʿilm* among the local Tablīghī *dāʿī-s* in the following way:

> Well, well … there are no real learned individuals in the whole of Tablīghī movement in the area. May be a few are. The leaders are not sheikhs per se. They have been given these titles due to age and association they have with sheikhs as well as their steadfast attendance and participation in Muslim religious activities such as prayers, meetings and so on. Just like Sheikh Buke, the Muezzin, he is by the virtue of his position, he has been absorbed into the class of the *ʿulamāʾ*. Same case with the people associated with Tablīghī activities, for instance, Aw Bidu, Aw Kombola. The title of 'Sheikh' and 'Aw' has always been extended to regular elderly mosque attendants. The titles are in simple words honorary and have little to do with *ʿilm*.[12]

---

12   Sheikh Abdub, personal communication, August, 2009, Merti.

The underlying discourse on right *'ilm* are the following questions: is *da'wa* an obligatory act (*farḍ 'ayn*) or an optional act (*farḍ kifāya*)? Is missionary work the obligatory duty of every individual or should it be done by a special group of people from among the community? Who are the most appropriate persons to conduct *da'wa*? Tablīghī position is that *da'wa* is *farḍ 'ayn* while the majority of the *Qalole* would insist that it is *farḍ kifāya*. *Qalole* are of the opinion they are endowed with cultural and religious capital and therefore the most legitimate custodians and revivers of the faith, although they welcome the efforts of enthusiastic *dā'ī-s* of the movement. The *Qalole* have accumulated cultural capital through years of investment in recognized centers of religious learning in Kenya and in countries like Sudan and Saudi Arabia. They have certificates to demonstrate their competence. They are well versed in use of religious texts and proficient in use of Arabic language. They are also the dispensers of knowledge as teachers in local *madrasas* and recognized interpreters of all matters of religion through sermons and informal consultations. They are therefore naturally inclined to view lay members who want to use the public space for religious instructions with suspicion. Sheikh Abdub laments the lack of knowledge in the following manner:

> A number of moments, the sayings of the prophets are narrated without chain of transmissions and mostly out of context. I have personally witnessed false *ḥadīth*s or ideas being preached to unsuspecting attendants. I do not blame such a preacher. But it would have been a good thing to acquire right faith and right attitude and right knowledge before one can stand up and preach. We had to correct them on numerous occasions.

The local Tablīghīs appear independent and no longer look to the non-Tablīghī sheikhs for guidance, religious training and advice on best texts and methods to use in proselytism. For all these matters, they look to their Kenya's national council composed of select Asian and non-Asian 'elders' and 'elders' from IPB. To the opponents, Tablīghīs have not only initiated alternative religious bureaucracy but also erode their religious authority as custodians of knowledge. Most sheikhs dislike the influential role Tablīghī elders have on practices and decisions of local adherents of the movement. Abdub Boru, a disenfranchised scholar says that:

> The most serious thing that the religious scholars do not want to hear is these emphases so called *jarole/wazee* (elders). They do not call them sheikhs. They do not refer to them as *'ulamā'*. They do not label them as the Muslim jurists (*muftī*) who deliver *fatwā* (ar. legal ruling). They just

call them elders. In simple terms, we the *madrasa* teachers, we the *'ulamā'*, our faith is not tied to some elders out there. Our religion is tied to Quran and Sunna. Our faith is based on Allah and the teaching of his prophet but not on elders of any kind. Above that, we may debate that these verses of the Quran was commented upon by certain renowned scholar in this manner and so on.[13]

Secondly, the majority of the *Qalole* question the legitimacy of the Tablīghī Jamā'at system as based on innovation in religion (*bid'a*) and not anchored on the correct Islamic thoughts and practices.[14] The Tablīghīs are accused of creating new religious practices such as *khurūj* (*da'wa* excursions for 3, 10, 40 days or 4 months), *jowla* (neighborhood tours/patrols), *ijtimā'* and *jor* (regular gatherings), *siffa sittah* (six virtues), *karguzari* (status review), *ḥalqa* (reterritorialization of national space for purpose of movement's activities) *ta'līm* and *bayān* (forms of preaching), and *tashkīl* (recruitment drive). *Ijtimā'*s and *jor*s are congregational gatherings lasting 3–5 days attended by Tablīghīs and non-Tablīghīs alike and which aims at mobilizing preaching teams to be sent within the country and to other countries. The apex of Tablīghī gatherings in Kenya is the annual national *ijtimā'* held at Baitul-Maal, the headquarters of the movement in Nairobi. After every few months, *jor* (a mini-*ijtimā'*) is held on rotational basis in towns such as Merti, Kinna, Garba Tulla and Isiolo. Creation of *ḥalqa* units are spatial innovation in management of religious space. It creates alternative imagination of proselytism and chains of command that ignores existing *Qalole* decision making structures. *Ta'līm* and *bayān* are motivational talks and sermons given by members of the movement to the general public in mosques in order to call on the audience to be steadfast in their religious observance and to motivate them to volunteer for preaching tours and gradually join the movement as self-sponsored lay preachers. Often to give these talks, Tablīghīs ask local *Qalole* for permission thereby acknowledging their authority as managers of mosques. These and many others practices instituted by Tablīghīs via translocal apprenticeship are relatively new and associated with their entry into the region. They are accused of not only symbolically creating these practices but also aspiring to recruit the laity to recognize them as legitimate practices to be emulated in every day religious life. Symbolic power,

---

13 Personal conversation with Abdub Boru, Kinna, October 2009.
14 To accuse one of innovation in religion (*bid'a*) is to accuse one of introducing new practices not revealed and carried out or encouraged by Prophet Muhammad. It is a statement of heresy and illegitimacy of unwarranted practice and hence viewed as evil. A number of prophetic traditions warn the *umma* against *bid'a*.

notes Bourdieu, is power of imposing on other minds a vision whether old or new, it is power of constitution, of creating things with words, ultimately of consecration or revelation, a power to conceal or reveal things which are already there (Bourdieu 1990a: 138).

Thirdly, the *Qalole*-Tablīghī tussle concerns legitimacy of source materials for *da'wa*. They both agree on centrality of the Quran and Prophetic Traditions (*Hadith*) as the main source of Islamic teachings. The *Qalole* however doubt the authenticity of some *Hadith* contained in some of the Tablīghī core texts. A case in point is *Faza'il-e-A'amal*, a collection of *Hadith* commentaries written by Muhammad Zakariyya Kaandhlawi, one of the early leaders of the movement. Also known as Tablīghī *Niṣāb* (Curriculum), the text is widely used in every day *da'wa* of the movement. The local Tablīghīs read and preach from this book more than from any other whether at home, in their local mosque or while on missionary tour. To the *Qalole*, this text and many others often used by the movement are ridden with weak *Hadīth* that cannot be used for spiritual guidance.

Fourthly, to bring on board more people onto the path of reform, Tablīghī methodology insists on two important aspects: a disinterested attitude to matters political and an emphasis on the benefits of the performance of religious duties (*faza'il*) rather than the doctrinal rationale of those actions (*masa'il*).[15] In the understanding of the *Qalole, dīn* and *dawla* are intertwined, i.e. religion and socio-political engagement cannot be separated. The members of the movement distance themselves from sectarian and doctrinal controversies and would not participate in such debates when on travel. This aloofness has been interpreted by local *'ulamā'* as unhealthy while the movement perceives it as strategy for mobilizing *dai*s on broadly agreed fundamentals of Islam. The fact that the Tablīghīs insist on spiritual revitalization and avoid all forms of socio-political activism on behalf of the *umma* is interpreted by the *Qaloles* as a proof of the defect of their rivals' approach.

The fifth issue is on what constitutes *da'wa*. What constitutes *da'wa* is varied and subject to debates. The basic objective remains that of calling, reminding, inviting, informing Muslims and non-Muslims about the truth of Islam. *Qalole* point out that *da'wa* is part and parcel of their lives: they lead prayers, they conduct marriages, arbitrate in social and marital conflict; they teach at local *madrasa*s, they lead by example. *Da'wa* without travel outside one's every day space is considered by the Tablīghī *dā'ī-s* as ineffective. Individuals must dedicate time to teach and learn from others and mainly away from home. Mobility for the sake of calling others back to faith is prioritized and contrasted with

---

15   Maalim Ali, personal communication, July 2010, Moyale.

'sedentarized' every day religious leadership of mosque-based *Qalole*. The former is celebrated as involving great sacrifice and commitment while the latter is frowned upon as non-transformative due to 'comfort of home and every day spaces'. One sheikh opines that the Tablīghīs that make travelling and preaching obligatory (*farḍ 'ayn*) and think that the Muslims who do not travel like them to spread the faith are not true Muslim. He adds that they place a great deal of emphasis on their system of travel tours of 3, 10, 40 days and 4 months and it is not written anywhere else except in their books and therefore a practice not legitimized by tradition.[16]

The sixth issue is a clash of origin. The *Qalole*, although a heterogeneous group, are largely associated with *salafī* influenced thoughts traceable to traditional centers of Islamic learning such as the Sudan, Saudi Arabia, Egypt or even Kuwait through humanitarian assistances and training of *'ulamā'*. In fact MQC is a testimony of such transnational cooperation, as some of the prominent clerics are products of educational institutions in the Middle East and the Sudan, or of affiliated local institutions. Compared with such a background, new groups originating from alternative Islamic centers face a great credibility test. The headquarters of the movement are in Nizamuddin, New Delhi, India, and other major centers are Pakistan and Bangladesh. The Indian subcontinent remains central to the movement's history and organization and is viewed by some *Qalole* as outside the traditional abode of Islamic revivalism and learning. What is more, for the greater part of Tablīghī Jamā'at history in the region it was preachers from IPB and of Kenyan Muslims of Asian origin carried out *da'wa* often *Urdu* or English instead of Arabic. Things have not changed much with the entry of local *dā'ī-s*. Thus the *Qalole*, who regard knowledge of Arabic and the Quran as the cultural capital that legitimizes their position as religious leaders, accuse the Tablīghīs of illiteracy and ignorance. The Tablīghīs, on the other hand, counter that accusation by pointing to the deficiencies of established, Arabic-centered Islam:

> Arabs and Muslims in other parts of the world have been sleeping for a long time. They have followed the path of pleasure and self indulgence. They had ceased to help in the way of Allah. Now those in opposition to *da'wa* still stick to the idea that out of India only cow worship and ignorance can come out. But it is in the Indian subcontinent that the best *da'wa* efforts, *'ulamā'* and adherents have to the preaching of the religion, reform of the individual and progress of Islam to many parts of the world. Thanks to them *da'wa* has reached everywhere.[17]

---

16 Sheikh Abdub, personal conversations, September 2009, Merti.
17 Personal interview with Muhammed Qalla, September 2009, Moyale.

The Strategies of Contests and Collaborations

Both the Tablīghīs and *Qalole* seek legitimacy and acknowledgement through reference to the sacred texts. The need to legitimate their practices fall more on the Tablīghīs than the *Qalole*. Tablīghīs often use select verses of the Quran and prophetic traditions to give credibility to their practices as authentic and orthodox. As discussed earlier, the *Qalole* invoke the same source to delegitimatize the approach of the Tablīghīs and guard their monopolization of the capital and its resultant privileges. The Tablīghīs strategize to recruit new members into a class of committed lay preachers ready to engage in regular travels and manage affairs of the movement in local mosques. They regularly meet to discuss progress and targets for growth. On the other hand, the *Qalole* guard their position as legitimate voice of authority by safeguarding the use of pulpit ensuring that the sacredness of mosques is not fringed upon. They also engage in regular mosque-based preaching and voicing socio-political concerns of the *umma*. Depicting themselves as custodians of right *'ilm*, they encourage locals to engage in religious learning before they could travel for preaching tours organized by the Tablīghī Jamā'at.

The notion of taking a lay person out of his every day life in order to enhance his religious practice is what the Tablīghī activists consider as a best way to remold the religious habitus of the laity. He travels to different mosques, learns Quran and *Hadīth*, builds regional and transnational durable network of lay preachers with others and inculcates a durable set of daily exercises and rituals that include *ziyāra* (visits) to fellow Tablīghīs. He initiates reading of the Tablīghī recommended texts at home, plays a central role in transforming his local mosque for Tablīghī work and transforms his manner of dressing and speaking and managing time. His reform of the habitus is reinforced by frequent visits of foreign and regional *jamā'ats* at the local mosque and his own travels on missionary tours and thus his experience of being as a lay preacher part of a large community, a larger group than the local rivals, the *salafī Qalole*.

The *Qalole* being dominant class have been relatively tolerant of the challenge to their hegemony. They could preach against them, but they do not do that. The nature of constraints and opportunities in the structure of the field do not allow for an all-out showdown but instead nurture gradual orientation towards collaboration. Tablīghīs, whether local or visiting ones, are always on some form of religious travel. Hospitality to all categories of travelers is held with high esteem within Islamic traditions. Those on travels whatever reasons are indeed exempted from a number of religious obligations such as fasting and are even allowed to combine and shorten prayers and are legally eligible recipients for *zakāt*, annual Islam alms. Therefore whenever foreign *jamā'ats* arrive at the door step of local mosques, the *Qalole* are bound to offer assistance however minimal based on pan-Islamic egalitarianism and brotherhood. Another reason is that the *Qalole* class appreciates the number of ordinary believers flocking mosques due to Tablīghī mobilization are immense and target to take over surging number of mosque attendants and guide them towards 'proper' religious guidance. The Tablīghīs have portrayed themselves as a group out to win back the neglected segments within the society such as drunkards and unruly youth.

Perhaps the appreciation of the Tablīghī strategies, as noted by one informant, stems from the positive transformation in the lives of some wayward persons in the local community.[18] The movement, hence, has sort of served as a rehabilitation program especially when such reformed persons take pivotal role in *daʿwa* efforts among the Borana.

The Tablīghīs attribute their relative success to self-sufficiency and bearing personal costs for their activities unlike religious scholars who gets some form of stipends. In other words, they draw themselves as selfless individuals out to spread the messages of the faith without incentives such as positions within religious institutions and financial benefits. One informant reflecting on issue mentioned above says:

> *Abbo injirru, Qalole nu hat!* You see the *Qalole* are fighting us! They are against us because we are doing good work! They are fighting us because we are doing what they refused to do! They are fighting us because they think we want their position of leadership! They are fighting us because unlike them we are not interested in power and money in to *daʿwa*; we do it for the sake of God![19]

The *ʿulamāʾ* on the other hand strategize that the reform of the laity is too delicate a work to be left unsupervised. To them, the Tablīghīs, though using a good *daʿwa* method, must be regulated with continuous guidance from them. They argue that the Tablīghīs do not wish to be corrected because they take every person who critiques their approach to proselytism as fighting them. The *ʿulamāʾ*, especially the youthful ones, think that the members of the movement suffer from some sort of collective persecution anxiety or complex. The *Qalole* are not comfortable with the idea circulated by the Tablīghīs among the laity

---

18   Sheikh Hussein notes that Tablīghīs had successfully reformed a number of persons that the society had given up hope on them into religious and responsible individuals. He posits that the movement is also a mobile school for adult Muslims. Personal conversations, September 2009, Garba Tulla.

19   Ali Mohamed, personal conversations, September 2009, Merti.

that outside their movement the laity cannot access God's bounties.[20] They are accused of preaching that they have the best methods with the best results. This echoes the famous Roman Catholic Church dictum '*Extra Ecclesiam nula salus*' that outside the Church there is no salvation. Commenting on this claim, one sheikh says that 'the *Qaloles* have always been in *daʿwa*. They live *daʿwa*. However the group considers their way of doing things as the only real way.'[21]

Though local *Qalole* have not produced polemical materials against the Tablīghī Jamāʿat, they possibly have access to audio cassettes and compact discs as well as written materials. This accommodative and inclusive attitude of the *Qalole* are informed by the temporality with which the view the new lay movement and being established players they do not feel the need to contest directly with the new comers. On the other hand, the Tablīghīs are aggressive in their claim to legitimacy because being new comers; they aspire to ground their practices in the core sources of Islamic authority, Quran and *Sunna*. As newcomers they feel compelled to market their practices as the most legitimate, attract as many lay people as possible as preachers, contest the use of mosques for their functions and transform the religious adherence of the masses to conform to their ideological basis.

The Tablīghīs and the *Qalole* carry out their strategies in tandem with time and space. There is a personal cost involved. In both traditions, time forms a central part of the management of practice, for instance, the required punctuality and consistency in performance of five daily prayers, personal and collective dedication of time for reading of respective texts at home, time for giving of *zakāt*, greetings based on time, *adhān* etc. What sets the Tablīghīs apart is travelling to places away from home for sole purpose of calling others to the faith. Novices as well as regular Tablīghīs pay for their travel expenses transforming economic capital into cultural capital. Self-financing of travel tours enhances commitment and ownership of the missionary outfit. Other benefits are accruable to committed individuals: leadership position such as *amīr*s of mosque-based Jamāʿat, area or even sub-*ḥalqa*, prestige and honor as reputable public preachers, experience of travelling to new regions and countries and above all reputation among fellow Tablīghīs and non-Tablīghīs as pious men of the faith. In addition, the movement has alternative forms of travel modules and practices that target to transform lives of their womenfolk. *Masturat jamāʿats*, for instance, involves groups of Tablīghī men and their wives travelling for a period of up to a month. There are also home-based teachings and text readings that incorporate women within the socialization

---

20   Sheikh Kallow, personal conversations, October 2009, Moyale.
21   Maalim Ibrahim, personal conversations, July 2010, Isiolo.

process. However despite deliberate efforts made to reach out to women, a considerable number of Tablīghī practices involve prominent participation of men (Wario 2012).

The aim of both *Qalole* and Tablīghī preaching is on how to mould the lives of the laity and leaders of local people so that they fulfill the religious obligations for their success here on earth and in the hereafter. Tablīghīs explicit avoids matters of political and social nature. More than *Qalole* for whom the mundane is as important as the sacred, Tablīghīs appear to be more inclined towards other-worldliness. There is a sense of temporality that is attached to the present time. 'Here and now' become a place for preparation for 'hereafter'. Tablīghī travels built the religious habitus of those who undertake the journey on regular basis. They gradually learn and master the Tablīghī practices. Regions that once are far are linked through such itinerancy. The recruit as regular consumer of such goods becomes accustomed to the belief that the movement is indeed the only legitimate way of 'doing' religion. The *Qalole* and the local Tablīghī activists come into the field of the game with different dispositions and strategies. They apply different forms of social and cultural capital when they compete or collaborate in the field. *Qalole* for instance have access to certain forms of institutionalized cultural capital, e.g. certificates from outstanding universities in the Sudan or Saudi Arabia, or from advanced *madrasa* colleges in Mombasa, Lamu, and Isiolo. They are in charge of dispensation of religious capital as tutors and mentors at local Islamic schools (*madrasas*). They conduct a range of social obligations such as leading prayers, burying the dead, uniting families in marriage; they participate in politics and act as social advocates on behalf of their constituencies. The Tablīghī *dāʿī-s*, as local Muslims, are a product of the *Qalole* training as well, they are locals who went through *madrasa* but lack university education. Instead, they have been exposed to the self-reform approaches marketed by the Tablīghī Jamāʿat. They have traveled the world (albeit to selected places and for certain periods of time), they have increased their social and cultural capital by self-training, reading Islamic texts and preaching in mosques. They feel that the *Qalole* have not done much and it is time to liberate the laity from their slumber so that they can take control of their own religiosity.

Qalole utilize networks of mosques and *madrasas* in the Waso region to proselytize on daily basis. On occasion, actors from both groups join hands to drive the forces of religious reform in the region. The *Qalole* as religious elites enjoy privileged positions in the Tablīghī gatherings and welcome the group to proselytize among the masses as the initial upsurge in membership normalize and excitement and contestation arising out of the growth decrease.

Conclusion

Merti is one of the most Islamized Borana regions that stretch from Southern Ethiopia to Northern Kenya. With its local clerical class running a number of institutions through Merti Quran Centre and its local Tablīghīs coordinating da'wa activities for the Waso region from their Markaz, it represent a fusion of local and transnational struggles over the nature of religious practices deemed fit for the laity. The *Qalole* and Tablīghīs strategize to increase piety and adherence to religious duties and values among the local population. Such strategies have ranged from the introduction of new religious practices to the reinforcement of the existing ones. Appeal to authenticity and orthodoxy forms one way of 'othering' rival group within the field of competitive proselytism. The relationship between the two groups is largely ambivalent fluctuating between latent conflicts to mutual cooperation in order to entrench greater religious observance in the town.

References

Aguilar, Mario. 1998. *Being Oromo in Kenya*. Trenton and Asmara: Africa World Press.

Bourdieu, Pierre. 1987. Legitimation and Structured Interests in Weber's Sociology of Religion. In *Max Weber, Rationality, and Modernity*, edited by Scott Lash and Sam Whimster, 119–136. London: Allen and Unwin.

———. 1990a. *In the Other Words: Essays towards a Reflexive Sociology*, Cambridge: Polity Press.

———. 1990b. *The Logic of Practice*. Stanford, Calif.: Stanford Univ. Press.

Bourdieu Pierre, and Loic J. D. Wacquant. 1992. *An Invitation to Reflective Sociology*, Chicago: University of Chicago Press.

Dickson, Rory. 2009. The Tablīghī Jamā'at in Southwestern Ontario: Making Muslim Identities and Networks in Canadian Urban Spaces. *Contemporary Islam* 3: 99–112.

Horstmann, A. 2007. The Tablīghī Jamā'at, Transnational Islam, and the Transformation of the Self between Southern Thailand and South Asia. *Comparative Studies of South Asia, Africa and the Middle East* 27(1): 26–40.

Janson, Marloes. 2005. Roaming about for God's Sake: The Upsurge of the Tablīghī Jamā'at in the Gambia. *Journal of Religion in Africa* 35(4): 450–481.

Jenkins, Richard. 2002. *Pierre Bourdieu*. London and New York: Routledge.

Masud, M. K., ed. 2000. *Travellers in Faith: Studies of the Tablīghī Jamā'at as a Transnational Islamic Movement for Faith Renewal*. Leiden: Brill.

Moosa, Ebrahim. 1997. Worlds 'Apart': The Tablīgh Jamāt in South Africa under Apartheid 1963–1993. *Journal for Islamic Studies* 17: 28–48.

Metcalf, Barbara D. 2003. Living Hadith in the Tablīghī Jamāʻat. *Journal of Asian Studies* 52(3): 584–608.

Racius, Edgunas. 2004. "Multiple Nature of Islamic Daʻwa." PhD Diss., University of Helsinki.

Reetz, Deitrich. 2008. The 'Faith Bureaucracy' of Tablīghī Jamāʻat: An Insight into their system of Self-Organization. In *Colonialism, Modernity, and Religious Identities: Religious Reform Movements in South Asia*, edited by Gwilym Beckerlegge, 98–124. Oxford, Delhi: Oxford University Press.

Salvadori, C. 1989. *Through Open Doors: A View of Asian Cultures in Kenya*. Nairobi: Kenway Publ.

———. 2000. *We Came in Dhows*. Nairobi: Paperchase Kenya.

Sikand, Yoginder. 2002. *The Origins and Development of the Tablighi Jamaʻat (1920s–1990): A Cross-Country Comparative Study*. New Delhi: Orient Longman.

———. 2006. The Tablīghī Jamʻāt and Politics: A Critical Appraisal. *The Muslim World* 96: 175–195.

Wario, Halkano. 2012. Reforming Men, Refining Umma: Tablīghī Jamāʻat and Novel Visions of Islamic Masculinity. *Religion and Gender* 2(2): 231–253.

Inter-Field Dynamics

∴

CHAPTER 6

The Bishop and the Politician: Intra- and Inter-Field Dynamics in 19th Century Natal, South Africa

Ulrich Berner

Introduction: Agents in Different Fields: J. W. Colenso and Th. Shepstone

Bishop John William Colenso (1814–1883) is well known in South Africa, at least among theologians of the Anglican Church and among historians working on British Imperialism. Jonathan Draper and Jeff Guy have done groundbreaking work to re-appreciate Colenso as a critic of conservative theology and as a critic of colonial policies of his time (Draper 2003; Guy 1983). Having been elected and consecrated as the first Anglican Bishop of Natal in 1853, Colenso was excommunicated for heresy by the Archbishop of Cape Town in 1862. This fact alone would make the case of Colenso an interesting object for studying the dynamics of the religious field: the conflict between orthodoxy and heresy, being, according to Bourdieu, homologous to the conflict between priest and prophet (Bourdieu 1991: 26). The impression that it was an intra-religious conflict, is confirmed, it seems, when it is realized that Colenso during the time of his heresy trial was still cooperating with an influential agent in the political field: Theophile Shepstone (1817–1893), Secretary for Native Affairs.

However, the case of Colenso might also be an object for studying the dynamics between different fields—the religious and the political. For it was only the support from the Privy Council of the Crown, a political body, that enabled Colenso to continue functioning as an Anglican bishop in Natal, although excommunicated and declared an heretic by the ecclesiastical hierarchy of the Anglican Church in South Africa. In any case, for the last ten years of his life Colenso emerged as a critic of the policies of the colonial Government in Natal, thus transgressing the borders of the religious field and initiating controversies that might be described as an expression of inter-field dynamics. The relationship between Colenso and Shepstone, at that period of time, changed from friendship into bitter animosity: "war to the knife".[1] Jeff Guy

---

1   Rees 1958, 283 (Letter of Colenso's wife to her brother, May 31, 1874). Cf. Guest 1976, 87–89; Guy 1983, 212.

already has analyzed Colenso's dissension with Shepstone and his fight against British imperialism (See Guy 1983, Part 3). Without claiming to go beyond Guy's knowledge of the colonial history of 19th century Natal, it may be rewarding to take a fresh look at this case by applying some concepts of Bourdieu's theory of religion.

Basic to Bourdieu's theory of religion, and most relevant for investigating the case of Colenso, is the metaphor of the field in general, and the concept of the "relatively autonomous" religious field in particular (Bourdieu 1991: 5; 7f). Concerning the dynamics inside the religious field, Bourdieu gives much attention to the opposition between priest and prophet, drawing upon Max Weber's typology of religious actors and touching only briefly upon the opposition between orthodoxy and heresy which, he thinks, is to be regarded as "homologous" (Bourdieu 1987: 126; 1991: 26). Another concept that might be of relevance is the notion of the game which plays a more important role in his 'Theory of Practice'. Basically, it is also a metaphor, like the notion of the 'field', used to conceptualize the practical sense "as a proleptic adjustment to the demands of a field" (Bourdieu 1990: 66).

In applying Bourdieu's theory, the concept of the field, being basically a spatial metaphor, will be taken primarily as related to the concept of the game. That means, 'field' will be conceptualized as a space for games like football or baseball, each one of these games having its own set of rules which the actors are expected to obey. Conceptualized in this way, the notion of 'field' implies reference to the rules of the game that determine the relations between the positions and the movements in the respective social field, as, for instance, the religious or the political field. It follows, that actors in the various fields, when transgressing the borders and entering another field are expected to change their performance by adjusting to the specific rules of the game—be it from football to baseball or from religion to politics.

The Bishop and the Politician in Cooperation (1854–1873)

Soon after being consecrated Bishop, Colenso in 1854 visited for the first time the newly created diocese of Natal. There he met and travelled together with Theophile Shepstone who had grown up in South Africa as the son of a missionary, thus being already well acquainted with Zulu culture and language. As the Secretary for Native Affairs, this man would play an important role in the administration of the colony, functioning as an adviser to the colonial government for many years. At that time, in 1854, Shepstone was working on the proposal to create a "Black Kingdom" under his own government, in a location southern to Natal, in order to relieve the colony of a considerable part of the African population (McClendon 2010: 32–43).

Colenso was impressed by the "noble self-sacrifice" involved in such an enterprise, and in his report on the visit to Natal, he gave some biographical details about Shepstone, in order "to show how strangely he has been formed, by the course of God's providence, for undertaking so momentous a work" (Colenso 1855a: 145). Colenso was sure that Shepstone, the politician, as a "devout Christian" was pursuing the same aim as the missionary with regard to the African peoples: "Their ultimate reception into the church of Christ he looks for as the great reward [...] of all his self-denying labours." (Colenso 1855a: 150).

There was indeed a basic agreement in their attitude towards Zulu culture and customs: both of them were ready and willing, for instance, to tolerate the polygamous marriage system of the Zulus, a highly controversial point, of course, opposed by the majority of the missionaries and of the colonists in Natal (See Colenso 1855b; cf. Ngewu 2003). Therefore, it is understandable that Colenso was looking forward to a close cooperation with Shepstone, both of them contributing to "the peaceful steps of commerce, civilisation, and Christianity" (Colenso 1855a: 150; cf. Etherington 1978: 42).

After having been informed that the colonial government had turned down Shepstone's proposal, Colenso was disappointed. He found comfort, however, in the confidence that in carrying on his missionary work he would in any case have "the presence and help of Mr. Shepstone himself" (Colenso 1855a: 158).

In addition to giving some biographical details, Colenso quoted a section from a personal letter, which, it seems at first sight, confirms the impression that Shepstone, the politician, as "a devout Christian", was sharing with the Bishop the same religious convictions: writing before his plans failed, Shepstone revealed to Colenso that he was discussing in his own mind "the question, as to whether it really was the path of my duty or not. I dared not decide this in the negative; for, if I had, I could not reasonably expect God's blessing upon my undertaking;...". (Colenso 1855a: 157). And he concluded by thanking Colenso for including him in his prayers.

Regarding this correspondence and especially Colenso's praise of his "dear friend" Shepstone, it may look the more surprising that friendship would later change into animosity, cooperation into antagonism.[2] The question is whether this dissension was brought about by personal emotions or by structural

---

2 On the Zulu side, they had been perceived as being "one person and only distinguished by being two separate heads" (Mokoena 2008, 324).

conditions and, if the latter was the case, whether it can be explained in concepts of Bourdieu's theory.

Looking more closely at Colenso's report on his first encounter with African culture, it may be possible, however, to discover the roots of the future disagreement and dissension between the Bishop and the politician. When reflecting on a possible successor who would be able to carry on Shepstone's work, Colenso seriously considered the possibility that Shepstone would be replaced by "a Christian Kaffir". Obviously, he regarded an African as an equivalent alternative to "an Englishman", thus from the very beginning showing his immunity towards any racist prejudices (Colenso 1855a: 151). It is not very likely that Shepstone who introduced the British system of 'indirect rule' would have consented to this idea.[3] In any case, it seems obvious that Colenso from the very beginning of his stay in Natal entertained ideas that would not contribute "to the perpetuation and reproduction of the social order," according to Bourdieu belonging to the social functions of religion (Bourdieu 1991: 19).

At that early period of time, when Colenso was still preparing for his missionary work in Natal, Shepstone was quarrelling with a Wesleyan missionary, and this conflict might be regarded as foreshadowing the future conflict with the Bishop of Natal. The previous conflict arose in March 1855, about three Zulus who had taken refuge to the nearest Wesleyan mission station after having been "smelt out" as having caused the illness of their chief.[4] The chief demanded that the refugees should be removed from this mission station, since he feared for his life as long as they were staying on the land of his chiefdom where the mission station was situated. The Wesleyan missionary, however, "allowed the men to remain at the Station until the case was brought before the Magistrate" (SNA 1/3/4 (6.3.1855)). The chief kept begging for the removal of the men from the mission station, and this request was answered positively by the Magistrate who ordered that the refugees should be transferred to another locality far away from the land of the respective chiefdom. The Wesleyan missionary, however, opposed this order and wrote an application to the Lieutenant-Governor to have the case reviewed. One of his reasons was the argument that "moral and religious principles" would be involved in such a case that was related to belief in witchcraft (SNA 1/7/2 (12.9.1855), § 16,3; 21). Obviously he was anxious not to give the slightest impression that witchcraft would be taken seriously. For some time there was "a complex and

---

3   Cf. Etherington 1989, 172; Myers 2008, 11; McClendon 2004; 2010, 2; for racist ideas of Shepstone see Guy 1983, 315.
4   For details see McClendon 2010, 53–57.

inconclusive contest of wills", in the course of which the chief died (McClendon 2010: 54).

In September 1855, shortly after the death of the chief, Shepstone wrote a report, strongly opposing the standpoint of the Wesleyan missionary and defending the policy of the magistrate:

> The object therefore of the Government was to do away with the probability of further collision, and as far as it could do so, to relieve the apprehensions of the dying man, by simply removing the parties to some other locality; (SNA 1/7/2 (12.9.1855), § 12).

As a politician, Shepstone obviously felt first of all responsible for peace and order in the colony, and therefore, he was willing to take seriously the belief in witchcraft as a social reality:

> The order of removal "was dictated by no desire on the part of the Government to afford the least sanction to the belief in witchcraft, but it was made with the knowledge that however our higher enlightenment and Civilisation may contemn the notion, it is nevertheless fully accepted and believed in with very few exceptions by all the colored population of the District." (Ibid., § 9).

So far, Colenso might have consented to Shepstone's argument, sympathizing with the "dying man" and opposing the strict theological principles of the Wesleyan missionary. However, where Colenso might have begun disagreeing with Shepstone is the emphasis the latter was putting on the absolute authority of the government, including authority over mission stations:

> ... wherever they were living, provided they were within the boundaries of the District, they were equally liable to the duty of obedience to any order the Government might think it necessary to issue ... (Ibid., § 19).

The reasoning of the Wesleyan missionary "ousts not only the authority of the Chief, but by inference that of the Government from lands to which he conceives the Wesleyan Society have a right of control;—a position utterly inadmissible if the supremacy of the Government of the District over the Natives is to be maintained." (Ibid., § 20).

In October 1855, Shepstone wrote a personal letter to the Wesleyan missionary, repeating the arguments of his earlier report and communicating to him the opinion of the governor. This letter contains a new argument which seems to foreshadow the future conflict with Colenso who was to become the 'guardian' of the Zulu population against the colonial government:

> Your insisting on becoming the guardian of the men in despite of the Government order for their proper disposal, appears to exhibit a desire to assume functions which it would be neither safe for the Government to delegate, nor, His Honor is persuaded good to the cause of Missions that you should possess (SNA 1/8/5 (16.10.1855), p. 446).

This "contest of wills" between the missionary and the politician was not carried further on, since the chief whose illness had given rise to the conflict had died in the mean time. In any case, Colenso would cooperate with Shepstone for nearly twenty years, and he could rely on this friendship even at the time of his trial, when he came into conflict with the ecclesiastical hierarchy.

In his work of translating the Bible, Colenso was cooperating with a native speaker, a Zulu convert, who used to ask critical questions, particularly concerning the ethics of the Old Testament.[5] The Bishop was impressed by the high intelligence of his "Zulu philosopher" as he used to call him, and this encounter resulted in critical reflections on Biblical hermeneutics in general and on the doctrine of Biblical Inspiration in particular.[6] After some time Colenso emerged as a forerunner of Biblical criticism, denying, for instance, Moses' authorship of the Pentateuch, and denying that baptism and formal conversion to Christianity would be necessary for salvation (Cf. Colenso 2003: 138; Darby 2003: 185f).

The Archbishop of Cape Town regarded such a theological position as heretic, arguing that it would undermine the whole idea of Christian missions.[7] Colenso kept defending his theological position, but without success, and he could not escape excommunication by the majority of the bishops of the Anglican Church. However, his appeal to the Privy Council of the Crown was successful, so that he could maintain his ecclesiastical position as the Bishop of Natal. It was a strange position, highly controversial among the clergy and lay people of his diocese and giving rise to a schism in the Anglican Church of South Africa, since another bishop was elected as a rival to Colenso. His

---

5 See Colenso 1862, VIIf; 9. Cf. Colenso 2003, 154f; Berner 2009, 82.
6 See, for instance, Colenso's statement, that it is not necessary feeling obliged "to maintain every part of the Bible as infallible record of past history, and every word as the sacred utterance of the Spirit of God" (1862, 150).
7 See Colenso's letter to Archbishop Gray, August 7, 1861 (Cox 1888 II. Appendix 697–706), discussing the various points of theological dissension.

opponents in the Anglican Church did everything to impede Colenso's work, cutting down the financial support for his mission station and fighting with him over the Church properties in his diocese.[8]

The dynamics of the religious field, in this case is determined not only by controversies in the subfield of theology and/or by the struggle for ecclesiastical power, but also by external forces, since the Privy Council as a political body prevented the Anglican Church from removing Colenso from his ecclesiastical position. Respecting the decision of the Privy Council, the colonial government of Natal continued to treat Colenso as "the Lord Bishop of Natal," even at later times when he was opposing colonial policies. Thus there was only a relative autonomy of the religious field: it was autonomous as far as the theological controversies and the trial of heresy itself were concerned; the limits of this autonomy are recognizable in the fact that the state provided the bishop with legal grounds to maintain his ecclesiastical position. A different phase and kind of inter-field dynamics was to begin in 1873 when Colenso ran into conflict with the colonial government, thereby losing the support from Shepstone, the Secretary for Native Affairs, and alienating himself from the majority of European settlers in the colony.

With regard to the inter-field dynamics in this earlier period of time, it may be also interesting to look at the neighboring field of literature and the subfield of religious literature. As an author, publishing theological books that rose great interest among the lay people, Colenso had entered the field of literature and encountered heavy critique. Matthew Arnold, a famous English literary critic, maintained that a theological book such as Colenso's Commentary on the Pentateuch "which all England is now reading", has to be judged not only from a theological point of view but also "before the Republic of Letters" (Arnold [1863] 1973: 43; 40). The principles or laws of this republic are, according to Arnold who claimed being its spokesperson, that such a book must either edify the uninstructed or inform the instructed. After reviewing Colenso's commentary on the Pentateuch, Arnold's scathing judgment was: "Fulfilling neither of these conditions, the Bishop of Natal's book cannot justify itself for existing" (Arnold [1863] 1973: 53). What Arnold metaphorically refers to as the "Republic of Letters", introducing himself as "a humble citizen of that republic", can nicely be described in Bourdieu's terms as a field: the literary critic would then appear as a main agent in this field, trying to push the author of the reviewed

---

8   See Rees 1958, 125–127 on the cathedral in Pietermaritzburg as a "battle-ground"; cf. Guy 1983, 154–158.

book beyond the borders by blaming him for not having played according to the rules of the game.[9]

Arnold's scathing and polemic criticism was also directed against Colenso's revaluation of non-Christian religions, and this new theological approach might be regarded as having been another transgression of borders and a violation of rules (Arnold [1863] 1973: 47). Towards the end of his biblical commentary, Colenso had quoted from sources of pre- or non-Christian religions, from Rome and India, presenting them as a divine revelation, not inferior to Christianity (Colenso 1862: 152–157). Thus it might be argued he entered the emerging field of the 'Science of Religion' as a comparative discipline, distinct from (Christian) theology. Max Müller, known as the 'father' of this discipline (Sharpe 1991: 35f), who spent the greatest part of his life in England, was well acquainted with the case of Colenso and expressed his basic agreement and appreciation (Cox 1888: II, 215; Guy 1983: 227).

Knowing or not knowing it, Colenso was anticipating and acting in accordance with 'the rules of the game' in this new field: He applied the principle that had been introduced by Max Müller as an axiom of this new science: the principle of applying the same measure to all religions, not giving any preference or immunity to Christianity (cf. Berner 2004a: 41f). Even James George Frazer, another 'father' of this emerging field of studies and himself a skeptic or even critic of religion, would have consented to Colenso's theological approach (cf. Berner 2012: 143f). In any case, during the time of the heresy trial, Colenso could still count on the friendship with and support from the Secretary for Native Affairs, Theophile Shepstone, as an influential agent in the political field.[10]

The anti-imperialist implications of Colenso's theological position became recognizable much later. His opponents and enemies would say "that the Pentateuch being played out, Dr. Colenso seeks a new sensation".[11] His adherents and friends would say that the bishop continued to act in accordance with his religious convictions and without any consideration of public

---

9 South African historian Jeff Guy has given an alternative, ideology critical analysis of Arnold's review: "…the roots of this controversy do indeed lie deep in matters of class, and in the fear that the erosion of belief in the bible would undermine the power of those who used the bible in the exercise of authority" (1997, 236).
10 See Shepstone's letter to Mr. Domville, December 7, 1867 (Cox 1888 II, 188–190).
11 Told as a "popular theory" from Natal (British Parliamentary Papers C. 1121: Inclosure 7 in No. 5: Lieutenant-Governor Sir B. C. C. Pine to the Earl of Carnarvon, July 16, 1874).

opinion.[12] The crisis in the relationship between Colenso and Shepstone began in 1873 when the colonial government deposed Langalibalele, a Zulu chief, deporting him after a trial of rebellion and breaking up his tribe. The process of growing antagonism culminated in 1879 when the colonial government invaded Zululand and deposed Cetshwayo, the Zulu king, deporting him and destroying the Zulu kingdom which had been independent up to that time. In both cases, Shepstone had been involved in the decision making, supporting and, later on, justifying all the violent measures taken by the government. Colenso intervened in both cases in defense of the accused, so that a conflict was unavoidable.

The Bishop and the Politician in Conflict (1873–1883)

The Langalibalele affair was presented by the colonial government as a case of rebellion that had to be suppressed by violence for the maintenance of the political order.[13] The authority of the government, it was argued, would be undermined if cases of disobedience remained unpunished.

Relations between Zulu chief Langalibalele and Secretary for Native Affairs Th. Shepstone had already been known as being strained (Guy 1983: 199), and the tension grew as the chief did not obey immediately when he was summoned to appear before the British magistrate. There he would have had to defend himself against certain charges concerning the registration of guns by members of his tribe. The conflict culminated when the messenger who had been sent by the colonial government, afterwards reported that he had been mistreated and heavily insulted by chief Langalibalele. Based on this report from the official messenger, the decision was taken that the insubordinate chief had to be punished severely.[14] Confronted with an ultimatum, the chief, however, for fear of his life made efforts to leave the colony with his tribe and all his properties. When trying to prevent the tribe from leaving the colony, some members of the military detachment sent by the colonial government were killed by Zulu warriors, without their chief having been present and informed

---

12   See Magema Fuze's, his former pupil's comments, quoted in Zulu and translated by Mokoena 2008, 330f.
13   For a short summary of the proceedings see Rees 1958, 258–270.
14   See British Parliamentary Papers C. 1025, Enclosure 2 in No. 35 (Shepstone's letter of November 2, 1873). Cf. Guy 1983, 201.

about this violent encounter. Later on, during his trial, chief Langalibalele would claim not having been responsible for the acts of violence.

This escalation to violence, of course, caused even more severe measures by the government. In the efforts to break any resistance, not only Zulu warriors were killed but also women and children who had taken refuge in caves. In addition to that, all the cattle of the tribe were confiscated by the government; surviving women and children were distributed to white farmers as "apprentices". Langalibalele, the chief, was captured and put on trial for rebellion, and without having been allowed counsel for his defense, he was sentenced to lifelong banishment. The legal procedure was following "native law", the Lieutenant Governor of the colony acting as "Supreme Chief" and heading the court. Th. Shepstone, however, the Secretary for Native Affairs, was arguably the most influential member of the court.[15]

Bishop Colenso intervened in defense of Langalibalele, after he had been informed by a Zulu convert who lived in his mission station, that the trial and sentence had been based on false information.[16] According to this new and—as the bishop thought—totally reliable version of the story, the messenger had greatly exaggerated in his report about the mistreatment he had suffered by Langalibalele. When facts were established later on by interrogating several other witnesses, it became clear that the messenger had not been "stripped naked" as he had complained of, but only asked to take off his coat, in order to show that there was no weapon hidden under it (Colenso 1875: BPP C. 114 § 83; 98). And there was some evidence for the assumption that Langalibalele had serious reasons to be afraid of such a maneuver, since rumor had it that a brother of the Secretary of Native Affairs, on a similar occasion had hidden a gun and tried to kill a Zulu chief (Guy 1983: 208). When Shepstone later on was confronted with the corrected version of the report, he felt not much impressed, insisting that in any case the chief had shown disobedience and the assembled portion of the tribe had treated the messenger "with disrespect in several ways" (BPP 1875: C. 1121, Enclosure 3 in No. 5, § 21). This element of the Langalibalele affair, the significance given initially to the clothes of the official messenger, it might be argued, could be used as an example of "political mythology em-bodied," according to Bourdieu.

By intervening in this affair, Bishop Colenso was beginning to oppose Shepstone's policies as the Secretary for Native Affairs. The conflict became unavoidable when Colenso accused the court of having intimidated the

---

15 For more details see Guy 1983, 205–213.
16 Colenso's informant was Magema Fuze, the famous convert and Zulu intellectual. See Mokoena 2011: 113.

witnesses he had sent afterwards, in order to forward a petition concerning the right of appeal to a higher court (Guy 1983: 210f). The growing tension can be seen in the correspondence between Shepstone and Colenso. Shepstone wrote to Colenso:

> The Lieutenant-Governor requests me to acknowledge your Lordship's letter..., and to inform you that the very grave imputation which you have cast upon the honour of myself and other officers, of having by intimidation attempted to impede the course of justice, will receive His Excellency's serious attention (BPP 1875: C. 1141, Appendix p. 132).

Colenso replied immediately, assuring Shepstone that the charge of intimidation had not been directed against him and other European officers, who might have been unaware that the witnesses had been intimidated by native members of the court. However, he felt offended himself and added that he had considered it necessary "to represent the fact of the intimidation in question... also because it seemed to be an imputation on my own honour that I had forwarded to His Excellency a frivolous and fictitious Petition..." (Ibid., Appendix p. 132f).

Regarding the further development of the conflict between Colenso and Shepstone, it seems to be clear that the growing tension was not just resulting from a personal reaction to an offence—the mutual reproach of an imputation on his honor—but resulting from different and diverging principles of action, related to the different fields in which they were acting.

In the preface to his report on the trial of Langalibalele, written later during his stay at London, the Bishop protested "against the whole processing as exceedingly unfair and unjust", and he defended himself against the reproach that he was dealing with matters that lie outside his "path of duty":

> I saw that my fellow-man was being unfairly treated and unjustly condemned, in a tumult of popular excitement and frenzy; and I believe that it did "lie in my path of duty", at all cost as an Englishman no less than as a minister of religion and a missionary, to raise my voice as strongly as I could against it (Colenso 1875, IV).

This statement shows that the Bishop was not willing to accept different rules as governing the different fields of politics and religion. His was a version of Christianity that did not allow of any encroachment on Christian ethics by pragmatic considerations that take into account political conditions and interests. His assurance to the reader that he would never act against "the peace and safety of the Colony" was based on the conviction that "Natives have a keen sense of justice" (Ibid.), and that it is only by acting "in accordance with strict principles of justice" that the colonial government can maintain its authority (Colenso 1875: 60).[17] In his view, British dominion could only be justified by "enforcing justice" and "practicing mercy".[18] On a different occasion, in a sermon preached to his (Zulu) congregation and still remembered by one of his converts after many years, the Bishop was going so far as indicating that Britain might be deprived of her dominion by God Himself. He is reported to have said:

> You see, my English nation has long been the chosen to rule. But when it also deviates from the path of benevolent rule He will depose it and place another nation that will obey the laws (rules) of governing lesser nations. If you choose the good, and act righteously, he may well give you the power to rule, provided you obey him and do what is good.[19]

What is provided from the memory of one of his early converts is totally consistent with Colenso' theological position as reconstructed from his own writings. Although he is not preaching revolution, in the sense of calling upon the end of the British Empire, he is by no means willing to stabilize and perpetuate the political order by "consecrating" it, as he was expected by the colonists to do. He makes again use of the principle of "applying the same measure", as in his view upon the world of religions, making clear to the dominated classes that the present political order is justified not absolutely but only if the dominating class rules in accordance with the principles of justice. And justice, in the eyes of Colenso, presupposes the unity and equality of humankind, the doctrine of the "Brotherhood of Man" being one of the central tenets of Christianity.[20]

In his report upon the trial of Langalibalele, Colenso quoted extensively from the accusations brought against the chief, as, for instance, the charge that "Langalibalele ever manifested an independent spirit" (Colenso 1875: BPP 1875 C. 1141, § 10). In his critical comment, the bishop does not deny the existence of such a spirit. However, he gives a contrary valuation, indicating that he views an independent spirit as something positive:

---

17 After the British invasion of Zululand, in 1879, Colenso lamented that the "considerations of fairplay and justice must give way to a crafty and, ... a ruthless, and bloody, policy" (Colenso: 1880, 133).
18 See Colenso quoted by Cox II, 334.
19 Magema Fuze, quoted in the original Zulu and translated by Mokoena 2008, 327.
20 See Colenso 1862, XV; 1868, 142 (sermon on Lucas 11,9 (8.4.1866)); 325.

> ... by those who regard the Natives as dogs, who should only cringe and fawn before a white man, such a spirit will be condemned, though perhaps in reality more worthy of respect than the servile obsequiousness of some others of the Chiefs and Indunas in the Colony (Ibid., § 11; cf. § 156).

What Colenso devaluates as "servile obsequiousness", Shepstone would appreciate as the obedience of the native chiefs that is necessary for the stability of the political order. And what Colenso appreciates as an "independent spirit", Shepstone would condemn as a "rebellious spirit" that endangers stability and peace.

Before reading "the Lord Bishop of Natal's pamphlet", Shepstone had already given his own account of the alleged rebellion and the trial of Langalibalele. First of all, he defends the application of native law in the trial, by arguing that this law—whether it is good or bad—"has been the means by which a native barbarous population...has been kept under control, and the peace of the colony maintained..." (BPP 1875: C. 1121, Enclosure 1 in No. 5, § 3). He continues arguing pragmatically, by pointing to the economic advantage of applying native law: "It has supplied the place of large military force at Imperial expense, and an enormous police establishment at the cost of the Colony" (Ibid., § 4).

Apart from using pragmatic arguments in defense of the governmental policies, Shepstone emphasizes the necessity for the government "to maintain, at any risk, its authority" (Ibid., § 17). With regard to the charge of atrocities having been committed by the colonial forces, Shepstone argues that the government in "carrying out the necessities" could not have avoided such "casualties" as are quite natural and occur in any kind of warfare (Ibid., § 51). Having in mind primarily the peace of the colony and the stability of the political order, Shepstone does not reflect upon the unequal treatment of the various tribes—this was an argument raised by Colenso—, simply insisting "that it was necessary to subdue a rebellious spirit in one tribe to secure future obedience in all the others" (Ibid., § 65). The key concepts in Shepstone's defensive report are "authority" and "obedience", in sharp contrast to Colenso's critical report that emphasizes the principles of "justice" and "fairness".

Colenso's activities—agitations as his opponents would say—were not confined to the colony of Natal. His critical report in defense of Langalibalele was circulated as a "pamphlet" also in England, so that Shepstone had to respond to it officially when the document had been sent back to Natal by the Secretary of State for the colonies (Ibid., Inclosure 3 in No. 5). In his response, Shepstone rejected, of course, all the critical assertions by Colenso, and expressed his conviction that there had been no alternative way of acting for the colonial government "without compromising its position" (Ibid., § 39).

By sending critical reports to London, Colenso was able to mobilize political pressure groups in England. The Anti-Slavery Society, for instance, sent a letter to the colonial Office, complaining about "a violation of those principles of justice which should ever be observed even in war with uncivilized tribes"; more particularly, the "memorialists" submitted that "in taking away the means of existence, and then seizing the women and children, carrying them away and parcelling them out to enforced servitude, a course has been pursued utterly unworthy a civilized people,..." (BPP 1874: C. 1025, No. 22). The Secretary of State had to react to such a letter and had to instruct the Lieutenant Governor of Natal, to give "a full explanation of what has occurred" (Ibid., No. 25). The Aborigines Protection Society approached the colonial office, too, requesting even for the appointment of "a Royal Commission to visit the Colony and report on these occurrences" (Ibid., No. 44).

Another incident of this kind was an article published by the Peace Society, in the "European Mail" of the 26th January 1874, reporting on "Atrocities in Natal". This article gave rise to a "counterstatement" signed by sixty church ministers and missionaries from Natal. In defense of the colonial policies, they declared "that the action of the Natal Government was throughout humane, lenient, just, and urgently necessary", and they insisted that "repressive measures" are "sometimes necessary to protect a Christian Government and civilize a people deeply sunk in barbarism and sensuality" (BPP 1875: C. 1119, No. 18).

Among the letters written by church ministers who supported the counterstatement, the letter of S. L. Doehne is of special interest: he designated Langalibalele as an "abominable rainmaker" and accused him of having drawn tributes from his people, "these heathens"; he came to the conclusion that "it is God Almighty in his righteous judgment who has come down upon him, and the Government of Natal only his instrument. Those that are against the Natal Government in this case, are actually against the Almighty God." (Ibid., p. 56). A copy of this letter to "The Times" with all the documents included was sent to the Lieutenant Governor of Natal who did not hesitate to forward it to the Secretary of State at London, drawing special attention to the "very important" remarks of Mr. Doehne "on the dangerous influence exercised by Langalibalele as a witch doctor" (Ibid., No. 18). This devaluation of Zulu culture and religion as "heathenism" stands in sharp contrast to Colenso's view of a universal divine revelation as a basis for salvation beyond confession to Christianity.[21]

Enclosed in a letter to the Secretary of State, from Lieutenant Governor of Natal, Sir Benjamin Pine was another counter-statement to the accusations

---

21 See, for instance, Colenso's assertion that there have been prophets "amongst all peoples" (1868, 201).

raised by the Peace Society's report on "Atrocities in Natal". In defense of the colonial government, the author of this counter-statement argues pragmatically by emphasizing the economic advantage: he draws attention to the fact that the government and colonists of Natal have "crushed the rebellion and punished the offenders without burdening the tax-payers of this country with one additional penny of expenditure", and "at their own cost" have "re-established the prestige of the British name in South Africa". With regard to the accusations denouncing the colonists as guilty of atrocities, the author states rhetorically: "is this the way to knit the bonds of union throughout the Empire—to show brotherly kindness towards our fellow countrymen struggling in distant colonies...!" (BPP 1875: C. 1121, Inclosure 7 in No. 5).

The obligation of "brotherly kindness" here is limited to (English) "fellow-countrymen", contrary to Colenso who had widened the concept of "fellow-man" to include Zulu chief Langalibalele, thus postulating a basic unity of humankind, finding support at least from some humanist associations like the Aborigines Protection Society.[22] Not surprisingly, the author of the counter-statement does not conclude without critical remarks and imputations upon Colenso, maintaining that "Throughout South Africa,... the Bishop's assertions are held disproved,... and his whole line of conduct stigmatized as little less than treasonable".

Given this controversial public debate among different political pressure groups in England, it was not an easy task for the Secretary of State to find a solution that would satisfy both parties. Shepstone and Colenso both travelled to London and were given the opportunity to explain their respective view to the Colonial Office. Secretary of State for the colonies, the Earl of Carnavon, listened carefully to both of them, and his final judgment was obviously an effort to achieve some kind of compromise:

> He stated that the trial of the Zulu chief had not been correct in all respects, referring, for instance, to the absence of counsel in defense of the accused. Although admitting that punishment had been necessary, he expressed his firm opinion that the sentence had been far too severe. Also, he disapproved entirely "of any compulsory assignation of prisoners as servants to individuals". In conclusion, he tried to confirm both the divergent views of the opponents, Shepstone and Colenso: on the one hand, he emphasized "the necessity of maintaining, in every legitimate

---

22 See Colenso's remark about an "act of plain justice and right between men and men", referring to agreements and negotiations between the British and the Zulu (letter to Sir Bartle Frere, 14.1.1879) (Archives of Zululand Volume 6, 18).

way, the prestige of the Government in the eyes of the vast number of natives"; on the other hand, he stated that "inordinate punishments inflicted on the guilty, and still more, punishment inflicted on those to whom no substantial guilt can be imputed, must tend rather to weaken than to increase the credit of the Government and its power for good" (BPP 1875: C. 1119, No. 26).

Although Shepstone was criticized, at least to some extent, for his part in the trial of Langalibalele, he was some time later honored by being knighted, the blame having been shifted to the Lieutenant-Governor Benjamin Pine, who was removed from his position. Colenso, although having come through with his accusations, at least to some extent, and having been honored by an appreciative message from the Queen herself, some time later felt "humbugged and deceived", since the administrational reforms that had been promised by the Secretary of State were not carried out satisfyingly (Guy 1983: 215–233). In any event, the trial of Langalibalele and its aftermath is another example of the dynamics between the fields of religion and politics in 19th century Natal.

These inter-field dynamics become even more visible in a later period of time, when the colonial government invaded Zululand and deposed the Zulu king Cetshwayo. The Bishop intervened again, when he came to the conclusion that the king was treated unfairly, being only the victim of the aggressive and expansionist policies on the British side (Guy 1983: 284f). Th. Shepstone, even after retirement from his position as Secretary for Native Affairs still an influential actor in the political field, was again defending and justifying the policies of the government (Guy 1983: 254f). Colenso again tried everything to contest the justice of the trial, and he was partly successful in causing the punishment to be mitigated. However, the troubles did not come to an end with the release and restoration of the Zulu king. Colenso did not live to witness the further development in Zululand and "the end of the Zulu Kingdom" (Guy 1994: 183–214). His daughters would take over the task of fighting for the rights of the Zulu king, however being in a much weaker position after the death of the bishop in 1883 (Guy 2002; 2003).

In 1882, when the Zulu king was still a prisoner in the Cape Colony, Sir Henry Bulwer, then Lieutenant Governor of Natal, transmitted to the Earl of Kimberley, then Secretary of State for the colonies, a letter from the British Resident in Zululand "reporting the arrival there of a messenger from the Bishop of Natal" to some Zulu chief, bringing a message which contained directives, from the Zulu (ex)King (BPP 1882: C. 3247, No. 55). This report gave rise to a correspondence that might be interesting with regard to the borders between the fields of politics and religion.

In his response to the British resident in Zululand, Governor Bulwer states that a message from the ex-King to any person in Zululand had to be sent "through the proper channel of the Government", whereas a message "sent through the Bishop of Natal" had to be considered as "wholly unauthorized" (Ibid., Enclosure 2 in No. 55). The next day he wrote a letter to Colenso, requesting an explanation, since he found it "difficult to believe" that the bishop had conveyed a message concerning the government of Zululand (Ibid., Enclosure 3). Colenso replied immediately, stating that the message as it had been conveyed to the governor, was totally distorted and by no means had been intended as an interference of the "king" in the Government of Zululand (Ibid., Enclosure 1 in No. 58). Governor Bulwer replied immediately again, trying to make clear to the bishop that any "unauthorized" message sent "through other than the proper channel of communication" would be dangerous and requesting him to "be so good" as not to send "any more messages on the part of the ex-king to anyone in Zululand as the proceeding is one calculated to lead to unsettlement and disorder". He concluded by pointing again to the government—the Governor and the British resident—as "the proper channel of such communications" (Ibid., Enclosure 2 in No. 58).

The notion of the "(proper) channel of communication" is basically a metaphor used by a leading agent in the political field to define and defend the borders of this field. This kind of 'boundary work' is even more visible in a letter of the same Governor to the Secretary of State, complaining about the intervention of the bishop in political affairs.

The Governor expresses his conviction—"formed very reluctantly"—that "the Bishop's intervention in the political affairs of the Zulu country" has caused "the agitation that has of late disturbed that country", and he is sure that there is "nothing more calculated to do harm in dealing with the native populations of South Africa than any unauthorised and irresponsible interference or interposition in matters pertaining to the province of the Government,..." (BPP 1882: C. 3466, No. 42, § 2/3). Although he does not impute to the bishop any intention to do harm (Ibid., § 27), and although he does not deny him "the right of the free expression of his opinion on political matters" (Ibid., § 21), the Governor cannot accept that the Bishop establishes relations to the Zulu that make them carry on communication with him "as if he were a rival authority to the government of the Colony" (Ibid., § 23).[23] He regards such an

---

23   Ibid., § 23. Sir Garnet Wolseley, High Commissioner for the colony in 1879/80, in his diary expressed the same opinion, though in a less sophisticated manner, speaking about that "pestilent Bishop" as "a busybody and meddler in affairs with which he has no concern" (Preston 1973, 79).

"interposition" as very dangerous, arguing that it places the Zulu "in a false position" towards the Governor, and the Governor "in a false position towards them" (Ibid., § 24).

Summarizing his views, the governor states that he "can ill find the words" to express his "sense of the inconvenience and danger that may arise from unauthorized relations with any portion of the Zulu people in political matters" (Ibid., § 25). When objecting to the bishop's "interposition" in matters "which are the province of responsible authorities appointed by Her Majesty's Government", the governor does not, of course, deny the bishop free space for any activities in the religious field, his main point being to draw clear boundaries between the different fields of religion and politics (Ibid., § 27). All the concepts he uses are basically spatial metaphors—channel, province, interposition—that can easily be translated into Bourdieu's concept and theory of the 'field', the more so since the governor also emphasized the concept of 'relation', thus coming near to an inter-actionist view of society.

These efforts of the governor obviously are intended to define and defend the borders of his field, counteracting the alleged efforts of the Bishop to transgress the borders and invade the field of politics. The Bishop, however, it will be recalled, was not willing to acknowledge such boundaries at all. Using another spatial metaphor, he was speaking about his "path" of duty as an Englishman and as a minister of religion, indicating that he accepted only one set of rules, derived from the idea of the "Brotherhood of Man" which, according to his conviction had to be the governing principle in the religious and in the political field—a principle, ultimately irreconcilable with the political order of colonialism.[24] Shepstone, it will be recalled, had also reflected upon his "path of duty", not distinguishing between the rules governing different fields. However, his understanding of the duty of an Englishman and of a Christian differed from Colenso's, and this dissension made his path lead in a different direction, supporting the political order of colonialism and serving the interest of British imperialism.[25]

The most basic dissension, perhaps, between Governor Bulwer and Bishop Colenso lies with the view of the (dis)unity of the human mind. Contrary to Colenso, Governor Bulwer regards the "native mind" as being different: according to him, it would be a mistake "to suppose that their ways of thought are as our ways of thought, that their modes of procedure are as ours" (BPP 1882:

---

[24] Guy's critical assessment is that Colenso "never reached a deeper insight into the nature of colonialism" (1994, 91; cf. 1983, 355).

[25] Indicative of this attitude is Shepstone's change in his policies towards the Zulu, after the annexation of the Transvaal. According to Guy, he was an "expansionist" (1983, 85).

C. 3466, No. 42, § 19). His disbelief in Colenso's contention that the Zulu people want their deposed king back was based on this assumption about the native mind which "if left to itself, depends entirely upon the will and direction of the power which it recognizes as its superior". Governor Bulwer is coming even near to Bourdieu's concept of habitus, when he goes on to say about the native mind: "It is not habituated to have any wish of its own in such matters or, if it has one, it refrains from expressing it" (Ibid.).

Conclusion: Bourdieu on the Social Functions of Religion, and the 'Alternative Tradition' in the History of Religions

The case of Colenso, it seems reasonable to conclude, provides a whole set of historical examples that are nicely suitable for applying some basic concepts of Bourdieu's theory of the religious field. First, there are some examples of intra-field dynamics: the (partly successful) effort to move him out of the religious field by putting him on trial for heresy and, finally, the excommunication—clearly an act of "symbolic violence" (Bourdieu 1991, 25); the (unsuccessful) effort to prevent him from preaching in his cathedral and, the (successful) effort to cut down his financial resources, in order to reduce his capacities for educational and pastoral work in his mission station—clearly a "struggle for power and positions" within the church.

Second, there are some examples of inter-field dynamics: the controversy over Colenso's interpretation of Christianity did not remain confined to the discourse within theology, be it in the church or in the university. For by addressing a wider audience of the laity, Colenso had entered the field of literature, thereby raising opposition from experts in a neighboring, relatively autonomous field: literary critic Matthew Arnold condemned Colenso's books as not having any right of existence. This criticism, aimed at destroying part of the cultural capital of the Bishop, is related to the conflict between science and religion in the 19th century, another kind of inter-field dynamics: Colenso was among the first theologians who did not see any problem in integrating the new and controversial theory of Darwinism into the Christian worldview, a decision that raised opposition from the conservative fraction of the clergy and laity.

Another example of inter-field dynamics is the intervention of the Privy Council, a political institution, resulting in the strange situation that Colenso, although excommunicated for heresy by his church, was not deposed from his position as Bishop. Keeping this ecclesiastical position, as much as it was contested within the church, Colenso transgressed the borders of the religious field and became an actor in the political field, thus giving rise to a new phase and a different kind of inter-field dynamics—perhaps the most interesting one. The members of the Privy Council, who saved the Bishop from deposition, could not have foreseen that he would use his position to intervene in politics and develop into a critic of the British colonial policies.

Bourdieu's view of the social functions of religion, it seems, needs some correction or at least refinement: at first sight, his theory seems perfectly well confirmed, since the overwhelming majority of the clergy in the colony, through its ardent support of the colonial government provided just that "consecration" which is needed for the "maintenance of the political order". This consecrating or legitimizing function of religion is even made explicit in the statement of one church minister, who declared publicly that resistance against the government is resistance "against the Almighty God" (BPP 1875: C. 1119, No. 18), thus contributing to the "misrecognition of the arbitrariness of the domination" (Bourdieu 1991, 31). Another missionary among the supporters of the governmental policies, contributed nicely to this misrecognition by stating explicitly that Christianity, though it is "a manly thing" is "also an inculcator of submission to the powers that be, which are ordained of God..." (BPP 1875: C. 1119, No. 18).

However, just the case of Colenso shows that the function of religion cannot be reduced to consecration, since the resistance, aimed at obstructing the misrecognition of colonial domination as natural or God-given, was coming not only from secular humanistic organizations, as, for instance, the Aborigines Protection Society, but also and foremost from a member of the ecclesiastical hierarchy, though a controversial one: still holding a high ecclesiastical position, Colenso was unwilling to give members of the dominating class a justification of their social position, thus refusing to provide the legitimation of the social order by sanctification and consecration. On the contrary, his interpretation of Christianity led him to the conviction that it was his obligation to defend the interests of the dominated class, the Zulu population. Thus it appears, contrary to Bourdieu's view, that theodicies are not "always sociodicies" (Bourdieu 1991, 16), at least not with regard to the objective power relations: one could say that Colenso was giving the Zulu king—already deprived of his power by the colonial system—a justification of his social position.

The social function of religion, in this case obviously is ambivalent: on the one side, there is strong support for constructing the misrecognition of the arbitrary as God-given, since the majority of the colonial clergy kept strengthening, even consecrating the political order; on the other side, there is an equally strong, though exceptional, effort within the same church, to obstruct this misrecognition, since Colenso kept criticizing the colonial government, thereby threatening the political order. Representatives of both sides, Colenso and his opponents, of course, were totally sure that they were fulfilling "the proper function of the church" (Bourdieu 1991: 31).

The most significant point is the fact that the obstructive and innovating initiative in this case was not coming from a member of the lower clergy, nor from a prophet outside the church, as Bourdieu's theory would have predicted, but from a member of the higher clergy, though a controversial one, who was declared an heretic by the majority of the clergy. Thus, it seems, it will not be sufficient, and could be misleading, to follow Bourdieu—who was drawing upon Max Weber's sociology of religion—in elaborating extensively on the opposition between priest and prophet, just maintaining without going into details that the opposition between church and heresy is 'homologous'.

Contrary to the 'priest', the 'prophet' is defined as a religious agent who acts independently, not being integrated into religious institutions which he challenges through his personal charisma. Modeled as homologous, then, 'heresy' might be understood as referring only to the founder/leaders and adherents of movements that challenge established religious institutions from outside. This would apply to Catharism, a religious movement in medieval Southern France, suppressed as a 'heresy' by the Roman Catholic Church in the 13th century. Bourdieu probably was thinking of Catharism when he touched briefly on medieval Christianity (Bourdieu 1991: 26).

Colenso's case, it seems, does not fit into a typology based upon the distinction between priest and prophet, since he was still belonging to the 'body of priests' when he was acting like a prophet by destroying the consecration of the arbitrary social order which he was expected to give as a member of the higher clergy. However, the 'homology' maintained by Bourdieu could be understood or constructed in such a way as to include the assumption that there may emerge critics inside the church who share essential features with the prophet outside the church and, therefore, will be put on trial for heresy. And the case of Colenso, the 'heretical' Bishop, is not a singular event in the religious history of Europe. There are comparable examples already from medieval Christianity, just that period in European history which Bourdieu has shown some interest in.

A first example for comparison might be William of Tyre, who held a high ecclesiastical position, as Archbishop of Tyre, being an agent in the political field, too, as chancellor of the Christian kingdom of Jerusalem. He resisted the crusading ideology in the 12th century and propagated a policy of cooperation across the borders between Christianity and Islam (cf. Berner 2005: 22–24). His project, however, did not come to fruition, and, like Colenso, in the end he was put on trial for heresy.

The best medieval example for comparison, however, might be the case of Bernard Delicieux, a member of the Franciscan order: in the early 14th century he emerged in Southern France as a critic of the Inquisition, openly criticizing the arbitrariness of inquisitorial activities and decisions. Thus he was opposing an institution of the Roman Catholic Church that was legitimized by the pope himself. Like Colenso he was cooperating successfully, for a period of time, with an influential agent in the political field who was legitimized by the French king himself. However, he lost any support from the political field when he began criticizing the politics of the French government, even coming under suspicion of high treason. Thus he was not able to keep his position in the ecclesiastical hierarchy and could not escape a trial for heresy. He was found guilty and sentenced to lifelong imprisonment—for having impeded the work of the inquisition, especially through his critical reports to the king; he was praised as a martyr, however, by those members of the Franciscan order who kept criticizing the ecclesiastical hierarchy and blaming it for deviating from the genuine intentions of St. Francis and of Christ himself (cf. Friedlander 2000: 254–256; 290–292).

An example for comparison from the early phase of European imperialism, might be the case of Bartholome de Las Casas, who resisted the imperial policies of the Spanish colonists in 16th century Latin America. He joined a monastic order, which gave him some backing in his political activities, and he was raised even to the rank of Bishop, a position he used to defend the interests of the dominated class. Like Colenso he refused to provide the consecration of the social order which had developed in the new colonies. And like Colenso he was actively trying to intervene in the political field, appealed to the Emperor himself and argued openly against his opponent Sepulveda who defended, on theological and philosophical grounds, the imperial policies in the recently conquered colonies (cf. Berner 2007: 58–60). Compared to Colenso, Las Casas was more successful in his efforts to influence political decisions pertaining to legislation, if only for a limited period of time.

The case of Colenso, it appears, is just one example of an alternative tradition within religious institutions: the emergence of that spirit of opposition which is normally ascribed to 'the prophet', regarded as an independent religious entrepreneur who calls into question the legitimacy of ecclesiastical decisions and, thereby, if successful, preventing the church from fulfilling the function of consecrating the social order. Focusing exclusively on the opposition between priest and prophet, as Bourdieu was inclined to do following closely Max Weber, would be misleading since it neglects the opposition that may arise within the 'body of priests' itself.

Controversies among members of the ecclesiastical hierarchy, leading to trials for heresy, are not confined to discourses on orthodoxy and/or struggles for power and positions; they may also reflect totally different views on the social function of religion, the 'heretic' within the church partly fulfilling the function of the prophet. Therefore, it is not sufficient to describe the social function of religion as 'consecration' which reflects only the attitude of the dominating class in the ecclesiastical hierarchy. Those critical minds within the church that are marginalized or even eliminated—by trials for heresy—have to be taken into account, too, the more so, since their deviant religious ideas may have effects beyond the borders of the religious field:

Although Colenso had not been able to change the politics of the colonial government, his interpretation of Christianity had some impact and influence on Zulu culture and politics, mediated mainly through a former pupil of his mission school, Magema Fuze (cf. Mokoena 2011: 61f). Later on, his legacy was carried on through his daughter Harriette who was in contact with the founders of the ANC (cf. Marks 1963: 409f). Thus a political movement in South Africa, in the beginning apparently was drawing some inspiration from the religious heritage of Colenso's mission station (cf. Marks 1975). Again, the case of Colenso can be seen as just an example of an 'alternative tradition' that crosses the borders between religion and neighboring fields:

An example for comparison might be Sebastian Castellio, humanist and theologian of the Reformation Era, who protested against the burning of heretics and propagated tolerance and religious freedom (Guggisberg 1997: 89–106; Berner 2004b: 26–29). The idea of tolerance was rejected by the leaders of the various ecclesiastical hierarchies, later on, however, transferred to the field of political philosophy: English philosopher John Locke, for instance, was well acquainted with the work of Castellio (cf. Guggisberg 1997: 282). It seems even quite reasonable, trying to reconstruct a line of continuity, from the discourse on tolerance among theologians of the Reformation Era, to the American constitution (cf. Hillar 1994: 51–57).

Thus it appears that Bourdieu's view on the relationship between church and heresy, modeled as homologous to priest and prophet, needs some correction or at least elaboration and refinement. In any event, his theory of the religious field still has much to contribute to Religious Studies: First, the very metaphor of the field already can help to evade the danger of reifying religion "as though it were an autonomous reality" (Fitzgerald 2007: 2). For fields do not exist as 'autonomous realities', as they emerge and/or exist only through the boundary work carried out by individuals or groups, trying to defend the borders and to enforce rules of the game.

Second, his contention that every religion will take on totally different meanings in the process of reinterpretation, helps to avoid the danger of essentializing religious traditions as if each one had an identity of its own (Bourdieu 1991: 19; 29). Again, the case of Colenso provides a good example: the dissension between him and the majority of the clergy of Natal, concerning the right attitude towards the policies of the colonial government—regarding the violent operations of the government either as deviation from or as fulfillment of the will of God—indicates that they were constructing or falling back on entirely different concepts of God, while interpreting the same religious tradition. This particular aspect of Bourdieu's theory has to be given much more attention in the Study of Religion.[26]

References

Archival Sources
SNA = Secretary for Native Affairs. Pietermaritzburg Archives Repository.

Published Primary Sources
Archives 1879 = Archives of Zululand. The Anglo-Zulu War 1879. Volume 6. ed. Ian Knight. Archival Publications International 2000.

Arnold, Matthew. [1863] 1973. The Bishop and the Philosopher. In *Lectures and Essays in Criticism*, edited by R. H. Super, 40–55. Ann Arbor: The University of Michigan Press.

BPP 1874 = British Parliamentary Papers 1874 C. 1025: Papers relating to the late Kafir outbreak in Natal.

BPP 1875 = British Parliamentary Papers 1875. C. 1119; C. 1121; C. 1158; C. 1187: Further Papers relating to the Kafir outbreak in Natal.

BPP 1882 = British Parliamentary Papers 1882. C. 3247; C. 3466: Correspondence respecting the Affairs of Zululand.

Chesson, F. W. 1879. The War in Zululand: A Brief Review of Sir Bartle Frere's Policy. Drawn from Official Documents. In *Archives of Zululand* 6: 51–76.

Colenso, John William. 1855a. *Ten Weeks in Natal. A Journal of a first Tour of Visitation among the Colonists and Zulu Kafirs of Natal*. Cambridge: McMillan & CO.

———. 1855b. *Remarks on the Proper Treatment of Polygamy. As found already existing in Converts from Heathenism*. Pietermaritzburg: May & Davis.

———. 1861. *First Lessons in Science. Designed for the Use of Children and Adult Natives*. Part I. Second Edition. Natal: Ekukanyeni.

---

26 Cf. Fitzgerald on the "fallacy of the world religion approach" (1997, 106).

———. 1862. *The Pentateuch and Book of Joshua Critically Examined*. Second edition, Revised London.

———. 1868. *Natal Sermons. Second Series of Discourses preached in the Cathedral Church of St. Peter's, Maritzburg*. London: N. Trübner & co.

———. 1875. Langalibalele and the Amahlubi Tribe: Remarks upon the Official Record of the Trials of the Cief, his Sons and Induna, and other Members of the Amahlubi Tribe. London (British Parliamentary Papers C. 1141).

———. 1880. Cetshwayo's Dutchman. Being the Journal of a White Trader in Zululand during the British Invasion by Cornelius Vijn. Translated from the Dutch and edited with Preface and Notes by the Right Rev. J. W. Colenso. In *Archives of Zululand* 6: 359–570.

Haggard, H. Rider. 1926. *The Days of my Life. An Autobiography*. Volume I. London: Longmans, Green and Co. Ltd.

Preston, Adrian, ed. 1973. *The South African Journal of Sir Garnet Wolseley 1879–1880*. Cape Town: A. A. Balkema.

Rees, Wyn, ed. 1958. *Colenso Letters from Natal*. Pietermaritzburg: Shuter and Shooter.

Secondary Literature

Berner, Ulrich. 2004a. Africa and the Origin of the Science of Religion. Max Müller (1823–1900) and James George Frazer (1854–1941) on African Religions. In: *European Traditions in the Study of Religion in Africa*, edited by Frieder Ludwig and Afe Adogame, 141–149. Wiesbaden: Harrassowitz.

———. 2004b. Kreuzzug und Ketzerbekämpfung. Das Alte Testament in der theologischen Argumentation des Mittelalters und der Frühen Neuzeit. *In Impuls oder Hindernis? Mit dem Alten Testament in multireligiöser Zeit*, edited by Joachim Kügler, 17–30. Münster: LIT Verlag.

———. 2005. Die Bibel in der mittelalterlichen Diskussion um Ketzer und Muslime. In *Auf Leben und Tod oder völlig egal. Kritisches und Nachdenkliches zur Bedeutung der Bibel*, edited by Joachim Kügler and Werner H. Ritter, 11–24. Münster: LIT Verlag.

———. 2007. Synkretismus—Begegnung der Religionen. In *Kultur und Religion in der Begegnung mit dem Fremden*, edited by Joachim G. Piepke, 47–74. Nettetal: Steyler Verlag.

———. 2009. Die christliche Missionsstation—ein Ort interkultureller Kommunikation? In *Kommunikation über Grenzen*, edited by Friedrich Schweitzer, 72–89. Gütersloh: Gütersloher Verlagshaus.

———. 2012. Religiosität und Rationalität. Reginald Scot und die Kritik des Hexenglaubens in der Frühen Neuzeit. In *Religion und Kritik in der Moderne*, edited by Ulrich Berrner and Johannes Quack, 141–179. Berlin: LIT Verlag.

Bourdieu, Pierre. 1979. Symbolic Power. *Critique of Anthropology* 13: 77–85.

---. 1987. Legitimation and Structured Interests in Weber's Sociology of Religion. In *Max Weber, Rationality and Modernity*, edited by Scott Lash and Sam Whimster, 119–136. London: Allen & Unwin.

---. 1990. *The Logic of Practice*. Stanford: Stanford University Press.

---. 1991. Genesis and Structure of the Religious Field. *Comparative Social Research* 13: 1–44.

---. 1993. From Ruling Class to Field of Power: An Interview with Pierre Bourdieu on La noblesse d'Etat. *Theory, Culture & Society* 10: 19–44.

Colenso, Gwilym. 2003. The Pentateuch in Perspective: Bishop Colenso's Biblical Criticism in its Colonial Context. In *The Eye of the Storm*, edited by Jonathan A. Draper, 136–167. London: T&T Clark.

Cox, George W. 1888. *The Life of John William Colenso Bishop of Natal*. Two Volumes. London: W. Ridgway.

Darby, Ian. 2003. Colenso the Sacramentalist. In *The Eye of the Storm*, edited by Jonathan A. Draper, 182–193. London: T&T Clark.

Draper, Jonathan A. 2003. The Trial of Bishop John William Colenso. In *The Eye of the Storm*, edited by Jonathan A. Draper, 306–325. London: T&T Clark.

Engler, Steven. 2003. Modern Times: Religion, Consecration and the State in Bourdieu. *Cultural Studies* 17: 445–467.

Etherington, Norman. 1989. The 'Shepstone System' in the Colony of Natal and beyond the Borders. In *Natal and Zululand from Earliest Times to 1910. A New History*, edited by Andrew Duminy and Bill Guest, 170–192. Pietermaritzburg: University of Natal Press/Shuter & Shooter.

Fitzgerald, Timothy. 1997. A Critique of "Religion" as a Cross-Cultural Category. *Method and Theory in the Study of Religion* 9: 91–110.

---. 2007. Encompassing Religion, Privatized Religions and the Invention of Modern Politics. In *Religion and the Secular. Historical and Colonial Formations*, edited by Timothy Fitzgerald, 211–240. London/Oakville: Equinox.

Friedlander, Alan. 2000. *The Hammer of the Inquisitors. Brother Bernard Delicieux and the Struggle against the Inquisition in Fourteenth Centrury France*. Leiden: Brill.

Guest, R. W. 1976. *Langalibalele. The Crisis in Natal 1873–1875*. Durban: Department of History and Political Science, University of Natal. Research Monograph No. 2.

Guggisberg, Hans R. 1997. *Sebastian Castellio. Humanist und Verteidiger der religiösen Toleranz*. Göttingen: Vandenhoeck und Ruprecht.

Guy, Jeff. 1983. *The Heretic. A Study of the Life of John William Colenso 1814–1883*. Pietermaritzburg: The University of Natal Press.

---. 1994. *The Destruction of the Zulu Kingdom. The Civil War in Zululand 1879–1884*. Pietermaritzburg: University of Natal Press.

———. 2002. *The View across the River. Harriette Colenso and the Zulu Struggle against Imperialism*. Oxford: James Currey.

———. 2003. The Colenso Daughters: Three Women Confront Imperialism. In *The Eye of the Storm*, edited by Jonathan A. Draper, 345–363. London: T&T Clark.

Hillar, Marian. 1994. From the Polish Socinians to the American Constitution. *Journal from the Radical Reformation* 3: 22–57.

Hinchliff, Peter. 1964. *John William Colenso Bishop of Natal*. London: Nelson.

Marks, Shula. 1963. Harriette Colenso and the Zulus, 1874–1913. *Journal of African History* 4: 403–411.

———. 1975. The Ambiguities of Dependence: John L. Dube of Natal. *Journal of Southern African Studies* 1: 162–180.

McClendon, Thomas V. 2004. The Man Who Would Be Inkosi: Civilizing Missions in Shepstone's Early Career. *Journal of Southern African Studies* 30: 339–358.

———. 2010. *White Chief, Black Lords. Shepstone and the Colonial State in Natal, South Africa 1845–1878*. Rochester: University of Rochester Press.

Mokoena, Hlonipha. 2008. The Queen's Bishop: A Convert's Memoir of John W. Colenso. *Journal of Religion in Africa* 38: 312–342.

———. 2011. *Magema Fuze. The Making of a* Kholwa *Intellectual*. Scottsville: University of KwaZulu-Natal Press.

Myers, J. C. 2008. *Indirect Rule in South Africa. Tradition, Modernity, and the Costuming of Political Power*. Rochester: University of Rochester Press.

Rey, Terry. 2007. *Bourdieu on Religion. Imposing Faith and Legitimacy*. London/Oakville: Equinox.

Sharpe, Eric J. 1991. *Comparative Religion. A History*. Second Edition. London: Gerald Duckworth & Co.

Swartz, David. 1996. Bridging the Study of Culture and Religion: Pierre Bourdieu's Political Economy of Symbolic Power. *Sociology of Religion* 57: 71–85.

CHAPTER 7

Healers or Heretics: Diviners and Pagans Contest the Law in a Post-1994 Religious Field in South Africa

Dale Wallace

Preamble

On April 27th, 2004, a gathering took place in a park in Johannesburg, South Africa. The occasion was Freedom Day and the event organized by local Pagans in celebration of 10 years of religious freedom as guaranteed in the new Constitution of 1996. This act of celebration was an implicit statement of perceptions of pre-1994 marginalization and/or exclusion from the religious field in South Africa. Whilst similar Pagan gatherings were held in all major centers in the country, what differentiated the Johannesburg gathering was the invitation to co-share the celebration with a large number of Traditional Healers; most of whom were known as Izangoma/diviners, and, in some quarters, by the colonial designation of 'witchdoctors'. There were only isolated objections to the fact that Pagans, almost exclusively white practitioners of Wicca and modern Witchcraft, celebrated their achievement of religious freedom with African sacred specialists who depended largely, for both their status and their income, on the recognition of their ability to identify witches in their community, and to prescribe treatment and protective measures to victims of malevolent witchcraft.

The shared camaraderie between Pagans and Izangoma as they drummed together in celebration of what they understood to be a realization of equal social and legal recognition for their religious beliefs and practices was relatively short-lived. The changes in this relationship can be traced in the genesis of a 'religious field' in a colonial South Africa, and to the consequences of colonial legislation and post-colonial, post-apartheid developments.

Introduction

The preamble discusses events that took place one decade into South Africa's new democracy and will serve as a framework for discussion in this chapter. The focus is on contemporary Pagans/modern Witches and African diviners (hereafter referred to as Izangoma)[1] as they negotiated their positions in a radically changed religious field still weighted by the influences of its colonial past alongside sweeping post-colonial political and legal changes. My usage of the term 'field' is drawn from the Theory of Practice of social theorist Pierre Bourdieu (1930–2002) who draws on this spatial metaphor as a tool for measuring social space empirically, and who defined a field as "a network, or a configuration, of objective relations between positions" (Bourdieu and Wacquant 1992: 97). What is so significant about the religious field in post-colonial South Africa is the rapidity with which political change—marked by the demand to redress the multiple effects of racially enforced segregation—challenged dominant positions in the field previously taken as self-evident. These processes destabilized what Bourdieu referred to as a doxic practice: a situation in which the arbitrariness of the structures in a field has been naturalized to such an extent that they become invisible to the actor (1977: 164). The impact of rapid political change on all fields of social life was evidenced in power struggles and conflicts as social agents competed to assume a position, or to assert, retain, or alter their incumbent positions in order to accrue the benefits of stakes in the nascent field. Bourdieu uses the term 'capital'[2] to describe the distribution of power relationships that inhered in the above strategies and suggests that forms of capital are drawn upon by social actors; not only to access stakes in and across fields, but also as strategies of dominance and advantage. There is considerable methodological value in the primacy Bourdieu gives to relationships between social actors, and to human agency, within a structuralist framework. He makes the salient point that,

> *social agents are not "particles"* that are mechanically pushed and pulled about by external forces. They are rather, bearers of capitals and, depending on the trajectory and on the position they occupy in the field by virtue of their endowment (volume and structure) in capital, they have a propensity to orient themselves actively either toward the preservation of the distribution of capital or toward the subversion of this distribution (Bourdieu and Wacquant 1992: 108–9).

---

1   Izangoma is the Zulu word for the African sacred specialist, or diviner. This is the plural term, with the singular being Isangoma. The term differs in various Bantu languages (e.g. Boloi in Sotho), but Izangoma remains the most widely recognized term.
2   These forms of capital are accumulated in material objectified form, or in incorporated, subjectified form. Bourdieu (1992: 97) says that the possession of these forms of capital "commands access to the specific profits that are at stake in the field, as well as by their objective relation to other positions (domination, subordination, homology, etc.)".

It is this perspective that allows me to discuss the reconfiguration of the religious field in post-colonial South Africa through the interplay between the objective structure of the field and the subjective systems of expectations and predispositions of human agents, that Bourdieu termed *habitus*. The ensuing power struggles within the web of relationships between Izangoma, Pagans and those who assert the hegemony of a religious Christian orthodoxy, is considered in terms of the spatial concepts of center, margins and boundaries.

The Genesis of a 'Religious Field'

No discussion of the 'religious field' in either colonial or post-colonial South Africa can be undertaken without reference to the complex debates on the definition of 'religion' itself, and is a topic raised through this chapter. The defining of terms is not merely the clarification of meaning of words, but is recognized by Bourdieu as a medium of power through which individuals pursue their own interests and exhibit their competencies. For a definition to function as true is largely dependent on the speaker's relational position in social space and, as such, is able to conceal systems of privilege and subordination. It is also capable of operating as a symbolic signifier of strategic domination. These difficulties in definition have, in the past as much as in the present, been reflected in the study of religion since the late nineteenth century. In global colonial encounters the definition of 'religion' was mostly void of contestation, and was grounded in the distinctly Protestant Christian understanding of what constituted religion, and of categories of beliefs and practices that therefore were excluded. Within such understandings lay distinct binaries such as insider/outsider, true/false, orthodoxy/heresy and orthopraxy/diabolism and magic. Pierre Bourdieu's sociology of religion does not engage directly with the issue of definition, and whether he focused extensively beyond Roman Catholicism in France and Islam in Algeria, must remain conjectural (Turner 2011: 109). What does, nonetheless, have salience in the application of Bourdieu's conceptual framework in the context of religion in Africa, is the emphasis he gives to religion as 'systems of embodied practices', rather than privileging the term as 'belief' as had been the case when colonists and missionaries demarcated the new boundaries of an emerging religious field. Accordingly, this chapter brings attention to issues situated in a time of radical social and political change, in which magic practices remained criminalized in legislation and conflated with the practice of witchcraft. With particular attention on the words religion, superstition, pagan, heresy, witches and witchcraft, I question who defines these terms and in what context these definitions are employed? Whose definition is made to function as true, and what role does this play in the construction of dominant and subordinate positions in the field? It is in the outcome of related struggles and strategies that the exclusion of individuals and groups from full participation in the stakes in the religious field in democratic South Africa can be traced.

Although Bourdieu's concept of field implies a clearly delineated space, he explains that "A field consists of a set of objective, historical relations between positions anchored in certain forms of power (or capital)..." (Bourdieu and Wacquant 1992: 16). As such the boundaries of the field can only be understood in the context of an investigation into the genesis, or history, of the field (Bourdieu 1985: 22). Such an investigation must focus on the historical development of sets of relationships. Prior to the colonization of South Africa by the Dutch (1652), and later the British (1814), the Khoisan[3] and various Nguni-Bantu[4] peoples who were inhabitants of the region from the Cape through to Natal, engaged in practices that were constitutive of the sustaining of the relationship between the living and the departed ancestors in the spirit realm. Although being ethnically distinct groups, both the Khoisan and Nguni-Bantu made little to no distinction between the secular visible world and the spirit-populated invisible world. A network of relationships existed between the individual and the community, through the animistic notions of a spirit-populated material world.[5] Fetishism,[6] incidents of totemism,[7] and the ubiquitous practice of divinatory systems were means of participating in, and communicating with, the spirit realm. They underpinned 'ways of being in the world' that were orally transmitted rather than codified systems of beliefs and

---

3   The Khoisan are recognized as the indigenous peoples of southern Africa, and are divided into two distinct groups; namely the Khoi-Khoi, or Hottentots, and the San. The latter later became known by the derogatory appellation of San Bushmen.
4   The Nguni-Bantu is a broad term for a diversity of linguistically distinct agriculturalist and herder groups who migrated southwards in search of grazing and available land. For more on Khoisan and Nguni-Bantu see Chidester (1992: 2–3).
5   Animism is a term developed by anthropologist E. B. Tylor to refer to the belief that the individual *anima*, or spirit, is distinct from the body and may wander in dreams, and wander permanently in death. It also includes the notion that the natural world is infused with spirits with which humans can participate in relationship.
6   Fetishism is the practice of worshipping an object believed to be inhabited by a spirit, or that has magical properties. It resembles totemism, but includes other aspects in the scholarship of J. F. McLennan and Emile Durkheim.
7   Totemism is the practice of venerating or worshipping an object or natural phenomenon as a symbol of a group or kinship community. It was emphasized in the sociology of religion of Emile Durkheim.

practices. The words themselves lacked equivalency in Nguni-Bantu languages and operated as colonial ascriptions of a range of 'primitive' practices in the colonies. Lacking the historical verification afforded by the texts of the Judeo-Christian traditions, it is worthwhile to note the caution of Chidester who says that, "any attempt to reconstruct pre-colonial African Religion, therefore, must remain conjectural" (1992: 3). In their encounters with the Khoisan and Nguni-Bantu, colonists and missionaries held no such conjectural thoughts and the early construction of an 'African Religion' developed in two distinct ways:

1. Early colonists and missionaries to Africa brought with them a variety of Protestant forms of Christianity that became synonymous with the colonial project. Constructing a 'religious field' where inclusion rested on adherence to Christian orthodoxy, colonists and missionaries exercised a denial that Africans had any religion at all (Chidester 1996: 234), effectively placing them beyond the boundaries of the emergent field. Animism was viewed as a blasphemy and a myriad of practices were seen as commensurate with heretical diabolism. Various forms of legislation were to ratify this position.

2. The publication of Darwin's *Origin of Species* in 1859, gave impetus and direction to the emerging social sciences (Sharpe 1992: 48). Taking inspiration from Darwin's evolutionary model, the critical error was made in presupposing that biological evolution could be mirrored in human social systems and structures. As a consequence, writings of encounters with indigenous peoples that fed back to Europe from colonial territories were drawn on as evidence that the roots of the apex of human religious expression, namely Christian monotheism, lay in the practices of animism, fetishism, totemism and magic; namely in the religion of the 'primitives'.

The colonial interpretation of many African practices as 'magic', contributed to a denial and delegitimation of an African religion on the one hand, and, on the other, was used as evidence of a 'primitive origin' of religion (Chidester: 1995). Anthropologist Sir James Frazer published *The Golden Bough* in 1890, from which scholars derived a working definition of magic (Sharpe 1992: 90). Describing magic as a 'false science' and as a distinctly primitive stage in the history of human religious thought ratified the growing power of the church that, since the eighteenth century, had not only placed magic outside the category of religion, but in opposition to it. As Knott says, "And yet such antipathy and fear developed within religious circles against magic (or certain types of it) that they took on the appearance of ideological separation, indeed opposition" (2005: 172). Certain types of magical practices—such as divination, conjuration, charms and fortune-telling—were designated as heretical. Importantly these practices also absorbed the legacy of the medieval Witchcraft era[8] that linked such practices to witchcraft. From the fifteenth to the seventeenth century, magic, now firmly linked to heresy, was beyond the boundaries of the new religious orthodoxy and orthopraxy. During these centuries ecclesiastical authorities were successful in converting their cultural capital (such as preaching, praying and reading the bible) into symbolic capital (status as legitimate religious leaders), and in exercising this capital as forms of power in the contiguous political and judicial fields. This was evidenced in the sixteenth century by the emergence of civil courts to try persons accused of the practice of witchcraft (Ellis 2007: 39). It was in the records of judicial proceedings brought against individuals accused of witchcraft that the influential power of ecclesiastical authorities can be witnessed. Persons accused of witchcraft, many of whom had held valuable cultural capital in their communities as traditional healers, herbalists and midwives, were negatively interpolated as agents of evil who conspired to wreak harm and even death on others. The cultural capital of witches came to include the ability to poison, to shape-shift and fly at night on damaging errands, to bring drought, and even hail to destroy crops. The negative constructions of the 'witch' and 'witchcraft' were ratified and extended in the Malleus Maleficarum, written in 1484 by Inquisitors Heinrich Kramer and James Sprenger, and which came to serve as an authoritative text on witchcraft in civil courts. An outcome of this was the conversion of the cultural capital of witches into negative symbolic capital through the accompanying charge of heresy. The power to identify and punish heresy no longer lay solely with church authorities, but was exercised in civil courts. Such legislation in turn formalized the boundaries of religious orthodoxy that could now be policed in religious and secular society.

Colonists and missionaries brought with them a mélange of notions underpinned by a Christian orthodoxy that included the historical constructions of the heretic, the witch and witchcraft and the 'pagan' in their epistemological field. Many, carrying the heritage of scientific rationalism of the Enlightenment,

---

8   The Witchcraft era refers to the historical period in Europe between the late 14th century and the 17th century. Known as the Great European Witch Hunt, it refers to the persecution of individuals under the accusation of heretical witchcraft. It overlapped Catholic and Protestant Europe and some 160,000 individuals (of whom most were women) are known to have lost their lives. Although executions dwindled by the end of the 17th century, charges of witchcraft continued to be brought against individuals across Europe well into the 18th century. The last execution took place in Poland in 1783.

considered the aforementioned as forms of primitive, base superstition. The religious field in colonial territories was constituted by adherence to a biblically-based Christian orthodoxy. 'Belief' in these emerging religious fields was in a universal God whose mercy, forgiveness and promise of human salvation, both denigrated and subsumed all other systems of interpretation and understanding. Entry into the field required a reconfiguration of African conceptions of causation as much as the sublimation of propitiatory practices associated with ancestor veneration. The fact that these practices constituted heresy through a Christian colonial lens was a viewpoint held in the *habitus* of colonial agents who carried with them notions of Christian heresy from the historical witchcraft persecutions in Europe. In terms of *habitus*, as a "set of historical relations 'deposited' within individual bodies in a form of mental and corporeal schemata of perception, appreciation, and action" (Bourdieu and Wacquant 1992: 16), these notions can be interpreted as the 'doxic' nature of this particular colonial thinking. They were taken-for-granted, self-evident knowledge of the boundaries of orthodoxy. Bourdieu and Wacquant argue for the necessity to,

> sociologize the phenomenological analysis of doxa as an uncontested acceptance of the daily lifeworld, not simply to establish that it is not universally valid for all perceiving and acting subjects, but also to consider that, when it realises itself in certain social positions, among the dominated in particular, it represents the most radical form of acceptance of the world, the most absolute form of conservatism (1992: 73–74).

Orthopraxy in the emerging field was constituted by adherence to Christian modes of worship, as well as to Christian modes of behavior, dress, and to Christian practices that generated familial and community relationships, such as marriage, baptism and burial. Those who held symbolic capital in this field, exercised this as the power to impose their categories and perceptions of meaning on those practices that were different from, or failed to conform to, the aforementioned. The power to do so would constitute what Bourdieu terms 'symbolic violence'. Bourdieu extends the concept of symbolic violence by stating that it is seldom recognized as 'violence'. Modes of social and cultural domination are 'misrecognized' as such, which allows for symbolic violence to be concealed within dominant discourses. The skills, competencies and qualifications (cultural capital) required for inclusion in developing fields, can be viewed as sources of symbolic violence and misrecognition when nascent political, economic and social structures excluded those who held less of these competencies from any form of legitimate inclusion. Inhering in all these processes was the 'non-recognition' of an existing 'religious' field in the colony, as colonists held a mélange of notions about African beliefs and practices as being primeval, superstitious, and even naive. As such, their practitioners were excluded from stakes available in the nascent 'religious field'; effectively further excluding them from the political and judicial advantages available to legitimately recognized religious leaders and their communities.

African Mediation with the Spirit Realm

To construct a 'religious field' in pre-colonial Africa necessitates the postcolonial shift from substantive definitions of religion, and requires a caution in interpretation due to the lack of first-hand primary written data. The hierarchical structures in African encounters with the spirit realm were integrated and intertwined with their economic, political and judicial systems, and, as "a set of objective, historical relations between positions anchored in certain forms of power (or capital)" (Bourdieu and Wacquant 1992: 16) are available for analysis as a religious field. There were two primary sacred specialists in African societies, namely the Isangoma/diviner and the Inyanga[9]/herbalist. Exclusionary mechanisms could be found in early recognitions of Izinyanga who undertook a rigorous training in the medicinal and magical properties of plants, herbs, minerals and animal parts, and in their expert combination in order to treat a range of physical, social and psychic afflictions. These traditional medical products are known as muthi.[10] Izinyanga were not called to this role from the spirit realm, nor did they employ divinatory methods to communicate with the spirit realm for their diagnosis, prescription and treatment. It was this distinction that privileged Izinyanga in colonial territories. From the outset, it was the magico-spiritual practices of Izangoma that were systematically criminalized. According to the Natal Code of Native Law No. 19 of 1891, "the practice and trade in philtres (magical charms), divining and witchcraft" (Xaba 2007: 332) was prohibited, thereby giving recognition to muthi practices solely within a context stripped of their spiritual underpinnings that, in being associated with magic, superstition and witchcraft, were duly criminalized. With the need for supernatural diagnosis unabated, Xaba points to an outcome of this legislation as being that Izinyanga began doing their own divining (ibid.: 333) and Izangoma in turn advanced their knowledge of muthi products. In such

---

9   Inyanga is the singular term for an African herbalist. The plural is Izinyanga.
10 The word muthi is drawn from the Nguni-Bantu stem –*thi*, signifying tree. It is interchangeably spelled as muti.

legislation lay the foundations for the current difficulty in clearly distinguishing between these two types of practitioners today. Whilst meeting requirements of legislation would benefit certain individuals who were able to convert their cultural capital in one field into forms of symbolic capital in the other, for the most part, legislation had little impact on the symbolic capital held in their communities by Izangoma who embodied the knowledge/power of mediating ancestral protection, punishment and guidance.

The Izangoma, as community mediators to the spirit realm, held authority across traditional structures of life; and their skills were highly valued by individuals, homestead elders and chiefs. African social life was hierarchically structured down; from the tribal chiefs, to elders of family lineages, to older individuals, and then down to infants. Chiefs, whose authority absorbed more homesteads, held more powerful forms of economic and cultural capital than those who absorbed fewer. This hierarchical order was sustained, not only through the living, but in the spirit realm after death. Material, physical, social and spiritual advantage in life depended on maintaining balance and harmony across these relationships; be it with the living or with the departed, or "living dead".[11] This relied on sustaining the reciprocal relationship between these two realms, with the departed ancestors bestowing protection from harm, physical well-being, and harmonious social relationships on the living in return for their being remembered and honored through ritual observance and their sustained inclusion in the lives of their living descendents. Lapses in the latter could result in ancestors withdrawing their protection, leaving the individual vulnerable to multiple forms of misfortune, including witchcraft. The power of ancestors to punish the living meant that they were as feared by the living as much as they were needed, and could be approached through the specialist mediation of the diviners. Whilst chiefs and elders could ritually approach ancestors with thanks, or to invite them to participate in functions with their living descendents, the divinatory skills of Izangoma were critical when causal explanation was required for inexplicable and/or unfortunate events. The Isangoma, who was called to his/her position by the ancestors, underwent a rigorous training in the achieving of altered states of consciousness in order to communicate with the spirit realm, and in the learning of the language of the ancestors for prophecy, diagnosis and prescription. Prescription could include

---

11   The term "living dead" is attributed to J. S. Mbiti (1990). Mbiti's use of this term refers to the African notion that the deceased continue to live in the spirit realm, and maintain their influence on the living, until they are no longer remembered by their communities.

forms of ritual observance and/or the inhalation or ingestion of muthi, and, prior to the Natal Native Code of 1891, it was common for Izangoma to refer clients to Izinyanga for muthi products once the supernatural diagnosis was completed. Additional treatments could include the bestowing of protective power to the client in the form of amulets, charms, incisions made on the flesh, and/or powders to inhale or ingest. The mystical power of Izangoma was authenticated by their ancestral connection and was an embodied power that could be harnessed, apportioned and channeled according to the client's needs. In the colonial construction of an African religion, which was constructed on Western Christian categories and drawn from the tales and writings of travelers, missionaries, traders and colonial agents, 'belief' in ancestors was a turn of phrase imposed on deeply embedded systems of meaning and practice that were themselves embedded in everyday life. The relationship between the living and the departed was less a body of 'beliefs', but rather an embodied knowledge system that was experienced through the fluctuating effects of fortune/misfortune and good physical and mental health or illness from birth through to death. Practices related to this relationship arose as a response to the vagaries of life, and to the learned obligations that would ensure guidance and protection in life and an individual's personal immortality beyond death. It was through a practical knowledge of how the reciprocal relationship between the living and the departed was affirmed, enacted, and integrated, that the totality of social life was experienced.

Bourdieu compares a field to a 'game' in which social actors (players) strategize for positions in a field, and in so doing, engage in systems of relations, alliances, and power struggles. It is the state of relations between positions that "defines the structure of the field" (Bourdieu and Wacquant 1992: 99). In the context of an 'African' religious field, the practices associated with securing ancestral guidance and protection were foundational to balance and health in this life, and to the assurance of personal immortality in the next. These were stakes available in the field to those who followed 'the rules of the game' that were mediated through the knowledge/power of chiefs, elders and sacred specialists; most importantly the Izangoma. Relational positions in the traditional context therefore cannot be separated from the hierarchy of positions between the living and the departed ancestors. To fully understand 'religion' in the traditional African context necessitates recognition of the extent to which individual capital is accrued and exercised, not only in social life, but through relational positions and interplay with the spirit realm. As a field of play, those who transgressed the rules risked exclusion from ancestral protection that would render the individual vulnerable to misfortune and/or to the malevolent practice of witches. Witches, or *abathakathi*,[12] were very much part of this religious field wherein they were recognized as the primary anti-social agents who, as players in the game, held the power to destabilize the game through the transgression and inversion of the rules.

Witchcraft in the African Context

Witchcraft in African communities is a complex phenomenon that is difficult to define as the term fails to refer to a coherent system of beliefs. Despite ambiguities, the overriding association of witchcraft is with the malicious practices of individuals who manipulate supernatural forces with ill-intent. Whether such beliefs are grounded in empirical reality or not, the witch as a manifestation of personalized evil is the predominant understanding of the term across Africa (Wallace 2009: 130). The belief in the reality of witchcraft has served many individual and community functions, including an explanation for illness, death and misfortune; as well as reinforcing the boundaries around communities by excluding destabilizing forces. How this operates cannot be adequately understood outside of discussions of power relationships, poverty and social change (Dovlo 2007: 69). Izangoma have been, and continue to be, implicated in the phenomenon of witchcraft persecution and violence. Positioned within the African religious field itself, the identity and the practices of the witch were clouded in secrecy and required the specialist skills of the Izangoma in confirming witchcraft suspicions and accusations, and in naming the culprit(s). According to van Beek,

> some societies purport to have the means to detect 'witches' and to be able to select between the guilty and the innocent. In such cases, the role of diviners is crucial—both as persons who are believed to embody power, and as people who depend on witchcraft violence for status and income (2007: 305).

Witchcraft accusations and fears in communities had historically been the responsibility of chiefs to address through the mediation of an Isangoma. This authority was lessened by the promulgation of the Bantu Authorities Act (68) of 1951 that delimited their power in the adjudication of witchcraft accusations. The technologies of diviners in the aforementioned processes were not

---

12   In Zulu the singular 'witch' is *umthakathi*. To 'practice witchcraft' is *ukuthakatha*. The term also refers to a wizard or sorcerer.

defined as 'magic', but as propitiatory mechanisms both understood and communicated by those in the spirit world. In fact, Bantu languages had a number of different words to distinguish between a range of practices that later were defined as 'magic' in the colonial context. Whilst African languages employed a number of words to describe the moral intent inherent in a variety of different beliefs and practices, these were subsumed under the single category 'witchcraft' through a colonial Christian gaze. Stressing the need for a careful use of language in witchcraft studies,[13] Gerrie ter Haar states that,

> it is not insignificant... to refer to the observation that the term 'witchcraft' was popularized in regard to Africa only in the later nineteenth century by Europeans who were applying to Africa ideas derived from their own historical memory of witchcraft in Europe. Before the mid- or late- nineteenth century, some aspects of African religious or spiritual beliefs that were subsequently labeled as 'witchcraft' did not go under that name (2007: 15).

Despite this caution, clearly identifiable 'language games'[14] operated to legitimate the forms of belief that upheld recognition of a legitimate religious field. The influence of Izangoma, which attracted the attention of colonial agents and early settler communities as they engaged in conflict and negotiation with African chiefs and homestead elders over land and other material resources in colonial territories, was seen as a threat to these processes. A result was that the practices of Izangoma soon were subsumed into a pejorative category of magic, witchcraft and/or heresy.

It was the enactment of legislation during the colonial and apartheid years (1948–1992) that clearly endorsed that an entity such as a 'legitimate religious field' was now in place. For the first time in South African history many beliefs and practices within African communities were criminalized as the state interfered to regulate religion in the public domain. Witchcraft Suppression Acts had already been implemented in many states across colonial Africa when the Witchcraft Suppression Act (3) of 1957[15] (hereafter referred to as the WSA (3) of 1957) came into effect in South Africa. Words used in the Act became operative without consultation over the meaning they had for the very individuals

---

13   This point is also made by Ellis (2007: 45).
14   For Bourdieu's discussion of language and dominance see Bourdieu 1991.
15   This Act was later amended by The Witchcraft Suppression Amendment Act (50) of 1970 that made it an offence to 'pretend to exercise supernatural powers'. The WSA (3) of 1957 is available on the website www.justice.gov.za/legislation/acts/1957-003.pdf.

and communities whose lives were subsequently to be negatively affected. Legislation was a particularly effective form of exercising powers of exclusion. Bourdieu comments that,

> Law thus adds its specific symbolic force to the action of the whole set of mechanisms which render it superfluous constantly to reassert power relations through the overt use of force (Bourdieu and Wacquant 1992: 132).

Izangoma and the Witchcraft Suppression Act (3) of 1957

It was during the apartheid era that regional legislation governing the practices of Izangoma was subsumed under the WSA (3) of 1957. Consistent with the anti-witchcraft legislation promulgated across Africa during the colonial years, this Act directly targeted the practices of Izangoma, upon which their economic, social, and symbolic capital rested. The primary offence in the WSA (3) of 1957 reads as follows:

> 1 (a) Any person who imputes to any other person the causing, by supernatural means, of any disease in or injury or damage to any person or thing, or who names or indicates any other person as a wizard.

Although the word 'magic' itself is not used in the Act, much of what constitutes magical practice is clearly criminalized. Offences 1 (d) and 1 (f) read as follows:

> 1 (d) Professes a knowledge of witchcraft, or the use of charms, advises any person how to bewitch, injure or damage any person or thing, or supplies any person with any pretended means of witchcraft.

> 1 (f) For gain pretends to exercise or use any supernatural powers, witchcraft, sorcery, enchantment or conjuration, or undertakes to tell fortunes, or pretends from his skill in or knowledge of any occult science to discover where and in what manner anything supposed to have been stolen or lost may be found, shall be guilty of an offence and liable on conviction.

The Act also makes it illegal to solicit or employ a 'witchdoctor'[16] and provides no exclusion for Izangoma whose function it is to allay and address the fears of bewitchment in their communities. The WSA (3) of 1957 has been cited as contributing to the escalation in witchcraft related violence and persecution; both of which are known to escalate in times of social and political change and insecurity.[17] The tone of denial of witchcraft that inheres in the Act left African communities feeling abandoned to the capricious powers of witches, against whom they had no legal defense. Whatever defensive measures were taken by them would be implemented outside of the formal jurisdiction of colonial law. A unique feature of the WSA (3) of 1957 is the absence of any definitions of terms, leading judges and magistrates to make recourse to the Oxford Dictionary when cases under this Act have come before the courts. The definition inevitably read as a heretic, or 'as one who makes a pact with the devil'. Notwithstanding the criminalization of most of their practices, Izangoma have sustained the vital cultural and symbolic capital embedded in their role and function. Xaba (2007: 322) notes that when Izangoma were banned through various Anti-Witchcraft Acts, the need for divination and healing did not suddenly disappear. In a rapidly changing society, Christian diviners, known as *Abathandazi*, were newcomers to secure positions in the field of spiritual healing. Wearing church garments and developing a clearly defined church structure and liturgy, the *Abathandazi* established a place in a changing religious field, notwithstanding their incorporation of divinatory techniques, and, in many cases, the prescription and dispensing of indigenous medicine, or muthi. *Abathandazi* further heard and responded to the fears of witchcraft in their growing communities. In many instances, the concepts of Satan and the devil that were historically absent in an African cosmology, were included in their preachings. These churches have achieved substantial social recognition, despite their retaining of many indigenous practices that were nevertheless legally criminalized. Such recognition was achieved through the symbolic capital accrued by African priests and healers who recontextualized the meaning of their practices within a Christian religious framework.

Notwithstanding the moral underpinnings of the WSA (3) of 1957 regarding the practices of Izangoma, the fact that numerous political and economic issues lay behind its promulgation, is obscured. As the power relations in colonial territories were irrevocably altered by advancing capitalist Christian

---

16   Clause 1 (c) lists as an offence, anyone who "employs or solicits any witchdoctor, witchfinder, or any other person to name or indicate any person as a wizard".

17   This fact underpins Isak Niehaus' 2001 study on witchcraft in the South African Lowveld.

colonial expansion (Chidester 1992: 20), it was in the profound interest of colonial agents to delimit the influence of Izangoma conterminously with their territorial expansion. What was deemed practice grounded in baseless superstitions became recognized as an agency of resistance against white control. It was from this point that Izangoma were firmly positioned on, or beyond, the newly legislated boundaries of the colonial religious field; a position from where they nonetheless sustained their economic, cultural and symbolic capital in African communities. Notwithstanding that the rationale behind anti-witchcraft legislation extended beyond the religious, the WSA (3) of 1957 was a salient indicator of colonial recognition of the power and influence of the Izangoma in African lives. Legislation was a means of exercising the power of colonists to establish and define the boundaries of the religious field, but ultimately failed to achieve its intended outcomes. Inhering in the legislation was the non-recognition of the coherence and durability of African beliefs and practices as they related to the spirit realm, and to their understandings of mystical causation. Jural authority came from the ancestral realm in a field which continued to establish and monitor its own boundaries accordingly, and not through formal institutional mechanisms. There was a radical disjunction between an African *habitus* and the external structures of the colonial field.

South Africa Pre- and Post-1994

In changing circumstances, it was the Izangoma whose skills and technologies were not only in of even more demand in times of political, social and economic crisis, but were also to prove adaptable in including new threats to individual balance and harmony in a changed world order. Lakoff and Johnson (1980) suggest that metaphors help understand aspects of a concept or thing, at the cost of hiding others, and can be a useful heuristic device to be strategically employed. In a strategy to dissociate their identities from the colonial conflation of their practices with witchcraft and heresy, Izangoma and Izinyanga became known collectively as Traditional Healers from the 1970s, and officially as individuals who "engage in indigenous medical practice" (Devenish 2005: 244). It is as 'healers' that Izangoma find their place on the negotiated boundaries of the two recognized parts to official State law in post-1994 South Africa. The first is the endorsement by the African National Congress (ANC) of Western Roman Dutch Law (within which the WSA (3) of 1957 is located) and the second is new initiatives in the recognition of African law based on the written and unwritten law of traditional communities. Customary Law, as it has come to be known, has constitutional recognition and yet its full application in South Africa has been fraught with difficulties as African systems of thought attempt to meet the requirements of empirically based, rational systems of law. Healing is a term that has salience in a society still in recovery from impacts of its colonial and apartheid history, with alarming statistics in HIV/AIDS, and high unemployment in the face of a European dominated political and social economy. It is at the official level that an herbalist/healer finds a 'magical fit' with the requirements in the medico-legal domains. In the same context Izangoma, as healers, find a way to circumvent attention being focused on the 'how' of what they do. Divinatory practices, the production and supply of magical paraphernalia, and their role in addressing witchcraft concerns and afflictions, are, for the most part, sublimated in official discourses. There are over 200 Traditional Healers Organizations registered with the Companies Act in South Africa. Many practitioners actively distance themselves from registered organizations in order to avoid the rules, regulations and fees imposed on members, and reject what they see as interference in their practices. Many healers comment on how the overtly legal-political focus of organizations is at odds with the work they do in the spirit realm, and caution against the risk that indigenous healing practices and treatments will lose their economic and cultural capital if incorporated in a system alongside Western scientific requirements and method.

The growth of such organizations must also be seen as responses to calls to professionalize the practices of herbalists and diviners in relation to the muthi industry that has burgeoned alongside increasing witchcraft fears, the need for protection in an unpredictable world and the phenomenon of harvesting human body parts in what are known as muthi murders.[18] Meeting requirements has been an easier task for herbalists who dominate the organizations in terms of leadership and number. Their practices conform more easily to the scrutiny of the scientific bio-medicine industry, under whose gaze the spiritual practices of diviners continue to fall short of official recognition. In 2004 the Traditional Health Practitioners Act (35) was passed and, once fully implemented, will make it illegal to practice as a Healer outside of organizational membership. This effort to set parameters for official recognition opens the door to wider abuses in practices as Izangoma fail to meet requirements for uniform standards in their training and practices; both of which find their starting point in the spirit realm. Standing outside of official bodies, the majority of Izangoma exercise a deviance from attempts to regulate the field from the center. Izangoma either refuse, or are unable to, meet the requirements that would legitimate their inclusion in the bio-medical field. Those who do comply with the new 'rules of the game' in meeting requirements, 'play for gain' to secure new positions in the field that they then are able to translate into symbolic

---

18 For more on the pandemic of muthi murders see Minaar (2003).

capital. It is legislation that often confers recognition of legitimacy on bearers of new symbolic capital to exercise this as power to effect changes in the field. In this way, legal mechanisms become a means of conflict resolution over the 'rules of the game' across a number of fields, and inevitably privilege, not necessarily the most numerically significant systems of thought and groups, but those most able to exert their symbolic capital into forms of knowledge/power. Once legislation is in place, objections are relocated from intra-field debates and become the jurisdiction of the courts that are sanctioned to monitor and police observance and transgression of the legal boundaries of any given field.

Sweeping changes were brought to the new Constitution of 1996, in the quest to redress previous inequalities based on race, religion or ethnicity. Although it was the Izangoma who were directly targeted in the WSA (3) of 1957, at no point had they, individually or collectively, lobbied for its repeal. Bourdieu and Wacquant (1992: 25–26) speak of social agents who appear disinterested in aspects of a field, whereas the appearance of disinterest could itself obscure strategies of social agents as to what actions serve their best interests. There was little benefit, and perhaps even potential harm, for Izangoma to engage in official state processes when their divinatory skills for causal explanation were in even more demand in changing circumstances. Witchcraft accusations have historically been known to escalate in times of social change and crisis (van Beek 2007: 292–315) and this was no different in South Africa, from the 1980s in particular. The Izangoma, no longer solely bound to rural communities, found even greater demand for their skills in the midst of transitions to the vagaries of urban living.[19]

Contemporary Paganism

The public emergence of the New Religious Movement,[20] Paganism, in South Africa in June 1996, was directly related to the change in dispensation in the

---

19 In urban centers, in particular, this function was simultaneously assumed by the *Abathandazi*—priests/preachers—in a range of African Initiated Churches. These churches have also been known as African Independent Churches and as African Indigenous Churches, and have their roots in African breakaways from mainstream churches since the late nineteenth century. The two largest are the Zion Christian Church and the Nazareth Baptist Church (Shembe).

20 The designation of Paganism as a New Religious Movement is not without debate, as its development can be traced to individuals and events from the late nineteenth century. In 1996, it can certainly be seen as a new religious movement in South Africa.

country and to the religious freedoms provided for in the new Constitution. Paganism is an umbrella term for a diversity of traditions; the largest of which are the traditions of Wicca and Witchcraft that made their public appearance in Britain after the 1951 repeal of the Witchcraft Act.[21] Wiccan traditions drew features from the pre-Christian mystery religions, from the history of High Ritual Magic and folk magic, and from ancient pagan nature-venerating traditions. At first a small and rather closed community, from the 1970s Wicca/Witchcraft[22] became one of the fastest growing new religions in the West, and was incorporated under the broader term 'Paganism'.[23] The features that unite most Pagan and Witchcraft traditions are the recognition of a) the masculine and feminine aspects of divine reality, b) the belief that the divine is immanent in the natural world, and c) the belief in the efficacy of magical practice for holistic healing and transformation.

Entry requirements to a field form part of the 'rules of the game' and recognition of legitimacy in the field becomes dependent on the extent to which newcomers align themselves with existing power relations in the field, or challenge them through multiple strategies of resistance. The legitimacy of Pagans to assume a position in the religious field in South Africa in the 1990s was secured by constitutional provisions of religious equality, and yet was not necessarily commensurate with recognition and acceptance within the religious field itself. Power relations in a field follow from the ability to mobilize capital and Pagans, as newcomers to the field, were disadvantaged by the relational position of those in incumbent positions who contested their terms of self-identity. Through the colonial and apartheid years, colonial Christian meanings associated with pagans, heretics, witches and magic had acquired legitimacy within and across fields of social life, and resistance to the lifting of these meanings from their imperialist foundations, were visible in all early attempts by Pagans to secure their religious rights in the field. These processes underscored the degree to which the boundaries of the category 'religion' were unresolved and policed in the new democracy, the renewed strategies to sustain the exclusion

---

21 The founding of Wicca is attributed to Gerald B. Gardner who, in the 1950s, published *Witchcraft Today* and *The Meaning of Witchcraft*, after the repeal of this Act. He claimed initiation into a coven of hereditary witches in the New Forest area of Hampshire, England. He used the terms 'witch' and 'wiccan' interchangeably.

22 The words Witch and Witchcraft are capitalized in the Pagan context in order to differentiate them as terms of self-identity from all other uses of the terms.

23 The umbrella term 'Paganism' emerged after Gardner's Wicca was taken to the United States by Raymond Buckland in the 1960s where it found congruence with the developing feminist and environmental movements.

of magic from the category religion, and its perpetual conflation of magic practices with malevolent witchcraft and evil. From the outset, Pagans attracted substantial attention from the media and from many religious quarters. Media attention seldom focused on their identification as Pagans, a term that had been pejoratively applied to indigenous peoples and their practices; as meaning those who had no religion at all. The attention was on their appropriation of the term 'Witch' as one of religious self-identity, and focused largely on what they *do*. Pagan Witches do magic. Seldom, if ever, questioned about beliefs and practices they shared with African traditionalists, they were ubiquitously cast as Satanists in most of their public encounters. In 1999 they participated in the World Parliament of Religion in Cape Town, an event aimed at highlighting the diversity in religious expression in the new South Africa. The organizers of this event—held every six years since 1993—opened invitation to individuals and groups of any religious or spiritual traditions that wished to engage in inter-religious dialogue and understanding. How religion and spirituality are defined at this event is subjective and broad. In an article in a leading newspaper (Sunday Times 12-12-99),[24] Anglican Archbishop Ndungane and the late Chief Rabbi Cyril Harris were quoted as expressing disappointment at the number of 'unorthodox' religious groups allowed to attend. Talking of the Pagans, Archbishop Ndungane was further quoted as saying,

> I don't think that's a religion. As we understand it here and if we look at it in the South African context, people will say it's not on. I think we need to sit down and work out criteria for what needs to be included and excluded. It should not be open to everybody who says they are a religion (ibid.: 1).

According to Chief Rabbi Harris, the presence of Izangoma and Pagans detracted from what the Parliament set out to achieve. He felt that,

> Religions should be democratic, but the wider the definition the more one loses depth—the whole thing becomes an exercise in artificiality. I would much prefer it to be more mainstream (ibid.: 1–2).

The fact that Rabbi Harris included Izangoma along with Pagans in whom he felt should be excluded from the Parliament, initiated Pagan support

---

24 The Sunday Times has the highest circulation of all Sunday newspapers in South Africa.

from Philip Kubukeli, president of the Western Cape Traditional Healers and Herbalists Association, who in retort said of Harris,

> He has still got apartheid. All the religions were invited to take part in the Parliament—they wanted an indication of the religions which we have in the new South Africa (ibid.: 2).

This dialogue engendered a mutual support between two religious groupings through the common denial of their authenticity as religions, and the sustained privileging of mainstream religions in our democratic society. Less than a decade before this exchange Philip Kubukeli would not have held the symbolic capital, as he now did as President of a Traditional Healers organization, to validate his participation in a 'religious' event. New guarantees of religious freedom had, however, enabled him to (re)position himself in the field, and to transfer the commensurate new forms of capital across fields; particularly evidenced in the assertion to have his rights to belief and practice recognized and included in the 'religious field'.

In their endeavors to counter discrimination in both the private and the public sphere, and to secure their rights in terms of the new Constitution, Pagans have found that the opinions of Archbishop Ndungane and Rabbi Harris are not isolated, but operate as normative at the highest organizational levels; including the judicial system, education, law enforcement, social welfare, home affairs, and in the various media. As they moved across social fields, Pagans, who had generally internalized negative expectations of their reception in the public sphere, soon developed strategies to enhance their symbolic capital. The most evident strategies were, 1) to give public emphasis to their identity firstly as a nature religion, 2) to distance themselves historically and theologically from association with Satanism and the Christian devil, and, 3) to associate their traditions with the practices of past and present indigenous peoples who lived in a close and reciprocal relationship with the natural world.

What can be evidenced by the above is a tacit opposition to the dominant discourses on Paganism and Witchcraft in the field. In the context of newly guaranteed religious freedoms, many Pagans actively engaged in public religious and legal challenges from the boundaries of the field. These were challenges to the prevailing definition of religion itself, and a claim to the right to self-identify as Pagans and/or Witches, albeit these terms were imbued with meanings historically and culturally different from how they operated in Africa. It was not until 2007 that Pagans gave attention to the WSA (3) of 1957 that, in part, equally criminalized many of their own practices.

New Legislation Changes the Field

Through the 1990s a small number of Pagans had established relationships with their fellow non-Christian magical practitioners, Izangoma, in order to understand and explore congruencies in their worldview and practices. These included the achieving of trance states, divinatory methods and natural healing technologies. Competing for various recognitions in the legal field, events of 2007 created new alliances, deep divisions, and began to reshape the borders of the religio-legal field. Recourse was made by the State to secular provincial officials to regulate the phenomenon of witchcraft that finds expression in religious, political, economic and social fields in South Africa, through legislation. Authorized by central government "to come up with something" to address the pandemic of witchcraft persecution and violence in the province, the provincial government of Mpumalanga presented a Draft Bill called the Mpumalanga Witchcraft Suppression Bill 2007[25] to replace the existing Act. This Bill ratified, word for word, the offences in the existing Act. The notable change was firstly the inclusion of a definition of terms that included muthi in the definition of witchcraft itself. Witchcraft was defined as,

> [...] the secret use of muti, zombies, spells, spirits, magic powders, water, mixtures, etc., by any person with the purpose of causing harm, damage, sickness to others or their property.

Muthi is the material culture of African magic, and the Draft Bill patently identified muthi practices as complicit in harmful activities increasingly labeled as 'witchcraft'. No definition of Isangoma was provided whilst Inyanga was defined as a healing practitioner, as well as "a person who uses muthi to cause harm, protect from evil spirits and ... who perform spells for good and/or evil purposes". The legal enforcement of this definition is singularly prejudicial to Izinyanga, and compromises the already protracted processes towards the formal recognition of traditional medicine. In addition, as with the WSA (3) that prejudiced Izangoma, it could prove to be a legal loophole within which to conduct certain practices under another name, as had resulted from the Natal Native Code of 1891. Secondly, the Draft Bill also included a code of conduct for Traditional Healers, within which their muthi practices were prominently featured. This pointed directly at "the antithetical relationship between the

---

[25] The Draft Mpumalanga Witchcraft Suppression Bill of 2007 was not officially distributed but can be accessed on http://methodius.blogspot.com/2007/07/mpumalanga-witchcraft-suppression-bill.html.

witch and the healer" (Ashforth 2005: 215), both of whom are recognized to possess the knowledge, power and skill to manipulate the magical and medicinal properties of muthi into a potent supernatural commodity that could cause harm or even death to its consumer. In terms of Bourdieu's Theory of Practice it also indicates the symbolic capital of individuals who hold positions in official organizations to wield this as a power to make a distinction between those who are members of Traditional Healers' associations and those who are not, whilst simultaneously inferring that this distinction further implies that those who belong practice legitimate (good/white) healing magic, and those who don't, are vulnerable to constant suspicion that they, like the witch, are involved in practices that are not only illegal, but are potentially evil (black). Initially sharing discussion of events at a conference in Gauteng,[26] Pagans and the Traditional Healers Organization (THO) both submitted their formal objections to the Draft Bill, as well as their own proposals for new legislation. In the THO objections to the Draft Bill[27] they firstly objected to the specific inclusion of Traditional Healers in the Bill as this directly infers their role in witchcraft accusations and violence. Secondly, they opposed the tone of denial of witchcraft that inheres in both the existing Act and the Mpumalanga Draft Bill and urged the Mpumalanga legislature to,

> Make a paradigm shift from the denial and channel the anger and frustration of the people who have a justifiable belief that they are bewitched within the legal framework.

Acknowledging the challenges for the legal system regarding the recognition of evidence in a court of law, in their objections to the Mpumalanga Draft Bill, the THO stated that,

> The standard of proof beyond reasonable doubt is not recommended in this instance as it may prejudice the parties concerned and fail the objectives of the legislation.

Accordingly, they recommend the establishing and strengthening of traditional witchcraft courts in which all diagnoses of Traditional Healers should constitute *prima facie* proof in any and all allegations of bewitchment brought

---

26   A detailed discussion of this conference can be found in Wallace (2008).

27   The THO objections, that include the two quotations below, were available on http://www.pagancouncil.co.za and on http://www.sapra.org.za until 2008. They were never printed for wider circulation.

before the courts. This creates a conflict between the norms of 'popular' belief and legal state norms, wherein clear rules of evidence apply (Diwan 2004: 287).

Pagans and Traditional Healers have pursued their objections at provincial government level, as well as to Lawyers for Human Rights and to the South African Law Reform Commission. Initially finding allies in their joint rejection of anti-witchcraft legislation, the different grounds on which these objections are based inspired a growing conflict between these two groups of magic practitioners. The two groups failed to reach consensus on a definition of witchcraft, and Pagans strongly objected to the THO's definition of witchcraft in their own proposal for changed legislation wherein it is defined as *'the harmful use of medicine, charms, and/or magic'*.[28] By this point in our history, the term 'witchcraft' had achieved a functional equivalency with a number of Nguni-Bantu words that signified a range of harmful actions, whilst in the vernacular, the term 'magic' continued to refer only to sleight of hand trickery. Its appropriation by those engaged in official debates is interesting as it indicates the complexity Traditional Healers have in claiming the right to collapse the boundaries of religion and magic that had been historically imposed upon them, and simultaneously seeking legal recognition for a distinction to be made between their own magic practices, and the same practices performed with ill-intent. The conflict that developed in the light of these events was rooted in deep divisions over a definition of terms. It also gave rise to new forms of power strategies as Pagans, whose attempts to attain their religious and legal rights in South Africa, would be hindered should the WSA (3) of 1957 either not be repealed, or be replaced with one even more deleterious to their practices. The power strategies exercised by Pagans and the THO are at odds with a blanket application of Bourdieu's notion of 'misrecognition' of symbolic violence by subordinate actors in the field. Neither group were complicit with the attempts of dominant agents to subordinate their rights or discourses in post-1994 developments in the religious or legal fields, but provoked legitimate debates between themselves, and with the shifting centers of the field. Based on the formal objections by Pagans and the THO, the Mpumalanga legislature withdrew the Draft Bill. However, it must be noted that the THO is the single

---

[28] The THO submitted their own draft proposal to challenge the Draft Mpumalanga Bill which they then made available to Pagans who lobbied for a blanket repeal of the WSA (3) of 1957. As a conciliatory gesture to self-defining Pagan Witches, the THO titled their Draft as the Control of Butsakatsi Practices Bill. *Butsakatsi* is a Swazi word for witchcraft/malevolent sorcery but is little known outside of its geographical location. Despite using this word in their title, the word 'witchcraft' is included in their definitions (see above). For more detail see http://www.vuya.net/node/3161.

Traditional Healers association to object to proposed changes to witchcraft legislation. With a lack of cohesion between the many associations, and with varying degrees of transferable capital to influence changes in the legal field, no other organization has passed comment, and the overwhelming majority of registered and unregistered healers remain silent on the issue. Similarly, it is a significant and yet small group of Pagan Witches who pursue their rights at the official level. The larger majority, as with Traditional Healers, is silent and chooses to continue their practices irrespective of strategies to exclude them from legal and religious recognition. Such recognitions require a clear definition of terms and, in this respect, struggles and conflicts that occur between individuals and groups are situated as much on the boundaries, as they are exerted from the center. In the case of the Izangoma, there is enormous economic benefit in practicing their skills without overt attention or interference. In negotiations with Izangoma over anti-Witchcraft legislation, modern Pagan Witches are caught in the dilemma as to what role they could play in the pandemic of witchcraft-related violence. Each group confronts difficulties in how the words 'witch' and 'witchcraft' are operationalized. For Pagan Witches they are terms of self-identity of their spiritual worldview and of their practices. For the THO, as across most of Africa, they are harmful practices associated with a malevolent agency that is always a threat to human lives. Both objectors are members of officially recognized organizations that are not fully representative of their traditions, and yet hold the symbolic capital in the religious field that has the potential to influence legislation. If consensus that the word 'witch' is legally defined as an agent of evil is a prerequisite "rule of the game" in order to effect changes in legislation, then Pagan Witches withdraw their participation. Their strategies instead turn to the rules of the highest court in land; namely the Constitutional Court that endorses the freedom of religion and practice in the Bill of Rights. A disconcerting current development is that some Pagans who are engaged in official debates with Traditional Healers have begun to label the African belief in witchcraft as a base superstition that can be overcome through appropriate education. The fact that the meanings that inhere in each of their definitions of the 'witch' and 'magic', are informed by vastly different cultural and religious histories, is obscured in most of their dialogues. The bearer(s) of mastery over meaning and definition of terms harness a power that can be exercised as symbolic violence. Bourdieu and Wacquant succinctly capture this in the following quotation:

> Even the simplest linguistic exchange brings into play a complex and ramifying web of historical power relations between a speaker, endowed with a specific social authority, and an audience which recognizes this

authority to varying degrees, as well as between the groups to which they respectively belong. What I sought to demonstrate is that a very important part of what goes on in verbal communication, even the content of the message itself, remains unintelligible as long as one does not take into account the totality of the structure of power relations that is present, yet invisible in the exchange (1992: 142–143).

In a changing post-1994 religious field in South Africa there is evidence that symbolic violence is, in many instances, recognized as such, and is openly contested. Complicity and misrecognition are not constants. A growing polycentrism can be evidenced and there are radically altered positions in the field. The mainstream Christian center has been numerically replaced by African Initiated Churches that have absorbed many African traditional beliefs and practices in a new biblical context. One of these was the ubiquitous understanding of a witch as an agent of evil. New and rising demonologies and anti-witchcraft rhetoric emerged in many of these churches and among the African Pentecostal and Charismatic churches that have grown exponentially since 1994. Many traditional African practices have garnered cultural, social and symbolic capital in a number of fields in a progressively Africanized society, and are sustained beyond the category 'African (Traditional) Religion'. Notwithstanding continuing contestation from exclusively Christian perspectives, the strategic employment of these forms of capital by Africans in numerous social fields, has largely enabled them to overcome their colonial interpolations as 'pagans', 'unbelievers' and/or 'heretics'. However, as muthi is increasingly implicated in negative outcomes associated with witchcraft, Izangoma and Izinyanga appear unable to overcome the legal conflation of many of these practices with witchcraft in official discourses. It is the contemporary Pagans who remain on the boundaries of the larger religious field and of most sub-fields. From most Christian perspectives, including those of the African Christian churches, and in the media, Pagans are ubiquitously (although inaccurately) seen as heretics and/or Satanists, and significantly less as healers. Notwithstanding this, they are supported by the constitutional recognition of religious freedom to pursue their aims in all public and institutional domains.

Conclusion

The boundaries between religion and magic in the religious field in a post-apartheid South Africa are indistinct and lack uniformity in intra-field discourses and debates. These difficulties are particularly evident in Africa where the post-colonial recognition of African Religion requires an incorporation of the magical worldview. The role of magic in the phenomenon of witchcraft violence and persecution makes the relationship more complex. Divination, magic and spells are integral to African and modern Pagan religious practice, just as they persist on the boundaries of most religions, both past and present. What is important is that as Traditional Healers join modern Pagans and others in collapsing the religion/magic divide, they too find the need to construct their own 'agents of evil' and their own definition of terms. For modern Pagans in South Africa, the fact that some Izangoma now call to legislate against 'the witch', and claim the magical technology by which such an individual can be identified and punished, adds a new dimension to debates on witchcraft in Africa. Jeffrey Russell (1980: 8) identified three conceptualizations of 'the witch': as a sorcerer, the anthropological approach; the witch as a Satanist, the historical approach; and the modern Pagan Witch. Although Russell's categories are grounded in western history, all three find expression in the religious field in Africa. It must be noted, however, that in most South African contexts, no linguistic or applied distinction is made between witchcraft and sorcery, and that there is a growing tendency to conflate witchcraft with Satanism. Similarly, magic continues to lack recognition as an authentic sub-set of religion from most theological, academic and legal perspectives. Many practices that have been defined as 'magic' are included in the category of 'witchcraft', and they remain a criminal offence in terms of the law. They simultaneously remain central to, or the center of, religio-spiritual practices for a growing majority of South African citizens. Whether such individuals, including Izangoma and Pagan Witches, are healers, religious functionaries, practitioners of evil or heretics depends on subjective interpretation and on the symbolic capital they have accrued in the field. Those who hold dominant positions in the field are most able to translate this advantage into forms of symbolic capital that can be exercised as power and influence, both within and across fields. The WSA (3) of 1957 remains in place and the future will unveil those whose voices will be influential in processes to effect changes in its repeal or replacement. Those whose influence is ultimately successful in the forms in which legislation is drafted and/or amended, will further endorse the legitimacy of their positions and power. Mpumalanga legislature has withdrawn its Draft Bill on objections.

The application of Pierre Bourdieu's theoretical and methodological framework to an analysis of social spaces as 'fields' of specific interests and relationships, is highly applicable in assessing the impact of rapid social change on the structures of a field. Analyzing attendant power relations and strategies in terms of the location (center, margin and boundary) of social actors in the field has salience in studies of domination and subordination, and on the analysis of social mechanisms directed at the inclusion or exclusion of certain individuals and/or groups from full and equal participation in various fields of interest. What constitutes 'religion' at the center of any given field is always culturally and historically contingent. What appears inevitable is that claims to legitimacy, made from any given center, require the marking of a boundary for all that is excluded. At different periods throughout history, magic has occupied the center, has often maintained a comfortable, symbiotic position on the boundary, and at other times, been interpolated as the wholly negative, anti-religious 'Other'. In terms of the law in South Africa, it remains the latter.

In South Africa today, the plurality and diversity of expression in human thoughts and actions that can be situated in, or surrounding, a 'religious field' provide evidence of the ongoing dialectic of privileging 'beliefs' over 'practices'. This privileging is often evidenced in conflicts over definition of terms, is strategically exercised as a power to retain capital resources in the field, and used as a rationale for establishing and policing the boundaries of the field. Legislation has had limited impact on a field wherein individuals and groups exercise their constitutional rights to the freedom of religion and practice, and draw on strategies to secure, challenge and retain the positions they hold within their communities. The individual right to self-define the terms 'religion' and 'spirituality' is affirmed within the law. The unique challenge presented is, however, in order to legally secure the advantages and rights accorded to religion(s) in the Constitution, the onus is on the individual/group to conform to legally worded definitions of what constitutes 'religion'. Those who identify their worldview and practices as 'spiritual' and not 'religious', are consequently excluded from all legally accorded benefits. These are 'the rules of the game' established on inter-field boundaries, and those who comply with the rules for legal advantage, have had to bring many of their beliefs and practices within an officially recognized, more normative, framework. Among Traditional Healers/Izangoma, organizations such as the THO have succeeded in doing so, as have a minority of the more activist Pagan organizations. These processes effect changes to the structure of the field and have the potential to generate new intra- and inter-group conflicts. They also reflect the dynamics of power in social life, as it is those who find *doxa*, or a 'magical fit,' between their *habitus* (subjective dispositions/internal structure) and the semantics and advantage of the legal boundaries of the field (objective structure), who most benefit from their application.

References

Ashforth, Adam. 2005. Muthi, Medicine and Witchcraft: Regulating 'African Science' in Post-Apartheid South Africa? *Social Dynamics* 31 (2): 211–242.

Bourdieu, Pierre. 1977. *Outline of a Theory of Practice*. Cambridge: Cambridge University Press.

———. 1985. The Genesis of the Concepts of Habitus and Field. *Sociocriticism* 2 (2): 11–24.

———. 1991. *Language and Symbolic Power*. Cambridge Massachusetts: Polity Press.

Bourdieu, Pierre, and Loïc J. D. Wacquant. 1992. *An Invitation to Reflexive Sociology*. Chicago: University of Chicago.

Chidester, David. 1992. *Religions of South Africa*. London: Routledge.

———. 1995. Gestures of Dismissal, Policies of Containment: From Denial to Discovery in Southern African Comparative Religion. In *Religion and the Reconstruction of Civil Society*, edited by John de Gruchy and Stephen Martin, 90–108. Pretoria: University of South Africa.

———. 1996. *Savage Systems: Colonialism and Comparative Religion in Southern Africa*. Charlottesville: The University Press of Virginia.

Devenish, Anne. 2005. Negotiating Healing: Understanding the Dynamics Amongst Traditional Healers in KwaZulu-Natal as they Engage with Professionalization. *Social Dynamics* 31 (2): 243–284.

Diwan, Mohammed A. 2004. Conflict between State Legal Norms and Norms Underlying Popular Beliefs: Witchcraft in Africa as a Case Study. *Duke Journal of Comparative and International Law* 14 (2): 351–387.

Dovlo, Elom. 2007. Witchcraft in Contemporary Ghana. In *Imagining Evil: Witchcraft Beliefs and Accusations in Contemporary Africa*, edited by Gerrie ter Haar, 67–92. Trenton NJ: Africa World Press, Inc.

Ellis, Stephen. 2007. Witching-Times: A Theme in the Histories of Africa and Europe. In *Imagining Evil: Witchcraft Beliefs and Accusations in Contemporary Africa*, edited by Gerrie ter Haar, 31–52. Trenton NJ: Africa World Press, Inc.

Gardner, Gerald. 1954. *Witchcraft Today*. Great Britain: Rider and Company.

———. 1959. *The Meaning of Witchcraft*. London: Aquarian Press.

Haar, Gerrie ter, ed. 2007. *Imagining Evil: Witchcraft Beliefs and Accusations in Contemporary Africa*. Trenton NJ: Africa World Press, Inc.

Knott, Kim. 2005. *The Location of Religion: A Spatial Analysis*. London: UK Equinox Publishing Limited.

Kramer, Heinrich, and James Sprenger. 1971. *The Malleus Maleficarum*. New York: Dover Publications, Inc.

Lakoff, George, and Mark Johnson. 1980. *Metaphors We Live By*. Chicago: University of Chicago Press.

Mbiti, J. S. 1990. *African Religions and Philosophy*. London: Heinemann.

Minaar, Anthony. 2003. Legislation and Legal Challenges to Combating Witch Purging and Muti Murder in South Africa. In *Witchcraft Violence and the Law in South Africa*, edited by John Hund, 86–91. Johannesburg: Protea Book House.

Niehaus, Isak. 2001. *Witchcraft, Power and Politics: Exploring the Occult in the South African Lowveld*. Claremont: David Philip Publishers.

Russell, Jeffrey. 1980. *A History of Witchcraft: Sorcerers, Heretics and Pagans*. London: Thames and Hudson Limited.

Sharpe, Eric. 1992. *Comparative Religion: A History*. London: Gerald Duckworth and Co. Limited.

Turner, Bryan S. 2011. *Religion and Modern Society: Citizenship, Secularization and the State*. Cambridge: Cambridge University Press.

Van Beek, Walter E. A. 2007. The Escalation of Witchcraft Accusations. In *Imagining Evil: Witchcraft Beliefs and Accusations in Contemporary Africa*, edited by Gerrie ter Haar, 293–315. Trenton NJ: Africa World Press, Inc.

Wallace, Dale. 2008. Debating the Witch in the South African Context: Issues Arising from the South African Pagan Council Conference of 2007. *The Pomegranate: International Journal of Pagan Studies* 10 (1): 104–121.

———. 2009. The Modern Pagan Witch: Negotiating a Contested Religious Identity in Post-Apartheid South Africa. In *Religion and Spirituality in South Africa: New Perspectives*, edited by Duncan Brown, 124–144. Scottsville Pietermaritzburg: University of KwaZulu-Natal Press.

Xaba, Thokozani. 2007. Marginalised Medical Practice: The Marginalisation and Transformation of Indigenous Medicine in South Africa. In *Another Knowledge is Possible beyond Northern Epistemologies*, edited by Boaventura de Sousa Santos, 317–334. New York: Verso.

CHAPTER 8

The False Messiah—Evangelicalism, Youth and Politics in Eritrea

Magnus Treiber

Other than in most African contexts Evangelical congregations in independent Eritrea have neither been able to establish a permanent presence in public life—by building prestigious churches or maintenance of schools, libraries and social clubs—nor to display accumulated wealth or exert direct political influence (cf. Ukah 2005; Van Dijk 2004; Meyer 1998; Marshall-Fratani 1998; de Boeck & Plissart 2004). Here Evangelical congregations have always been explicitly apolitical, while being identified as a political enemy by the country's post-revolutionary government. This has to do with their perceived foreign sources of influence and character, ideological rivalry and incompatibility on the one hand, and the churches' success among the young urban generation on the other—leading to their decisive role in escape and migration from Eritrea in more recent years. Pierre Bourdieu's theoretical design may help to access and better understand an unusual case.

According to Bourdieu dynamic rivalry between orthodox and heretic forces is a decisive trait of a 'field'. Contents of what is at stake are subject to political praxis, debate and struggle, while an implicit, but general consent on the games' rules, capitals and field positions can be taken for granted. Where orthodoxy tries to keep its monopoly to define, to position and legitimize,

---

* I am indebted to the editors of this book for their helpful comments. A first draft of this article has been presented at the workshop "New Religiosity and Inter-Generational Conflict in Northeast Africa", 26–28 April 2006 at Max Planck Institute for Social Anthropology, Halle/Saale, Germany, organized by Günther Schlee, Data Dea, Christiane Falge. Further research has been conducted within the research project "Dynamic worlds of imagination—learning processes, knowledge and communication among young urban migrants from Eritrea and Ethiopia". The project was situated at the Bayreuth University's Chair of Anthropology, run by Kurt Beck, Délia Nicoué and myself, and formed part of the Bavarian academic research network "Migration and Knowledge" (ForMig 2009–2013). Fieldwork in Asmara/Eritrea took place between 2001 and 2005 in several stays of different lengths, in Cairo/Egypt in 2008, in Khartoum/Sudan in 2009 and 2011 as well as in Shimelba and Addis Ababa/Ethiopia in 2007, 2010 and 2012 (Treiber 2010, 2009, 2007, 2005; Treiber, Tesfaye 2008). Transcription from Tigrinya follows either ITYOPIS journal or commonly used forms.

heretics will advertise their will for power, leadership and succession, presenting themselves as a true alternative and conservative innovators for the field's common good and consistency (Bourdieu 2003). In the Eritrean situation an uneasy entanglement of the political and the religious field seems to unfold: Political orthodoxy clashed with religious heresy over their fields' borderlines, autonomy and capital. Remarkably, both parties possess similar traits and so does their fields' symbolic capital. This may remind of Don Camillo's and Peppone's difficult, but hearty rivalry; here unfortunately lives are at stake.[1] Legitimacy and affection seem to have been converted and transferred from the political into the religious field and are claimed back by political orthodoxy. Fault lines open up between former guerrilla-fighters and Evangelical Christians (perceived counter-revolutionaries), between collectivist and individualist thought, between the older and the younger urban generation and between national and international actors.

While Swedish missionaries introduced the Protestant Lutheran faith into Eritrea in the late 19th century, the more radical Evangelical congregations date back to the presence of US-American soldiers and missionaries in Asmara during the 1960s. Then a number of smaller house churches had been established, which again lost influence after the Ethiopian revolution in 1974 and Ethiopia's subsequent turn to the Soviet Union (cf. Conrad 2005: 223–224).[2] Post-independence missionary initiatives revived different congregations during the 1990s after decades of war, including Adventists, Pentecostals, Jehovah's Witnesses, followers of Rhema-Gospel- or Kale-Hiwot-Churches and others.[3] In Asmara these were usually referred to with the depreciative term *pentes*— an expression already used in the late 1970s, when Ethiopia's new military leadership consolidated power and campaigned "against 'foreign' religions and their Ethiopian converts" (Donham 1999: 143, cf. Hepner 2003).[4]

---

1 Giovannino Guareschi, *Don Camillo und Peppone*, Roman. [1948] Salzburg 1950.
2 Eritrea's national territory is the historical product of Italian colonization (1890–1941). The country was federated with imperial Ethiopia after WWII and annexed in 1962. The Ethiopian revolution of 1974 did not end the already ongoing civil war. As Moscow eventually supported the new Ethiopian government, fighting intensified instead. The Eritrean People's Liberation Front (EPLF) won the country's independence only in 1991 (Killion 1998: xxiii–xli; Quehl 2005).
3 Amnesty International: Rundbrief Eritrea 2003: 12.
4 Ethiopia's then revolutionary government—known as the Derg—ousted Emperor Haile Selassie from power in 1974. Its campaign against 'foreign' *pente*-congregations during the late 1970s and early 1980s included the Lutheran Mekane Yesus Church, which had already been banned by Haile Selassie from the traditionally orthodox highlands (cf. Launhardt 2005). Thus Protestantism in Ethiopia was soon identified with political opposition from the state's

One of my first contacts with Evangelical youth occurred when I met Samuel, a young Pentecostal, at a bus stop in summer 2001. I was trying to guess what the title of the book he was reading might mean: "Prepare for war"[5]—an eye-catching title, only six months after the ceasefire following the devastating Ethiopian-Eritrean border war (1998–2000, cf. O'Kane 2006). He showed me that he was up to date with Evangelical ideology, using the occasion for his missionary intentions: Human beings are separated from God by sin; only the uncompromising shift towards Jesus can save one's soul. The official aim of Evangelical missionary activity is to convert as many people as possible regardless what their current faith might be (the harder to win, the better), in order to establish a morally disciplined world pleasing God. The world, as it is, is to a large extent under Satan's influence, or even control, so that all missionary engagement has actually to be seen as a war against evil. Being fully committed to his faith and demanding radical conversion and clear social separation Samuel had to delay any discussion on the topic to the period following my conversion, so that we have not been able to establish a relationship of mutual trust and further interest: "Magnus", he told me with a shake of the head— to my dismay quite publicly in Asmara's City Park—"I love you, but devil is behind you!"

Jersilem, a young student of arts at that time, was more open and showed me that a somehow traditional past was just one ideological enemy of the *pentes* and probably not even the most important today. The phenomenon of Evangelicalism in Eritrea is intertwined with national policy and cannot be understood without it. When asking Jersilem (an alias name she chose by herself) about her social environment she developed a categorization of 'influenced people', open-minded, showing external influences in clothing, language, life-style and equal treatment of men and women versus 'not influenced people', afraid to 'lose their culture'. Education for Jersilem was not only

---

periphery. In Eritrea Swedish missionaries' had even been temporarily expulsed during the late Italian period. However, the Lutheran congregation in Eritrea is traditionally rooted in its own neighborhood *Geza Khenisha* in Asmara. As Protestantism offered education to the urban elites throughout much of the 20th century, a considerable part of Eritrea's intelligentsia, including EPLF-cadres, has been of Lutheran faith. A famous example was Wolde-Ab Wolde-Mariam (1905–1995), an early intellectual promoting Eritrean independence already in the late 1940s (cf. Killion 1998: 170–175 Education; 349–359 Protestant Christianity; 430–434 Wolde-Ab Wolde-Mariam). The Lutheran church is too much involved in Eritrean history for today's *pentes*. In fact the Lutheran Church is represented in today's official Eritrean Church Council (further comprising the Roman Catholic Church, the Orthodox Tewadho Church and the Islamic Mufti of Eritrea) and is not considered a *pente* congregation.

5   Rebecca Brown, *Prepare for war*, 1993.

a question of access, but a choice which could be accepted or refused; education was the key to social change towards tolerance and individualization (or as van Dijk would put it "individual self-making", 2004: 171), liberating oneself from material dependence and the older generations' symbolic supremacy.

Jersilem considered education to be the gap between her friends, student colleagues as well as congregation members, and—in her eyes—the brutally stupid, narrow-minded and finally uncivilized rest of the Eritrean society. The *Shaebia*-government of course was the first to be blamed. *Shaebia* is Arabic for 'popular' and has been the vernacular name for the Eritrean People's Liberation Front (EPLF) during the liberation struggle (cf. Pool 2001). Until today Eritrea's post-war government is led by the former guerrilla leader, President Isayas Afeworki, while the EPLF has transformed itself in 1994 into the People's Front for Democracy and Justice (PFDJ), the country's single political party.

Jersilem expressed her contempt and hatred quite openly: In a café mostly attended by former guerrilla fighters and government officials she insisted to show me that her perception was appropriate, suddenly blustering "We are all living in jail. Look at them, they are so stupid, they cannot even understand what I am saying. You can say about them whatever you like as long as you say it in English." Jersilem did not differentiate between the former EPLF, the present-day PFDJ, government authorities, the Eritrean Defense Forces (EDF) or the officially independent mass unions like the National Union of Eritrean Women (NUEW) or the National Union of Eritrean Youths and Students (NUEYS), she subsumed them all under a collective subject, 'they'[6] or *shaebia*. Finally, to establish a clear separation between herself and 'them' she converted to a *pente* denomination, the so-called Memphis-Church, in summer 2001. Self-confidently she chose to open up for an ideological 'influence from outside'—at the same time healing and progressive in her perception, foreign and alien in *shaebia's* view. In spring 2002 these *pentes*, at least twelve different religious denominations, were suspended until officially registered with detailed documents on membership and funding. Since then none of them has been re-approved.

---

6 With the personal pronoun in the distanced 3rd person plural, Jersilem uses the same collective subject to speak about the Eritrean government, that was commonly used to speak about the Ethiopian government before liberation. Indeed, circumstances of daily life today and then show some striking similarities. See e.g. Alemseged Tesfai's character Kidisti in his play "Le'ul", documenting Eritrean urban life during the Derg period: "Of course, in the Haile Selassie years, when Asrate Kassa was the governor here, I used to earn one Birr and ten cents a day at the time... but let me tell you, I used to buy more with that meagre amount than what I buy with the 1.90 Birr *they* throw at us today. Sweat and backaches through winter and summer and what do we get? Fines, deductions, no food on the plates, hungry children.... This is no life, Le'ul." (Italics by M. T., Tesfai 2002: 140).

National Myth and Project

The official Eritrean national myth is a narrative on 30 years of liberation struggle, lasting from 1961 to 1991. The EPLF, its victorious party, campaigned for a self-relying, self-confident, secular and gender-equal nation, independent from Ethiopian and international imperialism. In the local language Tigrinya its committed and disciplined freedom fighters were celebrated as *yikealo*—'those who can do everything'—or *tegadelti*—'problem solvers'. Independence, peace and the promised future pay-off were the outcome of their dedication, sacrifice and martyrdom.

In the perception of the Eritrean leadership, however, the struggle has never ended. The national project is still at stake, independence and development have to be defended and fought for as in the days of the armed struggle—an ideological strategy borrowed from Mao Tse-Tung (cf. Pool 2001; Mao Tse-Tung 1967; Treiber and Abdela 2008). Step by step alternative political voices had to give way to a historiography highlighting the EPLF's finally successful revolutionary nationalism, claiming to represent Eritrea once and for all (cf. Araya 1997; Gilkes 1991). In September 2001 the former guerrilla leader and president of the state, Isayas Afeworki, consequently swept away emerging internal rivals and established autocratic control over the national political field by force. One of the first measures to ensure the continuation of national struggle after independence has been the creation of a national service in 1994, in Tigrinya-language *agelgulot*, demanding every man and woman between 18 and 40 to undergo 6 months of military training and 12 months of civil work in government institutions or in countrywide development projects.

In the official Eritrean terminology these national service conscripts are called *warsay*, literally meaning 'emulating' or as a noun 'inheritors'. Their educational preparation by the Eritrean leadership to take over the national project in future is far more than just symbolic. Being Eritrean in this perception means always to place the interest of the nation above religion, ethnicity or individual needs and to be ready to be steeled in the self-discipline and asceticism the heroic EPLF-guerrilla once proved in the field—far away from the capital (Riggan 2013; Müller 2009; cf. Pool 2001: 105–131). Lessons to train and incorporate those values and thus to produce a fitting habitus could not be harsh enough. Subjectified and objectified structures should perfectly correlate in Eritrea's political field.

> As the Government is undertaking a major campaign to provide nationals with knowledge, skill and professional competence, the public itself needs to meet certain obligations. We must realize that these human resources-oriented projects will play a big role in improving the people's

standard of living in the not-too distant future. [...] Progress and advancement are the fruits of toil and knowledge. So in order to improve our lives and catch up with the developed nations, let us work hard and eagerly to seek knowledge.[7]

Current Eritrean leadership could well be considered a communion ("Bund"); it claims to represent the whole older *yikealo*-generation—now in their fifties and sixties—and their collective identity-molding field experiences. In its propaganda a seemingly homogeneous as well as continuous class situation ("Klassenlage", Mannheim 1978: 44–49) is evoked. This leads to the problem of transfer of power, culture and resource control to the successive generation. The (inexorably ageing) Eritrean leadership obviously tries to safeguard its monopoly of legitimate physical and symbolic violence over territory and population and to extend it into the future. To this end an official, sanitized and standardized memory of EPLF's struggle is promoted and a permanent foreign threat is staged. Anyone pulling her/himself out of the ongoing national project—that claims body and mind of the individual and subsumes every action and every thought—therefore has to be considered a traitor to the nation, of its ideals, values and its *semaetat*, its 'martyrs' in its two large-scale wars. In combination with imperialist enemies from the outside treason from within (e.g. supposed collaboration with foreign and hostile powers or institutions) is the main danger of a guerrilla movement. Therefore not only the constant reference to the past gains a legitimizing effect, so do current restraints, harsh persecution of political opponents, strict ideological discipline, control of every private or public space and place, full dedication to the national project and so forth. In a word guerrilla-politics is continued.

Crackdown on Evangelical Churches

After eradicating any formal and open political opposition from public life—especially in September 2001 with two well-prepared crack-downs on dissidents and journalists, emphasizing the damage these would inflict on the nation's security, sovereignty and pride—the state's security authorities seemed to concentrate on another ideological enemy who managed to

---

7 Shabait (*Ministry of Information*): Human Resources Development. A priority of Warsay-Yikaalo Campaign. 05.02.2004 (www.shabait.com). See also Daniel Mebrahtu: National Service—the facts. In: Eritrea Profile. 04.06.94 or Adem Berhan: Sahel and Sawa, Eritrea's Symbols of Pride. 05.02.2004 (www.shaebia.org).

attract more youths than the loyalist National Union of Eritrean Youths and Students (NUEYS) could have ever dreamed of, especially during and after the war years: Evangelical churches, the so-called *pentes*. This outcome was not entirely unexpected. Soon after independence, if not already during liberation struggle, Islamic fundamentalists and Jehovah's witnesses have more or less been openly declared public enemies for being actively or passively opposed to the *shaebia*-state, and therefore excluded from the national project as early as 1977,[8] persecuted, incarcerated, executed and, in case of the Jehovah's witnesses, stripped off their civil rights (Mekonnen & van Reisen 2014; Tronvoll 2009: 90–105; Hepner 2014; Tronvoll 1996: 23–67).

Since spring 2002, secret prayer meetings as well as public weddings have been brutally assaulted by police and the military. Pupils have been locked up in shipping containers or underground cells for the possession of a bible. In 2011 Amnesty International estimated some 3,000 mostly young Evangelical Christians, pastors and laymen as well, to be in prison.[9] Despite the government's denials global Evangelical organizations have documented such incidents and arrests as persecution of the Christian faith, and the United States Foreign Secretary was successfully urged by the United States Commission on International Religious Freedom to declare Eritrea a 'country of particular concern' since 2004.[10] International actors obviously try to safeguard the autonomy of the religious field and its experts' legitimacy, whereas government representatives regard pastors and followers as political players and prosecute them accordingly.

The *shaebia*-government consequently attacked an officially apolitical religious movement as fundamental political opposition—denying commitment to the national project, while loyal to an ideological and imperialist alternative. Partly similar symbolic features were occupied such as martyrdom, full commitment to an invulnerable leader and uncompromising morality—Bourdieu reminds us that efforts for separation might be especially strong, where

---

[8] "Strictly oppose all the imperialist-created new counter-revolutionary faiths, such as Jehovah's Witness, Pentecostal, Bahai, etc." EPLF 1977: 163. 1987's 2nd National Democratic Program just mentions the separation from religion and state, cf. EPLF 1987: 174; Hepner 2003.

[9] Amnesty International: Report 2011. Zur weltweiten Lage der Menschenrechte. Frankfurt/Main 2011: Eritrea. (www.amnesty.de/amnesty-international-report-2011). Also: Amnesty International: ERITREA. Religious Persecution. AFR 64/013/2005. 07.12.05 (web.amnesty.org/library/print/ENGAFR640132005).

[10] U.S. Department of State, Bureau of Democracy, Human Rights, and Labor: International Religious Freedom Report. 07-12/2010. 13.09.2011: Eritrea (www.state.gov/g/drl/rls/irf/2010_5/168406.htm).

similarities and proximities are most obvious (1990: 137). Finally, *pentes* in Eritrea have largely become attractive to the young generation. The successful integration of young people in their twenties and thirties fundamentally subverted *shaebia's* generational policy and mission.

From outside, however, the persecution of the *pentes* might nevertheless look irrational. *Pentes* in Eritrea object to *shaebia's* revolutionary nationalism, but they are neither a direct and concrete danger to Eritrea's authoritarian leadership nor do Evangelical congregations generally object to the idea of statehood and secular government. To some extent the Eritrean persecution resembles revolutionary Ethiopia's campaign against *pentes* in the late 1970s. But in contrast to historic Ethiopia, where Evangelicals identified with the revolution, hoped for social modernization and change and were among the first to take office in the new revolutionary organizations and campaigns (Donham 1999), the young people joining the Eritrean *pentes* are disillusioned by the Eritrean national revolution and its outcomes, they share other generation-formative experiences[11] than the revolutionists and have other ideas about life in modern times. Bourdieu describes symbolic capital as a credit or advance, based on common belief and trusting support (1990: 120). For the young generation *sheabia* lost its legitimation and potential to guarantee for it.

Revolutionary Prophecy and the Mergence of the Political and the Religious

In the first years after the border war (1998–2000), Eritrea's revolutionary nationalists have not been ousted, but were seriously challenged by a young élite and its rigid alternative values and moral. Attempting to educate and orientate the next generation *shaebia* and its once broad base of supporters among the parents' generation tried to reify their own temporal group experiences and identity from the days of the liberation struggle into eternal values of national culture, ruling far into the future. From their perspective the urban

---

11   Mannheim speaks of "Erlebnisschichtung", 'layer of experiences', to describe the different perception and importance of historical events and experiences for different age-groups, Mannheim [1928] 1978: 46–47. While the border war with Ethiopia 1998–2000 was a new and dramatic experience for the young generation at the frontline, it might not have been much more than a well-known reiteration of the past for the yikealo-generation in the army. Also Bourdieu and Bude highlight the formative character of early experiences considering development and consolidation of a specific habitus or biographical self-evaluation, cf. Bourdieu 1990: 60–61; Bude 1984.

based *pentes* could clearly be identified as attacking heretics in the nation's political field. The Evangelical pastors and their followers, however, tried to evade this dangerous stranglehold and presented themselves as players in the religious and therefore indisputably different field, craftily denying any rivalry in this world. Maybe less witty but in control of the guns, the political leaders had already and since long diagnosed common objects of interests nevertheless. As the guerrilla war for liberation could not be won without a strong and unifying ideology, a charismatic political prophecy, *shaebia* conquered the religious field and merged the political and the religious field (cf. Bourdieu 1987: 127–128; Weber 1922: 140–148). In addition independence did not bring overall economic prosperity, but renewed endurance rallying, rendering the promised goods of political salvation into quite abstract and quasi-religious hopes and beliefs (cf. Bourdieu 1987: 133; 1991: 22–23). Thus the religious field could simply not be allowed autonomy.

Other religious denominations—the Orthodox Church, Islam, Lutheranism and the Catholic Church—also got sooner or later in the government's way, but were intimidated and played off against each other more easily and were then pushed aside into a less important subfield, where they could provide mere religious cult and care for religious needs under the always suspicious eyes of the political leaders. Also Evangelical pastors did not mix political and religious spheres. It was the striking success and growth of Evangelical communities that openly challenged the government and made *shaebia's* prophecy look profane and out-dated. Its overall ideological monopoly and authority was shattered, while Evangelical missionary activities became more and more self-confident and ostensible. A competition for the allegiance of the youth, moral and life-style and finally on the social order and its legitimacy itself was kicked off and *shaebia* obviously was afraid to loose. Its' symbolic violence— the capacity to define what is worthy of acknowledgement—successively failed. In the name of the revolution, political martyrdom and national independence the government resorted to physical violence.

Views from Below

There are different views on the daily reality in Eritrea and *shaebia's* propaganda is not the most popular among them. Torture, lawlessness, rape and extrajudicial executions form an essential part of other narratives not only given by the worldwide Evangelical movement, but by field informants (Bozzini 2011, Hirt, Mohammad 2013, Hepner 2009; Treiber 2009, 2007, 2005; Treiber and Tesfaye 2008), by refugees' self-help initiatives (e.g. Eritrean Anti-Military Initiative in

Frankfurt/Main, established by political asylum-seekers) or in regular reports by Amnesty International, Human Rights Watch, Reporters Without Borders and others.

Above all national service is considered an existential burden. Demobilization age for women seems to be in their mid-twenties; for men it has been moved well beyond 40. Their pay is 60 to 600 Nakfa (roughly 5 to 50 Euro) depending on their assignment. Most of the conscripts remain in the military, some for more than a decade now, isolated in remote army camps and at the arbitrary and high-handed military officers' mercy, bored, devilled and without future prospects. Fearsome stories of violence, rape and suicide are common and shared by the whole young generation as common and collective knowledge beyond differing group and milieu identities (Mannheim 1978: 38–40). The Warsay-Yikealo-Campaign's 'development projects' are more likely to be forced labor on commercial farms owned by the PFDJ and corrupt military commanders (Kibreab 2009). Despite draconian punishment like torture or execution, desertion from national service is a common phenomenon. Between 2001 and 2005 hundreds of illegal young people were still hiding in Asmara, but illegal emigration has increased tremendously. Since then hundreds of thousands of *warsay* have fled to Sudan or Ethiopia.[12] These hideaway outcasts and deserters are called *koblīlom*, estrays, in Tigrinya, or *kidaʿit*, traitors.

The more fortunate few are those who enjoyed an academic or college education and have been assigned to the capital's bureaucracy in Asmara, which offers all the choices and possibilities of urban life—despite poor pay and a material impotence that barely sustains family life or academic education, and that demands daily subordination and incapacitation in government offices under the allegedly omnipresent control of the secret service. For these assignments in urban areas or nearby family homes the payment of high bribes seems to have become normal. It is in the few urban centers, especially Asmara, that the Evangelical faith and community is still attractive to Eritrean youths. Today, students are absent, as the university has been incrementally shut down. Since educational reforms in 2003 (cf. Riggan 2009) students have been concentrated in the Warsay-Yikealo-School in Sawa-military camp or in down-graded and decentralized technical colleges, which are headed by military officials and at first were surrounded by fences and armed guards (Müller 2009: 65–67; 2012: 455–456).

---

12   Concerning Eritrean refugees the latest UNHCR Statistical Yearbook (2013) gives a figure of 337,256 unsettled cases in the category 'total population of concern'. During the last decade between 10,000 and 20,000 new Eritrean refugees have been registered yearly in Sudan as well as in Ethiopia, despite the Eritrean government's 'shoot to kill'-policy.

Becoming *pente* is not the only choice to join a specific milieu or concrete group, young urbanites also meet in respective public places such as certain bars or cafés in order to create and to celebrate their own life-style milieus and life concepts, e.g. pretending an upper-class life-style in chic bars, which these *warsay* and *koblïlom* are not really able to realize (Treiber 2010, 2005). "It's just politics..." was a sentence I often heard among young urbanites during my field work in Asmara between 2001 and 2005, mostly expressed in a resigned voice, often combined with a shrug of the shoulders. Politics is considered a sphere of danger, where you should not burn your fingers by getting to close to the one or the other side. There is not a lot the individual can actually do to express his or her exasperation with the government's policy, so young urbanites try to ban it as far as possible from their daily lives, while others become interested in Evangelical faith (cf. Clapham 1988: 155–156).[13]

Different from other African contexts *pente*-followers here form part of a whole generation of deprived youths, forced into a national service of unpredictable duration, that leaves them dependent and poor. While Eritrean propaganda claims body and life of its citizens for higher ends, corruption and arbitrariness have become a well-known reality. By aiming at full and unlimited commitment, propaganda ends up planting the seed of resistance and subversion deep into the young generation's consciousness and habitus.[14] The *pentes'* success in mobilizing such frustrated youths even after having been banned is watched jealously by the government, unable to interest youths in its own youth movement. Although the remaining leadership is still called *shaebia* (Arabic for 'popular') the former guerrilla front, the EPLF, does not exist

---

13   Abbebe Kifleyesus' article on Pentecostalism in Asmara ("Cosmologies in Collision") is itself a good example of what can and what cannot be said under dictatorial rule. Kifleyesus acknowledges an experienced "gap between [...] dream and actual futures possible" (2006: 79) as well as "socioeconomic transformations and their repercussions" (88), but refrains from of identifying Evangelicalism as one way to express critique and address the Eritrean government. Instead he portrays government policy as a necessary attempt to restore peace and social harmony: "The majority of traditional Christians in Asmara and in other parts of the country consider Pentecostalism a foreign and dangerous presence and an unwanted competitor to the orthodox Tāwahdo and Catholic churches. Many Eritreans of these denominations have encountered converts in crowds spilling onto the streets from Pentecostal churches, prayer houses, and tent revivals. These are common scenes in many communities and neighborhoods in Asmara, and they reinforce the impression of Pentecostalists as intrusive" (87).
14   Discussing political jokes about Eritrea's government Bozzini stresses, however, that joking entails both, hidden critique and acceptance of seemingly unchangeable circumstances (2013).

anymore. On the one hand it has been formally transformed into the a political party, on the other a lot of its former leading or rank and file members simply gave up or were marginalized, went into exile or prison—much to the benefit of Isayas Afewerki and his ruling clique.

Of course Eritrea's different Evangelical congregations are open for converts of all age-groups; they may even rival for members and lack a unifying collective agenda. However, as they contrast the government's explicit generational policy and its flagging 'mass organizations' *pentes* at least appear to be an effective youth movement.

Alternative Evangelicalism

Pente churches have always claimed with ostentation a solely religious and apolitical motivation. Joining the *pentes* meant—at least until their ban in 2002—one possibility to express open, and in contrast to PFDJ dissidents or the banned students' union, apolitical opposition to the national project and to politics and policy in general. At the same time the *pentes* have not become just another splinter group of Eritrea's exiled political opposition, which is rarely hoped for as an alternative. The *pentes* do not aim at profane political power and access to corrupt resource distribution, but offer an attractive program, regardless of their respective denomination:

First of all, the churches have marked a generation gap. They allowed educated young urbanites to actively and collectively free themselves ideologically and socially from 'father's rule' and paternalism. Amaniel, a young deacon of a refugee church community in Khartoum explained to me in September 2009, how religion had become a major topic of debate within his family. In his adolescence he started to express doubts about the Christian character of his parents' orthodox belief, which he perceived as religion for the illiterate, close to paganism. In fact, Ethiopian (and post-1991 Eritrean) Orthodox clergy, always supportive of the state and mostly close to the respective political power in place, had never experienced Catholicism's traumatic schism and subsequent reforms (cf. Haile 2005, Red. Encyclopaedia Aethiopica. 2005). Humble subordination to an authoritative priest, silent and awesome adoration of colorful icons, imperative belief in holy water, strict liturgical rituals, angels and the Mother of God did not answer Amaniel's questions (cf. Conrad 2005: 227). "They did not really know the Bible", he told me. Reading for them meant worshipping the book as any other sacred item, not trying to understand its spirit through reflection, discussion, rationalization and consequent practice (cf. Bourdieu 1991: 6–7). Evangelicalism for him and other curious and motivated disciples provided an alternative, constitutive and participatory learning process.

Second, a certain therapeutic effect of collective gospel singing and praying should not be underestimated in a military dictatorship, which forced its youths into a full-scale war without providing any kind of psychotherapeutic help thereafter, but a national propaganda keeping the danger of the next war alive.

Furthermore the *pente*-congregations offer to their members a social community life with strong community bonds shaped by mutual trust and reliability, a community always promised by *shaebia* on the national level but never realized. While *shaebia* has to blame the external enemy, Ethiopia, for Eritrea's lack of development and democratization, the *pentes* stay clean, straight and uncorrupted in a daily reality of despair, corruption, repression, torture and death.

Jersilem approves that being part of such a community makes her feel respected, balanced and in a way self-contented. The official ban, the danger of meeting in private, the risk of arrest and torture, considered by Samuel as the natural and real martyrdom Christians have to face, confirm Jersilem in her perception of 'them' as narrow-minded, intolerant, uneducated or as she would say "not influenced"—hinting already to an outside world, which also she finally seeks to emigrate.[15]

As Ethiopia's military regime did after Somalia's invasion in 1977 (Donham 1999: 142–150; Zewde 2002: 249), *shaebia* in fact tried to use the Christian Orthodox Tewadho Church as a centralized institution with authoritarian tradition in control of symbolic resources.[16] After independence pro-Ethiopian clergymen had already been silenced,[17] however unprecedented disapproval was provoked, when patriarch Abune Antonios was sacked in 2006 after criticizing *shaebia's* influence undermining his position.[18] The *pentes* proved to be much more difficult to control. A decentralized organizational structure,

---

15 "[Persecution] drove them [the Ethiopian pentes during the Derg period] underground (people began to worship in their own houses) and the persecution played exactly into evangelical narratives and stories about how [the] Bible prophecized that the faithful would be persecuted, particularly as the end of the world neared. State repression actually made religion more deeply meaningful." Donham, Donald: Comments on Halle Conference. Unpublished Document. 05/2006.

16 For a parallel to the Soviet Union under Stalin see Clapham 2006: 237.

17 The Derg as well as *shaebia* were hoped to value Islam, however the Somali invasion in Ethiopia and the threat posed by jihad insurgency to Eritrea didn't lead to this effect.

18 Letter from His Holiness Abune Antonios, Patriarch of the Eritrean Orthodox Tewahdo Church. 22.01.06. (news.asmarino.com).

relative independence, and transnational links to Evangelical congregations and religious media networks on the global level helped the *pentes* to survive the recent ban and subsequent persecution, despite constant danger and arrests. The extremely flexible communities do not need a fixed church building or a lot of mobile or immobile ritual material. As a church is where the congregation meets, any place can be turned into a religious space. So the clandestine meetings go on. Closure and strict loyalty at least in the inner circles keep the communities widely spy-free, and the government has to rely on neighborhood denunciation, for which grain and sugar have been granted.[19] This technique had already been used during the liberation struggle to find political opponents or jihad-members.

Although the pentes are themselves an urban phenomenon, they are not only mistrusted by the unpopular *shaebia* government, but in fact also by large parts of the urban population (cf. Kifleyesus 2006: 87). Their rigid morality is considered arrogant, declaring life concepts and experience before conversion null, void and evil. Their strict assimilation policy demands as much commitment as the *shaebia* propaganda, and tries to cut believers out of their former social environment, bringing the political (and generational) conflict as well as the security risks into the family. Rumors in the neighborhood damage not only the young follower's reputation but also affects parents and relatives. Israel told me that his parents with whom he used to live in *Geza Banda*, a middle-class quarter of Asmara, asked him insistently not go to church any more or at least stop singing gospel songs in the house, as the neighbors would start to talk about it. When he tried to move to a room of his own then, he faced explicit discrimination, as no one wanted to rent a room to a *pente*. Israel was one of around 70,000 individuals to have been deported from Ethiopia to Eritrea during the border war from 1998–2000 and chose to convert already in Ethiopia because of a personal crisis and alcohol abuse. Ironically, he found himself confronted with the rigid morality and the demand for full religious commitment when having a beer and smoking a cigarette with other young deportees in Asmara's well-known Bar Diana. Suddenly a delegation from his congregation came in to denounce him publicly—a story his friends told me in confidence. Obviously he felt embarrassed. After all, this example shows that the *pentes'* assimilation policy is also just a project in the making. The heretic party is also trying "to impose faith" (Bourdieu 1991: 21), seeking control over the individual, her/his social environment and her/his needs, but cannot always fully succeed. Believers such as Israel or Jersilem use religion for their

---

19   Compass Direct: Evangelicals face Neighborhood 'Spying', More Arrests. 13.02.2004. (www.compassdirect.org).

own purposes, benefits and well-being and such keep certain independence after conversion. This is also the starting point of the Eritrean government, forcing arrested *pentes* to make vital decisions.

> Fifty-seven young male and female members of minority Christian churches are being held in metal shipping containers at Sawa military camp in western Eritrea. [...] The 57 prisoners of conscience are school students from all over Eritrea who were sent to Sawa Military Camp in western Eritrea for a compulsory 3-month summer course under new pre-National Service education regulations. They were arrested in the camp for possessing bibles in the Tigrinya language (although this is not illegal) and are imprisoned in metal shipping containers. [...] They are being pressurized to sign statements to abandon their religion and rejoin the majority Eritrean Orthodox Church. Five others arrested with them were allowed to go free when they signed the statements (Amnesty International. September 2003).[20]

In contrast to Amnesty International's allegation, Eritrean youths know well enough that the possession of the Bible and the Quran in military camps is strictly forbidden, regardless of whether it may be an official restriction or not. Whosoever acts against this rule can clearly be identified as a religious fundamentalist and, as has been illustrated in this contribution, an ideological opponent. In its Maoist tradition *shaebia* sometimes accepts excuse and self-criticism so they set the arrested students mentioned above under pressure,[21] who then face an ideological dilemma. For them, deciding pragmatically and signing whatever to be freed immediately means betraying their faith, their Messiah and their community, while they should take 'destiny' as their 'choice' (Bourdieu 1991: 19).[22] More dogmatic prisoners will exert ideological and social pressure.

---

20 Amnesty International: ERITREA 57 male and female students—members of minority Christian churches. AFR 64/006/2003. UA 269/03. 18.09.03. Cf. Amnesty International: ERITREA: 75 evangelical Christians (37 female, 38 male). AFR 64/001/2006. UA 40/06. 17.02.06.

21 After temporary arrest one of Donham's interviewees accused of being pente during the Derg's persecution campaign in Ethiopia also mentions that he was ordered to sign a statement renouncing his faith (cf. Donham 1999: 145–146).

22 Originally Bourdieu refers to the "exaltation of asceticism" (1991: 19); however I found his wording also fitting here. After all, imprisonment entails asceticism—especially in cases of religious persecution.

Two years after her conversion and still in Asmara, Jersilem argued more radically in our discussions. She openly expressed her will to help topple President Isayas Afewerki, whom she called "the false Messiah", referring to the widespread sympathy towards him and his seemingly charismatic leadership. Especially women used to express their support enthusiastically, Jersilem explained, albeit this phenomenon seems to decline in urban centers during recent years.[23] In this perception the imprisoned students have to side with the 'false Messiah', a representative of the Devil himself, to get free. This is a sin that is hard to forget in one of those small religious communities to which one promised loyalty and often gave up family and former friends, irrespective of moral self-reproaches.

In the given political situation the *pentes* within Eritrea cannot promise economic success and prosperity to young and educated urbanites as there are few available and accessible resources, such as commodities or career networks. In contrast to present self-confidence and public activities of Pentecostal communities in neighboring Ethiopia or Sudan as well as their wealthy counterparts in West Africa, *pente* congregations within the country can only try to impart moral cleanliness where the blueprints of previous generations do not serve as a role-model. Outside the national territory and boundaries the situation is different.

Outbound Migration

Following Bourdieu, fields disclose current positions and objective strategies of its actors, who subjectively do not necessarily have to be aware of their inherent contribution to the field, its shape and dynamic (Bourdieu 2003: 127). Thus, the tense and difficult interrelation of the political and the religious field in Eritrea changed over time. After 2005 desertion from the national service and illegal emigration became a mass phenomenon. Vincent Crapanzano mentions "realism and resignation" as constitutive dimensions of hope: Young people did not want to become martyrs, neither for the nation nor for one's religious belief, but

---

23   Clashes of government-loyalists and opposition groups during an official festival on the occasion of 20 years of Eritrean independence in Giessen/Germany have shown that the idea of Isayas' charismatic leadership is still cultivated in pro-government diaspora communities (Jugendnetz Wetzlar: Demonstration gegen Militärdiktatur in Eritrea. Pro und Contra begegnen sich. www.youtube.com/watch?v=F8ThLSVguPs [accessed 17.06.2014]; Giessener Allgemeine: Handgemenge und Steinwürfe vor Hessenhallen. 04.10.2011).

had to reckon with it (Crapanzano 2003: 6; cf. Bourdieu 1990: 60, 62). Migration became the more promising option. Additionally, more and more parents in the urban middle-class changed from active or passive government supporters into active supporters of their children. Once elsewhere those could live a better life and support their parents in old-age. *Shaebia's* collectivist concept of a nation did not only open up an opposition between national politics and religion, between collectivism and individual life but also between national territory and the world. Evangelical belief outside Eritrea thus promises a specific social capital: access to a global and potentially resource-rich network of believers (centering in USA and Canada). Further more believers gain general respect for their explicitly religious reasons to seek refuge. Also, they can hope for religious freedom and the rule of law as well as collective therapeutic support in the exile congregations. And Evangelical belief always confirms one's way—migration then is a modern Via Dolorosa (cf. Nicoué 2011)—and one's ambitions of "individual self-making" (van Dijk 2004: 171), including "human security" (Mekonnen 2013: 2) and economic well-being. Bourdieu sees prophecy's habitus "objectively attuned to that of its addressees" (1987: 131). So, evasion from the political field in Eritrea has lead to the ideological mentoring of migration and a rapprochement of the rather isolated Eritrean situation to the broader transnational Evangelical discourse on modernity and consumerism elsewhere in Africa and the world (cf. Kastner 2011: 236–7; Nieswand 2008; Ukah 2005). Haves are provided with the legitimacy to possess and consume, while have-nots are motivated to dream of the possibility to do likewise (Bourdieu 1987: 127–128; Comaroff & Comaroff 2001; Jackson 2010: 284).

Of course there is a lively Evangelical Church and community in Shimelba refugee camp in Northern Ethiopia today, and a whole variety of congregations in Addis Ababa, where Eritrean and Ethiopian believers meet—both from the same urban milieu, educated and ambitious. In the Sudanese capital it takes several minibuses to bring believers from all over the city to the Tigrinya Sunday mess in Faith Mission Church in Khartoum Itneyn neighborhood—and it is only one of numerous Evangelical churches in town. Applicants for a visa to Canada, which allows legal immigration if religious communities there take over sponsorship for fellow Christians, have become that numerous that the Canadian Embassy in Khartoum issues file numbers that date processing several years ahead. Information on Canada's visa procedures can only be accessed by internet (embassy staff refuses any additional support) and there are reports among refugees in Khartoum that applications have already been declined in larger numbers—despite applicants insisting on their faith. Nevertheless almost all our informants in Khartoum already had such a "file number" and hung on it.

In Cairo, back in 2008, hundreds of Eritrean refugees were waiting for their legal visa applications to be processed; a large number among them were women waiting for family reunion with their—sometimes only nominal—husbands in the USA. As all of them are from time to time forced into informal, irregular and often illegal action, fellow migrants sometimes doubt the *pentes* sincerity. Informants in Cairo mocked the "fake pentes", and of course it is much easier and much more promising to be an Evangelical Christian outside than inside Eritrea. However this allegation only stresses the *pentes'* broad and unbowed attractiveness, winning their ideological struggle with Eritrean nationalism through the backdoor.

In Khartoum and Addis Ababa many Eritrean deserters insist on their political reasons to seek refuge and asylum abroad and emphatically express their willingness to fight the Isayas-regime back in Eritrea. Evangelical refugees seem to have left this national frame of reference much more easily. Their religious denomination and commitment and the well-known situation of their brothers and sisters in Eritrea are already well-promoted and legitimizing. Finally, those who have always claimed in Eritrea to be solely interested in the other world seem to be better prepared to prove themselves in a global reality. The false Messiah and his lost souls, however, are cursed to stay on their liberated soil and struggle for a paradise that has already lost credit and credibility. Facing continuous repression by political orthodoxy, the heretics redefined the borders of the field: the chosen people are moving out.

References

Araya, Mesfin. 1997. Issues of Hegemony in Post-Independent Eritrea. In *Ethiopia in Broader Perspective. Papers of the XIIIth International Conference of Ethiopian Studies*, Vol. II., edited by Katsuyoshi Fukui et al., 21–28. Kyoto: Shokado.

Boeck, Filip de, and Marie-Françoise Plissart. 2004. *Kinshasa. Tales of the Invisible City*. Ghent: Ludion.

Bourdieu, Pierre. 1987. Legitimation and Structured Interests in Weber's Sociology of Religion. In *Max Weber, Rationality and Modernity*, edited by Scott Lash and Sam Whimster, 119–136. London: Allen and Unwin.

———. 1990. *The Logic of Practice*. Stanford: Stanford University Press.

———. 1991. Genesis and Structure of the Religious Field. *Comparative Social Research* 13: 1–44.

———. 2003. Über einige Eigenschaften von Feldern. In *absolute Pierre Bourdieu*, edited by Joseph Jurt, 122–128. Freiburg: Orange-Press.

Bozzini, David M. 2011. Low-tech Surveillance and the Despotic State in Eritrea. *Surveillance & Society* 9 (1/2): 93–113.

———. 2013. The Catch-22 of Resistance. Jokes and the Political Imagination of Eritrean Conscripts. *Africa Today* 60 (2): 39–64.

Bude, Heinz. 1984. Rekonstruktion von Lebenskonstruktionen. Eine Antwort auf die Frage, was die Biographieforschung bringt. In *Biographie und soziale Wirklichkeit*, edited by Martin Kohli and Günther Robert, 7–28. Stuttgart: Metzler.

Clapham, Christopher. 2006. Afterword. In *Ethnic Federalism. The Ethiopian Experience in Comparative Perspective*, edited by David Turton, 231–240. Oxford: James Currey.

———. 1988. *Transformation and Continuity in Revolutionary Ethiopia*. Cambridge: Cambridge University Press.

Comaroff, Jean, and John L. Comaroff. 2001. Millenial Capitalism. First Thoughts on a Second Coming. In *Millenial Capitalism and the Culture of Neoliberalism*, edited by Jean Comaroff and John L. Comaroff, 1–56. Durham: Duke University Press.

Conrad, Bettina. 2005. From Revolution to Religion? The Politics of Religion in the Eritrean Diaspora in Germany. In *Religion in the Context of African Migration Studies*, edited by Afe Adogame and Cordula Weissköppel, 217–241. Bayreuth: Thielmann & Breitinger.

Crapanzano, Vincent. 2003. Reflections on Hope as a Category of Social and Psychological Analysis. *Cultural Anthropology* 18 (1): 3–32.

Dijk, Rijk van. 2004. 'Beyond the rivers of Ethiopia'. Pentecostal Pan-Africanism and Ghanaian Identities in the Transnational Domain. In *Situating Globality. African Agency in the Appropriation of Global Culture*, edited by Wim van Bimsberger and Rijk van Dijk, 163–189. Leiden, Boston: Brill.

Donham, Donald L. 1999. *Marxist Modern. An Ethnographic History of the Ethiopian Revolution*. Berkeley, Los Angeles, Oxford: University of California Press.

———. 2006. "Comments on Halle Conference." Paper presented at the Workshop New Religiosity and Inter-Generational Conflict in Northeast Africa, Max Planck Institute for Social Anthropology, Halle, April 26–28.

EPLF. 1977. *The National Democratic Programme of the Eritrean People's Liberation Front*. Pamphlet.

———. 1987. *The National Democratic Programme of the Eritrean People's Liberation Front*. Pamphlet.

Gilkes, Patrick. 1991. Eritrea. Historiography and Mythology. *African Affairs* 90, 361: 623–628.

Haile, Getachew. 2005. Ethiopian Orthodox (Täwahədo) Church. History from ancient times till the second half of the 19th cent. In *Encyclopaedia Aethiopica* 2, edited by Siegbert Uhlig, 414–421. Wiesbaden: Harrassowitz.

Hepner, Tricia R. 2003. Religion, Nationalism, and Transnational Civil Society in the Eritrean Diaspora. *Identities. Global Studies in Culture and Power* 10 (3): 269–295.

---. 2009. Seeking Asylum in a Transnational Social Field. New Refugees and Struggles for Autonomy and Human Rights. In *Biopolitics, Militarism and Development. Eritrea in the Twenty-First Century*, edited by David O'Kane and Tricia R. Hepner, 183–206. New York: Berghahn.

---. 2014. Religion, Repression and Human Rights in Eritrea and the Diaspora. *Journal of Religion in Africa* 44: 151–188.

Hepner, Tricia R., and David O'Kane. 2009. Biopolitics and Dilemmas of Development in Eritrea and Elsewhere. In *Biopolitics, Militarism and Development. Eritrea in the Twenty-First Century*, edited by David O'Kane and Tricia R. Hepner, 159–170. New York: Berghahn.

Hirt, Nicole, and Abdelkader Saleh Mohammad. 2013. 'Dreams Don't Come True in Eritrea'. Anomie and Family Disintegration due to the Structural Militarization of Society. *Journal of Modern African Studies* 51 (1): 139–168.

Jackson, John L. Jr. 2010. On Ethnographic Sincerity. *Current Anthropology* 51, S2: S279–S287.

Kastner, Kristin. 2011. "Zwischen Suffering und Styling. Nigerianische Migrantinnen beiderseits des Estrecho." PhD diss., University of Bayreuth.

Kibreab, Gaim. 2009. Forced Labour in Eritrea. *Journal of Modern African Studies* 47 (1): 41–72.

Ki[f]leyesus, Abbebe. 2006. Cosmologies in Collision. Pentecostal Conversion and Christian Cults in Asmara. *African Studies Review*. 49 (1): 75–92.

Killion, Tom. 1998. *Historical Dictionary of Eritrea*. African Historical Dictionaries, 75. Lanham Md., London: Scarecrow Press.

Launhardt, Johannes. 2005. Ethiopian Evangelical Church Mekane Yesus. In *Encyclopaedia Aethiopica* 2, edited by Siegbert Uhlig, 409–410. Wiesbaden: Harrassowitz.

Mannheim, Karl. 1978 [1928]. Das Problem der Generationen. In *Soziologie des Lebenslaufs*, edited by Martin Kohli, 38–50. Darmstadt: Luchterhand.

Mao Tse-Tung. 1967. On New Democracy. In *Selected Works* II, by Mao Tse-Tung, 339–384. Peking: Foreign Languages Press.

Marshall-Fratani, Ruth. 1998. Mediating the Global and Local in Nigerian Pentecostalism. *Journal of Religion in Africa* 28 (3): 278–315.

Mekonnen, Daniel R. 2013. Introduction. The Horn of Africa between endless conflicts and 'compassion fatigue'. In *The Horn of Africa at the Brink of the 21st Century. Coping with Fragmentation, Isolation and Marginalization in a Globalizing Environment*, edited by Daniel R. Mekonnen and Mussie Tesfagiorgis, 1–16. Felsberg: edition eins.

Mekonnen, Daniel R., and Mirjam van Reisen. 2014. Religious Persecution in Eritrea and the Role of the European Union in Tackling the Challenge. In *Religion, Gender, and the Public Sphere*, edited by Niamh Reilly and Stacey Scriver, 232–244. New York: Routledge.

Meyer, Birgit. 1998. 'Make a Complete Break with the Past.' Memory and Post-Colonial Modernity in Ghanaian Pentecostalist Discourse. *Journal of Religion in Africa* 28, 3: 316–349.

Müller, Tanja. 2009. Human Resource Development and the State. Higher Education in Postrevolutionary Eritrea. In *Biopolitics, Militarism and Development. Eritrea in the Twenty-First Century*, edited by David O'Kane and Tricia R. Hepner, 53–71. New York: Berghahn.

Nicoué, Délia. 2011. 'In Germany, I've never expected something like this to happen!' Studying Knowledge and the Narratives of Migrants on Their Way to Europe. In *Innovating Qualitative Research. New Directions in Migration*, edited by Miriam Busse et al., 35–51. ForMig. Forschungsverbund Migration und Wissen. Arbeitspapiere aus der Verbundforschung 1.

Nieswand, Boris. 2008. Ghanaian Migrants in Germany and the Social Construction of Diaspora. *African Diaspora* 1 (1–2): 28–52.

O'Kane, David. 2006. War in Africa. Space, Place and the Eritrea-Ethiopia War of 1998–2000. In *Borders and Borderlands in Contemporary Culture*, edited by Aoileann Ní Éigeartaigh and David Getty, 27–32. Newcastle: Cambridge Scholars Publishing.

Pool, David. 2001. *From Guerrilla to Government. The Eritrean People's Liberation Front*. Oxford: James Currey.

Quehl, Hartmut. 2005. *Kämpferinnen und Kämpfer im eritreischen Unabhängigkeitskrieg. 1961–1991*, 1–2. Faktoren der Diversität und der Kohärenz. Eine historische Untersuchung zu Alltags- und Sozialgeschichte des Krieges. Felsberg: editions eins.

Red. Encyclopaedia Aethiopica. 2005. Ethiopian Orthodox (Täwahedo) Church. History from 1959 to 1974. In *Encyclopaedia Aethiopica* 2424–426. Wiesbaden: Harrassowitz.

Riggan, Jennifer. 2009. Avoiding Wastage by Making Soldiers. Technologies of the State and the Imagination of the Educated Nation. In *Biopolitics, Militarism and Development. Eritrea in the Twenty-First Century*, edited by David O'Kane and Tricia R. Hepner, 72–91. New York: Berghahn.

———. 2013. Imagining Emigration. Debating National Duty in Eritrean Classrooms. *Africa Today* 60 (2): 85–106.

Stoffregen Pedersen, Kirsten. 2005. Evangeliska Fosterlands Stiftelsen. In *Encyclopaedia Aethiopica* 2, edited by Siegbert Uhlig, 459–460. Wiesbaden: Harrassowitz.

Tesfai, Alemseged. 2002. Le'ul. A One-Act-Play in Five Scenes. In *Two Weeks in the Trenches*, by Alemseged Tesfai Asmara, 139–165. Lawrenceville, NJ: Red Sea Press.

Treiber, Magnus. 2005. *Der Traum vom guten Leben. Die eritreische warsay-Generation im Asmara der zweiten Nachkriegszeit*. Münster: LIT.

———. 2007. Dreaming of a Good Life—Young Urban Refugees from the Horn of Africa between Refusal of Politics and Political Asylum Seeking. In *Cultures of Migration. African Perspectives*, edited by Hans-Peter Hahn and Georg Klute, 239–260. Berlin: LIT.

———. 2009. Trapped in Adolescence. The Post-War Urban Generation. In *Biopolitics, Militarism and Development. Eritrea in the Twenty-First Century*, edited by David O'Kane and Tricia R. Hepner, 92–114. New York: Berghahn.

———. 2010. The Choice of 'Clean' and 'Dirty'. Discourses of Aesthetics, Moral and Progress in Post-Revolutionary Asmara, Eritrea. In *Urban Pollution. Cultural Meanings, Social Practices*, edited by Eveline Dürr and Rivke Jaffe, 123–143. Oxford: Berghahn.

Treiber, Magnus, and Selahadin Abdela. 2008. Naqfa. In *Encyclopaedia Aethiopica* 3, edited by Siegbert Uhlig, 1141–1142. Wiesbaden: Harrassowitz.

Treiber, Magnus, and Lea Tesfaye. 2008. Step by Step. Migration from Eritrea. In *Hot Spot Horn of Africa Revisited. Approaches to Make Sense of Conflict*, edited by Eva-Maria Bruchhaus and Monika Sommer, 280–295. Berlin: LIT.

Tronvoll, Kjeti[l]. 1996. The Eritrean Referendum: Peasant Voices. *Eritrean Studies Review* 1 (1): 23–67.

———. 2009. *The Lasting Struggle for Freedom in Eritrea. Human Rights and Political Development 1991–2009*. Oslo: Oslo Center for Peace and Human Rights.

Ukah, Asonzeh. 2005. Mobilities, Migration and Multiplication. The Expansion of the Religious Field of the Redeemed Christian Church of God (RCCG), Nigeria. In *Religion in the Context of African Migration Studies*, edited by Afe Adogame and Cordula Weissköppel, 317–341. Bayreuth: Thielmann & Breitinger.

Weber, Max. *Wirtschaft und Gesellschaft*. Tübingen: Mohr 1922.

Zewde, Bahru. 2002. *A History of Modern Ethiopia. 1855–1991*. 2nd ed. Oxford, Addis Ababa: James Currey.

CHAPTER 9

Seclusion versus Education: Bourdieu's Perspective on Women Continuing Education Centers in Northern Nigeria

Chikas Danfulani

Introduction

This chapter relates Bourdieu's concept of 'Field' to Muslim women's education in northern Nigeria. Specifically, it focuses on Women Continuing Education Centers (WCECs) established since the re-implementation of Sharia in twelve states in northern Nigeria beginning in 1999. WCECs have been characterized by a large turnout of married women, mainly dropouts from formal education, as a result of early marriage. Several factors impede on women's education in northern Nigeria, chief among which are early marriage and seclusion—in addition to domestic responsibilities. The requirements of strict Islamic observance of the practice of seclusion perpetually hinder Muslim women's full participation in formal education programs and public life. Based on empirical data on women's education in two Sharia states—Kano and Zamfara of northern Nigeria between 2007 and 2008, the chapter argues that the participation of women in WCECs, which, according to policy makers and implementers is a structure of educating and preparing women for future responsibilities, serve to reproduce the long-existing cultural practice of seclusion prevalent in northern Nigeria and long-standing exclusion of women from the public sphere. With a focus on Bourdieu's concept of 'Modes of Domination,' the contribution demonstrates that although women's centers provide spaces where married women could actualize their dreams of access to education, the centers appear to be a customized form of *Kulle* (seclusion) due largely to their structure, content and women's perceptions of them. The study further shows how these women's centers lack the full capacity to prepare women for public responsibility because the brand of education and the atmosphere for receiving them perpetuate a one-sided form of education which in turn leads to a reproduction of social dominance of men over women.

The field as observed by Bourdieu is "a structured system of social positions—occupied either by individuals or institutions—the nature of which defines the situation for the occupants," but at the same time "a system of forces which exist between these positions [...] structured internally in terms of power relations [...] by virtue of the access they afford to the goods or resources (capital) which are at stake in the field" (Jenkins 1992: 85). This chapter discusses Bourdieu's concepts of field and symbolic violence or modes of domination in explaining how social relations are carried out in everyday life of Muslim in northern Nigeria, particularly in relation to their education. The concepts of 'field' and 'modes of domination' are important for this study because they explain the situation of Muslim women in northern Nigeria within the context of both the Sharia and women's education; and in relation to the cultural practice of seclusion (*kulle*) which is a prevalent practice in northern Nigeria. The practice of seclusion has been interpreted and perceived by a wider population of northern Nigerian Muslims as Islamic. This is also the case with several other cultural practices which have been fused into the religious field or been interpreted as religious practices, thereby becoming complex to distinguish between cultural and religious practices. One of the major challenges of this contribution is the fuzziness of the boarders of the field which Bourdieu argues is difficult to separate. Focal point of this chapter are the Women Continuing Education Centers which, although part of the educational field, are also located within the religious field in the form of Sharia, which in turn is intricately interwoven with the fields of law and state. According to Bourdieu and Wacquant:

> The school system, the state, the church, political parties, or unions are not apparatuses but fields. In a field, agents and institutions constantly struggle, according to the regulations and the rules constitutive of this play (and, in given conjunctures, over those rules themselves), with various degrees of strength and therefore diverse probabilities of success, to appropriate the specific products at stake in the game (Bourdieu and Wacquant 1992: 102).

The approach to the field of education in northern Nigeria is often viewed through religious lenses, leading to the fusion of the religious and the educational field. Another cultural practice within the broader religious field is the practice of seclusion (*kulle*). At this juncture, it is difficult to separate these boarders as they are in many ways interlinked with each other: law-religion-education-culture. This justifies the importance of analyzing women continuing education centers in the light of the religious field in northern Nigeria.

The theme of Muslim women's education in northern Nigeria has a prolong history. Earlier researches on the question of women's education date back to the colonial history of northern Nigeria and they indicate that Muslim women in northern Nigerian had limited access to "western education."[1] During the colonial era when western education was being introduced in northern Nigeria, the Emirs resisted it fearing it would come with Christianization; Lord Lugard as the Commissioner for northern Nigeria from 1900 onward actively shielded the north from educational initiatives pioneered by Christian missionaries till the 1930s. When the emirs finally agreed to have some western-type schools, only the children of emirs and political figures attended such schools while the rest of the population attended *madrassa* schools. When these restrictions were lifted for the rest of the general population, the educational gap between the northern and the southern regions of Nigeria was already too wide. Similarly, there evolved a wider disparity between males and females in the north, as girls were restricted for an extended period from attending western schools. In more advanced Islamic schools as well, girls were kept away, for cultural reasons, often given religious colorings or interpretations. This state of affairs led to a great deal of educational disparity between the northern and southern Nigeria (see Callaway 1987; Knipp 1987; Hubbard 2000). These studies also reveal several factors such as poverty, culture/tradition, early marriage and seclusion as responsible for the disparity. Recent research on Muslim women in northern Nigeria further unveils these earlier factors in addition to government policies and preference for Islamic education as responsible for perpetuating educational inequality (Nasir 2007; Umar 2004). These issues account for the current situation of northern Nigerian Muslim women who lack equal opportunity as the men and their female counterparts from other regions of Nigeria in terms of access to quality education instrumental to accessing resources and opportunities. This non-access to such opportunities is one of the main thrust of this contribution which shall be discussed within the educational field of northern Nigeria.

The continuity of certain cultural practices in the north have been difficult to erode. The re-introduction of Sharia in 12 northern states from 1999 onwards has further reinforced some of these practices. Structured in five main sections, the chapter employs Bourdieu's concepts of 'Field' and 'Symbolic Violence' to understand the multifaceted nature and structure of Women Continuing Education Centers (WCECS) in northern Nigeria, one out of the numerous

---

[1] The term "western education" means the formal system of secular education as introduced by the colonial administration in Nigeria. It is widely referred to as western education in Nigeria as opposed to other systems of education like Islamic education which is widely accepted in northern Nigeria.

reform programs of the Sharia states and situated within a strictly religious and patriarchal space. The contribution further illustrates how such programs although meant to close the educational gender gap are still reinforcing and perpetuating the cultural dominance of men over women due largely to the way these schools are structured as well as women and men's responses to the effectiveness of such schools in preparing women for future public responsibilities and participation.

Women's Education in Northern Nigeria: Problems and Prospects

The field of education in northern Nigeria has been a contested field of struggle between western versus religious education. This struggle is more apparent when it comes to the education of women due largely to the general view by a number of Muslims that educating a woman (especially in religious knowledge) means educating a nation. According to Bourdieu, the field is a field of struggle where different agents contest over specific resources. Situated within the religious field (Sharia states) the field of education in northern Nigeria consists of agents such as the state government and their respective policy makers, religious leaders, individuals (pupils; women, girls, boys, adults etc.), teachers and administrative who all act as players in the field. Several institutions also exist in the form of Schools, Sharia Commissions and Ministries of Education; others are Islamic Institutions such as the Izala Movement, the Jama'atu Nasir Islam (JNI) and the Federation of Muslim Women's Associations in Nigeria (FOMWAN) just to mention a few. All these are active agents contesting within the religious and secular educational fields in northern Nigeria.

The educational field in several of the Sharia states in northern Nigeria is linked to the religious and the political fields, giving rise to a mixture of religion, politics and education (Bourdieu and Passeron 2000). The arguments put forward for this fusion is the obvious fact that religion and the state are inseparable in the Muslim context. Although Bourdieu discusses extensively the political and religious field, there is no clear-cut concept of the field of education; however, Bourdieu and Passeron's *Reproduction in Education, Society and Culture* show some link between society, education and culture and since some cultures are often embedded within the belief system of a people, one can see the link in Bourdieu's work between the field of education and religion as is the case in the Sharia states of northern Nigeria.

This chapter focuses on the supposed secular education otherwise known as western education, which is a formal system of education introduced by the

Colonial authorities and some Christian missionary bodies. Bourdieu describes school as the field where knowledge and experiences are produced and where both cultural and social capital is acquired. According to Bourdieu, the values of the powerful in society are usually disseminated through the institutions of education such as schools. However, these educational structures—primary, secondary tertiary or women only—play a central role in the reproduction of social and cultural inequalities (Bourdieu and Passeron 2000: 71–72). Bourdieu and Passeron further note that the values of the powerful in the society are usually enforced on the children of the working class through the educational system, thereby perpetuating dominant values but also maintaining the status quo; and they note that the values of the powerful are disseminated through such school systems. This state of affairs in turn produces what he refers to as 'symbolic violence', a situation when holders of symbolic capital use such power against an agent who holds less (power), seeking to alter their actions, thus, in the long run children of the less privileged see the educational success of their privileged peers as legitimate social values to aspire to. Such actions often have discriminatory or injurious meanings or implication not only on class but also on gender dominance. As symbolic violence often forms the basis of gender inequality, the concept can be fruitfully used to account for the situation of Muslim women within the educational field in northern Nigeria. Bourdieu notes that the uneducated are always disadvantaged and in northern Nigeria the most disadvantaged group in terms of access to western form of education are women.

The history of education in northern Nigeria cannot be complete without looking at the various factors that have impeded on the education of Muslim women in northern Nigeria, as well as at several policies and practices introduced by the government, Nongovernmental organizations and Religious bodies in an attempt to solve the problems surrounding women's full participation. Whenever the topic of Muslim women's education and the obstacles they face in their struggle for equal opportunity in the public sphere comes up, one cannot avoid looking into the general history of education in northern Nigeria where it all began. A number of studies have been carried out on education in northern Nigeria and particularly women's education (see Fafunwa 1975; Hiskett 1975; Tibendarana 1976, 1985; 1985, Ozigi and Ocho 1981; Knipp 1981; 1987; Graham 1996); all focusing on Nigeria's educational situation with particular emphasis to the disparity existing between the northern and the southern region. There is a consensus among these authors that northern Nigeria's educational problems date back to the colonial era. They also consent to the fact that several cultural, social and political factors are responsible for the current state of affairs. Especially important to this contribution is the work of Merg Csapo (1981) who notes some basic hindrances to female education in northern Nigeria.

According Csapo (1981), one of the major aims of the Universal Primary Education (UPE) introduced in 1976 was to eliminate all political and social problems which gave rise to the imbalances of educational development between the northern and southern regions of Nigeria prior to the UPE. She remarks that the influence of the UPE program was not equally felt by the females who should have formed half of the school-aged population. This was because fewer girls were found in schools all over the country and especially in northern Nigeria. The rate of girls in schools in the north forty years after Csapo's study is still the lowest compared to other regions in the country because girls are not usually given the same priority as the boys. Csapo identifies several factors as responsible for this state of affairs which include; the place of women in Islam which often relegates them to a secondary place; the traditional antagonism towards western education which was viewed as synonymous with Christianity; marriage customs and practice of seclusion which perpetually relegate women to the background socially; the misconception of the Islamic view on the education of women which assumes that educating the female is not Islamic; the fear of moral laxity in western schools; the paucity of post-primary education; lukewarm support of political leaders, and economic factors. According to her, these factors repeatedly give the impression that investment in girls' education is a waste since girls were expected to be married off once they reach puberty (Csapo 1981: 312). These and many more factors are responsible for the existing great gender disparity in education in northern Nigeria. Recent studies on the subject of women's education in northern Nigeria also reveal that some of these factors are still impeding on women's education (Nasir 2007; Umar 2004; Werthmann 2005). They all show that several of the earlier factors such as poverty, culture/tradition, early marriage, seclusion and child bearing continue to pose great challenges to the education of women and girls.

Poverty has equally been a major factor that has impeded women's education in northern Nigeria. The economic status of most northern Nigerian families is relatively low and often times their earnings do not meet up with family needs. The women in their bid to augment the effort of their husbands in spite of their being in seclusion settle for petty-businesses mostly in snacks and often rely on their girls to hawk these items their behalf, thus, girls' engaged in these activities often stay out of school. Furthermore, in comparison to Islamic education, western education is considered too expensive. This view is best articulated by an informant who reasons that: "people here [in northern Nigeria—C.D.] are very poor. Islamic education is imparted cheaply. If somebody like me is married to four wives and have 25 children, if I send them to *Mallams* (religious teachers)to learn, it may not cost me much but if I send them to western education (schools) they will ask us to bring text books, bring uniform, etc."[2] This quotation shows that the reason behind parents' choice of Islamic schools over western schools is actually the existing poverty rate in northern Nigeria compelling some parents to send their children to traditional schools which are usually imparted cheaply.

Secondly, early marriage is another cultural practice in northern Nigeria that has remained hard to erode even with recent transformations in most contemporary societies with laws limiting the age of marriage for females to a minimum of eighteen years. Some cultural and Islamic practices which holds parents responsible for the moral laxity of unmarried girls compels majority of Muslim parents to marry off their girls at a very early age.[3] In addition to such Islamic injunctions, many northern Nigerian Muslims explain their actions and support for early marriage as being in conformity with the action of the prophet Mohammed who married his wife Aisha at a very early age; parallel to this conception is the belief that young girls who are not married off early in life acquire a lot of immoral behaviors if they remain unmarried beyond the age of puberty, especially when these girls are allowed to attend western schools where the atmosphere is unfavorable as they are exposed to western style of thinking and behavior. As a result, some parents would marry off their ages as young as 12 and once married they remain in seclusion and begin the process of child-bearing.

In most cases however, because these young girls are not fully matured at the time of childbirth, they are infected with Vesicovaginal Fistula (VVF), a pregnancy related disease which prevents young mothers from actively participating in the public due to the stigma related to the disease. For girls, marriage, which ideally coincides with puberty, marks the transition to adult status. If a girl is married off at age 12–15 she enters seclusion and loses the freedom of childhood. For many, the switch from childhood to motherhood is a difficult one. These and many more practices have hampered the education of women as most of them remain within the confines of their homes after marriage.

In addition to early marriage, the practice of seclusion has perpetually hindered women from accessing education. Seclusion is prevalent in many parts

---

[2] Interview with Alhaji Sani Usman (pseudonym) Director, Inspectorate Services, Ministry of Education, Sokoto. Sokoto state, 05.03.07.

[3] Interview with Mohammed Isa, (pseudonym), Principal, Women Center for Continuing Education, Gusau Zamfara state 07.03.2007.

of northern Nigeria. Introduced as far back as the 15th Century first in Kano, the observance of seclusion in Nigeria is represented not so much by the wearing of the veil but by the thick walls surrounding several homes and by the absence of women on streets as well as their non-participation in the public spheres (Werthmann 2005). What this implies is that once married, young Muslim women are bound to the rules of seclusion thereby limiting their chances for accessing education or fully participating in public social activities as these are disrupted at puberty.

However, the introduction of the Universal Primary Education (UPE) in early 1976 was a major challenge to the institution of seclusion and similar practices. The UPE program was expected to close the gap between the North and South in terms of educational disparity and to make primary education compulsory with the hope of retaining many girls in school (Clerk 1978). The program helped in relaxing earlier resistance to western education and prevention of girls from accessing it. This development however did not last because the program although a huge project, lacked continuity, especially due to the collapse of the Nigerian economy in the early 1980s (Umar 2004; Reichmuth 1989).

The emergence of Islamic schools in the late 1970s was also a major challenge to women's access to western education as parents preferred to send their girls to such schools due largely to a number of the factors discussed above. This new development led to a process of mass acquisition of Islamic education in the Islamic institutions which have today produced a large number of female (*ulama*) scholars (Umar 2004). This kind of liberation within the Muslim context is highly commendable because it has provided Muslim women the cultural capital to contribute to the society as well as to serve as academic mentors to other women; women who would otherwise not have such opportunities. These Islamic schools are scattered all over northern Nigeria today.

Impact of Sharia

The reimplementation of Sharia in northern Nigeria which began in 1999 brought about enormous changes such as the establishment of Sharia boards and commissions; the creation of several Islamic institutions; the formation of new committees on Sharia and the establishment of Islamic education boards. By this expansion in Sharia law, the secular state became an active provider of religion and religious education. These new policies were aimed at purifying the society as well as restoring the 'lost glory' of Islam which proponents felt was lost during the colonial era, thus, there was a clamor for the reform of the society to conform to the tenets of Islam. These changes led to the establishment of Sharia commissions in all the Sharia states. The commissions were responsible for creating and implementing programs, policies and projects of the various states. In particular, the education boards were charged with the responsibility of establishing more Islamic schools as well as incorporating Islamic knowledge into the existing western schools. Apart from these changes, there were numerous awareness programs on the need for women to get educated. Consequently, a number of these changes influenced women's education positively as more women were enrolled in schools all over the Sharia states. Statistics from four of the Sharia states show a rising awareness of western education since the reimplementation of Sharia. Also, official statistics of enrolment in public secondary schools and from the ministries of education in Zamfara, Kano and Kaduna show that more girls/women are getting educated. For instance Zamfara state enrolment figure in girl's school had 6,397 girls in 2001—about two years since the reimplementation of Sharia. By 2006, more than six years later, the figure had increased to 22,946, revealing an overwhelming increase in girl's school enrolment and by implication a rise in awareness of the importance of female education.[4] Important to the field of women's education in the Sharia states is the creation of several programs for married women such as the establishment of separate female education boards, creation of women continuing education centers and special programs for primary school girls aimed at improving women's education.

Description of Women Centers—Zamfara and Kano States

A common phenomenon observed while carrying out this research in the northern states is the existence of Women Continuing Education Centers. Several of these centers existed before the reimplementation of Sharia in northern Nigeria; established as crafts and skills acquisition centers where women attend to learn some skills such as knitting, sewing and baking as a way of empowering women. With the reimplementation of Sharia however, a good number of these centers received a lot of recognition as they were upgraded to very special centers where women are heavily populated and taught western education alongside other skills. The centers are an important factor for the improvement of women's education in the northern states, partly because they are accepted by the women's spouses. The main characteristics of these centers is that they are exclusively for married women who dropped out of school

---

4 Statistics from Women Education Board Gusau, Zamfara State, March 2007.

as a result of marriage and who could not continue due to constrains mostly related to the practice of seclusion; this being a qualification for admission in women centers.

Two centers were important for this study, namely *Women Continuing Education Center, Gusau* and *Kano City Women Center*. The centers in Kano and Zamfara have a lot in common yet differ in many ways; both centers received wide recognition and huge support by government since the reimplementation of Sharia.[5] These Centers are sponsored by the government and thus offered free of tuition fee. They have mostly female teachers with a handful of male teachers. They are characterized by a large number of Muslim women of different age groups. The Zamfara state center under inquiry has a total number of about 500 women, while Kano state City women center has over 800 women in attendance. Subjects taught at the centers are largely conventional subjects such as Mathematics, English, Biology, History and Physics. Authorities of the schools maintain they have no special emphasis on Islam but operate the western system of education, however, apart from the subjects mentioned above; other subjects such as specialized Islamic studies and Arabic literature are top priority subjects in the centers. Modes of dressing in the schools must conform to the Islamic conventional way of dressing for women—the wearing of the *hijab* (veil) which every married woman should wear. The principal of Zamfara women center sheds more light on the reason why women dress this way as she remarks;

> [...] a Muslim woman is not supposed to go out of her house without covering her body [...] this is the Muslim way of dressing and it does not matter if you are in primary or secondary school you have to cover your body [...] If you go round all the schools I mean female schools in Zamfara you will not see any women in school without the *hijab*, except for private schools but all government schools have to comply.[6]

The veil being an important part of Muslim women's dressing in northern Nigeria, is not only a mark of identity with the religion but also a major feature which distinguishes them from non-Muslim women and gives women the recognition of decency. The reinforcement of the wearing of *hijab* as a compulsory part of female dressing in northern Nigeria was a major part of the

---

[5] Interview with Principals of Zamfara and Kano WCEC, March, 2007 and November 2007.
[6] Interview with Sa'adatu Shehu (pseudonym), Principal, Women Center for Continuing Education Gusau, Zamfara state, 08.03.07.

reengineering programs of the Sharia States were all public schools including pupils from ages six onward had to include the veil as part of their uniforms.

The WCEC in Gusau, Zamfara state, is based on the formal system of western education. It differs from other public schools only insofar as the women in these centers are all married. Women admitted into these centers are accepted based on their previous qualification before dropping out of school. From the center, they are expected to steadily progress until they write the West African Examination Council (WAEC) and National Examination Council (NECO) examinations which qualifies them for entrance into other tertiary institutions. The Kano City women center shares the same concept, but differ to some extent because skills acquisitions remain a major part of the Kano center, thus besides the subjects mentioned above the center offers cooking, baking, tailoring and knitting skills and more, such that women could enroll for skills acquisition only. However, the Kano center is not fully funded as women have to pay certain levies in order to get admitted. Facilities in Kano are also inadequate thus the center is overly crowded due to lack of classrooms and seats as women often sit on floor mats to receive lectures. WCEC Gusau on the other hand does very little of skill acquisition except as found in some subjects which relates to basic skills although largely theoretical, subjects like home economics, clothing and textile and agriculture. The Zamfara center is also less crowded with better facilities and a more serene environment than the center in Kano.

Arguments for the Existence of Women Centers

Contrary to previous restriction of girls and women from accessing western education, the advocates of Sharia in northern Nigeria insist on the importance of educating women and have made a great deal of effort in improving of their educational chances. A number of arguments presented by proponents of Sharia for the establishment of women centers and the reasons behind their decision to invest in the education of women include the fact that the Quran in which the Sharia is based on greatly supports women's education. They expand on this point by maintaining that since the states are based on Sharia system of government they have to abide by the rule of the Sharia which is enshrined in the Qur'an.[7] They also argue that women are custodians of knowledge and play a prominent role in the development of their children by virtue of their being mothers and inculcators of knowledge in their children; so educating

---

7   Interview with the Director, Sharia Commission, Kano State, 16.03.2007.

them is as good as educating the world.[8] Another strand of argument states that the cultural and Islamic system of marriage in northern Nigeria has kept women in seclusion and has prevented them from acquiring basic education; the reimplementation of Sharia was therefore meant to correct some of these practices by providing women the opportunity to continue with their education in spite of the hindrances caused by marriage and seclusion. Furthermore, the proponents of Sharia argue that they envision women only institutions in the future because co-education as found in western schools is one of the factors that prevent parents from sending their girls to western schools and husbands from supporting their young wives to proceed with education after marriage. With the reimplementation of Sharia therefore, the separation of sexes became a major task of the Sharia proponents. For instance, Zamfara State government has since the reimplementation enforced the separation of all public primary and secondary schools according to gender. Before this period, boys and girls attended the same school with separate classes; according to authorities improved female enrolment figure in the state which statistics from the ministries seem to support. However, as would be revealed below, although these programs have in some way improved enrolment rates in girls schools and women centers, the idea of a women only institution appears to be a major agenda of the proponents of Sharia as articulated by one of the officials who feels is a sort of litmus test which he hopes would reflect in the wider society in the near future.[9]

Seclusion or Education?

As observed above, WCECs were established to address the problems of early marriage and seclusion and to allow female dropouts continue with their education, with the hope of reversing the shortcoming of the past.[10] However, majority of the women at the center reveal that their choice of WCECs were informed by their husbands' preference for these centers better than the usual girls school. An informant articulated the reason why husbands prefer to send women to WCECs when he says "Men have a duty to protect women from any form of external and negative influences especially from unmarried girls

---

8   This view was shared by a number of the informants interviewed for this study.
9   Interview with the Director, Sharia Research and Development Commission, Gusau, Zamfara State, 07.03.2007.
10 Interview with Principal, Women Center for Continuing Education, Gusau, Zamfara State, 08.03.2007.

which often times produce un-submissive wives."[11] Since most public schools are designed for and populated by young unmarried girls whom they considered would be major influencers of married women, it seems unwise then to allow married women attend the same regular schools attended by young girls. Although women seem to have no preference since the final decision to be enrolled in the centers are their husbands, yet women argue that their choice of these centers are influenced majorly by marriage and traditional practices of seclusion. When asked about their main reason for choosing this center instead of a regular female school, women's responses include: "I could not continue with school when I got married but this center has opened the way for me";[12] "when I got married, it was difficult to go back to school, but now my children have grown and when the center was opened my husband advised me to enroll."[13] Because a greater part of the women married early and have been accustomed to life in seclusion; a system of education which conforms to the one similar to what they have been used to and which they find more flexible as it accommodates their peculiar conditions as married women seem a good offer as one informant notes: "I chose to come here [meaning the Kano center] because as you can see we are all married women, we can share ideas as we learn."[14] Another informant at the center feels that "this place is better than other [female] schools because, you know, those girls they can look down on you, so I feel more comfortable [learning] with other women."[15] While women find it more comfortable to be in these centers, men also feel more at ease with their wives attending the schools because as the Principal of one of the schools comments "the environment is a well sanitized environment, there is no distraction from unmarried persons or persons of the opposite sex as you can see the women are enjoying it and with the number of women here, you know that it is favorable."[16]

While women seem happy with the development and in their comments praise government's initiative, these programs however have the propensity to conform to the traditional system of seclusion because they tend to overlook

---

11   Interview with Alhaji Sanni Usman (pseudonym), Director Inspectorate Services, Ministry of Education, Sokoto, Sokoto State, 05.03.2007.
12   Semi-structured interview with Hauwa B. Mada 21 years, Women Continuing Education Center Gusau, Zamfara State, 17.03.2008.
13   Interview with Zainab Alhassab 32 years, Women Continuing Education Center Gusau, Zamfara State, 17.03.2008.
14   Interview with Binta Ahmed 28 years, City women Center Kano, 14. 11.07.
15   Interview with Luba Mohammed 25 years, Women Continuing Education Center Gusau, Zamfara State, 17.03.2008.
16   Interview with the Principal Kano City Women Center, Kano State 13.11.2007.

the practice of early marriage, instead, creating an opportunity for combining early marriage with education. The provision of these kinds of schools by government rather than ending the practices that limit women's access—early marriage and seclusion, the Sharia governments are to some degree accentuating the traditional system of seclusion presented as women's education and which appears to be a reformed continuation of the system of *kulle*, as married women are restricted to these centers only. Furthermore, WCECs accommodate the *kulle* system by re-investing it with an academic aura, hence an expansion of the *kulle* moved outside the family homestead and funded by public funds.

Although the practice of seclusion is waning as more women are now allowed by their husbands to leave their homes and attend these center, however, limiting them to women only centers further reveals huge similarities between the practice of seclusion and style of education provided at the women centers. Women at the centers are not exposed to interaction with younger women from other public schools nor are they sent to such schools to proceed with the educational pursuit, but they are to remain within the confines of their school and only use Sharia approved public transportation back home. Similarly, the practice of seclusion demands that married women remain within the confines of their home and only leave the house for special reasons, with full approval of their husbands.[17] This limited interaction and complete segregation from the opposite sex in the process of acquiring education, limits women's prospects of full participation in the public sphere as majority of teachers at the centers are also females.[18] Government's choice of providing a form of education where the decision to get enrolled are made by women's husbands demonstrates how much the Sharia government maintains the status quo by providing the kind of education which conforms with the practice of seclusion; this perpetuates a practice which can be viewed as a form of "seclusion away from home," the old practice—seclusion without education—and the new—education in seclusion. In this way seclusion is perpetuated, but also substantially altered. However, those the Sharia governments assert could get educated in women only institution may hardly be able to fit into public service jobs with mixed sexes.

17 This practice of seclusion described by Barbara Callaway as *kullen tsari*—where "a wife may go out occasionally, with permission and accompanied by others to attend ceremonies and seek medical care" for more on this and different types of *kulle* (seclusion) see Callaway (1987).

18 Interview with Principals, Women Continuing Education Center, Gusau, Zamfara State. 08.03.2007, and Kano City Women Center, Kano State, 13.11.2007.

The idea of providing nannies (baby-sitters in the schools) for the women as they receive instruction also brings in the domestic into the public sphere. Women in seclusion often do not engage in economic enterprises outside the home, only small scale businesses such as knitting, sewing, mat-making and baking where they depend on their daughters as mentioned earlier. In like manner, WCECs especially those found in Kano stress on skill acquisition in sewing, knitting, baking and soap making. Emphasis on skills acquisition as means of improving women's efforts in learning domestically inclined skills in an academic environment, further illustrates how policy makers reinforce the existing practice during the inception of western education in northern Nigeria, where girls were only allowed to attend public schools to specialize in domestically inclined subjects in preparation for a possible future role as wives to the sons of the emirs.

Although the inclusions of male teachers in these centers have never been the wish of the initiators of Sharia, however, given the fact that less women are educated to tertiary level, it is inevitable to prevent male teachers from being employed in these centers; therefore, it is hoped that the education of women will produce more women in the state who would occupy positions in the civil service particularly as teachers in schools. Accordingly the proponents of Sharia say they anticipate a time when more women teachers would be produced who would take up teaching responsibility in women only schools with all female actors.[19] Following the issues raised the section below examines these practices in the light of Bourdieu's approach.

Implications of Bourdieu's Perspective

Women in the centers have come to appreciate learning at WCECs. They see government's effort in providing such options for women as good enough. When asked why they chose such centers and not other female schools, they responded "because it is a center for married women,"[20] or "because my husband supports it."[21] Since the centers are supported by their spouses, they feel

---

19 A view shared by the Director, Sharia Research and Development Commission, Gusau, Zamfara State, who holds that western education has for a long time provided an unfriendly atmosphere. The reintroduction of Sharia has however offered a comfortable (Sharia compliant) atmosphere for the education of women since the Sharia states have insisted on the separation of males and females in all public schools.

20 Interview with Zuwaira Gambo (pseudonym) WCEC Gusau, Zamfara state, 08.03.2007.

21 Interview with Amina Zubairu (pseudonym) WCEC Gusau, Zamfara state, 08.03.2007.

more confident that their wives are protected against external influences. In these centers however, Muslim women are expanding their options by stressing on their rights to be educated as guaranteed by the Quran. Many of them feel they are better wives and mothers since they started schools than when they were out of school.[22] They view the educational opportunity at the centers as enormous considering their current circumstances. However, a critical examination of the quality of education provided in terms of the mode of dissemination and the restricted atmosphere in which they are offered reveals that the quality is below the standard of education as these centers lack the basic facilities found in other public schools. Although they share the same curriculum as other public schools, the casual approach towards them demonstrates that they hardly implement the curriculum and policies guiding it to the latter. For instance, students are admitted based on their former qualification with no proper examination to determine their current performances; women can go on maternity leave for a whole semester and return whenever they are strong enough to attend, such flexibility in the implementation of academic program lowers the performance of women who end up graduating with grades too low for admission into tertiary institutions.

WCECs appear not fully equipped to prepare women for future public responsibility due largely to their continued existence as separate spaces for women to receive education and since women do not make the final decision in the choice of school, they have to comply to their spouses' choice, most of their academic values and excellence perpetuate their domestic and cultural values which serves to reinforce their subordinate roles as wives and mothers. Women however misrecognize the system as the best option. According to Bourdieu misrecognition arises where subordination to systems is reinforced by values that others accept as valid. In such a situation, the subordinated become complicit with the values, in which case *Symbolic Violence* is exerted—when holders of symbolic capital exert power against an agent who holds less, seeking to alter their actions. He further describes symbolic violence as

> gentle, invisible violence, unrecognized as such, chosen as much as undergone, that of trust, obligation, personal loyalty, hospitality, gifts, debts, piety, in a word, of all the virtues honoured by the ethic of honour, presents itself as the most economical mode of domination because it bests corresponds to the economy of the system (Bourdieu 1990: 127).

---

22 Several women at WCECs share this view.

Spouses' preference for women centers where their wives are kept away from public are viewed by these women as legitimate, thus they become complicit in their subordination and misunderstand or misrecognise the legitimacy of other types of school.

The implication of insisting on women-only educational centers is in its propensity of reproducing the social domination of women by men; since women at these centers do not have the freedom to make decision in terms of an alternative type of school which Bourdieu argues works to benefit those who dominate. According to him; "those who dominate in a given field are in a position to make it function to their advantage but they must always contend with the resistance, the claims, the contention, 'political' or otherwise, of the dominated" (Bourdieu and Wacquant 1992: 102). The Islamic injunction which places men a degree above women also has the tendency of reproducing the religious enforcement of female subordination as certain Islamic regulations are interpreted in the light of culture, frequently erasing the cultural base of the practice. This according Bourdieu can best be described as modes of domination; Bourdieu argues that the dominated in this circumstance accept the values and positions of the dominant to be legitimate. The consequence of this state of affairs in northern Nigeria is that it creates a male-centered system, whose values as sanctioned by religion and cultural norms that define the status of women as subordinate to that of men and restrict their lives to the domestic sphere (Callaway 1984). Bourdieu's views are further explained by Harker (1984) where he notes that formal education as those found in the centers represents key example of this process when he talks about the roles that schooling plays in reproducing social and cultural inequalities from one generation to the other. Harker explains that there is a tension between the conservative aspect of schooling (preservation of knowledge such as in Quranic/Islamic schools) and the dynamic innovative aspect of schooling (generation of new knowledge—as found in Western Schools) where the dominant group cultures are embodied in the schools (Harker 1984: 117–118).

Conclusion

The central argument of this chapter is the relationship between Women Continuing Education Centers in Sharia states of Nigeria and the cultural practice of seclusion. The contribution discussed the issues surrounding female education in northern Nigeria as well as how Sharia has impacted on women's education. It shows how several of the programs introduced since the reimplementation of Sharia has led to an unprecedented increase in female enrolment. Majority of the women who dropped out of school as a result of marriage run to these centers which somehow protects them from external influences as found in other schools. These types of schools viewed as legitimate for women by the dominant group—their spouses and policy makers (mostly males), compels women to be complicit in their subordination to the system. The study argues that the centers recreate a male centered system with its values sanctioned by religious and cultural norms, which in turn defines the status of women as subordinate to that of men and restricts their lives to the domestic sphere.

References

Bourdieu, Pierre. 1990. *The Logic of Practice*. Standford: Standford University Press.

Bourdieu, Pierre, and J. Pessaron, 2000. *Reproduction in Education, Society and Culture*. London: Sage Publication.

Bourdieu, Pierre, and Loïc Wacquant. 1992. *An Invitation to Reflexive Sociology*. Cambridge: Polity Press.

Callaway, Barbara J. 1987. *Muslim Hausa Women in Nigeria. Tradition and Change*. Syracuse, NY: Syracuse University Press.

Clerk, Peter B. 1978. Islam, Education and the Development Process in Nigeria. *Comparative Education*. 14(2): 133–141.

Csapo, Merg. 1981. Religious, Social and Economic Factors Hindering the Education of Girls in Northern Nigeria. *Comparative Education*. 17(3): 311–319.

Fafunwa, Babs A. 1975. *A History of Education in Nigeria*. London: George Allen & Unwin Press.

Graham, Sonia F. 1996. *Government and Mission Education in Nigeria 1900–1919*. Ibadan: Ibadan University Press.

Harker, Richard K. 1984. On Reproduction, Habitus and Education. *British Journal of Sociology of Education*. 5(2): 117–127.

Hiskett, M. 1975. Islamic Education in the Traditional and State Systems in Northern Nigeria. In *Conflict and Harmony in Education in Tropical Africa*, edited by Godfrey N. Brown and Mervyn Hiskett, 134–151. London: Allen & Unwin.

Hubbard, James P. 1975. Government and Islamic Education in Northern Nigeria (1900–1940). In *Conflict and Harmony in Education in Tropical Africa*, edited by Godfrey N. Brown and Mervyn Hiskett, 152–167. London: Allen & Unwin.

———. 2000. *Education under Colonial Rule, a History of Katsina College, 1921–1942*. USA: University Press of America.

Jenkins, Richard. 1992. *Pierre Bourdieu*. London: Routledge.

Kassam, Hauwa M. 1996. Some Aspects of Women's Voices from Northern Nigeria. *Gender and Popular Culture* 9(2): 111–125.

Knipp, Margaret M. 1981. West African Women and Change: A Synthesis. *The Bulletin of the Southern Associations of Africanists* 11(1): 7–18.

———. 1987. "Women, Western Education and Change: A Case Study of Hausa Fulani of Northern Nigeria." PhD diss., North-Western University, Evanston, Illinois.

Nasir, Jamila M. 2007. Sharia Implementation and Female Muslims in Nigeria's Sharia States. In *Sharia Implementation in Northern Nigeria 1999–2006. A Sourcebook.* Vol. 3, edited by Philip Ostien, 76–118. Ibadan: Spectrum Books.

Ozigi, Albert, and Lawrence Ocho. 1981. *Education in Northern Nigeria.* London: George Allen and Unwin Ltd.

Reichmuth, Stefan. 1989. New Trends in Islamic Education in Nigeria: Preliminary Account. *Die Welt das Islams* 29: 41–60.

Tibenderana, Peter K. 1976. The Emirs and the Spread of Western Education in Northern Nigeria 1910–1945. *Journal of African History* 24(3): 517–534.

———. 1985. The Beginning of Girls' Education in the Native Administrative Schools of Northern Nigeria 1930–1945. *Journal of African History* 26: 93–109.

Umar, Mohammad S. 2004. Mass Islamic Education and the Emergence of Female 'ulama' in Northern Nigeria: Background, Trends and Consequences. In *The Transmission of Learning in Islamic Africa*, edited by Scott Reese, 99–119. Leiden: Brill.

Werthmann, Katya. 2005. The Examples of Nana Asma'u. http://www.nmfuk.org/asmau/TheExampleofNanaAsmau.pdf. accessed 06.02.2010.

CHAPTER 10

Shembe is the Way: The Nazareth Baptist Church in the Religious Field and in Academic Discourse

Magnus Echtler

Shembe is the way

It wasn't the valley of death I was walking in.
It was the valley of confusion for many years.
Different religions different beliefs.
Undermining my culture.
Looking down upon my tradition.
Making fun of my language.
Telling my children, they have no God.
Finally I can tell them about, Shembe is the way.

Oh Shembe thank you for showing us the way. Shembe nobunazaretha.
Oh Shembe thank you for healing my people. Shembe nobunazaretha.
Shembe is the way.

I hear them shouting Amen, at the top of the mountain.
I hear them shouting Uyingcwele at the top of that mountain.
No one will undermine my religion.
No one will undermine my culture anymore,
Cause God sent him from above, to be with the people.
Bring them back to what is their own.
Take them back to the way of our forefathers.
Finally I can tell generations and generations that Shembe is the way.

Oh Shembe thank you for showing us the way. Shembe nobunazaretha.
    LUCKY DUBE. *Respect*. Gallo Record Company (South Africa). 2006.

Introduction

Lucky Dube (1964–2007) was the most famous reggae singer of South Africa, and he was also a member of the Nazareth Baptist Church, one of the biggest African Initiated Churches (AICs), or New Religious Movements in South Africa. His song takes us right into the middle of the problem addressed in this chapter. Is the Nazareth Baptist Church, founded in 1910 by Isaiah Shembe, an illiterate lay preacher and healer, a Christian church or a new religion? What does it mean when the members of the church shout 'You are holy' (*uyingcwele*)? Does it mean that the leader of the church is the Black Messiah?

In his poetic interpretation of his religion (*ubunazaretha*), Lucky Dube emphasized the liberation of his culture from suppression, and in the South African context that means the liberation of Black African culture from White apartheid suppression. And he states that Shembe is the way, not Jesus Christ, and that Shembe was sent by God to bring back the way of the forefathers.

All of these aspects will be considered in my analysis which focuses on the symbolic capital of Isaiah Shembe, his charisma, his social status as acknowledged by others.[1] I will argue that Isaiah Shembe's success in establishing his new church in the religious field was based on the invention of new religious practices that linked with pre-existing religious traditions, while at the same time served to distinguish the new church from both mission Christianity and Zulu religion. I will argue further that these very practices served to buttress his symbolic capital by connecting him and his new style of leadership with the dispositions of the part of the laity that formed the main portion of the church's membership, dispositions that were based on socio-political structures of pre-colonial Zulu society.

The second section of the chapter is concerned with symbolic violence, the inverse side of symbolic capital. I will show how the academic interpretations of the church, especially the controversy over the theological status of Isaiah Shembe and thus the classification of the church as Post-Christian or Christian both exerted symbolic violence, and functioned as excommunication and canonization, the structural responses of established players vis-à-vis heretical newcomers in the religious field. Finally, I will contrast the academic interpretations with emic views on the leaders of the church, views of which Lucky Dube's text formed the first example.

---

1 My analysis is based on extensive fieldwork in the Nazareth Baptist Church, *eBuhleni* faction, during the years 2007–2013, funded by the German Research Foundation (DFG). My thanks to all church members who let me partake in their lives, religious and otherwise, and who shared their views with me.

The Nazareth Baptist Church (NBC) in the Religious Field

Isaiah Shembe founded the Nazareth Baptist Church in 1910. Before that, he had been active as a travelling lay preacher and healer, and sent his converts to other churches for baptism. According to the oral traditions of the church, Shembe started his own church only after his converts were refused baptism by the American Zulu Mission because they dressed in traditional attire (Becken 1966: 103). This founding myth captures important features of the church's position within the religious field: the founder's proximity to Mission Christianity as well as his break with it over the question of African cultural traditions. It was in these borderlands that the church was to be thriving.

Isaiah Shembe, called 'the founder' (*uMqaliwendlela*) within the church, can be considered as a prophet from a social science perspective, as an innovator within the religious field who, thanks to his specific relations with the lay people, achieves the "initial accumulation of the capital of symbolic power" (Bourdieu 1987a: 130).[2] Pierre Bourdieu follows Max Weber in basing the dynamics of the religious field on the opposition between the priest and the prophet (Bourdieu 1987a: 127, 1991: 17, Weber 1972: 268–9). The two types of religious specialists differ with regard to their religious legitimacy: the prophet depends on his charisma, a personal quality that has to be continuously acknowledged by the laity, while the authority of the priest is based on his office in a religious institution. As both compete over the power to impose a religious habitus on the laity, a disposition to (mis)recognize the status of the religious experts as legitimate, the prophets, as the newcomers in the game, have to attack the routinized, institutionalized basis of the priests' power (Bourdieu 1987a: 126, 1991: 27). Their success depends on their ability to de-legitimize the priestly order through the mobilization of the deviant religious interests of a portion of the laity (Bourdieu 1991: 24). Thus the mobilizing force of the prophets' charisma is based on collective representations in Durkheim's sense, on the link between personal qualities of the prophet and dispositions present in parts of the laity. Bourdieu insists that the prophets' symbolic capital, their charisma, is based on this relation which explains why they are "*socially* predisposed" (Bourdieu 1987a: 131, emphasis in original) to express the dispositions present in the laity. Based on their ability to draw on latent dispositions and to mobilize deviant interests, successful prophets are often associated with moments

---

[2] As will become clear later on, the designation 'prophet' is rejected by some of his successors because from their perspective it does not do justice to his (and their) specific spiritual powers.

of social crisis, when the laity's dissatisfaction with the established order favors newcomers in the religious field and elsewhere (Bourdieu 1987a: 130).

The crisis that formed the backdrop for the founding and early history of the Nazareth Baptist Church was the destruction of Zulu society in the wake of the military defeat of the Zulu kingdom and the increasing incorporation of its people within the growing capitalist economy of South Africa, a process that entered its final stages when the last major uprising, called the Bambatha rebellion, had been forcefully put down in 1906 (Guy 1979, 2005, Marks 1970). As a result of this social upheaval, prophetic strategies proved successful in de-legitimizing the established positions within the religious field. With regard to the established order of pre-colonial Zulu religion, the first prophets had been the representatives of mission Christianity.[3] As newcomers the missionaries had tried to discredit the established religious experts (priests, elders, healers, diviners, witches, chiefs, etc.) by arguing first that the African people had no religion, and once the African laity was under the control of the colonial state, that there was religion, but of the wrong or inferior kind (idolatry, superstition), interpreted either as a degeneration of the original monotheism or as primitive form in the evolution of religion (animism, ancestor worship), as argued by Chidester (1996) for Southern Africa. This strategy proved successful only when the colonial state had destroyed the pre-existing social structure and thus created the specific religious interest in the laity that mission Christianity could satisfy: the justification for their status as colonized (Bourdieu 1987a: 124–5, 1991: 16). But while the mission churches excelled in legitimizing the social position of the colonizers, and consequently enjoyed state support in their quest for the monopoly on legitimate religious power, their justification for the position of the colonized proved wanting and invited the de-legitimizing strategies from the next type of prophets: African Christians within the mission churches. The problem for the white missionaries in monopolizing religious power was "to make known to those who are excluded from it the legitimacy of their exclusion, that is, to make them misrecognize the arbitrariness of the monopolization of a power and a competence that is in principle accessible to anyone" (Bourdieu 1991: 25). These African prophets—like John L. Dube, ordained minister, founder of a Zulu language newspaper and an

---

[3] Of course the missionaries were primarily priests in this sociological sense: as office-holders within a hierarchical institution whose position depended on formalized education. But it might prove fruitful to consider them as prophets in the sense of innovators—or as rather unsuccessful newcomers to the African field, especially in the early phases, when they failed to accumulate symbolic power because their religious message did not resonate with the religious interests of the laity.

industrial school and first president of the South African Native Congress (later ANC) as well as contemporary and neighbor of Isaiah Shembe in Inanda—challenged the monopoly of the whites not only in the religious but also in the political field, and their religious message mobilized the well educated and economically successful parts of the laity, i.e. the emergent African bourgeoisie (Cabrita 2008: 43–52, Marks 1975, 1986). Their religious message was labeled as 'Ethopianism' by the white establishment, and they were certainly regarded as a threat to colonial stability, yet their claim to religious authority followed the rules of the game of the white missionaries: they demanded an office because they possessed the right kind of cultural capital—a western education acquired in mission institutions (Etherington 1978, Chirenje 1987). But why should religious authority depend on western education? This brings us back to Isaiah Shembe and the role of African clothing in the Nazareth Baptist Church.

If one interprets the strategies of the players as conflicts over the borders of the religious field, then the missionaries excluded all pre-colonial practices from the field, and the African Christians demanded their inclusion in this new field. Isaiah Shembe invented religious practices for his church by using both Christian and African religious traditions, while at the same time distinguishing them from both strands, i.e. he shifted the borders of the field and changed the rules of the game. His success was based on the 'magical fit' between his religious message and the religious interest of his clientele, the portion of the laity that might roughly be characterized as 'rural traditionalists'.[4] But this fit, and therefore the success of the church, was not there from the beginning, but rather the result of a process, an interaction with the lay members that continues up to the present day.

When Isaiah Shembe started out with his own church, his clientele were the marginalized of colonial Natal, especially those at the fringes of the urban centre of Durban, and his ministry was certainly regarded as threat to social stability by state officials. Analyzing the correspondence of the Chief Native

---

4 By this I mean that many church members come from a rural, low income, low education background, and most consider African/Zulu cultural traditions as important. I cannot provide any quantitative data to back this proposition, which is rather based on my ethnographic fieldwork and especially on the interaction with my primary peer group: university students from the church. The highly educated members are growing in numbers but remain in a marginal position within the church. They are extremely sensitive with regard to this fact, especially as the outside perception of the church is dominated by the 'rural simpleton' stereotype (see Sithole 1999: 252). For church membership in the 1950s see Vilakazi & Mthethwa & Mpanza 1986: 53–58. The social position of the laity is central to Bourdieu's argument, which I follow here.

Commissioner (CNC) from 1912 to 1922, Liz Gunner concludes that these "letters give some evidence of the intense suspicion and hostility directed at Shembe from the highest official levels" (Gunner 1988: 215). But it is also interesting to see who urged the representatives of the state to take action against the unruly preacher. Not surprisingly, there were missionaries who wanted their competitor to be taken out of the game. In 1913 two clergymen of the American Zulu Mission visited the CNC and "complained that a native named Shembe, who is under no control or supervision by European missionaries, is carrying on preaching on the Reserves mentioned, and is having a bad influence amongst the Natives residing there" (C.N.C. 2155/12/30–13), a complaint that prompted the CNC to consult the Attorney General about how to best regain control over this independent religious entrepreneur.

But there were also some leaders of the pre-colonial social order who urged the colonial state to take action against Isaiah Shembe. And this is rather more surprising, because these were representatives of the portion of the African laity that formed the basis of the church's success later on. A case from 1915 contains the statements of two African men who complained about Shembe and his church undermining male authority. A chief pointed out that women and children left their homesteads to follow Shembe without the permission of their husbands or fathers, and that some families were evicted from mission reserves because the women left the mission churches, while another man who had just received his eviction notice complained that he had "been convicted for thrashing my wife because she is continually leaving home without my permission and staying away sometimes two or three weeks [...] preaching on behalf of a sect called 'The Nazareths' under the leadership of Isaiah Tshembe" (C.N.C. 2155/12/30–31). In the resultant letter to the Chief Native Commissioner, the Magistrate of Port Shepstone in southern Natal showed respect for the relative autonomy of the religious field by arguing that "[t]olerance, no doubt, is the keynote in all religious matters, but surely even that has its limits" and that he "would be the last to advocate any policy antagonistic to the teachings of true religion, but when we have a scurrilous fanatic like this man, Isaiah Tshembe, to deal with I consider that we should deal with this mischievous growth swiftly and destroy the trouble in its inception, root and branch" (C.N.C. 2155/12/30–31). He therefore asked the CNC for the authority to stop Shembe from entering his district, but that proved to be rather difficult. As Shembe was preaching primarily on private property and not on mission reserves, he could not legally be stopped from preaching. Instead, the CNC suggested to make use of the complaints of Zulu men about their wayward women in order to charge Shembe with "inciting women and girls to wander from their kraals," and, once in custody, have him medically examined and declared "a dangerous lunatic" (C.N.C. 2155/12/30–32). This case shows, next to the fact that Isaiah Shembe still had to win over his key constituency five years after the founding of his church, that the state agents respected the relative autonomy of the religious field—that made the complicated plan to take out Shembe necessary—even if the player in question was a lay preacher outside of European control.

Being acknowledged as an actor in the religious field by the state certainly helped Isaiah Shembe's career, but what ensured the success of the church was the introduction of new religious practices, the Sabbath service and religious dancing, which corresponded with the religious interests of certain portions of the laity. In the Nazareth Baptist Church, two forms of worship are distinguished: praying (*ukukhonza*) and dancing (*ukusina* or *umgidi*). Praying includes the daily prayers and the Sabbath services, while religious dancing takes place only at the church's festivals which form the yearly ritual cycle of the church. It is not entirely clear when the shift to Saturday services, including the observance of Sabbath taboos occurred, but the earliest historical evidence is from 1923 (Heuser 2003: 116). What is clear, however, is that this shift marked a break with mission Christianity, and also marks a difference to most African Initiated Churches. It is a religious practice that makes a difference; church members are concerned with church matters during the high time for social recreation from Friday evening until Saturday afternoon, and they are free to socialize outside church on Sunday, when the Christians are in church. It is also closely linked with the esteem placed on Old Testament taboos within the Nazareth Baptist Church, especially those linked with the Nazarenes, like the bare feet in the temples, and the prohibition to cut the hair, that likewise serve as marks of distinction.

Like the Sabbath service, dancing was not practiced from the beginning of the church. According to Johannes Galilee Shembe, the son and successor of Isaiah Shembe, his father was at first "totally opposed to all forms" of dancing, and introduced it only in 1919 (Fernandez 1973: 42). As Isaiah Shembe attracted converts from both mission churches and Zulu traditional religion, it is likely that some new members who were still grounded in the pre-Christian cultural traditions continued dancing within the church, a practice expressing lineage identity at wedding celebrations and regimental competition in the Zulu military (Berglund 1976: 198–9, Erlmann 1996: 189, Mthethwa 1989: 248). This dancing forced or inspired Isaiah Shembe to create religious dances for the Nazareth Baptist Church. At first, he introduced European-style dance uniforms, but by the early 1930s most dancers wore the neo-traditional uniforms for men, women, and virgins, which continue to dominate the performances until today (Brown 1995: 114–116, 129–130).[5] This reluctant decision to include dance as a form of worship as well as the move towards the neo-traditional attires reflected a shift in church membership as converts with a traditionalist outlook gained in influence (Brown 1995: 128–131, Heuser 2003: 224–227, Papini 2004: 49–52). It is this process of reintroducing practices and material objects into the religious field—practices and objects that had been excluded from the field as defined by the Christian missionaries—that creates the "quasi-miraculous harmony" between the form of the religious message and "the strictly religious interests of its privileged clientele" (Bourdieu 1991: 18). This move can be described as a concession to the religious believes of this key constituency, a growing constituency that increasingly included not only women and children but also the homestead heads and chiefs, a constituency that occupied a decisively different social position than the black bourgeoisie that formed the key clientele of the prophets from the African mission Christianity, and that therefore had decisively different religious interests. Any extension of the power of the experts over the laity, writes Bourdieu (1991: 29), "must be paid by a redoubling of the concessions granted [...] to the religious representations of the laypersons thus conquered." The reintroduced practices can also be interpreted as a revitalization of African society, but it has to be kept in mind that they marked a difference not only to mission Christianity but also to African Traditional Religions (Vilakazi & Mthethwa & Mpanza 1986, Roberts 1936: 62, 123). The religious dance is different from the cultural traditions it draws upon, most notably in the hymns that form its basis (Echtler 2010: 377, Heuser 2008: 46–7, Papini 2004: 55). While the musical form links with clan and regimental songs, it was Isaiah Shembe who created the texts, which combine an Old Testament feel of Babylonian loss and suffering with the lament of the disintegration of Zulu society and are considered as outstanding example of Zulu poetry and a testimony to Isaiah Shembe's artistic genius. But despite the transformations, the church members were still dancing, and dancing became effectively a religious practice, and thus altered the shape of the religious field, because it was a practice able to "mobilize the virtually heretical religious interests of determinate groups or classes of laypersons through the effect of consecration" (Bourdieu 1991: 24). Finally, the introduction of dancing as well as the introduction of the Sabbath services can be described as a strategic moves, based less on conscious deliberation than on the actors' habitus, as moves whose practical success depended on the concurrence of the habitus of

---

5 Only some of the young men dance in 'Scottish' attire (*isikoshi*), including pith helmet and military style boots. See front cover and Echtler 2014.

the prophet and the laity. With the invention of religious practices that marked a difference to pre-existing religious traditions, Shembe build a "(quasi-)system endowed with and itself bestowing meaning" which could play "an organizing and legitimating role" only because it had "as its own generative and unifying principle a *habitus* objectively attuned to that of its addressees" (Bourdieu 1987a: 131). With that in mind it is now possible to turn to the decisive factor for the success of the NBC in the religious field: the charisma of Isaiah Shembe and his successors.

With regard to Weber's concept of charismatic authority Bourdieu cautions against a "naïve representation of charisma as a mysterious quality inherent in a person or as a gift of nature" and against a concept of charismatic legitimacy "grounded solely in an act of 'recognition'" (Bourdieu 1987a: 129). Instead he suggests that "the word and the person of the prophet symbolize collective representations that, by virtue of the creative nature of symbolization, they contribute to constituting" (Bourdieu 1987a: 130). In order to solve the problem of the "initial accumulation of the capital of symbolic power" it is therefore necessary "to explain why a particular individual finds himself *socially* predisposed to live out and express with particular cogency and coherence, ethical or political dispositions that are already present in a latent state amongst all the members of the class or group of his addressees" (Bourdieu 1987a: 130–1, emphasis in original).

A longstanding though contested answer to this question in the literature on the NBC is the argument that in "Shembe the kingship type of leadership is combined with that of the *isangoma* (diviner)" (Oosthuizen 1968: 10, see also Sundkler 1961: 240, Vilakazi & Mthethwa & Mpanza 1986: 100, 157–8). In order to evaluate this proposed social disposition, it is necessary to look at pre-colonial Zulu religion. According to Bourdieu the religious field is constituted through the exclusion of the lay persons, who recognize the specialists as legitimate holders of religious capital (Bourdieu 1991: 9). There was little division of labor in Zulu society, and accordingly the religious specialists were part-time experts only, and there were no religious institutions in the strict sense. Nevertheless, two types of specialists can be distinguished. The first were the homestead heads and lineage seniors, the men who officiated at the sacrifices to the ancestors of this lineage (Krige 1950: 290, Berglund 1976: 225). By extension, the chiefs and the king were part of this system. They were the heads of the most important lineages and responsible for the well-being of the whole of their dominion. Especially in the case of the king this well-being had to be insured through elaborate rituals (Krige 1950: 249–60). These men were religious specialists because of their position within the lineage, that is, their social capital (see Bourdieu 1986: 248–52).

The second type of religious specialist was the diviner (*isangoma*).⁶ Both men and women could become diviners not by choice but by calling, through overcoming an affliction and serving an apprenticeship with an established healer/diviner (Berglund 1976: 136–62). Through this process they gained the cultural capital that made them religious experts (see Bourdieu 1986: 243–48). But there was also a link with social capital, because it would often be spirits from the diviners' lineages who afflicted and empowered them. Diviners diagnosed and dealt with all kinds of afflictions, they produced medicines (*muthi*), interceded with spirits and identified and fought witches (*abathakathi*) on behalf of their clients.

These practices did not end with the destruction of pre-colonial society, up to today laypeople consult diviners and sacrifice to the ancestors within the descent groups. However, the attitude of the NBC towards the two strands of tradition is very different. While the religious practices of the lineages are encouraged, and the ancestors are in fact considered to play an important role in bringing converts into the church, it is forbidden for church members to consult diviners, and if they do, they have to be cleansed before they may enter the sacred places of the church. In what sense, then, can Shembe's leadership be considered as combining that of the king and the diviner?

In supporting the religious traditions of the lineages and in teaching respect (*hlonipha*) towards their elders, Isaiah Shembe legitimized the traditional socio-political structure with the chiefs and the king on top (see Cabrita 2009, 2010). However, in his hymns and sermons he also attacked the Zulu royal house. In the liturgy for the Sabbath service, which forms part of the hymnbook of the church, verse 21 reads:

> Do not behave like your fathers, the Dinganas and Senzangakhonas, our fathers who hardened their hearts. Jehovah eventually punished them in this manner, now today we bear their sins (Muller 2010: 31).

In his interpretation of the destruction of Zulu society Isaiah Shembe put at least part of the responsibility on the sins of the forefathers, and especially on the Zulu kings—though their names were removed from the hymnbook in 2005 (Cabrita 2009: 620, note 75). Thus he suggested that any redemption of Zulu society would be achieved not through political but spiritual means, means that he and his church could provide (Cabrita 2009: 609, 624; Heuser

---

6 There were actually various sub-types of healers/diviners. See Krige 1950: 297–302, Berglund 1976: 185–90. For postmodern varieties see e.g. Flynt & Parle 2008, Steyn 2008.

2003: 215–20). Just like the ordinary lineages of commoners had been united under the patronage of the chiefs, who were in turn united under the king, the restored Zulu society would be united under Shembe's patronage. And according to the oral traditions of the church, Shembe could bring drought to the dominions of chiefs who opposed him, just like the Zulu king had been responsible for rain and the fertility of the land (Cabrita 2010: 21, Krige 1950: 247–8). Like the king who moved between his numerous residences and performed the first fruit ceremonies for the whole nation, Shembe moved between his temples throughout South Africa and performed the rituals of his church's ritual cycle. And the chiefs did come and join his church. For the chiefs, who were in need of a boost of their authority in the wake of colonization, the NBC provided a stage where they "instructed and exhorted their constituencies into submission to their rule, not only as a secular obligation but also a spiritual virtue" (Cabrita 2010: 22). For the church the chiefs provided an avenue to proselytize the rural laity beyond the women and the young people and to acquire the credibility of "an institution of national standing" (Cabrita 2010: 27). Isaiah Shembe was like the Zulu king insofar as he occupied a similar position within a transformed social structure. This predisposed him to express dispositions already present in his clientele, which added to his symbolic capital, his charisma (Bourdieu 1987a: 131). *INkosi*, the title of the pre-colonial Zulu kings and chiefs, is also the title of the leader of the NBC. When he sits in front of his congregation, with the Zulu chiefs in the front row, he is King of kings (*iNkosi yamaKosi*)—one of his praises—not only in the biblical sense, but also in relation to Zulu social structure.

A similar argument can be made with regard to Isaiah Shembe's relation to the diviners. As mentioned before, members of the NBC are not allowed to consult diviners, but they do not need them anyway, because Isaiah Shembe and his successors can deal with any affliction they might suffer from. Isaiah Shembe was a healer from the beginning, and in the oral traditions of the church there are many such stories of miraculous healings, of how he deals with witches, or how he bests diviners or Christian pastors in spiritual competitions (Hexham & Oosthuizen 1996: 59–62, 103–106, 134–140; 2001: 19–25; Sithole 2009). This calls to mind Weber's idea that charisma is acknowledged willingly because it proves itself, a proof that originally took the form of miracles (Weber 1972: 140). Shembe's role as a worker of miracles made the diviners superfluous because he like them dealt with this-worldly afflictions, but he did not heal like them, he did not employ their techniques or materials, he healed simply by saying "*iNkosi ikubusise*—May the Lord bless you." Of course healing added to his charisma, because it satisfied the demands or religious interests of parts of the laity, interests that had been banned, together with the diviners, from the religious field by mission Christianity. With regard to the powers of the prophet Bourdieu argues that

> [...] the basis of the relation among interest, belief, and symbolic power must be found [...] in the dialectic of inner experience and social image, a quasi-magical circulation of powers in the course of which the group produces and projects the symbolic power that will be exercised upon itself and in the terms of which is constituted, for the prophet as for his followers, the experience of prophetic power that produces the whole reality of this power (Bourdieu 1991: 21).

I argued elsewhere how the telling of the miracle stories—common not only in church services but also in everyday interaction among church members—interconnects the life-histories of the members with church doctrine, thus charging the religious message with lived emotion and producing the symbolic capital of the church leader (Echtler 2010: 383–4). In the context of the social production of symbolic power Bourdieu also refers to Levi-Strauss' famous example of the skeptical sorcerer who did not become a sorcerer because he healed people, but who healed people because he had become a sorcerer (Bourdieu 1991: 42, note 44). There is a similar example from the NBC from the time when Johannes Galilee Shembe, the son of Isaiah, followed his father as leader of the church:

> It was only after his father's death that Johannes Shembe discovered that he, also, possessed the gift of healing, or, perhaps it would be more correct to say, the gift of inspiring the emotion which makes it possible for healing to take place. His ability to carry on this branch of his father's work has done a great deal to strengthen his position as head of the church (Roberts 1936: 111).

This example leads to a decisive factor for the position of the NBC within the religious field, the routinization or banalization of the founder's charisma. Bourdieu follows Weber in regarding this process as one of the regular transformations of the religious field, based on the structural opposition of prophet and church. In order to succeed, every prophetic movement has to ensure continuity; it has to become a church, an institution with a bureaucratic character, a hierarchy of functions and positions, and a codified doctrine (Bourdieu 1987a: 127, 1991: 24). Within the NBC this happened primarily during the reign of Johannes Galilee Shembe (1936–1976). I argued above how Isaiah Shembe and the laity stabilized the new religious order of the church in interconnection and distinction to pre-existing religious traditions, both through the new practices of the church and the dialectical construction of Shembe's symbolic capital. But it was Johannes Galilee Shembe who established the extended hierarchical and patriarchal order of the church, with the female heads of the virgins' and women's groups subordinated to the male hierarchy of preachers, evangelists and ministers, who headed the temples and regions, or were appointed special functions. And it was Johannes Galilee who codified the church's doctrine, especially within the hymnbook, which was first printed in 1940, and which serves since then as the cornerstone of the teachings of the church (see Heuser & Hexham 2005, Muller 2010). However, he also retained the extraordinary charisma of his father as a worker of miracles, and this was expressed in church doctrine as the concept of the singular and eternal spiritual Shembe, who is present in the leader of the church. This emic representation of the church leader's spiritual power is neatly captured in hymn 220, composed by Johannes Galilee Shembe in 1938, two years into his church leadership: "My flesh is weary, it will lie in the grave, my spirit will rise and be clothed with a new flesh. I was born in eternity, at all times I shall be there" (Muller 2010: 201). But the concept proved problematic after his death in 1976, when both his brother Amos Shembe and his son Londa Shembe claimed to be the church leader in whom the spiritual Shembe is present. This succession conflict led to a split in the church, in which the vast majority of church members followed Amos Shembe because he was able to secure the support of the church's priesthood, that is he was able to secure his charisma through the bureaucracy of the church (Echtler 2010: 388). Despite the inner-church conflicts—and this structural problem remained, in March 2011, after the death of Vimbeni Shembe, the son of Amos, another succession conflict arose—the NBC, or its various factions, continued to grow. Church membership received a further boost with the end of apartheid, when the reinterpretation of the South African history increased the social standing of the NBC. Liz Gunner (2002: 1) argues that "the church's public 'gravitas', its growing numbers (it may well have over a million members now) and its success in presenting a religious presence which is distinctively African, make it a force to be reckoned with in social, religious and political terms" in the new South Africa.

At the funeral of Vimbeni Shembe, taking place in eBuhleni on 3 April 2011, Jacob Zuma, the president of South Africa, acknowledged the historical significance of the NBC:

> The founder of this church will always be remembered in the history of this country as one of the brave and important leaders. Black people knew that they were being robbed when they were told that in order to worship they must change their cultures (Zuma 2011).

But he also acknowledged the charisma of the late leader of the church:

> You might recall, especially the ministers, I used to come here at different times with different situations. In some of my visits I asked the *iNkosi* [Vimbeni Shembe] to pray for me as I was facing charges, I wanted him to hear it from me rather than just reading about it in the newspapers. I wanted to tell him the true story. He would always pray and say that nothing is impossible with God (Zuma 2011).

With this statement he identified with the hundreds of people who stand in line each Saturday to meet with the leader of the NBC, in order to tell him their problems and receive his blessing *"iNkosi ikubusise*—May the Lord bless you." Thus Zuma acknowledged the symbolic capital of the *iNkosi*, the extraordinary ability to work miracles, in a form understandable to all familiar with the practices of the church—and of course his audience at this occasion consisted primarily of church members. Now Jacob Zuma cannot exactly count as an emic voice with regard to the status of the leader of the NBC, although he certainly is an expert in using his Zulu background to full political advantage. But before turning to emic views proper, I will discuss how the status of the leader of the NBC has been interpreted within academic discourse.

The NBC in the Academic Field

This section is concerned with symbolic violence, the reverse side of symbolic capital, that is "the power to recognize, to consecrate, to state, with success, what merits being known and recognized" (Bourdieu 2000: 242). I discuss how academics used their position within the academic field to pass judgments on the NBC, and how these judgments were perceived from within the religious field. I argue that the controversy over the theological status of the church's leader was shaped primarily by the structure of the academic field, rather than the structure of religious field, and that emic views were in fact declared irrelevant for the question of the leader's status. While my discussion here focuses on a mainly theological discourse, the general argument that academic concepts and distinctions exert symbolic violence over the social realities they propose to describe objectively is of wider relevance, as the recent controversy over the question what should form the object of the academic study of 'African religions' shows (See Ranger 2007, Haar & Ellis 2009).

The Nazareth Baptist Church is arguably the most researched African Initiated Church. The most famous part of its academic treatment has been the 'Black Messiah' controversy that debated the status of the church's leader.

Starting point of this debate was Bengt Sundkler's classic *Bantu Prophets in South Africa*, first published in 1948. The conclusion contained Sundkler's famous theological judgment on AICs which gave the concept of syncretism its bad name in the study of religion in Africa:

> The behaviour and activities of the Zionist prophet and his church reveal that, in certain cases, the deepest cause of the emergence of Independent churches is a nativistic-syncretistic interpretation of the Christian religion [...] *The syncretistic sect becomes the bridge over which African are brought back to heathenism*—a viewpoint which stresses the seriousness of the whole situation. (Sundkler 1961: 297, emphasis in original)

That Sundkler judged the situation to be serious was based on his vested interest in the religious field: to defend the fruits of Christian mission against the inroads made by nativistic movements. The Nazareth Baptist Church was for Sundkler the prime example for the "Black Christ ideology" (Sundkler 1961: 281). Based on the interpretation of the church's hymns, but also on interviews with Johannes Galilee Shembe and other informants, Sundkler concluded that in the hymns "Shembe is represented as the Christ of the Zulus" and that in "the belief of his followers Shembe becomes co-creator with God, and he is the mediator in heaven" (Sundkler 1961: 284–5). On top of that Sundkler provided information about how a church member managed the insider-outsiders divide in order not to jeopardize the church's position within the religious field dominated by Christian interpretations:

> Because of the opposition which these dogmatic statements call forth among other Christians, Nazarites are sometimes careful not to call him God [i.e. Isaiah Shembe]. "It is this way," one informant told me; "he *is* God, but in *inhlonipho*-language we call him prophet" (Sundkler 1961: 285–6).

This interpretation of the Messianic character or deification of Isaiah Shembe was later repeated by Gerhardus Oosthuizen in his analysis of the hymns of the NBC. He summarizes his interpretation—backed also by a small empirical study (Oosthuizen 1974)—as follows:

> Shembe I [i.e. Isaiah Shembe] is not only Mediator but is Messiah, the manifestation of God. Shembe II [i.e. Johannes Galilee Shembe] in a sermon stated inter alia that "Isaiah Shembe showed you a God who walks on feet and heals with his hands". The listeners naturally had Shembe I

in mind. To this association of the Supreme Being and Shembe I his Izl [*izihlabelelo*—hymns] contributed. Shembe I is to the Nazarites the personification of Supreme power (Oosthuizen 1967: 3).

For Oosthuizen "every religion is an organic whole" and the Nazareth Baptist Church "is a Zuluized religion!" But this has consequences from a theological perspective, because "as far as the creed is concerned no borrowing is possible for Christianity unless one wishes to establish a new religion" (Oosthuizen 1967: 10). As a result, he labeled the NBC and other AICs like it as "Post-Christian":

Many form easy bridges back to nativism. They are neither Christian nor traditional, but a syncretism of both, and thus a new religion (Oosthuizen 1968: xi).

Both Sundkler and Oosthuizen classified AICs, and both excluded the NBC from the Christian category, that is they exerted symbolic violence, the power to define who is worthy of acknowledgement, which is based on their symbolic capital, on their standing as academics, as scholars of religion and theologians who pass disinterested judgments on what constitutes objective truth—according to the rules of the academic game (Bourdieu 2000: 242).

However, by the late 1960s the critical reflections on the link between anthropology and colonialism had led to post-colonial positions within the academic field, and the academic authorities who passed judgment on the subalterns were increasingly called into question. Consequently, Oosthuizen's judgments did not go unchallenged. The first critic was Sundkler, who had reconsidered classifying Shembe as the Black Messiah and now suggested "the Biblical, and, indeed, African, concept of the *eikon*, i.e. the mask, and in this case the mask of the Black Christ" which allows the Africans to worship the Christian God beyond "the heavy, artificial rules of the Whites" (Sundkler 1976: 193). He arrived at this new interpretation thanks to two methodological considerations, both of which he claimed Oosthuizen overlooked:

(1) One must *distinguish* between the prophet's own personal faith and expressions of faith *and* the testimony of his followers. (2) The principle of *ambiguity of meaning*: there is a constant oscillation in these terms, a double-meaning which cannot be grasped by stereotype, ready-made phrases (Sundkler 1976: 193, emphasis in original).

Oosthuizen was also criticized by Absolom Vilakazi, Bongani Mthethwa and Mthembeni Mpanza, who argued that his misrepresentation of Shembe stemmed from his lack of understanding the Zulu language and from his Christian bias (Vilakazi, Mthethwa & Mpanza 1986: 89). They classified Shembe as "a prophet in the nature of the biblical prophets" (Vilakazi, Mthethwa & Mpanza 1986: 104), and argued that the classification of Shembe as Messiah could not be based on either Shembe's statements or the hymns, but only on what his followers said. These statements they regarded as evidence for the "sacralisation of Shembe" but they considered it "unfair to blame Shembe I for what people, who came under his influence, said about him" (Vilakazi, Mthethwa & Mpanza 1986: 115). And they certainly took issue with symbolic violence exerted over Africans by Western scholars:

> [The] Christian theological obsession with the theme of the usurpation of Christ's place in African independent churches arises from western ethnocentric bias and arrogant assumptions that somehow they have the 'pure' Christianity and that their perspectives on Christianity are the only valid ones. This, of course, would deny non-western interpretations of Christianity which could come out of socio-cultural perspectives of other peoples (Vilakazi, Mthethwa & Mpanza 1986: 113).

This interpretive frame has remained the dominant one for the academic classification of the Nazareth Baptist Church. Allan Anderson included the NBC not only in the Christian but in the Pentecostal fold, based on his findings that "[i]nstead of being a 'Messiah' or 'Black Christ', Isaiah Shembe is the 'servant of the lord', 'the man sent by God' who is obedient to the bidding of God" in most of the oral traditions of the church (Anderson 2000: 226). At the beginning of his book he emphasized that his "use of this terminology [African Pentecostal / Pentecostal-type churches] was definitely not an attempt to claim ownership of Zionist churches by Pentecostals, but simply to describe the fact of affinity between Pentecostals and Zionists" (Anderson 2000: 9), but then again disinterestedness is the basic rule in the academic game. A number of recent theological dissertations on the NBC likewise retained the inclusive frame (Thisken 2002, Heuser 2003, Cabrita 2008).

However, inclusion, just like exclusion, is a classification that exerts symbolic violence, and that might be rejected by the people so classified:

> In the past Christians used a stick to beat us. They said we were pagans and that our followers ought to join *real* churches. Now they are using a carrot. They say we are just another Christian denomination. In this way they are trying to bring us under their control by using promises of recognition and financial assistance to lead our people back into their

churches [...] only Oosthuizen understands us. The others want to remake us in their own image (Hexham 1997: 363–4, emphasis in original).

This is a statement of Londa Shembe, the leader of one faction of the church from 1977–1989. According to Hexham, both Londa and Amos Shembe, the leader of the other faction (1977–1994), agreed that Oosthuizen rather than Vilakazi or Sundkler understood their religion, which Amos considered to be a new form of Christianity, and Londa to be a new religion (Hexham 1997: 363). If one considers the academics involved in this controversy to be players in the religious field, it becomes clear that they represent the structural responses of the church to the prophetical challenge:

> When the relations of force are in favour of the church, prophetic contestations can end only in the suppression of the prophet (or the sect), by physical or symbolic violence (excommunication), unless the submission of the prophet (or the reformer)—that is, recognition of the legitimacy of the ecclesiastical monopoly (and of the hierarchy that guarantees it)— authorizes annexation by canonization (Bourdieu 1991: 25).

When the scholars classify, as players in the academic field, when they exclude or include, they are in effect, from the perspective inside the religious field, excommunicating or canonizing. The problem with the inclusive interpretation—and the corresponding downplay of the Messianic character of the church's leader—is that at least some of the (prominent) players of the religious field from within the NBC reject the Christian monopoly of definition, and do not want to be canonized, but rather prefer to be excommunicated, because that entails more of a recognition of what they consider to be the status of the spiritual Shembe. But what, then is the (more or less) objective truth? How do we as academics deal with the fuzzy borders, the feedback loops between the academic field and the field under study?

Bourdieu's answer is participant objectivation, which requires that not only the objective structure of the field in question is analyzed, but also the position of the researcher within the academic field, and within any other social field relevant for the current research:

> What needs to be objectified, then, is not the anthropologist performing the anthropological analysis of a foreign world but the social world that has made both the anthropologist and the conscious or unconscious anthropology that she (or he) engages in her anthropological practice— not only her social origin, her position and trajectory in social space, her

social and religious memberships and beliefs, gender, age, nationality, etc., but also, and most importantly, her particular position within the microcosm of anthropologists (Bourdieu 2003: 283).

If the structure of the microcosm of scholars of religion can be characterized by the tension between apologetic / theological and critical / secularist approaches or insider and outsider perspectives (see Bourdieu 1987b: 106, King 2013: 139), then the approach pursued here certainly tends towards the secular social science pole, aimed at reducing religious phenomena to objective social structures beyond the individual experiences. However, Bourdieu warns that the break with religious institutions does not foreclose one's interest and investment in the religious field, as in the case of the secular science of religion's tense relation to theology over the insider-outsider issue (Bourdieu 1987b: 107). Consequently, Bourdieu's theory of practice does not only require a break with the phenomenological truth of the primary experience of the social world but with objectivist theories of action as well (Bourdieu 1977: 3, 1990: 135). Participant objectivation requires the conscious mastery of the interests of both insiders and outsiders, and especially of the social determinants of the scientific practice (Bourdieu 1987b: 109, 111), and it requires the scholar to draw upon his "own primary experience of the world", because otherwise "he cannot recognize the universal logic of practice in modes of thought and action (such as magical ones) that he describes as pre-logical or primitive" (Bourdieu 2003: 286). In the case of the NBC it is rather not helpful to cleanse the emic perspectives of all views of ordinary church members that contradict the interpretation serving one's own theological interests, because it is their views that allow us to understand the *illusio* of the social game and the mis-recognition of the positions of the actors in the field. In order to arrive at a better truth—that is, for the purposes of my analysis here, a social science rather than a theological one—it is therefore necessary to take into account emic views on the church's leader, which constitute his (mis-)recognitions, his acknowledgement through the church members, and which form the basis of his standing, his charisma, his symbolic capital, and thus his objective position within the religious field in relation to its other players. So it is the emic views that I now turn to for the final section of the chapter.

Emic Views of the NBC

Who, then, was Isaiah Shembe? What is the status of the leaders of the church? Londa Shembe answered this question in letters to Irving Hexham, scholar of religion and editor of the publications of the oral traditions of the church, in 1988:

> "Europeans", he said, "call Isaiah Shembe a prophet". But, this term, he insisted, did not convey the full meaning of the reality of Shembe. Who was Isaiah Shembe? To this question Londa Shembe answered "I have made it plain to you again and again who I think Shembe was within the bounds of safety which the cultural domination of the West permits me (at the cost of my being called a lunatic)". On another occasion he wrote "Think about me as being both Londa Shembe and Isaiah Shembe and then you will understand... Then move on and think again that to you I am Londa Shembe (or Johannes Galilee Shembe for that matter) and then you will see... I am making an attempt to make you see my God through my eyes..." (Hexham 1997: 366).

This is certainly an ambiguous statement. This ambiguity might be due to the fact that Londa Shembe explained Isaiah Shembe's and his own status to an outsider, an academic, who might, or might not, in Londa's view belong to the group of Christians who call Shembe a prophet, and who are now using the carrot to lure them back into their church. But the ambiguity might also be a functional requirement of prophetic speech: to be open to various interpretations in order to link with the dispositions of a wide range of addressees (Bourdieu 1987a: 131). If this is the case, one should not expect decisive statements regarding their status from the leaders of the church, and as far as I know there is none. Nor are the statements of the leaders decisive, at least not from a social science perspective. Sundkler (1976: 196) wrote: "Johannes Galilee Shembe has every right to be believed when he declares emphatically: 'Some of our people say 'Shembe is God'. But no, Isaiah never wanted to accept that.' From the social science perspective it is precisely the belief of the laity, their acknowledgement that determines the objective position of Shembe within the religious field. And there is ambiguity even in Sundkler's account, as he quotes another statement of Johannes Galilee Shembe on the same page: "Shembe was not born as you or I. He was born of Spirit and was Spirit" (Sundkler 1976: 196). The status of the leader, his charisma, his symbolic capital depends on the acknowledgement by the laity as framed within the objective structure of the religious field, as I have tried to show above. An important aspect of the objective structure of the field is its subjectified form, the habitus of the church members, including their views of the world and their views of their leader. The methodological challenge here is how to get data on the member's views.

The solution I propose here is to analyze the views of two individuals as they present them to other church members. One is a speech given to university students by one of the leading intellectuals of the church, the other a sermon by an Evangelist of the church delivered in the temple of eBuhleni, the church's headquarters, during one of the major festivals.

On 8 June 2008, J. J. M. Vilakazi, Minister (*umfundisi*) of the Nazareth Baptist Church, delivered a speech at the launch of a branch of the church's university students organization (NaTesA: Nazareth Tertiary Students Association) at the Tshwane University of Technology. Vilakazi was one of the leading intellectuals of the church. He was one of four young school teachers who Johannes Galilee Shembe selected to study theology, and who in 1984 was ordained Minister of the church by Amos Shembe—against the resistance of the established church hierarchy (Interview with Vilakazi, 9 July 2008). During the time of my research, he was one of the leaders within the eBuhleni branch of the church, and master of ceremony at the funeral of Vimbeni Shembe in March 2011.

I was not present when Vilakazi delivered the speech; he just gave me the 10 page printout of it after our interview. Therefore I cannot judge the exact context of its deliverance. I assume that with the speech Vilakazi aimed at representing the church to outsiders within the frame of an institution of higher learning, but also targeted the students from the church who hosted the event.[7]

The speech was divided in two main sections, the first one entitled "Shembe human divinity and Shembe spiritual divinity," and the second one "Ubunazaretha [i.e. the religion of the NBC] including the practical instance." The sub-section on human divinity starts out with the statement that there are different religions as well as different concepts of what religion is, and that the history of religions teaches that the first prophet of monotheism was Zoroaster. Vilakazi argues that "[r]esearch reveals that Judaism, Christianity, Islam and Nazariety have been build on the foundations of the teachings of this prophet of old [Nazariety is his translation of *ubunazaretha*, the religion/faith of the *amanazaretha*, the Nazarites, the members of the NBC]" (Vilakazi 2008:1). He lists the features that are shared by these religions, like one supreme God, Satan, an immortal soul and the day of judgment, and concludes that they "are not different from the religion that Isaiah Shembe came up with" (Vilakazi

---

7 I attended numerous functions of NaTesA at the University of KwaZulu-Natal. They served to present the church within the public sphere of the university, but also functioned as social events for the students, with delegations visiting from other universities, and refreshments being served after the main events. On all those occasions, the vast majority of the participants were members of the NBC.

2008: 2). He states that Nazariety is based on the Bible, but that Isaiah Shembe sometimes corrected the Bible although he was uneducated, which shows the superior knowledge of the prophets. Then he discusses that according to the Bible, God can take many forms like fire, human or animal form, or refer to different things, like an angel or prophets "when they perform supernatural acts," and concludes that because of that "the Nazarites believe that God is one but can assume different forms" (Vilakazi 2008: 3–4).

In the sub-section on spiritual divinity Vilakazi uses various oral traditions of the church to show how the Holy Spirit entered Isaiah Shembe's mother when she ate a flower, and how miracles from Shembe's youth show that the Holy Spirit resided in him (Vilakazi 2008: 5–6). He finally relates the vision that called Shembe to become a prophet, and argues that in that vision "a spiritual Shembe showed that he dwells in a human Shembe and that a human Shembe is one with a spiritual Shembe" (Vilakazi 2008: 7).

In the second section of his speech Vilakazi develops the concept of *ubunazaretha* and shows its practical consequences. He explains that the term comes from the Hebrew nazar, meaning to abstain, and refers to the Bible to show that Nazarites were people who dedicated themselves to God and in whom the Holy Spirit dwelled. He points out that in the New Testament John and Jesus Christ where Nazarites. He concludes that *ubunazaretha* "refers to holiness and to live and dedicate yourself to the Lord and to submit to his commandments" (Vilakazi 2008: 9). This dedication has practical consequences: Nazarites are not allowed to eat forbidden food, drink alcohol, cut their hair, wear shoes in the places of worship, smoke or have pre-marital sex. He then points out that the Nazarites keep the Ten Commandments, are allowed to sacrifice to the ancestors and follow cultural traditions unless they violate rules of the bible, and must acquire African attires used in the holy dances of the church.

Vilakazi ends his speech by quoting almost verbatim from the article by Hans-Jürgen Becken that opens the edition of the oral histories of the church:

> This church is the fruit of an organic growth of Christianity in the African soil, an institution in which the gospel message incarnated in African culture and milieu, mentality and community life. She worships God in an African manner and addresses the mentality and the needs of the Africans in the way they themselves sense them. Therefore this movement can be termed properly the African reformation of the century, resembling the indigenization of the Gospel in the European Reformation of the 16th century (Vilakazi 2008: 10; see also Hexham & Oosthuizen 1996: ix).

In his speech Vilakazi paints an ambiguous picture of the Nazareth Baptist Church and the church's founder. One the one hand he portrays the church as a new religion, an equal among the world religions, on the other, in the somewhat surprising turnaround at the end, as the African reformation, equally impressive, but within the Christian fold. Both these conceptions he backs with reference to academia, quite aptly given the context of his speech. He also uses the oral traditions of the church to support his arguments, especially when talking about the special nature of Isaiah Shembe. The traditions he uses are the ones from the very centre of the church's oral history, the story of the life of the founder as told by himself (see Papini 1999). There is certainly something divine about Shembe in Vilakazi's portrayal, and he mentions some miracles, on the other hand he calls him a prophet throughout, and counters the possible critique of a deification of Shembe with reference to the many forms that God takes in the Bible. The Bible is his main source to validate the rules that govern the life of the Nazareth Baptist Church. He does not mention the Sabbath, and the dancing and the African attires only briefly, that is he is deemphasizing the break with Christianity. He does not stress the African character of the church, which would be an obvious choice for an aggressive marketing of the church in the new South Africa, but that runs the risk of adding to the 'uncivilized' stereotype that dominates the outside perception of the church and that many of the students are extremely sensitive about. Overall, Vilakazi emphasized the greatness of the church and its founder, while at the same time guarding his church against possible attacks, and avoiding some contentious issues altogether.

In my next example, the situation was rather different. On 31 January 2009, I attended the Sabbath service at the temple in eBuhleni, during which Evangelist (*uMvangeli*) Cele delivered a sermon. The congregation had just returned from the yearly pilgrimage to the holy mountain, the temple was packed with people, and Vimbeni Shembe, the leader of the church, was present. Evangelist Cele is from Kwa Mashu, a township in the north of Durban, just south from Inanda, where the holy city of eBuhleni and the original one of eKuphakameni are located. And the stories he told during the sermon were also located in that region.

The first story was about white astronomers who followed an unusual star which fell from the sky close to Inanda. The white astronomers enlisted the help of the local rulers and the police, in order to get everyone to keep the Sabbath, because they wanted to approach the star during the Sabbath. But someone lighted a fire, and all who broke the Sabbath were imprisoned for 6 months. Finally, the white astronomers approached the star, and they learned about the Messiah (*umumesia* was the Zulu term used) who would come to the area and who would be greater than great (*mkhulu kakhulu*). There was one problem, however: he would be Black (*kodwa umnyama*), and they, as Whites, could not be his followers. Cele then started singing hymn 139, verse 2, and the congregation joined in: "He has arrived, who is spoken about by the prophets. Acclaim him, you men, acclaim him, all you nations" (Muller 2010: 141). He ended his first story with the following remarks:

> The Nazarites say that Shembe came in 1910 but this incident with the star occurred before 1910. But as Nazarites we know that Shembe had always been around. It is just that we did not know him and we could not see him. When Shembe arrived in Inanda problems began because Shembe began doing miracles to everyone, even people from other churches. As a result the leaders of the other churches began to see Shembe as an insult or a threat to them (Cele 2009).

The second story centered on a woman from Inanda who, after being sick with the flu, passed away. When she was about to be buried, she woke up, and everyone was shocked and stunned. The lady did not belong to the Shembe congregation but to a mission church. When she awoke, the people from her congregation gathered around her, but she began screaming and chased them away. Later she explained to her family that she had gone to heaven, where she saw a house brighter than the sun and the moon. She heard drums and flutes playing inside that house, and people in traditional dance dresses (*imvunulo*) danced in praise of their God. Then the gate opened and someone came out and greeted her, referring to her as his child. He told her that on earth he was known as Shembe. He also told her that as she did not have the white church dress (*umnazaretha*) and a ticket as receipt of church membership she would have to return back to earth. He also told her that he had not arrived on earth, and that she had to wait for him. After that she woke up. She broke all contact with the mission church and waited for Shembe, and she waited for over 18 years, because it was still not 1910.

Finally she heard of someone who had amazing healing powers, while others called this man mad. This man came to heal a blind child of the lady's neighbor. After the successful healing, everybody was excited and people crowded the neighbor's yard:

> When she got there, the founder [*uMqaliwendlela*, Isaiah Shembe] signaled for her to come towards him. She was in shock. The founder said to

her: "Lady, remind me, have we met before?" The lady began crying and could not believe what was in front of her eyes. She said "We have seen each other in heaven" (Cele 2009).

In his sermon Cele made use of well established topics in the oral histories of the church. The prediction of the coming of Shembe is a common subject, though it is usually foretold by African prophets (see Hexham & Oosthuizen 1996: 37–41, 47). And in hymn 34 the church headquarter eKuphakameni in the hills of Ohlange is linked with the biblical Bethlehem, as the place from where "shall emerge the prophets who will redeem the village of Ohlange" (Muller 2010: 73). In his first story, Cele combined the biblical motif of the star with South African race relations with the twist that the Whites identify Shembe as the Black Messiah—and, as far as I could tell, it was not problematic to identify Isaiah Shembe as the Messiah in the January 2009 sermon in front of a large congregation and Vimbeni Shembe. Cele's second story also draws upon a genre within the oral traditions: stories about resurrected people reporting from heaven (see Sithole 2009). What is special in Cele's story is that it happened before 1910, before the founding of the church. The eternal existence of the spiritual Shembe formed the main message of the sermon. And this eternal spiritual Shembe formed also part of the explanations of Minister Vilakazi during his speech at the university, although in a somewhat more downsized version. The spiritual Shembe, present in all the leaders of the church, I would argue, forms one of the basic tenets of the Nazareth Baptist Church.

When Vilakazi explained to me how he was send to study theology by Johannes Galilee Shembe, and then made Minister by Amos Shembe, he said:

> You know when a prophet in this church dies only the flesh goes into the grave, but that spirit, the prophetic spirit, remains hanging somewhere, now when God chooses anyone to be a bishop, a leader of this church, a spiritual leader, that hanging, that suspended, that spirit descends into him and he will start to do things, supernatural things that other people can't do, that's what happened when the third Shembe came, he knew already that there were young men who were chosen to be priests by his predecessor. How he knew is because that spirit knows everything of what the other one has done (Interview with Vilakazi, 9 July 2008).

This is the charisma of the leader, his symbolic capital as it is acknowledged by the members of the church: the spiritual Shembe, who might then be variously interpreted as being the Messiah, the Holy Spirit, or some prophetic power—an ambiguity in meaning that hardly matters from a sociological point of view.

What matters, however, is that the charisma is restricted to the leader only. And the leader has to prove his power, especially in times of succession. The social mechanism making this happen becomes clear in the account given by Nonhlanhla, a leader of the virgin group, of how Vimbeni followed his father Amos in 1996:

> We just heard the praising [*uyingcwele*—you are holy], and later on we heard that a blind person had been saved, that his eyes had been opened. And secondly another person, who was in his wheelchair and could not walk, stood up and left his wheelchair and walked. The same thing happened during *iLanga*'s [the sun: Johannes Galilee Shembe] and *uMqaliwendlela*'s [the founder: Isaiah Shembe] era (Interview with Nonhlanhla, 23 July 2008).

This is the dialectic of inner experience and social image: Vimbeni does not become the leader because he heals, he heals because he is the *iNkosi*. And he becomes the *iNkosi* in practice by public acclaim, when the church members fall to their knees and shout 'You are holy'! This acknowledgement proves that the spiritual Shembe resides in him to all present. This bodily hexis and linguistic habitus (Bourdieu 1987b: 111) form the centre of the religious belief in the NBC, and they produce the charisma, the symbolic capital of the church's leader in practice.

Conclusion

Isaiah Shembe's symbolic capital, his social standing and charismatic authority as founder of the Nazareth Baptist Church, depended on the acknowledgement of others, especially those who he managed to draw into his church. The success of his church was based upon the invention of religious practices— the observation of the Sabbath and the sacred dance, for example—that connected with pre-existing cultural and religious traditions, but also served to distinguish the new church from these traditions, notably from mission Christianity and Zulu traditional religion. His lasting success as a leader, his success in generating stable acknowledgement, depended on his ability to draw upon the dispositions of the section of the laity that was still grounded in the pre-colonial social structure. This constituted a shift from the earliest phase of his ministry when he was regarded as a threat to social order, both by colonial officials and Zulu chiefs. He remained a prophet in the sociological sense with regard to mission Christianity, but with his growing success he increasingly turned into a guardian of African tradition. His symbolic capital, his authority as church leader, remained charismatic, as acknowledged in the numerous miracle stories which form the core of the church's oral tradition, yet his authority increasingly turned traditional, being backed by and in turn supporting the social capital of the Zulu descent groups and their leaders. In other words, he successfully routinized his charisma. This process continued with his successors and the end of apartheid—with the proclaimed African renaissance highlighting a reappraisal of the value of African cultural and religious traditions—further added to the church's success.

The position of the church and the church leaders is not only dependent on the views of church members but also on the judgments of outsiders, both within the religious field and beyond. The judgments of academics carry a heavy weight because they are supposed to be objective and disinterested, according to the rules of the academic game. The treatment of the Nazareth Baptist Church within the academic discourse has centered on the theological evaluation of the status of Isaiah Shembe. Early theologians emphasized his Messianic character and excluded the church from Christianity, a judgment that was criticized within the post-colonial context, when the NBC was classified as a prime example of African Christianity. However, leaders of the church preferred the exclusive interpretation, because it rather gave justice to their own conceptions of the church's leadership. Both inclusive and exclusive classifications exert symbolic violence, and in fact reproduce the structural reactions of established players towards prophetic newcomers—excommunication and canonization—within the religious field.

The changes in academic representations of the NBC and its founder reflect changes in the academic field, but they have little to do with the emic representations of the church's leadership. Looking there one finds the concept of a singular and eternal spiritual Shembe, the church's version of hereditary charisma, expressed for example in speeches and sermons by church officials. This specific form of symbolic capital continues to be contested, as recurring succession conflicts in the church testify. In the end, it is produced in practice by public acclaim at the church's annual festivals.

As I started with a song, let me end with a painting. It is on the back of the travelling coach of the NBC and shows a steam train underneath a rainbow. Bombela the Pondoland train is one of the praise names of Isaiah Shembe, and rainbow (*uThingo lwenkozasana*) is the church's name for Vimbeni Shembe. So the painting shows the unity of the spiritual Shembe. Underneath is written: Shembe is the way. This represents the core of the doctrine of the Nazareth Baptist Church.

References

Archives

Natal Archives Depot, Chief Natives Commissioner, correspondence

Box 96, C.N.C. 2155/12/30 (Native Separatist Churches; The Nazarenes, Tshembe and Philious):

C.N.C. 2155/12/30–13: 24 September 1913, Chief Native Commissioner, Natal, to Attorney General, Natal.

C.N.C. 2155/12/30–31: 22 September 1915, Magistrate, Port Shepstone, to Chief Native Commissioner, Natal.

C.N.C. 2155/12/30–32: 24 September 1915, Chief Native Commissioner, Natal, to Magistrate, Port Shepstone.

Interviews

Vilakazi, minister of the NBC, 2008-07-09, eBuhleni, transcript by the author.

Nomhlanhla, leader of the virgins, 2008-07-23, eBuhleni, transcript and translation Sicelo Mpungose.

Other Primary Sources

Cele. 2009. Sermon delivered during the Sabbath service at the temple in eBuhleni, 31 January 2009, transcript Sicelo Mpungose, translation Zakhona Maduna.

Vilakazi, J. M. 2008. Type-script of speech delivered to the Nazareth Tertiary Students Association at the Tshwane University of Technology, 8 June 2008.

Zuma, Jacob. 2011. Speech delivered at the funeral service for Vimbeni Shembe in eBuhleni, 3 April 2011, transcript and translation Sicelo Mpungose.

Literature

Anderson, Allan. 2000. *Zion and Pentecost. The Spirituality and Experience of Pentecostal and Zionist/Apostolic Churches in South Africa.* Pretoria: Unisa Press.

Becken, Hans-Jürgen. 1966. The Nazareth Baptist Church of Shembe. In *Our Approach to the Independent Church Movement in South Africa*, edited by Hans-Jürgen Becken, 101–114. Mapumulo: Missiological Institute.

Berglund, Axel-Ivar. 1976. *Zulu Thought-Patterns and Symbolism.* London: Hurst.

Bourdieu, Pierre. 1977. *Outline of a Theory of Practice.* Cambridge: Cambridge University Press.

———. 1986. The Forms of Capital. In *Handbook of Theory and Research for the Sociology of Education*, edited by John Richardson, 241–258. New York: Greenwood Press.

———. 1987a. Legitimation and Structured Interests in Weber's Sociology of Religion. In *Max Weber, Rationality and Modernity*, edited by Scott Lash and Sam Whimster, 119–136. London: Allen & Unwin.

———. 1987b. Sociologues de la croyance et croyances de sociologues. *Choses dites*, 106–111. Paris: Éditions de Minuit.

———. 1990. *The Logic of Practice*. Stanford: Stanford University Press.

———. 1991. Genesis and Structure of the Religious Field. *Comparative Social Research* 13: 1–44.

———. 2000. *Pascalian Meditations*. Stanford: Stanford University Press.

———. 2003. Participant Objectivation. *Journal of the Royal Anthropological Institute* (N.S.) 9: 281–294.

Brown, Karen Hull. 1995. The Function of Dress and Ritual in the Nazareth Baptist Church of Isaiah Shembe (South Africa). PhD diss., Indiana University. Ann Arbor: UMI.

Cabrita, Joel. 2008. A Theological Biography of Isaiah Shembe, c. 1870–1935. PhD Dissertation, Trinity College, University of Cambridge.

———. 2009. Isaiah Shembe's Theological Nationalism, 1920s–1935. *Journal of Southern African Studies* 35 (3): 609–625.

———. 2010. Politics and Preaching: Chiefly Converts to the Nazaretha Church, Obedient Subjects, and Sermon Performance in South Africa. *Journal of African History* 51: 21–40.

Chidester, David. 1996. *Savage Systems. Colonialism and Comparative Religion in Southern Africa*. Charlottesville: University Press of Virginia.

Chirenje, J. Mutero. 1987. *Ethiopianism and Afro-Americans in Southern Africa, 1883–1916*. Baton Rouge: Louisiana State University Press.

Echtler, Magnus. 2010. A Real Mass Worship They Will Never Forget. Rituals and Cognition in the Nazareth Baptist Church, South Africa. In *Body, Performance, Agency, and Experience*. Vol. II of *Ritual Dynamics and the Science of Ritual*, edited by Angelos Chaniotis, Silke Leopold, Thomas Quartier, Joanna Wojtkowiak, Jan Weinhold and Geoffrey Samuel, 371–397. Wiesbaden: Harrassowitz.

———. 2014. Scottish Warriors in KwaZulu-Natal: Cultural Hermeneutics of the Scottish Dance (Isikoshi) in the Nazareth Baptist Church, South Africa. In *Africa in Scotland, Scotland in Africa: Historical Legacies and Contemporary Hybridities*, edited by Afe Adogame and Andrew Lawrence, 326–348. Leiden: Brill.

Erlmann, Veit. 1996. *Nightsong: Performance, Power, and Practice in South Africa*. Chicago: University of Chicago Press.

Etherington, Norman. 1978. *Preachers, Peasants, and Politics in Southeast Africa, 1835–1880: African Christian Communities in Natal, Pondoland, and Zululand*. London: Royal Historical Society.

Fernandez, James W. 1973. The Precincts of the Prophet: A day with Johannes Galilee Shembe. *Journal of Religion in Africa* 5 (1): 32–53.

Flint, Karen, and Julie Parle. 2008. Healing and Harming: Medicine, Madness, Witchcraft and Tradition. In *Zulu Identities. Being Zulu, Past and Present,* edited by Benedict Carton, John Laband and Jabulani Sithole, 312–321. Scottville: University of KwaZulu-Natal Press.

Gunner, Elizabeth. 1988. Power House, Prison House—An Oral Genre and its Use in Isaiah Shembe's Nazareth Baptist Church. *Journal of Southern African Studies* 14(2): 204–227.

———. 2002. *The Man of Heaven and the Beautiful Ones of God. Writings from Ibandla lamaNazaretha, a South African Church.* Leiden: Brill.

Guy, Jeff. 1979. *The Destruction of the Zulu Kingdom: The Civil War in Zululand 1879–1884.* London: Longman.

———. 2005. *The Maphumulo Uprising. War, Law and Ritual in the Zulu Rebellion.* Scottsville: University of KwaZulu-Natal Press.

Haar, Gerrieter, and Stephen Ellis. 2009. The Occult Does Not Exist. A Response to Terence Ranger. *Africa* 79 (3): 399–412.

Heuser, Andreas. 2003. *Shembe, Gandhi und die Soldaten Gottes. Wurzeln der Gewaltfreiheit in Südafrika.* Münster: Waxmann.

———. 2008. 'He Dances Like Isaiah Shembe!' Ritual Aesthetics as a Marker of Church Difference. *Studies in World Christianity* 14 (1): 35–54.

Heuser, Andreas, and Irving Hexham, eds. 2005. *The Hymns and Sabbath Liturgy for Morning and Evening Prayer of Isaiah Shembe's amaNazaretha.* Vol. 5 of *The Story of Isaiah Shembe.* Lewiston: Edwin Mellen Press.

Hexham, Irving. 1997. Isaiah Shembe, Zulu Religious Leader. *Religion* 27 (4): 361–373.

Hexham, Irving, and G. C. Oosthuizen, eds. 1996. *History and Traditions Centered on Ekuphakameni and Mount Nhlangakazi.* Vol. 1 of *The Story of Isaiah Shembe.* Lewiston: Edwin Mellen Press.

———, eds. 2001. *The Continuing Story of the Sun and the Moon.* Vol. 3 of *The Story of Isaiah Shembe.* Lewiston: Edwin Mellen Press.

King, Richard. 2013. The Copernican Turn in the Study of Religion. *Method and Theory in the Study of Religion* 25: 137–159.

Krige, Eileen Jensen. 1950. *The Social System of the Zulus.* Pietermaritzburg: Shuter & Shooter.

Marks, Shula. 1970. *Reluctant Rebellion. The 1906–8 Disturbances in Natal.* Oxford: Clarendon Press.

———. 1975. The Ambiguities of Dependence: John L. Dube of Natal. *Journal of Southern African Studies* 1 (2): 162–180.

———. 1986. *The Ambiguities of Dependence in South Africa: Class, Nationalism, and the State in Twentieth-Century Natal.* Baltimore: John Hopkins University Press.

Mthethwa, Bongani. 1989. Music and Dance as Therapy in African Traditional Societies with Special Reference to the *iBandla lamaNazaretha.* In *Afro-Christian Religion* and Healing in Southern Africa, edited by G. C. Oosthuizen, S. D. Edwards, W. H. Wessels and I. Hexham, 241–256. Lewiston: Edwin Mellen.

Muller, Carol, ed. 2010. *Shembe Hymns*. Trans. Bongani Mthethwa. Scottsville: University of KwaZulu-Natal Press.

Oosthuizen, Gerhardus C. 1967. *The Theology of a South African Messiah. An Analysis of the Hymnal of "The Church of the Nazarites"*. Leiden: Brill.

———. 1968. *Post-Christianity in Africa. A Theological and Anthropological Study*. London: Hurst.

———. 1974. Wie christlich ist die Kirche Shembes? *Evangelische Missionszeitschrift* 31 (3): 129–142.

Papini, Robert. 1999. Carl Faye's Transcript of Isaiah Shembe's Testimony of His Early Life and Calling. *Journal of Religion in Africa* 29 (3): 243–284.

———. 2004. The Move to Tradition. Dance Uniform History in the Church of Nazareth Baptists. *African Arts* 37/3: 48–61, 91–93.

Ranger, Terence. 2007. Scotland Yard in the Bush: Medicine Murders, Child Witches and the Construction of the Occult: A Literature Review. *Africa* 77 (2): 272–283.

Roberts, Esther. 1936. Shembe: The Man and his Work. Master thesis, University of South Africa.

Sithole, Nkosinathi. 2009. The Mediation of Public and Private Selves in the Performance of Sermons and Narratives of Near-Death Experiences in the Nazarite Church. In *Religion and Spirituality in South Africa. New Perspectives*, edited by Duncan Brown, 249–265. Scottsville: University of KwaZulu-Natal Press.

Steyn, H. Christina. 2008. Credo Mutwa. New Age Zulu. In *Zulu Identities. Being Zulu, Past and Present*, edited by Benedict Carton, John Laband and Jabulani Sithole, 304–311. Scottville: University of KwaZulu-Natal Press.

Sundkler, Bengt. 1961. *Bantu Prophets in South Africa*. Oxford: Oxford University Press (orig. pub. 1948).

———. 1976. *Zulu Zion and some Swazi Zionists*. London: Oxford University Press.

Tishken, Joel Edward. 2002. Prophecy and Power in Afro-Christian Churches: A Comparative Analysis of the Nazareth Baptist Church and the Église Kibanguiste. PhD diss., University of Texas at Austin.

Vilakazi, Absolom, M. Mthethwa, and M. Mpanza. 1986. *Shembe: The Revitalization of African Society*. Johannesburg: Skotaville.

Weber, Max. 1972. *Wirtschaft und Gesellschaft*. Tübingen: Mohr.

Index

Abathakathi   19, 176, 245
Abathandazi   19, 179
Actors
   Creative   52, 65–66, 243
   Disinterested   5, 89, 90, 129, 132, 149, 182, 252, 262
   Interest of   5–6, 75, 78, 119, 168, 182, 203, 238–239, 243, 246–247, 250, 254
   Position of   2–4, 38, 75–76, 99, 114, 118, 132, 167–168, 175, 185, 191, 207, 239, 243, 247, 249, 253–255, 262
   Strategic   4, 16, 38, 119, 125, 131, 134–135, 168, 175, 243
Afflictions   81, 111, 173, 181, 245–246
Africa
   Pre-colonial   10–11, 13, 19, 37, 42, 44, 170, 173, 237, 239, 241, 244–245, 261
   Religious fields in   10–15, 22, 175
   Study of Religion on   10–15, 249
African attire   238, 240, 242–243, 257–259
African Christianity
   African-Christian diviners (*abathandazi*)   19, 179
   African Converts   43–44, 46, 48, 58, 62, 142, 144, 150, 161, 196, 208–209, 238, 242–243, 245
   African Initiated Churches (AICS)   11–12, 16, 20–21, 24, 36, 38, 45, 61, 65–66, 77, 190, 237, 242, 249
   Apostolic   66–67
   Ethiopian   46, 240
   Evangelical   70, 195–197, 201–206, 208, 211–212
   Orthodox   96–99, 206–207
   Pentecostal/Charismatic   8, 12, 16, 36–39, 44–45, 51, 70–71, 77, 80–92, 190, 196–197, 201–203, 205–210, 212
   Zionist   35–40, 44–45, 51–53, 62, 65–67
African Churches
   AmaJericho   35, 63–66
   Believers LoveWorld (Christ Embassy)   82
   Christian Catholic (Apostolic) Holy Spirit Church of Zion   52, 54
   Christian Orthodox Tewadho Church   207
   Faith Mission Church   211
   Memphis Church   198
   Nazareth Baptist Church   21, 25, 62, 66, 237–242, 244–247, 250–251, 254, 256, 260–262
   Synagogue Church of all Nations   82
   Redeemed Christian Church of God   82
   Winners Chapel   82
   Zoe Ministries Worldwide   81–82
African Islam   8, 10, 120–121
African Traditional Religions   10, 12–13, 19, 73, 77, 87, 173, 175, 190–191, 237, 239–240, 242–244, 261
   See also *Abathakathi*; *Aggaafaariis*; Ancestors; *Babalawo*; *Izangoma*; *Izikhali*; *Izinyanga*; *Kaddamis*; *Karaama*; Magic, African; Material religion, colors, drums, staffs; *Muthi*; *Onisegun*; Religious specialist, chiefs; Witchcraft, African; *Zar*
Aggaafaariis   99
Alcohol   45, 257
Algeria   8, 41–42, 168
Allah   99, 128, 130
Amakholwa   43–44, 46, 48, 58, 62, 142, 144, 150, 161
Ambivalence   17, 21, 50, 61, 73, 135, 158, 253, 255, 258, 260
Ancestors   50, 56, 62, 65–66, 73, 169, 172, 174–175, 244–245, 257
Anderson, Allan   36–39, 46, 252
Apartheid   16, 54, 67, 73, 78–79, 88, 177–178, 185, 237, 248, 262
Arnold, Matthew   145–146, 157
Authority   78, 87–88, 90, 96, 113, 123, 125–128, 143, 147, 150–151, 155, 171, 174, 176, 180, 189, 198, 203, 240–241, 246, 251, 261–262

Babalawo   77
Baptism   45, 51, 53, 58, 144, 172, 238
Bare feet   52–53, 61–62, 104, 242, 257
Beliefs   13–14, 101, 105, 168, 172, 175, 180, 183, 187–188, 192, 203, 247, 255
Bible   44–46, 60, 85–86, 144, 146, 172, 190, 201, 206, 209, 246, 251, 257–258, 260

INDEX

Bitek, Okot p'   10, 13
Borana   120–121, 132, 135
Bourdieu, Pierre   1–10, 14–15, 37–38, 40–43, 50–51, 57, 67, 72–76, 86, 90, 92, 96, 102, 104, 114, 118, 125, 129, 139–140, 142, 145, 148, 156–162, 167–169, 172, 175, 182, 187, 191, 195, 201–202, 210, 217–218, 220–221, 232–233, 238, 244, 247, 254
Burial   99, 172, 259

Canonization   21, 237, 253, 262
Capital
　Conversion of   104, 114, 196
　Cultural   4, 11, 16–17, 26, 37–38, 40–41, 45, 49, 66–67, 74, 99–100, 104, 112, 114, 118, 126–127, 134, 157, 171–172, 174, 179, 190, 224, 240, 245
　Economic   4, 17, 26, 40, 66–67, 74, 104, 114, 118, 174
　Religious   78, 86–87, 89, 91, 119, 125, 127, 134, 244
　Social   4, 9, 11, 18, 21, 40, 74, 104, 114, 118, 134, 190, 211, 244–245, 262
　Symbolic   4, 6, 9, 11, 16–17, 21, 25–26, 39–40, 44, 50, 74, 102, 104, 114, 118, 171–172, 174, 179, 181–182, 185, 187, 189–191, 196, 202, 221, 232, 237–238, 244, 247–249, 251, 254–255, 260–262
　See also Power
Castellio, Sebastian   161
Categories   172, 249, 251, 256
Ceremonies   100, 103, 108, 110–111
Change   4, 8, 10–12, 24, 37, 39, 121–122, 167–168, 179, 182, 191, 198, 224, 262
Charisma   7, 9, 20–21, 87–88, 90, 93, 159, 203, 210, 237–238, 244, 246–249, 254–255, 260–262
Chidester, David   11, 43, 76–77
Christianity
　Anglican   48, 58, 139, 144–145, 184
　Catholic   8, 74, 133, 159–160, 168, 203, 206
　Evangelical   70, 195–197, 201–206, 208, 211–212
　Jehovah's Witnesses   196, 201
　Lutheran   196, 203
　Mission   11, 13, 16, 21, 44–45, 53, 73, 76–77, 88, 141–145, 150, 158, 170–172, 196, 219, 221, 237–243, 247, 250, 259, 261

　Orthodox   96–99, 203
　Pentecostal   8, 12, 16, 20, 44–48, 51, 74
　Protestant   168, 170, 196
　Reformed   47, 53, 58
　Wesleyan   142–143
　Western   61, 74
　Zionist   35–37, 39, 44–45, 51, 61
　See also African Christianity
Classification
　Academic   21, 25, 237, 251, 252–253, 262
　Emic   89, 92
Coffee   100, 102–103
Colenso, John William   18, 35, 43, 47–48, 54, 139–162
Collaboration   119, 125, 131, 134
Colonialism   8, 13, 18, 37, 39, 42, 66–67, 73, 76–77, 124, 140–141, 144–145, 147–155, 158, 161–162, 168, 170–171, 175, 177, 180, 219, 221, 239–241, 246, 251, 261
Color coding   54–58
Comaroff, Jean   37
Commitment   3, 85, 120, 130, 133, 201, 205, 212
Community   39, 49–50, 70, 122, 131, 169, 172, 203, 207–208, 211
Competition   1, 8–9, 19, 74, 119, 125–126, 134–135, 203
Congregations   118, 128, 195, 197–198, 202, 206–208, 258–260
Consciousness   65, 73, 205
Contestation   38–39, 48, 74
Creativity   52, 65–66, 243
Culture contact   41, 77

Dance   62, 64, 106, 108, 112, 242–243, 258–259, 261
Darwin, Charles   157, 170
Definitions   168, 188–189, 192
De-legitimization   16, 74, 88, 91, 131, 238–239
Delicieux, Bernard   160
Dialogue   49, 65
Diaspora   70–71
Discourse   57, 73–74, 77, 89–90, 172, 185, 190, 249, 262
Dispositions   2–3, 7, 14, 23, 54, 76, 134, 237–238, 261
Distinction   73, 76, 78, 89, 187, 198, 201, 237, 240, 242–243, 248–249, 261
Divination   173, 179, 181, 186, 191

INDEX

Division of labor   8–9, 100, 244
Doctrine   125, 247–248, 262
Domination   120–121, 125, 131, 167–169, 172, 185, 192, 217–218, 220, 233
Dowie, Alexander   46–47, 49, 61
Doxa   3, 15–16, 40–41, 45, 47–48, 57–58, 65, 167, 172, 192
Draper, Jonathan   139
Dreams   48, 56
Drums   62, 102, 107, 259
Dube, John L.   239
Dube, Lucky   236–237
Durkheim, Emile   1, 238
Dynamics
  Inner-field   3–4, 8–9, 73, 78, 90–93, 139–140, 145, 157, 182, 190, 192, 195, 238
  Inter-field   18, 20, 22, 139, 145, 148, 154, 157, 182, 192, 196, 203, 210

Economy   23, 66, 83–84, 90, 151, 153, 181, 203, 210–211, 222, 231, 239–240
Education
  Islamic   17, 20, 117, 120, 126–127, 130, 134, 219, 223–225, 233
  Missionary   40, 219, 240
  Western   20, 46, 81n, 197–198, 204, 219–227, 231, 233, 240
  Women's   217–218, 220–221, 224–229, 232–234
Egypt   17, 106–107, 120, 130
Ellis, Steven   10, 12–14
Embodiment   23, 36, 40, 96, 112, 148, 168, 172, 175, 261
Emic
  Classifications   89, 92
  Representations   254, 262
Enlightenment   48, 143, 171
Enyonini   52, 60–63, 66–67
Eritrea   20, 24, 195–203, 206–212
Eritrean People's Liberation Front (EPLF) / Shaebia   20, 198–203, 205, 207–208, 211
Essentialism   1, 15, 162
Ethiopia   17, 96–97, 99, 101, 106, 196, 199, 202, 204, 207–208, 210
Ethnocentrism   8, 13, 15, 252
Eve   107
Evil   176, 184, 187, 189–191, 197, 208
Evolution   170, 239

Exclusion   86, 168–169, 173, 179, 183, 187, 192, 217, 239–240, 243–244, 251–253, 262
Excommunication   18, 21, 139, 157, 237, 253, 262
Exorcism   46, 103, 105, 110–113
Experts, religious see Religious specialists

Faraqqasaa   17, 96–97, 99–102, 104–105, 107, 111–114
Fields
  Academic   5, 15, 21, 25–26, 237, 249, 253
  Autonomy of   6, 18, 23, 75, 140, 145, 201, 203, 241–242
  Borders of   4, 6, 10, 18, 23, 38, 42, 49, 139–140, 146, 154–157, 161, 168–170, 180, 182–183, 185, 192, 196, 212, 218, 240, 253
  Dynamics of   3–4, 8–9, 22, 73, 78, 90–93, 139, 154, 157, 192, 195–196, 210
  Economic   12, 186
  Educational   11, 218–221
  Interrelations between   6, 12, 20, 22, 149, 182, 185–186, 192, 195, 203, 210, 218, 220, 249, 253
  Judicial   171, 186, 218
  Literary   6, 9, 145, 157
  Medical   181
  Political   11–12, 18, 20, 139–140, 146, 149, 154–155, 158–160, 171, 186, 196, 199, 203, 210–211, 218, 220
  Power, Field of   6, 13, 19, 22
  Religious see Religious fields
  Scientific   15, 26, 146, 157, 254
  Social   2–7, 22–23, 118, 140, 185–186, 190, 253
  Structures of   76–77, 91, 168, 180, 191–192, 199, 253–255
Fogelqvist, Anders   35–39, 49
Frazer, James George   19, 146
Fuze, Magema   161

Game
  Feel for the   3, 5, 43, 49, 54, 63, 65, 73–74, 92
  Rules of the   4, 49, 89, 140, 146, 161, 175–176, 181–183, 189, 192, 195, 240, 251–252, 262
  Social   2–4, 6, 9, 14, 40, 175, 254
Generation   195–196, 200, 204–206, 210

Generational conflicts   20, 206, 208
Gender relations   54, 56–57, 63, 100, 107, 110, 123, 133–134, 183, 197, 199, 217, 219, 221, 228, 230–234, 241, 248
God   14, 43, 45, 47, 58, 62, 85–86, 99, 107, 132–133, 141, 150, 152, 158, 162, 172, 197, 206, 237, 249–250, 252, 255–257
Government   140–141, 143–145, 147–148, 150–155, 161–162, 186, 195, 199, 201–206, 208–209, 219, 221, 226, 230–231
Guerilla   196, 199–200, 203
Guy, Jeff   139

Haar, Gerrie ter   10, 12–14, 177
Habitus   2–3, 7, 9, 16–17, 23–24, 37, 39, 41–43, 47–49, 57–59, 65–66, 76, 89, 96, 102, 114, 119, 121–122, 134, 157, 168, 172, 180, 192, 199, 205, 211, 238, 243–244, 255, 261
Healing   17, 46, 50–51, 57–58, 96, 101–102, 104–106, 113–114, 179, 181, 183, 186–187, 198, 247, 259, 261
Heathenism   152, 250
Heaven   250, 259–260
Hegemony   14, 36, 46, 121, 131, 168
Hell   47–48
Heresy   139–140, 144–145, 157, 159–161, 168, 170–172, 177, 179, 183, 190–191, 195–196, 203, 207, 237, 243
Heterodoxy   40, 57
Hierarchy   44, 139, 144, 158, 160–161, 175, 247–248, 256
Hybridity   43–44, 65–66
Hymns   100–102, 243, 245, 250–251, 259–260
Hysteresis   24, 180

Identity   43, 73, 86, 162, 176, 183, 189, 200, 226, 242
Ideology   89, 123, 197–200, 203, 209, 211–212, 250
Idowu, E. Bolaji   10, 13, 76
Ikenga-Metuh, Emefie   10, 13
Illusio   3, 254
Inclusion   172, 192, 240, 243, 252–253, 262
India   18, 122, 124, 130
Inheritance   109–110, 112, 199, 262
Innovation / Invention   45, 91, 126, 128, 159, 196, 233, 237–238, 240, 242, 261
Institutions   238, 244, 246–247

Islam   8, 10, 96–100, 106, 122, 159, 201
    Allah   99, 128, 130
    Education   17, 20, 117, 120, 126–127, 130, 134, 219, 223–225, 233
    Dāʿī-s   124–127, 129, 130, 134
    Daʿwa   117–118, 121–122, 124–130, 132–133, 135
    Hadith   129, 131
    Hijab   226
    ʿIlm   123, 126–127
    Madrasa   17, 117, 120–121, 124, 127–129, 134, 219
    Markaz   121–122, 125, 135
    Merti Quran Center   117, 120–121, 125–126, 130, 135
    Mosques   117–118, 120–121, 131–132
    Qalole   117n3, 120–122, 125–128, 131–135
    Quran   100, 126, 128–129, 131, 133, 209, 232
    Salafī   117n2, 120, 125, 130–131
    Sharia   217–219, 224–225, 228, 230, 233
    Sheiks   117, 120, 126–127, 133
    Tablīghī Jamāʿat   17, 25, 117–119, 121–135
    ʿUlamā'   117–119, 123, 126–130, 132
Izangoma   19, 50, 56, 166, 168, 173–181, 184, 186, 190–192, 244–245
Izikhali   59–61, 64
Izinyanga   19, 56, 173, 175, 180, 186, 190

Jesus   45, 197, 237, 257

Kaddamis   99, 103
Kano   217, 224, 226–227
Karaama   96, 98–99, 101, 103
Kenya   17, 25, 118, 120, 124, 127
Khambule, George   59
Khat   101–102, 105
Knowledge   6, 17, 23, 44–45, 76, 86, 90, 112, 123, 126–127, 143, 174–175, 185, 199–200, 204, 220, 225, 233, 257

Laity   7, 16, 21, 24, 118–119, 123, 125–126, 128, 132–135, 157, 201, 238–247, 255, 261
Language   20, 35, 43, 111–112, 127, 170, 174, 177, 252
Las Casas, Bartholome de   160
Laws
    African   180
    Islamic   123, 125–126

INDEX

Native 148, 151
Witchcraft 168, 171, 173, 177–179, 186–189, 191
Lebaron, Frédéric 5
Legislation 19, 168, 170, 174, 177–178, 180, 182, 186–189, 192
Legitimacy 7, 9, 15, 21, 49, 71, 73–74, 85, 88, 92, 96, 119, 127–131, 133, 158, 160, 172–173, 177, 183, 187, 191–192, 196, 200, 202–203, 212, 221, 233, 238–239, 244–245
Le Roux, Peter 46–49, 51–53, 58
Lizardo, Omar 22

Magic
    African 177, 186–187, 191
    Pagan 183
    Religion and 7, 19, 77, 168, 170, 184, 188, 190
    Science and 19, 170
Mahon, Edgar 46–47
Makwerekwere 89–91
Market, religious 82, 85
Marriage 217, 222–223, 228–229, 234
Martyrs 199, 201, 203, 207, 210
Marx, Karl 1, 74
Material religion
    African attire 238, 240, 242–243, 257–259
    Colors 53–58
    Crosses 53, 58
    Drums 62, 102, 107, 259
    Hijab 226
    Perfume 104, 107–108
    Robes 51–53
    Staffs 52–53, 58–61
Mbiti, John 10, 13
Mediation 174, 250
Messiah 20–21, 25, 209–210, 212, 237, 250–253, 259–260, 262
Metaphors 4, 6, 140, 145, 155–156, 161, 180
Methodology 25, 35n, 80n10, 97n2, 118, 195n, 237n, 251, 253–255
Migrants
    Asian 124
    Eritrean 195, 204, 207, 210–212
    Nigerian 71–74, 78–80
Miracles 17, 86–87, 96, 101–104, 114, 246–249, 257–259, 262
Misfortune 103, 174–176

Misrecognition 4, 7–8, 15, 37, 39, 42, 52, 58, 158, 188, 190, 232–233, 238–239, 254
Mission 11, 13, 37, 40, 42, 44–46, 122, 124, 140–145, 148, 157, 161, 170–171, 197
Modernity 43, 67, 202, 211
Momina 96–105, 107, 112, 114
Morality 142, 177, 179, 197, 201, 203, 208, 210, 222–223
Morgan, David 14
Moses 45, 58–59, 144
Mudimbe, V.W. 12
Müller, Max 146
Murray, Andrew 51
Muthi 173, 179, 181, 186, 190, 245
Myth 44, 106, 148, 199, 238

Narratives 84–91, 199, 247, 258–260
Natal 46, 54, 139–142, 144–145, 151–155, 162, 169, 240–241
Nation 199, 202–203, 212, 246, 259
Newcomers 133, 179, 183, 237–239, 262
Nguni 37, 169–170
Nigeria 70, 78–79, 83–84, 107, 217–223
Nigerians 71–74, 78–92
Nkonyane, Daniel 37, 48–49, 52, 60

Onisegun 77
Oosthuizen, Gerhardus 250–251, 253
Oppositions, binary
    Colors 54, 56–57, 63–64
    Gender 54, 56–57, 63
    Hot/cold 57, 63, 66
    Spiritual 48–49, 57, 66
Oral traditions 42, 44, 55, 97, 169, 238, 246, 257–258, 260, 262
Orthodoxy 40, 57, 113, 131, 135, 139–140, 161, 167, 170–171, 195–196, 212
Orthopraxy 168, 171

Pagans 19, 24, 166, 168, 183–192, 252
Participant objectivation 25, 253–254
Peel, J.D.Y. 11
Perfume 104, 107–108
Pilgrimage 17, 83, 96, 98–101, 105, 113, 258
Pork 45, 52–53, 61
Post-apartheid 19, 24, 70, 73, 78, 92, 166
Post-colonial 10, 15, 25, 67, 191, 251

Power
  Relations   37, 73, 77, 89, 118, 158, 161, 167, 178–179, 183, 189–191, 218
  Spiritual   35–36, 39, 50, 65, 85–86, 88, 96, 98, 101, 104, 174–175, 187, 248, 261
  See also Karaama
  Symbolic   7, 128, 244, 247
Practical sense   3, 23, 74, 78, 140
  See also Game, feel for the
Prayer   86, 100, 102–103, 126, 129, 134, 201, 207, 242
Preaching   118, 121–123, 126–127, 130, 133–134
Pre-colonial   8, 10–11, 13, 19, 37, 42, 44, 170, 173, 237, 239, 241, 244–245, 261
Progress   198, 200
Prohibitions *see* Purity rules
Prophecy   46, 51, 203, 211
  See also religious specialist, prophets
Proselytism   117, 123–124, 126–127, 132, 134–135
Prosperity   81, 84, 86, 101, 203, 210
Public sphere   24, 224, 230
Purity rules
  Alcohol   45, 257
  Bare feet   52–53, 61–62, 104, 242, 257
  Pork   45, 52–53, 61
  Tobacco   45, 52, 62–63, 257

Racism   142, 260
  See also Xenophobia
Ray, Terry   8
Rebellion   148, 151, 239
Reductionism   5, 8, 254
Religion
  Abrahamic   8, 10, 14, 256
  Definition of   14, 168
  Denial of   76, 152, 184–185, 239
  Judaism   106, 184, 256
  Nature   185
  New Religious Movements   12, 72, 237
  Paganism   19, 182–183, 206
  Social function of   8, 142, 158, 161
  See also African Traditional Religion; Christianity; Islam
Religious fields
  Eritrean   196, 210
  Ethiopian   96–97, 99, 113–114
  General   4–5, 7–26, 74–76, 140, 238
  Kenyan   119, 125
  Nigerian   218, 220
  South African   37–40, 42–51, 65–67, 73–74, 87–93, 139–140, 145, 154, 156–157, 166–167, 173, 175, 177, 179–180, 183, 186, 189–190, 237, 239, 241, 244, 247, 250, 253, 255, 262
Religious freedom   166, 183, 189, 211
Religious objects
  see Material religion
Religious specialists
  Abathakathi   19, 176, 245
  Aggaafaariis   99, 107–108
  Chiefs   174–177, 239, 244
  Church leaders   16, 21, 24–25, 71–72, 237, 247–249, 258–261
  Church owners   72, 74, 83–84
  Clerics   130, 206–207
  Dāʿī-s   124–127, 129, 130, 134
  Diviners   19, 21, 24, 50, 56, 59–60, 77, 166, 173, 176, 181, 239, 246–247
  Entrepreneurs   74, 160
  Founders   17, 71, 96, 238, 258–259
  Healers   77, 111–112, 171, 179–181, 185–188, 190–192, 237–239, 245–247
  Herbalists   19, 56, 171, 173, 181
  Izangoma   19, 50, 56, 166, 168, 173–181, 184, 186, 190–192, 244–245
  Izinyanga   19, 56, 173, 175, 180, 186, 190
  Kaddamis   99, 103
  Missionaries   23, 25, 42, 47, 76–78, 85–87, 89, 91, 140–143, 149, 158, 239, 241, 243
  Pastors   16, 72–74, 78, 81–92, 201, 203, 246
  Pilgrims   96–98, 100–104, 107, 113–114
  Preachers   117, 130–131, 237–238, 241–242
  Priests   7–8, 139–140, 159, 179, 206, 238–239
  Prophets   7–9, 18, 57, 64, 139–140, 159–161, 238–239, 244, 247, 252–253, 255–257–261
  Qalole   117n3, 120–122, 125–128, 131–135
  Rabbis   184
  Scholars   118, 126, 251–252
  Sheiks   117, 120, 126–127, 133
  Sorcerers   7–8, 191, 247
  Spiritual leaders   96–97, 101, 104, 107, 110, 112–114
  ʿUlamāʾ   117–119, 123, 126–130, 132

INDEX

Witches   19, 23, 176, 185, 187, 189–191, 239, 245–246
Resistance   58, 77, 85, 90, 110, 148, 158, 180, 183, 205, 224, 233, 256
Revolution   123, 150, 196, 199, 202–203
Rhetoric   16, 71, 73–74, 88–92
Rituals   2, 17, 51, 62, 96, 98, 101, 105, 110–111, 174–175, 244, 246
Robes   51–53
Rural   240, 246

Sabbath   53, 61, 242, 258
Sacred space   114, 121–122, 125, 245
Sacrifice   17, 57, 63, 65–66, 102, 104, 108–110, 130, 199, 244, 257
Salvation   7–8, 70, 84–85, 90, 133, 144, 152, 172, 203
Saudi Arabia   17, 120, 122, 127, 130, 134
Seclusion   20, 217–218, 222–223, 228–229
Sermons   118, 122, 245, 256, 258, 260
Shaw, Rosalind   12–13
Shembe
   Amos   248, 253, 260
   Isaiah   20, 62, 66, 237–238, 242–246, 250, 252, 254–262
   Johannes Galilee   242, 247–248, 250, 255–256, 260–261
   Londa   248, 253–254
   Spiritual   20, 248, 253, 257, 260–262
   Vimbeni   248–249, 256, 258, 260, 262
Shepstone, Theophile   18, 139–149, 151, 153–154, 156
Singing   100–102, 207–208
Social
   Fields   2–7, 22–23, 118, 140, 185–186, 190, 253
   Forces   2, 16, 38, 75, 91, 145
   Structures   2–5, 22, 57, 76–77, 168, 180, 191–192, 199, 246, 253–255
   Struggles   2–3, 16, 19, 38, 75, 99, 118–119, 135, 167–169, 189, 195, 199, 220–221
Sociodicies   2, 8, 158
South Africa   16, 18–19, 22–24, 46, 64, 70, 78–79, 139, 144, 153, 155, 161, 180, 182, 184–185, 187, 237, 239, 248, 258
Speeches   256–258
Spirit
   Evil spirit   36, 48–49
   Holy   16, 35–36, 44–49, 65–66, 257, 260
   Zulu/Swathi (*umoya*)   36, 65–66
Spirit possession   17, 48–49, 63–64, 96, 99, 103–113
Spirit realm   169, 173
Spiritual beings
   Allah   99, 128
   Ancestors   50, 56, 62, 65–66, 73, 169, 172, 174–175, 244–245, 257
   Christ   237, 250–252, 257
   Demons   36, 45, 81, 106, 190
   Evil spirits   36, 48–49, 103, 107, 110, 113
   God   14, 43, 45, 47, 58, 62, 85–86, 99, 107, 132–133, 141, 150, 152, 158, 162, 172, 197, 206, 237, 249–250, 252, 255–257
   Guardian spirits   110, 113
   Queen of Heaven (*uNomkubulwane*)   49, 57
   Satan   36, 47, 49, 59, 179, 184–185, 190, 197, 210, 256
   Zar   103–113
Staffs   52–53, 58–61
State   7, 12, 18–20, 22–24, 83–84, 145, 152–154, 177, 180, 186–187, 199–202, 239–242
Status   4, 12, 44, 92, 97, 104, 110, 114, 119, 171, 176, 233, 237, 249, 254–255
Strategies   4, 16, 23–24, 38, 41, 73–74, 88–90, 119, 125, 131, 134–135, 168, 175, 185, 189, 199, 239, 243
Study of Religion   10–15, 146, 161–162, 168, 249, 254, 256
Subordination   233–234, 248
Succession   21, 112, 248, 261–262
Succession conflicts   21, 39, 248, 262
Sudan   17, 106–107, 120, 127, 130, 134, 203, 210–211
Sundkler, Bengt   35–36, 46, 250–251, 253
Superstition   168, 180, 239
Swazi   16, 39, 42, 49, 60, 65
Swazi kings   57, 60, 64
Swaziland   35, 64
Symbolic power   7, 128, 244, 247
Symbolic violence   6–9, 15, 19, 21, 25, 89n, 120, 157, 172, 188–190, 200, 203, 218, 232, 237, 249, 251–253, 262
Symbols   51–52, 56, 244
Syncretism   39, 65–66, 250–251

Teachings   123, 127, 133, 241, 248
Theology   143, 145–146, 150, 157, 161, 237, 249, 251–252, 254, 262
Theory of practice   22, 167, 187, 254
   See also Actors; Capital; Doxa; Fields; Game; Habitus; Illusio; Strategies
Tobacco   45, 52, 62–63, 257
Traditional Healers   166, 186–187, 191–192
Traditional medicine   104–105, 173, 181, 186, 245
Training   122, 127, 173, 199
Transnationalism   117, 122, 126, 135, 196, 208, 211
Travel   122–123, 126, 130–131, 133–134
Trees   49, 59, 101, 104
Turner, Byran   71, 74
Turner, Victor   51

Urban   80, 182, 195–196, 202, 204–206, 240

Vilikazi, Elias   35, 64
Vilakazi, Absolom   251, 253
Violence
   Physical   7, 72, 78, 147–148, 151–153, 176, 179, 186–187, 189, 191, 200, 203, 239, 253
   Symbolic   6–9, 15, 19, 21, 25, 89n, 120, 157, 172, 188–190, 200, 203, 218, 232, 237, 249, 251–253, 262

Wakkerstroom   37, 46, 48, 51, 54, 58, 62
War   197, 202–203
Weapons, spiritual   58–61, 64
Weber, Max   1, 8–9, 87, 159–160, 238, 244, 246–247

Wicca   19, 166, 183
William of Tyre   159
Witchcraft
   African   19, 36, 142–143, 166, 173, 176–177, 182
   European   47, 171, 177
   Laws   19, 171, 173, 177, 188–189
   Pagan   19, 166, 183, 188–189
   Violence   176, 179, 186–187, 189, 191
Witchdoctor   152, 166, 179
Women   54, 56–57, 63, 100, 133–134, 210, 217–225, 241
Women Continuing Education Centers, Nigeria   20, 217–218, 225–228, 230–233
World Parliament of Religions   19, 184
Worldview   7, 10, 48, 76, 119, 157, 186, 189, 191, 255

Xenophobia   72, 78
   See also Makwerekwere

Youth   20, 195, 197, 201, 204–207

Zamfara   226–227
Zar   103–113
Zulu   16, 18, 21, 35–37, 39, 42–43, 46–49, 51–52, 58–63, 142, 144, 147–148, 150, 152–153, 156–158, 161, 239, 241–246, 249, 261–262
Zululand   147, 154–155
Zulu kings   55–57, 147, 154–155, 157–158, 244–246
Zuma, Jacob   248–249

Printed in the United States
By Bookmasters